LIBRARY/NE

W9-ABK-824

3 0147 1003 9344 9

NA 737 .J6 S38 1996
Schulze, Franz, 1927-
Philip Johnson :
    life and work

NEW ENGLAND INSTITUTE OF TECHNOLOGY
LIBRARY

ALSO BY FRANZ SCHULZE

MIES VAN DER ROHE: *A Critical Biography*

FANTASTIC IMAGES: *Chicago Art Since 1945*

ONE HUNDRED YEARS OF CHICAGO ARCHITECTURE:
Continuity of Structure and Form

NEW ENGLAND INSTITUTE OF TECHNOLOGY
LIBRARY

PHILIP JOHNSON

PHILIP JOHNSON

LIFE AND WORK

by FRANZ SCHULZE

NEW ENGLAND INSTITUTE OF TECHNOLOGY
LIBRARY

The University of Chicago Press

copy.
7-13

#33441561

PUBLISHED BY ARRANGEMENT WITH ALFRED A. KNOPF, INC.

The University of Chicago Press, Chicago 60637

Copyright © 1994 by Franz Schulze
All rights reserved. Originally published 1994
University of Chicago Press Edition 1996
Printed in the United States of America
01 00 99 98 97 96   6 5 4 3 2 1
ISBN 0-226-74058-7 (pbk.)

Library of Congress Cataloging-in-Publication Data

Schulze, Franz, 1927–
Philip Johnson : life and work / by Franz Schulze.
p. cm.
Includes bibliographical references and index.
1. Johnson, Philip. 1906–   . 2. Architects—United States—
Biography. I. Title.
NA737.J6S38 1996
720'.92—dc20
[B]   95-43299
CIP

All permissions can be found on pages 466–470.

♾ The paper used in this publication meets the minimum requirements
of the American National Standard for Information Sciences—
Permanence of Paper for Printed Library Materials, ANSI Z39.48-1984.

To Stephanie

CONTENTS

ACKNOWLEDGMENTS ix

PROLOGUE 3

PART ONE: ORIGINS AND DIRECTIONS, 1652–1934 7

FROM NIEUW AMSTERDAM TO OVERLOOK ROAD 9

HOMER AND LOUISE 14

THE IRREPLACEABLE HEIR 22

HARVARD: COLLISION OF MIND AND HEART 33

ALFRED BARR 46

THE PILGRIMAGE ROADS 50

MoMA, RUSSELL, AND THE NEW STYLE 58

MIES 65

THE AMERICAN INVASION 70

THE 1932 SHOW: THE REVOLUTION GOES UPTOWN 75

THE RISE AND FALL OF ART 87

PART TWO: THE INGLORIOUS DETOUR, 1934–1946 102

ZARATHUSTRA AND THE KINGFISH 104

NEW LONDON AND THE RADIO PRIEST 120

TOMORROW THE WORLD 132

BACK TO HARVARD 147

THE PENITENTIAL PRIVATE 160

PART THREE: REBIRTH AND RENEWAL, 1946–1953 169

BARR AGAIN, MoMA AGAIN, MIES AGAIN 171

DOMESTICITY 184

OPUS IN VITRO 188

THE EARLY FIFTIES: WORK, PEOPLE, WORLDVIEW 199

PART FOUR: BREAK WITH MODERNISM, 1953–1967   228

"IT IS ALL SOCRATES'S FAULT"   230

YET AGAIN MIES: EASY TO SHOOT AT, HARD TO BRING DOWN   235

HISTOROPHILIA AND MONUMENTALITY   251

WANDERING MINSTREL   264

THE SIXTIES: LAURELS AND ASS'S EARS   273

NEW CANAAN   287

URBANISM AND ITS DISCONTENTS   294

OUTPACED AND RESTORED BY THE YOUNG   305

PART FIVE: SUPERSTARDOM, 1967–   318

BURGEE OF CHICAGO   320

RAISED UP AT AT&T, BROUGHT LOW AT MoMA   344

THE PoMo REVEL   357

PETER   371

PHILIP AND DAVID AT HOME   379

DECON   393

BURGEE: DISCARDED BY THE DISCARDED   401

THE SUMMING UP: BERLIN, 1993   408

WORK IN PROGRESS   415

NOTES   421

SELECTED BIBLIOGRAPHY   444

INDEX   451

PERMISSIONS ACKNOWLEDGMENTS   466

PHOTOGRAPH CREDITS   467

ACKNOWLEDGMENTS

The person most deserving of the author's gratitude for assistance in the completion of this study is its subject, Philip Johnson. Despite a daily schedule as robust as it was unrelieved, Johnson made himself consistently accessible to me over the eight years I needed for research and writing. Moreover, he voluntarily forwent seeing any of the text or the notes before the book was published. It is thus an independent and unauthorized work. I am indebted to Johnson not only for the generous allocation of his time, recollections, and opinions but for his simple good sense in realizing that his biography could not be taken seriously unless its readers were assured he exercised no editorial control over it.

Many others who imparted valuable information to me are professional practitioners of the art to which Johnson has devoted most of his adult life: architecture. They include Eli Attia, Edward Larrabee Barnes, John Burgee, George E. Danforth, Peter Eisenman, Paul Florian, Richard Foster, James Ingo Freed, Frank Gehry, the late Landis Gores, James Jarrett, John M. Johansen, William Keck, Robin Middleton, Peter Millard, the late William Peterson, Donald Porter, Jaquelin Robertson, Paul Rudolph, Denise Scott Brown, Emile Spira, Robert A. M. Stern, Jane Fiske Thompson, Stephen Wierzbowski, James Wines, and Evans Woollen.

While several of this group have written about architecture as surely as they have made it, it seems appropriate to distinguish them from those of their colleagues whose reputations rest mostly on their work in criticism and scholarship. I profited greatly from exchanges with critics Kurt Andersen, Rosamond Bernier, Peter Blake, John Brodie, Martin Filler, Paul Goldberger, Robert Hughes, Jeffrey Kipnis, Michael Sorkin,

Suzanne Stephens, and Carter Wiseman, while the historians I recall with similar gratitude and respect are Geoffrey Blodgett, Alan Brinkley, James Marston Fitch, Kenneth Frampton, George M. Goodwin, Thomas S. Hines, the late Henry-Russell Hitchcock, Carol Krinsky, Victoria Newhouse, Richard Plunz, the late Richard Pommer, Vincent Scully, Helen Searing, David Van Zanten, Ujjval K. Vyas, and Nicholas Fox Weber.

These last two lists do not take note of other professionals properly regarded as critics or historians but more standardly associated with art museums, especially with the great institution Johnson himself has served so long and with such distinction, The Museum of Modern Art. I am grateful to the following, who have variously and at various times past and present been curators, trustees, librarians, research associates, and administrative figures at MoMA: Mary Barnes, Mikki Carpenter, Aileen Chuk, Elizabeth (Eliza) Parkinson Cobb, Helen Franc, Wilder Green, Agnes Gund, Barbara Jakobson, Elizabeth Mock Kassler, Richard H. Koch, Porter McCray, Donald B. Marron, the late Elodie Courter Osborn, the late William S. Paley, Elizabeth Shaw, Daniel Starr, and John Trause. I must express special appreciation to the museum's archivist, Rona Roob, for her unfailing readiness both to guide and to assist me in my researches; to Harriet Schoenholz Bee of the Publications Department for her alertly intelligent reading of the manuscript; to Stuart Wrede, Terence Riley, and the late Arthur Drexler, who, like Johnson before them, have borne the title of director of the Department of Architecture and Design; lastly, to Richard Oldenburg, until late in 1994 the director of the museum, who made me welcome in all of my labors there. People in more nearly assistant capacity at the museum also merit thankful recognition: Jennifer Brody, Robert Coates, Marie-Anne Evans, Leslie Heitzman, Apphia Loo, and Rachel Wild.

Comparably, I am indebted to staff members of other museums: to William Lieberman of the Metropolitan Museum of Art and to Betty Blum, Jack Perry Brown, Mary Woolever, and John Zukowsky of the Art Institute of Chicago.

In his long, vigorous, and multifaceted life, Johnson has been a subject of singular interest to an army of friends, relatives, students, and observers at large, some of whom have shared their liveliest memories with me. I have been especially rewarded by the acquaintance I made with his sisters Jeannette Dempsey and Theodate Severns (likewise with the latter's husband, Scott Severns), by time spent with the late Margaret Scolari (Marga) Barr, Victoria Barr, Alan Blackburn, Richard Bowers, Nina Bremer, Mosette Broderick, John Hohnsbeen, Lee Ignat, Lincoln Kirstein, the late David Lloyd Kreeger, Sharon Maguire, Edith Morrill,

Susan Morris, Janet T. Phypers, Frank Sanchis, Arthur Schlesinger, Jr., Karl Schlubach, the late Carleton Sprague Smith, the late Jay Spectre, Anne and John W. Straus, Jon Stroup, the late Virgil Thomson, the late Edward M. M. Warburg, Mrs. Mary Warburg, Kay Warwick, Connie Weinzapfel, David Whitney, John Wisner, and Mrs. Douglas Wood.

People I have met in Johnson's office warrant grateful mention, as well: Janet Crowley, Debbie Green, the late Alan Haber, Joan Kane, Barbara Wolf, Linda Wool, and Ivan Zaknic. Aaron McDonald was uncommonly resourceful in helping me assemble the illustrations and miscellaneous material for the book.

The text was written at Lake Forest College, where as a faculty member I was consistently encouraged by president Eugene Hotchkiss and his successor, David Spadafora. Assistance was also generously provided by Professor William Moskoff as well as by head librarian Arthur Miller and his colleagues Susan Cloud, Dawn Diventi, Esther Keil, Rita Koller, Robin Leckbee, David Levinson, and Vanaja S. Menon.

I must also acknowledge the judiciousness with which my editor at Alfred A. Knopf, Ann Close, guided the book to conclusion. Thanks go as well to her assistant, Ann Kraybill, and to Carol Edwards for her scrupulous copyediting of the text. And finally, a salute of affection and respect to my agent, Maxine Groffsky, for her patience and encouragement.

PHILIP JOHNSON

Two events, one a disappointment, the other a near calamity, thwarted the plans Philip Johnson had made to celebrate his eightieth birthday with guests on the lawn of his Connecticut estate in the summer of 1986. The first was rain, which fell lightly but steadily during the day of the affair, leaving small pools and fens scattered throughout the property. The second was a heart collapse that Johnson suffered just hours earlier, requiring his hospitalization in New York and a hurried angioplasty.

The festivities went on anyhow. Hundreds of artists, architects, literati, and patrons at large—people of rank in the very activities in which Johnson had distinguished himself professionally—made the forty-mile trip from Manhattan to New Canaan. Many were his close associates and devoted friends, more than a few his outspoken enemies, but they stayed for hours, all of them, strolling the grounds under umbrellas, like figures in a Japanese print, nodding and bowing as they paid court to one another and homage to a guest of honor who wasn't even there. Conditions aside, there was much to look at, notably the eight buildings Johnson had designed over the course of four decades and put up on the estate for his own delight, each strikingly unlike the other: chiefly his house, a single large rectangular room enclosed fully by floor-to-ceiling walls of glass, and its almost totally opaque counterpart in brick, the so-called Guest House; a pair of repositories crammed with a glittering collection of contemporary art—the painting gallery, buried in an artificial hillside and detectable only by an entry cut into the earth, and the sharp-angled sculpture gallery, its several interior landings forming an ambiguously helical circulation pattern; the bone white library-study with its treasury of books, a bandbox in stucco, highly visible but isolated and standoffish in the landscape, with no telephone or lavatory or path leading to it through the tall grass; the cunning pavilion on the pond at the bottom of the hill, a *folie* built at a scale too small for people to stand in it comfortably; and two more oddments whose commonplace materials underscored the irony implicit in their pointedly unfunctional design: the "Gehry Ghost House," a mock miniature corncrib done in chain link fencing, and the thirty-six-foot Lincoln Kirstein Tower, made completely of concrete blocks and meant to be climbed—although potentially fatal to any climber not fully mindful of his footing.

These buildings, in turn, were parts of a larger architectural artifice, a rocky, mostly wooded parcel of thirty-three acres organized, trimmed, and cultivated by Johnson with as much care as he put into the constructed objects that punctuated it.

No architect of his time, neither Frank Lloyd Wright nor Le Corbusier nor Ludwig Mies van der Rohe, could have presided, especially at a distance and flat on his back, over such a spectacle. Yet aggrandized though he was, Johnson knew that so far as greatness in the profession is concerned, he was not the equal of any of these legendary figures. He had, in fact, already done as much as any single person in the twentieth century to promote the reputations of his betters, while generously bowing to their superiority. He was the kind of man who in revering others, and even imitating them, drew equal attention to himself. His genius was that of a singularly gifted harlequin who forever changed the masks of style on his own work and conducted his personal relationships with comparable whimsicality. Yet however just, the characterization fails to explain the steadfast commitments and loyalties, indeed the studied worldview, that animated all his movements. Possessed of a psyche of the most elaborate intricacy, he could not have reached old age without being enthralled by the scene he had so helped to shape, eager for more of it, proud, tough, immensely vital—and more deeply scarred than he knew.

Even so, he recognized and cherished a single day in his youth that more than any other turned his life around. On a spring afternoon in 1929, the strands of his troubled and disconnected emotions had suddenly drawn together, leaving him exhilarated and newly self-assured. Later they would come unraveled again, as they had much too often in the past, ever since he was old enough to take a measure of adult responsibility for himself. Six years earlier, having made an excellent record at boarding school in spite of a protractedly lonely existence there, he had matriculated at

Harvard College, where demons he had kept at bay rose up to assail him. His concentration blazed and dimmed erratically and his spirits vacillated between periods of conviction and spells of pathological lassitude and self-doubt.

On the sixteenth of June, as he drove from Cambridge to join his younger sister, Theodate, for her commencement exercises at Wellesley College, he was on leave of absence from his own studies and adrift, unsure of the rightness of his undergraduate program in classics and philosophy and tinkering with various alternative ambitions—law school or teaching Greek at a college back home in Ohio, even though he had no degree as yet, or simply doing nothing at all. He indulged himself such a desperate range of choice because he was outwardly quick-witted and arrogant enough to think himself capable of moving mountains, while inwardly anxious and insecure enough to doubt his capacity to kick over an anthill.

Theodate, whom he treasured, had done more than adequately at Wellesley. Especially, she had sparkled on the campus stage, where her performance as Catherine in Shakespeare's *Henry VIII* had earned the admiration of Alfred H. Barr, Jr., a young professor of art history shortly to become the first director and guiding spirit of The Museum of Modern Art. Following her graduation ceremonies, she encountered Barr, who paid her his compliments and whom she introduced to her brother. The two men promptly fell into spirited conversation.

Barr was a scholar with a wide-ranging command of the classics in his own right, but he was possessed as well of a special burning devotion to a subject of recent renown, modern art. Philip had taken only three formal courses at Harvard in the "fine arts" and dropped two of them, but he matched Barr's intellectual zeal with an intense and apparently natural sensibility of his own, and his willful, quixotic approach to self-education had left him with enough knowledge of the visual arts to seize Barr's rapt attention. While no one could later recall in detail what he and Barr had said, it was agreed that they had discussed art, more art, and still more of it, and that above all a gravitation of immense and abrupt force had developed between them.

Philip came away from Wellesley with a newly composed sense of what to do with himself. If it bears repeating that his certainty would lose its wholeness again later on, indeed that a scattering of his mental faculties proved an unalterable condition of his long life, it is no less evident in retrospect that his meeting with Barr did not just point out a direction to him that he had never discerned so clearly before. More than any event in his personal history, it persuaded him that the labyrinth of his mind had a center, where he might build a fire that would burn as brightly as Barr's, with a similarly sacred purpose. He spent the rest of his life seeking the center. He never found it. Instead, he learned to savor the search, which he conducted so indefatigably that it became at last an end in itself, with its own set of rewards. The sacred he learned to live without, even gladly, exchanging the prospects of it for the pleasure of riding his racehorse intelligence everywhere, through the worlds of art, high society, low politics, and back to art again. He committed most of his creative energies eventually to architecture, writing about it at first and later making it, sometimes brilliantly, sometimes badly, but always with an imagination capricious enough to conceal a subtly consistent philosophy of style and sufficiently constant in its drive to win him a place at the forefront of the international culture of his time. How he did it, and how it was done to him, make up the substance of this narrative.

PART ONE

ORIGINS AND DIRECTIONS

1652–1934

FROM NIEUW AMSTERDAM

TO OVERLOOK ROAD

Homer Hosea Johnson, father of Philip, was born in Hartland Township, Ohio, at a time, 1862, when pious and progressive Americans thought it fitting to anoint a child with both a classical and a biblical name. He lived to be ninety-seven. He could remember when Union soldiers returned from the Civil War and he followed the television coverage of the first launches of American satellites into outer space.

His own father, Alfred Stutts Johnson, enjoyed considerable material success in life, due largely to a knack for meeting good fortune with good sense. Having married Philothea Townsend, daughter of a local family more prominent than his own, he moved with her onto the Townsend farm, six miles northwest of New London, Ohio. The price of wheat rose steeply during the Civil War and Johnson made enough money to build a second house for his family in 1867, on Main Street in New London. He later became president of the local bank.

An only child, Homer spent his boyhood on the farm and in the town. He proved inept at the most rudimentary farming chores, but he performed well in school and exhibited a seemingly natural appetite for socializing, assets that prefigured an urban rather than a rural career. Appropriately, his father sent him to a boys' academy in Oberlin and later enrolled him in Oberlin College, whence after two years he transferred to Amherst College, some fifty miles from the ancient Townsend homestead in Great Barrington, Massachusetts. He returned for his senior year to Oberlin, graduating in 1885, exactly thirty years after his mother, Philothea, earned a diploma from the same school.

In another three decades, his son Philip would pass his own childhood

JOHNSON COUNTRY HOME, TOWNSEND FARM, NEAR NEW LONDON, OHIO, C. 1918

hours at Townsend Farm, which remains today a congenial and accommodating place, dominated by the Greek Revival house that the Townsends built in 1845. By the time it came into Homer's possession, it had enough history, together with its palpable charm, to become a fixture in the life of his own later family, a cherished possession put to constant good use.

Hosea Townsend, Philothea's father, bought the farm in 1815 and moved his own wife and children onto it one year later, all of them making the trip west by wagon from Great Barrington. At the time, Ohio had been a state for only twelve years. The farm was part of the old "fire lands" of the Western Reserve, ceded in 1792 by Connecticut to citizens whose property had been burned during the American Revolution. Thus the Townsends had been Ohioans nearly as long as any white folk living there. Philothea recalled that Native Americans passing through the district sometimes slept on the parlor floor of the original family cabin, while the Townsends, uneasy but unmolested, huddled in the loft.

Philothea's family traced its lineage to England and the seventeenth century, while Alfred, with genealogical pride of his own, could follow his clan back to the same period, when they were the Jansens of the Netherlands. Where and when Hendrix Jansen's great-grandson William married Lydia Cortelyou, who bore him Alfred Stutts, is unrecorded, but it is certain that Lydia was descended from the canny Huguenot Jacques Cortelyou, probably the most famous paternal ancestor of Philip Cortelyou Johnson and the first of the line to tempt the biographical historian to fantasize about the genetic transmission of a sensitivity to constructed form.

For Jacques Cortelyou, having arrived in the New Netherlands in 1652 as the tutor for an émigré Dutch family, became surveyor general of the province just five years later. In 1660, he furnished Governor Pieter Stuyvesant with the first town plan of Nieuw Amsterdam. Known as the Castello Plan, it organized all of lower Manhattan Island into a cityscape visible for many years in the Museum of the City of New York, where it took the form of a large three-dimensional model accompanied by a reproduction of a copy of Cortelyou's original drawing.

Two hundred twenty-five years and ten generations later, Homer Johnson had decided on law school. Harvard seemed within reach of his intellectual ambitions and, when his father gave him the rights to a large wooded section of the farm, of his wherewithal, as well. Homer sold the lumber steadily over several years, thus paying his way to Cambridge and through Harvard. He graduated in 1888 with a master of arts and a bachelor of laws, the latter granted summa cum laude.

At the time, his future wife and mother of Philip, Louise Pope, was completing her sophomore year at Wellesley College, just a few miles away from Harvard. Although she was from Cleveland, which was close enough to New London, there is no evidence that she and Homer met until later, after she returned home and he himself took up residence in Cleveland to begin the professional practice of law.

If Homer came from a good family, Louise came from a better one, more accustomed than his to urban ways and cultural refinements, and proud in its own right of a genealogy that carried back to seventeenth-century Britain. The Pope money came from industry, not farming, and was already being accumulated in the wool business in the mid-1800s. Alton Pope, Louise's grandfather, was a "belligerent" Quaker whose religious convictions brought him into conflict with his neighbors in North Vassalboro, Maine, and finally drove him to move, sometime before the Civil War, to a Quaker community in Baltimore.

One of Alton's three sons, Edward, had already left home to seek his fortune in Cleveland, but he reestablished contact with his parents after the war started, when he learned of their latest straits, now as Northerners living in Maryland. Entraining east, he managed to insinuate himself behind Confederate lines, rescued his family, and brought them all back to Ohio. By 1862, Alton had opened a new woollen mill in Salem. His youngest son, Alfred, joined the business but left it in 1869 to take a position with the new Cleveland Malleable Iron Company. His swift rise through the ranks earned him the presidency of the firm and a later life of affluence unmatched by any of his ancestors.

The Popes' entrepreneurial spirit was largely lost on brother Edward. By nature more dreamer than doer, he had some modest success in several business ventures, including even shipbuilding, but approximately as many failures. It didn't matter to his daughter Louise, who adored him anyhow. The cultivation of the mind and its corollary rewards were his chief gifts to her, and she regarded them later in life as an inheritance that had enriched her tenfold. By all reports, she was the brightest and most intellectually committed of Edward's children, all of whom he succeeded in getting through college, three boys to Cornell University and Louise and a sister to Wellesley. She graduated in 1891 and remained a year longer to pursue her studies in art history, whereupon Edward dipped deeper into whatever till he had access to—now and then it was his rich brother Alfred's—and helped her to further her education, in Italy. On her return, she taught mathematics at a coeducational private school in Springfield, Ohio, then signed on as an instructor in Miss Mittelberger's private school for girls in Cleveland. She continued her travels abroad during the summers, keeping a sketchbook filled with pen and pencil drawings that disclosed more than a little skill.

Homer, meanwhile, had gone directly back to Ohio after Harvard, and in the year of his graduation, 1888, renewed his acquaintance with Melvin Blake Johnson, no relation but a former college chum. Directly, the two men set up the M. B. and H. H. Johnson law firm in downtown Cleveland. Homer was the better educated of the two and the more winningly extroverted, but the subtler legal aptitude belonged to M. B., an autodidact who studied law by reading it in the back room of his office. Within a few years, they claimed as clients the White Sewing Machine Company and its more formidable offspring, the White Motor Company. At the dawn of the new century, Homer Johnson, by his own efforts, was developing into a man of independent financial substance.

He was also courting Louise Pope, although the record should show that before he ever got to know her well, he had already been widowed twice. In 1888, he had exchanged vows with Janet Whitcomb, who died of tuberculosis two years later, and in 1896 his second wife, Gertrude Beggs, succumbed to the same disease on her honeymoon in Paris. Gertrude must have been suffering even as she was joined to Homer, suggesting, especially in view of the unanimous reports of his lifelong conscientious nature, that he must have gone ahead with the ceremony as much out of pity as out of love.

By the time he and Louise were married on October 26, 1901, he was thirty-nine and she thirty-two. Each, as it were, stood on the brink—he of middle age, she of spinsterhood. It was no lightly considered union; indeed, nothing about it or their subsequent family life seems to have been undertaken frivolously or impulsively. Homer and Louise Johnson prided themselves on their backgrounds, their values, their accomplishments, and the pains they agreed to take in rearing their children, whom—since it was late—they promptly set about conceiving.

HOMER AND LOUISE

In view of their comfortable circumstances, the Johnsons had good reason to regard Cleveland as a fit place in which to establish themselves. While they had in common ancestral ties with New England as well as a measure of personal experience abroad, Ohio was native earth to both of them. More to the point, Homer's professional fortunes were manifestly bound to the future of the great city on Lake Erie.

Five years before his marriage to Louise, Cleveland had celebrated its centennial in a rush of optimism that seemed justified by a history of nearly unflagging material growth. A strategic location at the mouth of the Cuyahoga River, midway between the coal and oil fields of Pennsylvania and the iron ranges of Minnesota, had turned the city into a teeming transshipment center, the greatest iron ore market in the world. Industry grew and commerce with it; by 1900, Cleveland was one of young America's major fabricators of metals, a leader in iron and steel processing, oil refining, and chemical manufacturing.

Not only was it a good place for a good lawyer; Homer Johnson found it fully suited to his temperament, which was equal parts of pragmatism and idealism. His gift for maneuvering in the rapids of laissez-faire economics assured him a consistently handsome income, while a no less natural inclination to perform public service inspired him to works of demonstrable value to the commonweal. When he died in 1960, the Cleveland press composed encomiums to the memory of a privately successful, publicly dedicated man, "an aristocrat . . . and a sensitive man who never lost the common touch," as the *Plain Dealer* identified him in an editorial.

Newly married in 1901, he bought his bride and himself a substantial house in the Tudor manner at 2171 Overlook Road on the East Side. A generation earlier, he might have aspired to buy or to build on Euclid Avenue, the splendid concourse where the mansions of Cleveland's wealthiest citizens had gone up mostly between 1860 and 1880. But if he was well fixed, he was not yet rich. Moreover, the commercial growth of Cleveland in the last decades of the nineteenth century had already begun to encroach on Euclid Avenue just east of downtown. Tall commercial buildings, the most obvious evidence of aggressive capitalist instincts, fanned outward from the Public Square, invaded the precinct of the great houses, and forced the new wealth of Cleveland to move farther from the city center. Facilitating this dispersal, even encouraging it, was the development of street railways and interurban systems. Those that followed an easterly direction carried out to a 440-foot escarpment, the western edge of the Appalachian plateau. There a community took form, incorporating in 1903 as Cleveland Heights.

The Johnson house stood on the brow of the hill, formally part of Cleveland but literally within a few feet of the city limits of the Heights. Across the street was a park and beyond, a glorious, unimpeded view of Lake Erie. The new neighborhood was palpably prosperous, with the Johnsons occupying the "dollar end" of Overlook Road, some six or seven blocks west of the "penny end." Their immediate neighbor to the west was Myron T. Herrick, an officer of the Society for Savings Bank who in 1903 was elected governor of Ohio. Two doors east of 2171 lived M. B. Johnson, who had recommended the neighborhood to his partner, Homer, in the first place.

Louise and Homer settled in contentment on Overlook Road, remaining in the Tudor house until late in their lives. At the outset of their marriage, Louise had felt ambitious enough to hanker after an abode of a higher order. It was not grandeur she wanted but something that would signify the informed esthetic awareness she regarded as a crucial part of her dowry. Homer owned a lot a block away from 2171, and there Louise envisioned putting up a house by the thirty-four-year-old architect from Oak Park, Illinois, Frank Lloyd Wright, whose reputation was rapidly growing among people like Louise, who cared about that sort of thing. She was on the verge of offering Wright a commission when her first pregnancy commenced, so debilitating her that she gave up the idea of a new house altogether.

Still, she thought, her frustration need not be total. An addition to 2171 Overlook might do, which is what she commissioned and got from J. Milton Dyer of Cleveland, who transformed the Tudor house into something grander after all.

HOMER AND LOUISE JOHNSON RESIDENCE, 2171 OVERLOOK ROAD, CLEVELAND, C. 1915

Dyer was no Wright, nor even close to the architectural avant-garde. There was very little of that in Cleveland anyhow, a city whose tastes in building ran to staunch conservatism except in those rare cases when an adventurous designer from out of town—like John Wellborn Root of Chicago—was brought in to construct a commercial structure in the center of the city. Nevertheless, Dyer by reputation was one of the ablest local professionals, the first graduate of Paris's celebrated École des Beaux-Arts to practice in Cleveland. His conversance with the numerous stylistic options of the day inspired Louise to ask for something in Art Nouveau, a manner then past the crest of its popularity in international capitals, though still racy enough in Cleveland. Ten years later, she got something even more advanced from Louis Rohrheimer, a respected local designer-craftsman, who remodeled several of the Johnson rooms in a crisply simplified geometric decor not just in tune with contemporary modes but prophetic of the modern architecture Louise's son Philip would one day make the central issue of his life.

Aware of the lateness of their marriage and united in their intention to rear a family, Homer and Louise produced four children in little more than five years. The eldest, Jeannette, was born on July 26, 1902, nine months to the day after her parents' wedding. A son, Alfred, followed less than eleven months later, on June 18, 1903. Three years intervened, then a second son, Philip, born on July 8, 1906, preceded by only thirteen months a second daughter, Theodate, who arrived on August 13, 1907.

The symmetry of the order of these births—daughter/son, interval, son/daughter—had the effect of forming two pairs of children as surely as four individuals. Jeannette was devoted to Alfred, Philip even more attached to Theodate. Unsurprisingly, both alliances drew a measure of their strength negatively, with each child feeling closer to its intimate companion partly because it didn't care overmuch for one or the other of its counterparts.

The balance of this duality was upset when Alfred died of mastoiditis at the age of five, with the following consequences: Jeannette became increasingly independent. She was a typical firstborn anyhow, at once obliged and free to make her own way and, as a girl child, to care for little Alfred, the male who followed her. Even in her old age, she recalled him lovingly, dwelling on his apparently delicate turn of mind. "See," she recollected his saying tearfully of a bouquet of dead daisies, "how the flowers melted." She played with him, ministered to him, and was torn up by his death.

By contrast, Philip and Theodate lost not a loved one but only a presence, of whom Philip may have had no more than the faintest direct recollection—if that—and Theodate surely none at all. The two grew closer

HOMER HOSEA JOHNSON WITH ALFRED
AND JEANNETTE, 1904

PHILIP, C. 1908

to each other as they maintained their apartness from Jeannette, perceiving her as their bossy big sister. "Philip didn't wash under his armpits," Jeannette would tattle to her mother, and Philip would fall into a sulk, with Theodate hovering over him. While it is commonplace for any trio of children to split themselves occasionally into two confidants and a separated third, the players customarily change places with one another. In the Johnson family, the roles remained fixed, with Jeannette moving at all times free of the Philip-Theodate binary, and Alfred, even in death, preserving his alliance with Jeannette and his own unassailability. "Alfred would never do *that*"—Louise's standard way of scolding Philip and Theodate—left both youngsters with only a ghost to resent. As the three survivors grew older, the maturation process turned juvenile divisions into a familial bond, but it did not alter kinships of temperament.

Alfred haunted his parents as much as he did his siblings. When the child died, Homer was forty-six and Louise thirty-nine. Homer had already had two wives taken from him and Louise had been long enough in winning a husband. Realizing the time had passed for more children, they endeavored to cope compensatorily with the wound of Alfred's death and its threat to the integrity of their household. Thus Philip and Theodate, two years and one year old respectively when Alfred died, were subjected to an uncommonly protected upbringing, more studiously, one might say more defensively, imposed upon them than any regime Jeannette and probably Alfred had experienced. For Theodate, this meant chiefly an overload of fatherly affection that turned her into a pampered darling even as it deepened the self-sufficient Jeannette's impatience with her. With Philip, the

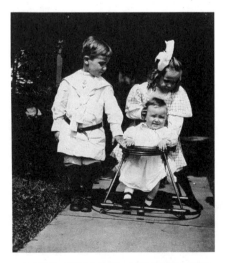

ALFRED, JEANNETTE, AND PHILIP, 1907

THEODATE AND PHILIP, C. 1911

effect was more complicated, since he was recognized by both parents as the only surviving son and preserver of the name, with all the implications of irreplaceability that such a designation carried in a day when family continuity was prized in proportion to the dread frequency of infant mortality. The attention paid his rearing was singular and intense, yet not without intimations of parental anxiety. Early in his childhood, his physical mannerisms were noticeably light and dainty, rather like a girl's. Homer never made his peace with such confounding behavior in his sole male heir, and while there is no way of knowing whether he purposely declined to lavish the voluntary little endearments on the boy that he could more easily afford with Theodate, it is certain that he was neither warm nor hearty with Philip. Gestures of closeness and closeness itself were left to Louise, who had her own way of showing, or of withholding, them.

For all their unity of purpose, then, the two Johnsons acted upon their children as distinct, in some major respects dissimilar, forces. Homer was lord of the manor, Louise his chief minister: He presided and she carried out, a distinction that awarded more direct familial influence to her. Their division of labor was not inconsistent with the customs of the time, but to Philip's parents it meant more than that. For Homer was in his element in the office, at the club, on the golf course, or on the many trips demanded of him. Louise was literally and figuratively much in place at the hearthside, where Homer might have been more comfortable than he was if she had entertained outsiders as cordially within the walls as he met them without. But there was little about her that was naturally gregarious. Company was welcome at Overlook Road on a carefully discriminating basis. Alcohol was never served. Home for Louise, and thus for Homer, was an enclave meant mostly for the members of the immediate family, where she would be a judicious companion and helpmate to him and a model to her children, a mother of majesty rather than intimacy. With cool relish, she instructed Jeannette, Philip, and Theodate in the good manners and lofty ideas appropriate to her concept of their station and mission in life. Since she understood more of the mind than of the heart, she looked upon Philip's special place in the family as an excuse, indeed an inspiration, to design his intellect first and worry over his psyche later, if at all. Homer countenanced this, without interference, or, it may be more accurate to say, he let it happen. Philip in his later years recalled one of the few conversations he ever had with his father in which the distance between them was narrowed, and even so, Homer's counsel was more pragmatic than affective. "Marry a woman with brains," he advised Philip. "I did, and I've never regretted it. It is a little hard at home. I like to see people. Your mother doesn't. But her intelligence makes up for it."

LOUISE POPE JOHNSON WITH (LEFT TO RIGHT) THEODATE, PHILIP,
AND JEANNETTE, C. 1917

The elder Johnsons looked as well as acted their separate parts. Homer had watery blue eyes in a ruddy, malleable, slightly porcine face that smiled naturally. An ordinary-looking man of average height, he was overweight by later standards, although not by those of the early 1900s, which admired the well-fed profile. If he did not stand out in the boardroom or the chambers of the court, he looked sufficiently at home in them.

Louise was far more physically arresting. If there is any truth to the notion that some people appear to belong to a particular period and to no other, she was the very image of a lady of means of the 1910s and 1920s—strikingly so, in no way routinely. An appropriate six inches shorter than Homer's five feet ten and broad rather than stout, she was preceded by an ample bosom that crowned a torso meant for corsets and baroque foundation garments. She locomoted with unerring deliberateness, like an ocean liner. Her face was finely proportioned, somehow generic rather than specific, with clear brown eyes and a gaze of imperturbable authority and alertness. Affecting pince-nez, she looked the headmistress she always longed to be.

Only with the help of their children's much later recollections can one speculate about the intimacies of Homer and Louise. By family consensus, Netty (Janet Whitcomb), his first wife, was the true love of his life; Louise is said to have known it as well as Homer did, but the two of them were prudent enough to accept the fact and let it go at that. Was there any truth to the family rumors that Louise was involved in at least one lesbian relationship? Philip and Theodate, more sensitive than Jeannette to sexual nuance, talked as if they were virtually sure of it, and Theodate even identified an old Wellesley associate of her mother's named Claudia as a friend who was more than a friend.

As for the Johnson children's eventual liaisons, Jeannette, who married once, was the only one to bear children and make her life as a wife and mother. Theodate became a singer, led a lively romantic life, and took three husbands. Philip, committing himself to homosexuality, claimed to be more limited to "serial monogamy" than he really was, while acknowledging a total of four "Mrs. Johnsons."

From the very beginning, Homer and Louise saw formal education as the only best road to their children's good fortune, and they left the early tending of it to well-trained governesses. Philip learned nursery German from a Fräulein Tietemann and a Fräulein Dorner, who made a sufficient impression upon him that he never forgot their names or the prayers ("*Ich bin klein, mein Herz ist rein . . .*") they drilled him in. When the time came for academic schooling, he and his sisters were enrolled in private institutions unless nothing else was available. Thus Philip was installed in Laurel School, the only respectable local kindergarten, but one where attendance was normally restricted to girls.

An exception was made in his case and he hated it, although he found himself hardly better off in first and second grades at the University School for Boys. There the newly appointed headmaster proved to be a believer in the special benefit of athletics and manual training, two activities for which Philip had an unqualifiedly negative aptitude. He was no better coordinated than his father had been around the Townsend Farm and his clumsiness at sports was total. The isolation he had felt at Laurel School only deepened. His parents, reacting to his indifferent grades, took him out of University School when he was in third grade and sent him, together with Theodate, to a highly regarded public school in Shaker Heights.

Since the school was at some distance from the Johnson neighborhood, special arrangements had to be made for the transfer. The family chauffeur was directed to transport Philip and Theodate by auto, a daily ritual that the children managed to manipulate by persuading the driver to let them alight a few blocks short of the school so that they could walk the last stretch more or less indistinguishable from their peers. In Philip's case, the effort was of little use, since he was regularly dressed in Brooks Brothers suits that only more conspicuously set him apart from his knicker-bocker-clad schoolmates. Much too often, he later recalled, he sat down

PHILIP, C. 1917

on the front steps of the school to eat his lunch, all neatly attired and quite alone. Compensation took the form of better grades, which hardly won him friends but gave him some reason for doing what he was doing. He was more than just intelligent. He was shrewd enough to realize that intelligence could protect him against forces over which he had no other control.

He had need of defenses. Obviously, Homer and Louise believed they were directing the exemplary upbringing of a family of cultivated children, but one can hardly avoid observing that Philip, while exquisitely fashioned, was very nearly suffocated in the process. The signs that might have alerted his parents to his condition were evidently ignored, or rationalized away, or regarded as a small price for a larger gain, or even as the disconnected, unalterable facts of life. Philip stuttered. By the age of eight or nine, he had also developed a tendency to fly into extravagant tantrums, which Homer at least once tried to cope with by hurling a glassful of cold water into his face. The rage only intensified as Philip ran shrieking and dripping from the room. Then, when the unpleasantness had passed, he resumed his place and his role: a dreamy but mentally quick model of a child, well mannered when he wanted to be or had no choice about it, and, haply, quite beautiful to look at. The family photograph albums show it: a brunette with an exquisitely shaped face, brown eyes from his mother, although little if anything from his father, and a pair of lips that bring Ganymede to mind. He is rarely seen smiling.

Still another well-intentioned policy of the Johnsons brought their offspring to grief, less because of the substance of it than of the excess. At a time when fresh air was widely regarded as a virtual guarantee of good health, Homer and Louise believed in fresh air, and since they could think of no better protection against that grimmest scourge of the times, tuberculosis, which had killed Homer's first two wives, they saw to it that their young became accustomed to sleeping on open screened-in porches during summers on the Townsend Farm and the rest of the year at the house on Overlook Road. In winter, the children sometimes awoke to find their counterpanes invisible beneath several inches of snow. It is not unlikely that little Alfred's death from mastoiditis was hastened by this regime, which Homer and Louise pursued anyhow, calling an end to it only when Philip and Theodate developed mastoid infections of their own. Both were plagued with ear trouble as late as their adult years, with Theodate suffering especially during her childhood. Again characteristically, her parents spirited her to the "better climates," variations, after all, on the fresh-air theme: to Atlantic City for the salt air, to the sandy hills of North Carolina for the purportedly dry air.

Homer and Louise found more than a few rewards of their own in the latter locale. Homer, much given to golf, fell in love with the links at Pinehurst and in 1915 bought a house there, where the whole family could spend time during the winter months. Theodate could take the air cure and he could improve his handicap. And Louise would prosper. She would start a cottage school of her own, fulfilling a hope she had long cherished and only lately refined in a number of inspiriting discussions with Mae Chapman, the principal of the Shaker Heights school Philip and Theodate were attending. (Jeannette, by now fourteen, was in residence at Westover School in Connecticut.) So Louise hired Chapman, and in 1916 the two women opened a facility in Pinehurst where Philip could be in attendance when the family was wintering there. (Theodate's ear condition called for a program less fixed.)

The new arrangement seemed something of a dream to Louise. Philip, less enthusiastic about it, was hardly in a position to alter it. Since the family spent only the colder months in North Carolina, he was obliged to

THEODATE AND PHILIP, C. 1917

LOUISE JOHNSON WITH JEANNETTE, THEODATE, AND PHILIP,
TOWNSEND FARM, C. 1918

JOHNSON FAMILY, TOWNSEND FARM, C. 1918.
LEFT TO RIGHT: LOUISE, HOMER, JEANNETTE, PHILIP, THEODATE

begin the school year in Cleveland in early fall, then move south for the winter and return to Cleveland in the spring. Thus he was removed from newly won acquaintances up north and dropped into a nest of strangers in Pinehurst, from whom, once they got to know him, he would again take leave, repairing to Cleveland and the first group that had spent the year together nicely enough without him. He did poorly at the cottage school, and in 1918 Louise and Homer transferred him to another private school, this one for boys, on the outskirts of Pinehurst.

One may wonder at last how he ever learned, as he later did, to thrive in a scholastic environment. During his Pinehurst years, he was a nearly breathless peripatetic, shuttling from one academic arena to another, rarely free from supervised education even during the summers on the farm, where he and his sisters were tutored by hired teachers in Latin and biology and by Louise herself, who fed them a steady diet of botany and Greek. And she could be a taskmistress sufficiently unyielding that Philip never forgot the occasion when she grew exasperated with his seeming inability to master a simple lesson in handwriting. "All right, Philip," she said, laying aside her instruction manual in a gesture of irritated resignation, "perhaps you are just not up to the problem." He recalled being stunned by her reaction, which he later described as "a look of such disappointment, such censure." He made no reply.

Even so, his mind remained his one possession that most commanded his mother's attention and solicitude. Yet the obligation worked both ways; since she had created and shaped his intelligence, she was as needful of him as he of her. Their mutuality endured, and she became his favorite correspondent throughout his school years away from home and his early professional life. Only in his middle years did he acknowledge to himself and others that he had not much liked either his mother or his father, that he thought of her as a "cold fish" who loved more from program than from impulse, and of his father as her distracted and seldom-accessible consort.

In her old age, Theodate confirmed Philip's recollection, recalling at the same time a day in Pinehurst when he was twelve and she eleven. In a confiding mood, he had told her—the soul he felt closest to—that he was having odd feelings about some of his classmates at the boys school, sensations that seemed close to thrills. "What do you think it means?" he asked her.

"Philip, how should I know?" she replied.

Jeannette was the first of the Johnson children to follow a path that Homer, even more than Louise, regarded as central to a sound education;

foreign travel. America could always be seen later in life, he reasoned; the place to go at the very time one was learning about it in school was Europe.

Thus, not yet quite twelve, in the spring of 1914, Jeannette had been bundled off to Germany in the company of the wife of an Oberlin College professor. Her trip was cut short by the onset of World War I, and at the end of August she was home again, where her father reflected sadly on the news of the cataclysm. Unlike most Americans, he felt no animus toward the Germans—nor toward their enemies, for that matter—since it was his respect for all of European culture that had prompted him to acquaint Jeannette with it. Berlin, where he sent her, was one of the capitals of Western civilization, but now he brooded on the destruction that all the great nations were likely to unleash upon one another.

This was the idealistic side of Homer Johnson, whose nativist instincts nonetheless led him to support the United States when it entered the war on the Allied side in 1917. His son Philip, as we will later record, would live to be affected by Homer's coexisting admiration for Germany and loyalty to the United States, but he would suffer more than his father from the conflict implicit in those two convictions. Homer, in fact, did not suffer, but profited. During the winter of 1918–1919, shortly after the war ended, Secretary of War Newton D. Baker appointed him to the so-called Liquidation Committee, a group of legal and military professionals who were charged with the responsibility of disposing of all the American military matériel that had been left on the battlefields during the war.

The task took him to Paris, requiring more of his time than he or Louise had anticipated. Accordingly, in the late spring she obtained four passports and, children in tow, sailed for France on the *Aquitania*. The family settled in at the elegant Hotel France et Choiseul, where they, too, stayed longer than planned, chiefly because Homer had meanwhile been given another assignment by the U.S. government, this one of major humanitarian significance. Joining Gen. Edgar Jadwin and Henry Morgenthau, Sr., he traveled to Warsaw to conduct a lengthy investigation into reports of wartime pogroms against the Jews in Poland.

At thirteen, Philip was only vaguely aware of what his father was doing, but he responded well to his new environment. Europe meant an invigorating change of scene, filled with more delights than duties. He drew free of his family long enough to discover and be captivated by the Paris Métro. Good at being alone, he rode it all over the city by himself, and nothing it led him to appealed more to his adolescent sensibility (and unconscious architectural predisposition?) than the fanciful Buttes Chaumont Park with its temple, lake, and artificial rocks, all arranged several generations earlier as part of Baron Haussmann's famous reorganization of the plan of Paris.

His personal idyll lasted about a month. Then in July, Louise, concerned as ever about proper rearing, packed all the children off to private schools in Geneva—the girls to Les Hirondelles, Philip to the Pensionat Thudicum. By November, Homer's obligations were fulfilled and the family was home for Thanksgiving. The imminence of winter dictated a return to Pinehurst rather than to Cleveland, but education resumed in any case, with Theodate back at Miss Chapman's, Philip at the boys' school. Jeannette was in the special tutorial keep of a recently demobilized American soldier who had been a junior faculty member at Harvard before the war and whom Homer had hired in Paris. Having accompanied the Johnsons back to the United States, the young instructor helped Jeannette to prepare for her matriculation at Wellesley in the fall of 1920.

In spirit, Philip left Cleveland well before he ever set out for boarding school. He never really knew the city to begin with, nor had any appreciation of its sweaty vitality. Having been carried by the dynamics of upward mobility to a suburban locale, his family gave him little choice but to lead a life of guarded privilege. He was at home in the Cleveland Museum of Art and at the concerts of the Cleveland Orchestra. He also listened to his mother as she lectured him and his sisters on the splendors of the Euclid Avenue mansions, which she knew by heart. But all these attractions lay well to the east of the center of the city. He had little reason to venture down there, still less to explore the brawling industrial area known as the "Flats," on the far side of the river.

Even some parts of town close by were off limits to him. At the foot of the hill on which Overlook Road ran was Little Italy, a tight, tough urban pocket filled with immigrants whose children sometimes invaded the Johnson neighborhood, where they dug dandelions and took them home for their parents to turn into salads. That the Italians were unwelcome was taken for granted along Overlook, where egalitarianism was not a practiced faith. The idealism of Homer and Louise Johnson was, after all, cultural rather than social. Moreover, if there was culture enough in Cleveland for family purposes, the time had come in Philip's personal development when it was better studied in an atmosphere more densely and consistently imbued with it.

Overlooking the Hudson River at Tarrytown, New York, Hackley was a boys' academy of solid, well-earned reputation. Its roughly ninety students and even its faculty of twelve came from families of established sub-stance, which in almost all cases meant Anglo-Saxon names and old money from the East Coast. Ohio was considered a rather remote province, and Minneapolis was identified in the 1923 Hackley annual "as far West as our class can boast of having a representative."

Philip spent three years at Hackley, where he showed signs of the behavior immediately recognizable to people who knew him as an adult. He came into full bloom as a student, an aggressive one at that, who seemed to have internalized not only his mother's values but the intensity, and the unsentimentality, with which she inculcated them. Not only were his grades rivaled by only one of his classmates; he became a provocative, highly verbal presence in the classroom. The first swift answer to an instructor's question usually came from him and was nearly as often accompanied by an unsolicited opinion derived from the inde-pendent reading that had become his consuming habit. He developed a cocky streak, comporting himself with such hauteur at times that he was at least once ejected from class. His earlier stutter straightened into nor-mal speech, rapid and precociously articulate. The pleasure he took in his ability to hold forth with teachers and fellow students alike led him to plunge headlong into the appropriate extracurricular activities: debating, drama, and writing for school publications. Apparently, he had gotten something from his father, too: a volubility, a social forwardness, expressed, however, not with the winning cheer that was Homer's wont, but instead with a pugnacity that was as much a rebutting response to his father as an emulation of him—and colored again by his recollection of the steely effectiveness of Louise.

HACKLEY SCHOOL,
TARRYTOWN,
NEW YORK,
1920

He was also a pianist, having once again followed his mother's example. Whether his talent was equal to his interest is unclear; once he gave up music following college, he did so for good, claiming later that he was a natural botch at it, a judgment disputed by one of his schoolmates at Hackley, Carleton Sprague Smith. Well after Smith became an internationally acclaimed flutist in his own right, he remembered Philip's teenage musicianship as, if not brilliant, altogether competent. Certainly Philip was good enough to be the Hackley Mandolin Club's pianist during both his junior and senior years. In the paragraphs devoted to him in the Hackley annual of 1923 (under the identifying title "A rhapsody of words"), he is assessed:

" 'Phil' is the intellectual type, rather than the athletic, his athletics being confined to the track squad of which he was manager. There were few limitations to his other, more essential fulfillments. Among these are his talent on the piano stool, his vocal trueness, the excellent roles he rendered in our most successful plays of the past two years, his work on the 'Annual,' and *The Hackley*, and his position at the scholastic head of the class. How we envy that youth (he's only sixteen, too) his brains."

Written in his senior year (anonymously), that statement bolsters the supposition that Philip was a force on campus, and indeed he made himself sufficiently felt among his peers that they voted him "brightest" and "most likely to succeed" among the class of 1923. What the annual does not recall as explicitly as he himself did in his later adulthood was the persistence of the loneliness that had hung over him ever since his earliest days in kindergarten and elementary school. If he was coping, it was at a cost. His bumptious, frenetic activity at Hackley was as much as anything a way of filling up an emptiness: If he could not make close friends with any of his fellow students—and he did not—he could at least command their respect. His social proclivities, in fact, were only confused by the kind of physical attraction he occasionally felt for a classmate—a feeling he understood well enough simply to know he could not act upon it. The strongest bonds he fashioned at boarding school were with his teachers. That much the annual hints at: "His favorite pastime is that of talking to the masters," among whom the unmarried instructor of English Frank Ellis Bogues—"Daddy," as he was known to all the students—stood out. Bogues enjoyed a mutual kinship with Philip. If it was sexual, it was never overt. The two maintained their association well after Philip left Hackley.

By the time he graduated, Philip's immediate future was set. Since Harvard College traditionally waived its admission examination requirement for the two top graduates of the best boys' academies, Hackley among them, he and Robert Sanford Riley knew well before they left Tarrytown that a place was waiting for them in Cambridge if they wanted it. Philip spent the summer of 1923 at Townsend Farm, making the necessary preparations for Harvard, which were interrupted by a rail trip to San Francisco in the company of his father. It was an event he preserved in his memory as the major occasion of his precollege youth when he was alone with Homer for any substantial period. "We got along all right," he later recalled, "but he was stiffer with me than with his friends at the club. Most of the time he talked pieties. Noble thoughts. Clichés."

HARVARD: COLLISION OF

MIND AND HEART

With the exception of a major event in Philip's personal economic fortunes, the record of his first year at Harvard is vague. Neither his own recollections nor those of his family have illuminated much of anything about the way he spent his days there. A transcript survives, which, in view of the fact that he had been valedictorian at Hackley, reads unimpressively. His program consisted mostly of courses in the humanities (English, Latin, Greek, history), in each of which he scored a grade of B, to go along with a wobbly D in chemistry. One is left mostly to speculate about his response to a collegiate environment, presuming that to some degree he was feeling his way, in the manner of many an insecure freshman. It is more certain, because he once admitted as much, that the loneliness he felt at Hackley remained with him at Harvard, where he discovered that he did not stand as high on the social ladder as he had in Cleveland or even in Tarrytown. Hackley, while a respected boys' academy, did not enjoy the gilt-edge reputation of a Phillips Exeter or a Groton. Philip received invitations from none of the Harvard clubs that signified upscale status.

Away from school, on the other hand, his life, at least its future, was affected dramatically by Homer Johnson's decision in 1924 to parcel out a very large portion of his worldly goods to his children. No believer in wills, Homer preferred to give what he had to his heirs while he was still alive and they were still young—that is, at a time when material wealth could provide each of them with an advantageous start in life. He was most considerate of Jeannette and Theodate, reasoning that females could not expect to make a living on their own as readily as males could. So

Homer gave them the most ironclad of his holdings, real estate in the heart of downtown Cleveland.

To Philip, he gave issues of stock in the Aluminum Corporation of America. Alcoa was already one of the largest industrial companies in the country, and the stock, on the face of it, was valuable. But it was common stock, more volatile and speculative than either bonds or preferred stock. That Homer owned it at all was not consistent with his suspicious opinion of the stock market in general. It was just that one of his clients had been his old college friend Charles Martin Hall, who, in 1886, shortly after he and Homer had graduated from Oberlin, had devised a process that eventually made possible the modern commercial production of aluminum. Hall sold the rights to his patent on the process to a group of investors who formed Alcoa and paid Hall with stock in the new corporation. In turn, Hall gave a portion of that stock to Homer in compensation for the latter's legal services, and Homer, having held it for years, passed it on to Philip in full awareness that it could fall in value as easily as rise. It rose, and then some. In the boom of the later 1920s, Alcoa stock soared, and by the time Philip graduated from Harvard, he was not only a wealthier man than his father but a millionaire, at a time when the word meant rich, not just comfortable.

Not to be outdone, his mother treated him in the summer of 1924 to his second trip abroad, a specially arranged student summer tour of Western Europe, following which he returned to Harvard for his sophomore year. Moving out of his freshman dormitory, he rented a private apartment in Cambridge, bought himself a Peerless motorcar, the first in a long line of luxury automobiles that he made a lifelong habit of owning, and added heaps of books to his personal library.

His indulgence, however, did not stop with himself. In fact, his new wealth helped to develop a singular habit of Philip's, a material generosity that began simply as a way of drawing attention to himself but that later in life became a uniquely personal trait that brought him greater profit than it did his beneficiaries. Even his destiny as a patron of the arts had a measure of its origins in the largesse he visited upon his Harvard classmates in the wake of his 1924 windfall.

He invited his friends in large numbers to his handsome private new digs as well as to concerts and the theater in Boston. Those gestures enabled him to grow closer to people rather than to overpower them as he had at Hackley.

But his very sociability proceeded to draw him into an emotional pit. As he communicated more with his contemporaries, he let down the guard he had long kept up, only to be overwhelmed by the feelings it had protected him against. He found himself possessed to utter distraction by a freshman man who had no idea how Philip felt about him and whom, therefore, Philip could not bring himself to touch. Other boys awakened his passions during his sophomore year and with some of them he permitted himself a bit of play that never got beyond furtive kisses and caresses. The social proscription of homosexuality left him caught during the early months of 1925 in a tormented conflict between desire and shame. The respectable record of his first semester declined in the second, when he dropped courses in Greek, history, and the fine arts and fell to a C in another history course he would normally have mastered easily. Finally, his despond was obvious enough to one of his best friends, Francesca Greene, and to her mother—the latter having become something of a surrogate parent to Philip—that the two women took him in hand. Get yourself some professional help, they counseled.

It was late winter when he visited a Boston neurologist, Dr. Sandy MacPherson, who concluded that Philip was suffering from cyclothymia, a manic-depressive syndrome intensified by his anxiety over his apparent homosexuality. Noting his intellectual interests, the doctor assured him that his condition was commonplace in the arts and constituted no cause for alarm. Many artists have been that way, he said, and they did very well with themselves. You can, too. Go home and give yourself several months' rest; you'll be better.

"That's all?" asked Philip.

"That's all," said Dr. MacPherson.

That was not all to Homer Johnson, who, hurrying to Cambridge, delivered his own advice in terms certain to deepen the gulf between himself and his son. "Boys don't fall in love with boys," he said. "Do something to get your mind off it. Forget about it. You'll be all right."

In March of 1925, Philip requested and received formal leave of absence from Harvard. He returned to Pinehurst, where the family was in residence, and settled into a routine that consisted of reading detective stories and weeping, more or less alternately, for several weeks. When he could no longer bear his distress, he telephoned Dr. MacPherson, who only repeated his prescription, together with the guarantee that rest would make all the misery go away. After several more weeks, it did.

The recovery may have been little more than what Dr. MacPherson anticipated—namely, a turn in the manic-depressive cycle—but to Philip's family, it seemed a small miracle, sufficient to itself. During the early summer, with all the Johnsons back in Ohio, Theodate invited one of her schoolmates from Abbott Academy, a vivacious brunette named Talita Jova, to spend several weeks at Townsend Farm. According to unanimous family reports, Philip no sooner met her than he succumbed to her. With nearly equal suddenness, the gloom of the neurological diagnosis was lifted from the minds of his parents, who were content to conclude that the boy's bizarre crisis of the previous spring was just that, an anomaly, a quirk, thus forgettable. Philip was a young colt, after all, and a thoroughbred at that, high-strung and impulsive, nothing more. Nor was anyone surprised when he interrupted his fling with Talita in midsummer to go off on a camping trip to Jackson Hole, Wyoming. By the time he returned, the girl had remembered she had another boyfriend back east, and she gave Philip the air. "As I prophesied the night she left Cleveland," he wrote Jeannette, "all is over. I am quite furious about it, because it would have been very nice this winter. But such is life, when I got back here I found that I did not give a continental about her and that is the whole story."

Philip's behavior would prove the neurologist a better prophet than the Johnson family. Talita never reappeared in his life, but neither did any other woman capture his fancy except as a very occasional diversion from what settled into an abiding homosexual orientation. To what extent he accepted that crucial fact of his personality by the time he returned to Harvard in the fall of 1925 is difficult to say. It would appear he began the adjustment, judging from his own memory of several brief crushes, each as unreciprocated or unfulfilled—in any case as unsatisfactory—as the encounters of his sophomore year, but none as emotionally jostling. All signs indicate that the 1925–1926 academic year was overall the happiest of his college career. He resumed dormitory living, taking over a spacious suite of rooms at a "gold coast" residence hall, Claverly, that was much nearer the heart of the campus than his earlier apartment had been. There he found it even easier to make new friends and no harder to entertain them. More and more he embraced society as less and less he felt the neglect of the clubs that earlier ignored him. He filled his evenings not only with the discussions he promoted among the brightest of his neighbors but with his own music making. Among his new possessions was a splendid Mason & Hamlin grand piano on which he labored earnestly enough to join in programs of chamber music with his accomplished classmate and fellow Hackley alumnus Carleton Smith. He even dreamed of life as a concert pianist.

That ambition was real, but it must be judged against the content of the letters he wrote to his most receptive correspondent, his mother, which record a mind flying all over the intellectual landscape, perching only fit-

fully in widely separated fields of the humanities: history, philosophy, languages, poetry, music, drama. His passion for learning exceeded his discipline in the ordering of it ("I have been so busy thinking that I have not done a thing"). He earned higher grades but not the highest, a reflection of an almost constitutionally unfocused temperament. While he admitted as much, he was capable of tossing off an arrogant rationalization: "I like to think I am not narrow enough to get all A's in my courses. Warren Farr gets A's but what does he know. He knows he knows much less than I do."

Philip's formal concentration was Greek, which, together with Latin, he had already mastered sufficiently that he read original texts in two of his courses. He captured the attention of a professor of philosophy, Raphael Demos, a noted authority on Plato. Homely, unkempt, and speech-impedimented but brilliant, Demos gained Philip's reciprocal admiration and steadfast loyalty, as if in a reprise of his relationships with the teachers at Hackley. Gradually, Philip united his interests in Greek and poetry to form a devotion to philosophy: "We must not forget that Plato loved poetry even though he wished to banish it," he wrote his mother. "He was a poet and couldn't help it. It was rather a poetic idea of his to abolish it."

It was Plato, in fact, to whom he surrendered himself, quickly and completely. The great Athenian's masterful advocacy of the absolute nature of right and wrong as well as his identification of virtue and knowledge carried a special appeal for Philip, whose own desire to attach himself to an authoritative moral position had already led him as a freshman into a brief affiliation with a Harvard chapter of the Buchmanite movement.

Sex was entangled in this, too, theoretically in the form of the homosexual society Plato, through Socrates, had treated with such easy cordiality in the dialogues, more immediately in the feelings that drew Philip to several young men among the Buchmanites.

Shortly before Christmas of 1925, Philip declared philosophy as his new formal academic concentration. Within several months, he had become a fixture in the Department of Philosophy and even a regular guest in the household of the most formidable philosopher at Harvard, Alfred North Whitehead ("with Bertrand Russell," Philip wrote to his mother, "the greatest philosopher we have today"). The celebrated professor found his new student's mental quickness fascinating; Mrs. Whitehead, like Francesca Greene's mother before her, was even more taken by a charming, vulnerable boyishness in the youth, which brought out the mother in her. Demos himself was pleased by Philip's move to philosophy, but he had no illusions about the constancy of it. " 'Just now he [Philip] is concentrating in Demos,' " Philip quoted his teacher in a letter, " 'next year in something else, I suppose.' " In fact, as matters developed, Philip never abandoned the philosophy major during the remainder of his stay at Harvard, but he continued feeding all the while from every trough within reach, and not always digesting what he took in. "I actually thought something out the other day," he wrote Louise in a manic moment of unwittingly precise, if conceited, self-characterization. "I was stinging under Raphael's reproach that I was a lazy thinker and never criticized my thoughts, so I got busy and thought for five minutes. As a consequence, I have a thorough knowledge of the psychological foundations of the state and got an A in the quiz this morning."

There was already one architect in Philip's family. Theodate Pope Riddle, Louise Pope Johnson's first cousin, had grown up in the midst of the wealth of her father, Alfred Atmore Pope, but she was never educated beyond finishing school and as an architect she was largely self-taught. Thus Louise was both jealous and contemptuous of her, with one feeling reinforcing the other, ever more insistently as Theodate grew in renown on the one hand and quirkiness on the other. She was an ardent believer in psychic phenomena and once offered her friend Henry James papers purporting to account for the appearance of his dead brother William at a séance she had attended. Archmaterialist that he was, Henry had written her back, with cruelly eloquent disdain:

"I return you the dreadful document, pronouncing it without hesitation the most abject and impudent, the hollowest, vulgarest, and basest rubbish I could possibly conceive. Utterly empty and illiterate, without substance or sense, a mere babble of platitudinous phrases, it is beneath comment or criticism, in short beneath contempt."

Her weakness for "rubbish" aside, Theodate was not without gifts as a designer. Her chef d'oeuvre, Avon Old Farms, a boys school in Farmington, Connecticut, is a fanciful sandstone olio of classical Greek and medieval English components. Its charm develops out of that very mixture of parts and styles, but Philip chose to see it otherwise when he visited it on a holiday outing with Daddy Bogues in October of 1925. He wrote home: "It is the purest mess you ever saw. It is built out of red stone and in no particular architecture that I could discover. Inside it is as dark as a pocket. . . . Daddy and I had a good talk with her [Mrs. Riddle] and both pronounced her thoroughly cracked when we got out."

Surely he meant what he said, although it is just as likely he was accommodating himself to his mother's feelings toward her cousin. Louise's values—her dearest devotion was the visual arts—were evidently working on him in another way: This letter is the first in which he mentions architecture. His interest was passing, but the knowledge he had to show for it better than idle. In the summer of 1926, having invited Daddy Bogues as his guest on a tour of England, his eyes were full of the Norman and Gothic, especially at Winchester and Canterbury: "Winchester, much maligned Winchester, is gorgeous. The Norman transept and the extra long nave are great. I had a chance of walking above the vaulting which I took. We clambered all over the place." There is more rhapsodizing about the countryside and the people ("all . . . wonderful to me"), including the Whiteheads, who were themselves in England for the summer and who "invited me to stay at their house overnight."

If these amiable remarks were meant to sit well with Louise, a later passage in the same letter suggests that mother and son shared unkindlier sentiments, which Philip expressed unashamedly, with typical gusto:

"When we meet these awful Americans in the cathedrals etc. I thank God I am not as other men and take my little car [Philip had bought a Morris Cowley convertible] and come into the country to some inn like this where no American has been this spring and sigh with relief. It is not that I mind Americans per se. But I hate the kind that comes from Kankakee and can't tell the difference between the nave and the transept and has to take up the verger's time by asking."

The total absence of letters from 1926–1927 makes it difficult to trace Philip's movements during that academic year. His Harvard transcript identifies him as a junior; clearly he required two years, 1924–1926, to complete his sophomore obligations in the wake of the breakdown he suffered in the winter of 1924–1925. The record also discloses his best grades to date, three B's and an A in four philosophy courses, a B in psychology, and an A in physics, this last remarkable enough in view of the distance he had previously kept from the natural sciences. No information could be gleaned from his sisters, who were in normal touch with him at the time. This paucity of recollection might signify little more than a period free of noteworthy incident. On the other hand, the very emptiness of the record arouses a premonitory suspicion, partly because the record is otherwise and elsewhere so full, partly because of the emotional crisis that did indeed develop in Philip's life beginning in the spring of 1927.

The overt onset was somatic. He was felled by an attack of mastoiditis. While it occurred late enough in the academic semester to permit him to finish his studies, nothing else about it was redeeming. He underwent a painful mastoidectomy that left him depleted spiritually as well as physically. His sister Theodate recalled that he languished in depression following the surgery and that the family decided on an appropriate therapeutic measure: another trip to Europe, a study trip, of course, as most of his travels were. Mindful of the time his son had spent in France in 1919 and England in 1926, Homer argued for Germany now, specifically for that Elysium of German cultural lore, Heidelberg. Since letters are missing for the summer of 1927, we are left knowing little more than that he spent his time working in Heidelberg with a private tutor in German.

Correspondence resumed in the autumn, following his return to Harvard for the beginning of his senior year, but it is noteworthy for the near absence of the skylarking cockiness and delight in learning that take up so much space in his communiqués of 1925–1926. Instead, his mood was lackluster and tentative. He was not certain he would stay at Harvard. The offer of a teaching assignment in beginning Greek at Oberlin College had been made by a professor of classics there—where, not incidentally, Homer Johnson was a trustee. Law school beckoned, too. That was his father's idea. Philip felt he might pursue it after the teaching, but not to the extent of adopting the legal profession: "Mr. Whitehead," he wrote in one of the rare letters addressed solely to his father, ". . . thinks it would be an excellent plan to take at least a year in the Law School [at Harvard]. . . . I myself feel that I would go back to philosophy freshened and with a good new point of view for a year in Law. I haven't for a minute gone back on Philosophy for a life work, but the field seems to extend itself the more I see of it. Unless you are a very sharp specialist in scientific metaphysics like Whitehead, the best you can do is be the other kind, the philosopher in Plato's sense of a man who correlates and because of his wide knowledge can correlate with more intelligence than his fellow men.

"The only thing I lack just now is, strange to say, self-confidence. I haven't Raphael here this year to back me up [Demos was on leave in Paris, victim of a nervous breakdown] and I get tremendously discouraged when I can't think things out the way I ought to be able. . . ."

Philip in law school? It is a senseless notion, at odds with nearly everything established thus far about him. His versatility notwithstanding, the study of law, for as little as a year, would have been more than his chronically short attention span could have tolerated. He was right about his wavering self-confidence, which would account for the unusual weight he seemed willing to assign his father's advice. Missing Demos and shaken by his breakdown, he relied instead, also unwisely, on Whitehead, who understood him no better than his father did and had less need to. Eventually, in fact, Philip and the great philosopher would have the good sense to part company, cordially but for good.

In the meantime, Philip's pain closed in on him as he suffered a second emotional collapse in the fall. No evidence of its exact nature survives beyond his own recollection that he "could feel the depression coming on, like a storm approaching over the mountains, within sight." No one else seems to have kept track of it. At the time, Theodate was occupied with her own undergraduate life at Wellesley, while Jeannette was even farther away, busy with graduate work in English at Oxford University during most of 1926 and by 1927 back in Ohio, where she was being courted by her future husband. It must suffice to say that Philip's misery was serious enough to prompt him to ask for another leave of absence from Harvard, which was granted on November 12, 1927. No letters document the remainder of the 1927–1928 academic year.

There is, however, ample record of another long trip to Europe that commenced early in 1928. Everything about it as it pertained to Philip fitted the pattern of a crisis deepening and as yet without resolution. It was a family trek, devoted with characteristic family thoroughness to the lands of the Mediterranean. Philip's rehabilitation was a motive secondary to Jeannette's forthcoming wedding, which would be the climax of the journey. Together with her and his mother, he set forth in January on the Italian Line, steering through the Strait of Gibraltar to Algeria, thence to Egypt, and later to Greece, where Homer joined the group in March. Sicily, Italy, and France followed and finally Paris, where Jeannette was married in July to John Dempsey, a Cleveland lawyer. Theodate remained stateside until she arrived in Paris in time to serve as one of Jeannette's bridesmaids.

By then, Philip had gone home, evidently in the trough of a rapidly vacillating manic-depressive cycle. Some weeks earlier in Egypt, he had become transfixed by the exoticism of the Arab population, and he took to dressing in their traditional regalia. He was now twenty-one, grown to manhood with, if anything, an increase in comeliness: Snapshots trace the looks of a striking young sheik in turban, caftan, and precisely trimmed mustache. Apparently identifying the foreignness of the environment with a freedom from constraint, he felt a renewed zest for living that had been missing from the letters he had written late in 1927. On an April day, he stole into a dark corner of the Cairo Museum with a museum guard for what he later called his first full-fledged, "consummated" sex-

PHILIP JOHNSON IN ARAB GARB,
CAIRO, 1928

PHILIP AND JEANNETTE, NICE, 1928

ual experience. Then, almost as quickly as the high phase of his behavior exhibited itself, the low followed in Italy, in a nightmarish reenactment of previous depressive attacks. He remained with his parents until they reached Paris, where it was expected he would attend Jeannette's nuptials. But he could not, and by midsummer he was back in Cleveland, prepared to spend the better part of what was left of his most tortured school year at the ancient family home on Overlook Road. He was in the grip of a dull desperation, confused by his own changeability, unsure of the nature of it, and quite as lonely as he had been at age eight when he ate his lunch by himself, in his natty little suits, on the steps of the school in Shaker Heights. Thus self-absorbed, he added hypochondria to his other griefs, from which he sought diversion, more likely relief, by falling back on one of his parents' favorite prophylactic measures. Suspecting that he was suffering from poisonous substances produced by all he ate and drank—"autointoxication," as it was popularly called and seriously regarded in some quarters at the time—he betook himself to a sanitarium in Battle Creek, Michigan, an establishment frequented by the family. There, properly flushed out and for the nonce buoyed up, he met a young actor from Kansas City, with whom he engaged in a fling of more comfortable duration than his hurried tryst in Cairo. The two drove in Philip's Peerless to the Finger Lakes in upper New York State, where they amused themselves for several weeks before returning the actor to his home in Kansas City. By the time Philip was back once again in Cleveland, his family was, too. He elected to sit out the autumn semester at Harvard.

While the frequency with which Alfred North Whitehead's name appears in Philip's Harvard correspondence is in part the measure of an intellectual closeness, it is even more a reflection of a social relationship that eventually extended to the families of both men, with visits and written pleasantries exchanged in the late 1920s. In the course of the friendship, in fact, Philip came to realize the limits of his talent for philosophy. Whitehead was far too monumental a thinker, too thorough a mathematician, too deadly sober a metaphysician for Philip, who in turn was much too impatient, mercurial, and even superficial in his thought processes for Whitehead. Neither the aging teacher—he was sixty-five when Philip met him—nor his wife could help liking his student's rapid wit, elegance, and cultivated good manners, but these assets by themselves were inadequate to a life in philosophy. "Whitehead never flunked his students," Philip recalled, "but if he gave you a B, it meant the same thing—that you didn't have what it takes. In 1927, he gave me a B. If I

JEANNETTE, C. 1928

was good in some species of philosophy, I was hopeless in metaphysics. He knew it."

The grade was, in fact, one of those that had made his 1926–1927 transcript look stronger than it was. Coming as it did in the spring of 1927, however, shortly before his mastoidectomy, it only added to the depression he suffered for most of the next year. Worse still, the European trip apparently had no curative effect, especially if we judge it by the desperate haste with which he broke it off. He did not return to Harvard until the second semester of 1928–1929.

It appears, however, that another change of heart in a most irresolute of young men was occurring in the very midst of his thrashing about. At first glance, it seems hardly different from other shifts of direction he had already taken, yet it set him on a course, crooked though it may have been, that governed his thoughts and movements over the next decade and even longer.

While he retained his philosophy major, he found himself drawing away from his once-beloved classics, especially from Plato, at about the same rate his interest in the arts grew. In a 1925 letter to his mother already cited here (see p. 37), he had sought to mediate Plato's low opinion of the esthetic impulse: "Plato loved poetry even though he wanted to banish it. . . . It was a rather poetic idea of his to abolish it."

Gradually, he found more rationalization than reason in that argument. He drew away from Plato, either because of his new passion for the arts or because he came under the spell of another, distinctly different philosopher. In any case, during the course of 1928, several events conjoined to reset his mental compass.

Salient among these was his ecstatic discovery of Friedrich Nietzsche's *Also sprach Zarathustra,* a work built upon ideas strikingly at odds with the moral absolutes Plato stood for. Nietzsche, moreover, wrote like a poet, with a poet's fervor, unlike the soberer Plato or, for that matter, any of Whitehead's metaphysicians. Philip, mindful of his own vaulting, frequently frustrated intellectual ambitions, not to mention his deeper psychic agonies, was swept away by such Nietzschean passages as:

"Whatever in me has feelings, suffers, and is in prison; but my will always comes to me as my liberator and joy-bringer. Willing liberates: that is the true teaching of will and liberty—thus Zarathustra teaches it. Willing no more and esteeming no more and creating no more—oh, that this great weariness might always remain far from me."

Nietzsche gave full-throated voice to his anti-Platonism: "Evil I call it, and misanthropic—all this teaching of the One and the Plenum and the Unmoved and the Sated and the Permanent." Clearly, Philip had found a thinker who not only spoke to his personal condition but preached the sacredness of creativity. The arts, especially music and poetry, had always occupied a comfortable but distant place on the edges of Philip's consciousness. Now the visual arts took command of the very center—not painting, which his mother had favored, but architecture, which would be his possession and no one else's.

In his later years, he remembered three events that awakened him to the art of building. One of these, his first sight of the cathedral at Chartres, which occurred when he was thirteen, seems to have been magnified in his mind more by mature reflection than by a reliable recollection of his feelings as an adolescent. His visit to the Parthenon in 1928, on the other hand, left him certainly and literally in tears, and while he was a weeper by habit, on this occasion once his eyes were dry, the image of the great temple remained undimmed in his memory. He later liked to claim a "Saul-Paul conversion" in 1928–1929, a simile inaccurate insofar as it suggests an antagonism to architecture prior to an embrace of it, but one that at least measures the force of the embrace.

Some months after his encounter with the Parthenon, he came across an article on architecture in *The Arts* of February 1928 that produced a similarly revelatory effect. The essay dealt not with old buildings but with the work of a living Dutchman, Jacobus Johannes Pieter Oud, and it bore the byline of an American architectural historian named Henry-Russell Hitchcock, Jr., who had graduated from Harvard in 1924, when Philip was already a student there. He knew Hitchcock no more than he knew Oud, but he was as arrested by the former's analytical insights as by the latter's crisply proportioned, startlingly unornamented structures. Oud was one of the major practitioners of the new European architecture, a movement that, if Philip knew nothing about it except the understated beauty he could see for himself in Oud's work, was familiar to only a handful of others in the United States.

At the time Philip met him, the twenty-seven-year-old Alfred Barr was recognized in the quarters that counted as one of the best-informed and most persuasive spokesmen in the United States for the cause of the painting and sculpture that had revolutionized Western art during the previous fifty years. He had recently completed a series of five well-advertised public lectures at Wellesley College that covered virtually the whole history of modernism, from Post-Impressionism through Cubism and the American schools to the Bauhaus and Russian Constructivism. Philip claimed he had heard nothing about the series or about Barr. Moreover, he was only marginally conscious of a related phenomenon that was closer to him than Wellesley—the Harvard Society for Contemporary Art, an association of Harvard students that began formal operations in February of 1929 in rented space above the Harvard Coop, where it staged several displays of modern painting, sculpture, prints, photographs, and even architecture, that had no local precedent for innovative exhibition fare. Shortly before he met Barr, Philip had visited the place, chiefly to look up the model of the Dymaxion House, a curiously futuristic concoction by the young R. Buckminster Fuller. He did not like it well enough to make a return visit.

The guiding spirits of the HSCA were a trio of undergraduates even younger than himself, Edward M. M. Warburg, John Walker, and, most prominently, Lincoln Kirstein, a nineteen-year-old Bostonian who was rather akin to Philip in the keenness of his intelligence and his quicksilver emotional metabolism, although more directed in his work habits, an authoritative figure among his campus peers. Philip knew who he was, but he was a little intimidated by Kirstein's imperious manner, and he declined to seek him out. If he met any of the three leaders of the HSCA before his afternoon with Barr, it must have been only cursorily. In short, he was almost completely without the sort of field experience sufficient by itself to attract Barr's attention.

Yet he appears to have attracted it. Our only account of his conversation with Barr at Wellesley is his own later recollection, which, in view of the long-lasting friendship that developed between the two men, has the ring of truth. Evidently, they did become involved in a matter of minutes in a conversation of unrelieved intensity. Philip made up for his ignorance of the specifics of painting, sculpture, and architecture with his wide-ranging conversance with the humanities and his newly formed fascination with modern building in Europe. He remembered being at his best with Barr, which meant behaving toward him with his mother's intellectual concentration, his father's sociability and extroversion, and the nervous vitality that was his own. He had a habit of seeking out authority figures (Bogues, Demos, Whitehead) who, as if reenacting Louise Johnson's role in his younger life, could take command of his emotional loyalties at the same time they nurtured his intellectual ambitions—could dominate him, that is, as they aggrandized him. Barr's soft-spokenness did not conceal—if anything, it illuminated—an excellence of mind and thoroughness of commitment, to which Philip eagerly surrendered. In turn, Barr, by nature responsive to anyone who showed an interest in the things he held dear, was drawn immediately to Philip's own mental fire, and he found himself more and more teaching him as he talked to him.

Philip's personal history, together with the fact that Barr was a bachelor at the time they met, are enough to arouse the suspicion that a sexual magnetism was also at work between them. There is no known evidence that it ever existed, either overtly or covertly. In fact, Philip, who in his mature years discussed his various liaisons with disarming and often sardonic frankness, spoke of Barr as he spoke of no one else, with a memorably guileless affection. He claimed he was never moved to touch Barr, who, relevantly or no, less than a year after their meeting married a woman to whom he appears to have been true his entire life and who in her own right became one of Philip's closest friends and companions.

The conversation with Barr led shortly to further communications that, more than any events of the period, brought Philip's mind into focus and gave shape to the summer trip he had planned to Europe. Judging from the letters he composed while abroad, moreover, Barr had inspired him to a still-sharper sense of purpose, a still-greater elation.

Writing from Berlin on November 8, at the end of his journey, he addressed his mother:

"I got your wonderful letter just after I sent off my last to you. I don't think I have ever had so much good news all at once. Of course I have known for months of Barr's appointment and strange that in my letter that crossed yours I should tell you about the same thing. . . . I would rather be connected with that Museum and especially with Barr than anything I could think of. I will have to hump myself and learn something in a hurry though."

Philip was referring to Barr's designation as the director of a new museum that had been organized by a group of major patrons in New York, a museum of modern art, the likes of which had never been realized in the United States. The appointment was made on July 9, several weeks before Philip, probably already apprised of the news, sailed for Europe. His later recollection that Barr had suggested the possibility of his working eventually in some capacity for the museum seems confirmed by the letter. So does his expression of the need to "learn something in a hurry."

Accordingly, before Philip departed, Barr pressed instructions on him, listing in detail what he should look at and contemplate on his imminent and now virtually annual transatlantic trip. He must visit museums he had not seen before and pay closer attention still to buildings, all the best of them, from all ages. Especially, he must find his way to those few sites where modern architecture, the stuff about which he had confessed such enthusiasm, had been constructed. Barr knew those places himself, having personally visited Rotterdam and the Hook of Holland, where the houses of Oud stood; Dessau, home of the revolutionary Bauhaus of Walter Gropius; and even the Soviet Union, where Constructivism was still more dream than reality, but nonetheless driven by a will to redesign the world. From close reading, he also knew of Stuttgart and its spectacular commune, the Weissenhofsiedlung, a collection of houses designed by the most daring architects of Europe and executed in a startlingly unified modern style.

This curriculum was laid down as Philip, newly galvanized, prepared for his trip. The fantasy of law school had dissolved, along with the prospect of returning to Ohio to teach Greek at Oberlin. Both futures suddenly seemed composed of the stuff of the past that had already not held together very well for him. Harvard as a whole felt stale. He had never really made more than a hobby of his piano, and once philosophy replaced Greek in his fancies, Raphael Demos faded somewhat from view and Whitehead deflated his balloon. Plato was gone, too, replaced by

Nietzsche and the arts. Worse luck, he was not yet finished with school; he had a full semester to complete that promised nothing more than a bachelor's degree with a concentration in classics and philosophy. What to do with himself when the summer was over—how to get closer to Barr, that is, and how to shoulder the remaining academic burden—was an issue he would deal with when the time came.

He headed straightway for New York, where he purchased a big Packard convertible touring car, hoisted it onto the proud new flagship of the German commercial fleet, the *Bremen,* and set sail. Once in Bremer-haven, he drove south to Heidelberg, meaning to make it his home base again, where he would resume his German and set out upon his search for great works.

THE PILGRIMAGE ROADS

Philip was a fast typist who wrote almost all the letters of his undergraduate years on a little portable that was an essential part of his traveling gear. He could put his thoughts on paper as rapidly as they came to him, and since he more or less free-associated in writing to those closest to him, his mail is a reliable measure of the things, or most of the things, that were overtly important to him.

Nothing about his letters is more striking than the contrast between his knowledge and the sophistication of his mental processes on the one hand and, on the other, an infantile self-indulgence aired almost proudly, especially in the correspondence with his mother. He learned quickly to speak with assurance about works of architectural renown (". . . the ninth century porch at Lorsch is a gem, with stolen or copied classical capitals and a zigzag architrave, all made out of chequered red and white stone") and many passages of his writing, obviously dashed off, were literate and suggestive of an almost instinctively critical mind-set: ". . . what I like about the Black Forest is that it is neither black nor a forest. It is folding hills, hills beyond hills, with houses slid down into the valleys, and their fields with them. On the crowns are woods, light straight, beautiful woods. And beautiful, so differently from ours. Perhaps not quite as lovely in their complete order, but there is something of grace about them that our wilds cannot give, not even a new forest with its heaths, which the German heart would never understand."

Meanwhile, he was forever the dutiful Johnson boychild, reporting not only on his lessons but on his ailments: He worried over a toothache and "the visions of what are to come [that] don't make me feel any better.

Anyhow, I rest a good deal with naps in the afternoon, and I never motor more than three hours in the day, and often none at all."

Since most of his letters were addressed specifically to "dear mother," the inference grows that by his early twenties he had devised two special ways of relating to the person who had long occupied the central place in his emotional life. To gain her respect and approval, moreover to magnify her in her own mind as well as in his own, he would demonstrate the intellectual prowess they both knew he owed to her. To win her affection and her sympathy, he would complain to her almost on cue, pamper himself, play the lamb, suffer a little—bravely: "I know you will be thinking that I am traveling too fast and that I am getting tired, but I really am not." Both modalities were of long standing, the one cognitive, the other affective. While we have no letters from her to him and thus cannot test this speculation, Philip's later criticism of her as more schoolmistress than mother might begin to explain why at this stage of his life his intellectualizing moved her and profited him, while his indebtedness to her was preserved by the gestures and sounds of his dependence. Did he seek from his age-mates and lovers the confirmation of his manhood that he could not gain fully from her, and even less from his father, whom he mentions comparatively seldom in his correspondence? How could he address her so adoringly in his early letters and as a man of middle years dismiss her with studious indifference?

His own later comment that "she was my invention; I invented her to write my letters to" is too oblique to be illuminating, but it does suggest that his way of dealing with the skewed affection of his parents, once he was on his own, ranged from indifference to manipulation. It is too late to know how fully they realized that or how deeply it affected them.

Once in Heidelberg ("My plans are still more or less vague"), he made contact with old acquaintances, and it seems to have been they who suggested the directions his first moves took. With Albert Kreusel, a local student, he made his first excursion, to Freiburg. There his lessons began, to which he made a characteristically opinionated response. The cathedral was "the most beautiful thing I have yet seen in Germany. . . . Being an awful prig, I think it is pretty good of me to say I like this Gothic thing [the Freiburg Cathedral]. But I do. To be sure the late Gothic [part of the building] is awful, but where is it not awful. The Romanesque is the best part. . . ."

Evidently, he had turned sour on the Gothic he once admired at Canterbury. So he pursued the Romanesque, to Worms, Speyer, and Mainz.

with brief visits along the way to the little Carolingian gatehouse at Lorsch and the protomodern housing colony put up in 1901 on the Mathildenhöhe in Darmstadt. By then, he had also been to Mannheim, where in one of the galleries of the museum he struck up a conversation with a young American of his own age, John McAndrew, who, it developed, was a fellow Harvardian, an architecture student at that. A friendship developed between the two travelers with a suddenness that recalled Philip's earlier meeting with Alfred Barr. Several days after Mannheim, he wrote his family that "in another month we [McAndrew and himself] meet to go all over Germany getting materials for popular articles on architecture."

That is, in fact, what they did—the going, if not the getting—since they observed a lot but never published a thing. In a midsummer letter, Philip reported his visit to Stuttgart, where he saw "a little suburb made by all the famous modern architects." It was the Weissenhofsiedlung, recommended to him by Barr, a housing colony completed in 1927 and widely hailed in Europe as the first major collective triumph of design in the modern idiom. Philip recognized it for its stylistic distillation of the features he had learned from Barr: A compacted group of houses and apartment buildings had been laid out informally on a hillside overlooking Stuttgart, its parts remarkably akin to one another in their unornamented, asymmetrical, rectilineally geometric volumes, their flat roofs and sleek unarticulated walls with surgically pierced windows and stucco exteriors painted for the most part white. Similarly free of historical detail, the Weissenhofsiedlung was architecture abstracted, "just perfect for me to begin on," as he wrote, adding that it was "my first view of things by Le Corbusier, Gropius and Oud, the three greatest living architects."

More exactly, they were the Europeans Barr had called "perhaps the finest masters" among the moderns, which is to say the three his eager disciple had heard the most about. Otherwise, it is hard to explain Philip's failure to mention Mies van der Rohe, who not only supervised the Weissenhof project but was responsible for the design of its remarkably free-flowing plan as well as of the biggest single building on the site, a three-story apartment block. Mies would soon become Philip's favorite living architect, but in mid-1929 he was not yet so well known to international audiences as Gropius, who "may be the greatest of them all," as Philip framed it, in a superlative typical of many he loved to confer, not always consistently.

Excursions continued from Heidelberg. Philip was charmed by Rothenburg's late medieval and Renaissance vernacular, and in Würzburg his delight turned to exultation: "I feel so festive and well-dressed in the presence of the Baroque . . . for town planning you must admit there is no better style."

Late in August, after about a month in Europe, self-indulgence shouldered dedication aside: "Heidelberg was getting more and more strenuous, so the day after I wrote you I up and left . . . the name Geneva sounded so nice, so I came as far as this for a rest." And then: "Once here I decided that it might be my teeth that had to do with my being tired and the Dutch boy [an unidentified friend] knows the best American dentist in London and I want to go to London sometime, so I am going day after tomorrow."

And so he did, for a two-week romp memorable for shopping ("My new suits are gorgeous, of course, but the total cost is as usual staggering") and a brief flirtation with the playwright Noël Coward, which he later claimed neither of them acted out. At last, his sobriety again intact, he returned to Germany—by the uncommon luxury of an airplane ride—to prepare himself for the expedition he and McAndrew had plotted.

By late September, the two pilgrims were in The Hague, having just seen the work of "the world's greatest architect, J. J. P. Oud," in Rotterdam. The ambition of their scholarship was now upgraded to the level of "a book, a fact-picture book, with a minimum of metaphysics and aesthetics in it. . . . we hope to include a short article of belief by each of the big men. . . ."

Less than a fortnight later, they reached Berlin.

It was the best of times. The German capital was at the peak of a cultural fever that had made it the most galvanic metropolis in Europe during the late 1920s. The great traditional German performance arts of music and drama were in full flower, sharing the *Berliner Luft* with an irreverent avant-garde that was active in all the creative fields, most aggressively in a wide-open cabaret scene where the collapse of middle-class morality was celebrated nightly.

To Philip, the setting was empyreal. He gorged himself on opera, ballet, and theater, took in every experimental film he could find, haunted the art galleries, and lounged in the cafés. His letters describe his activities in dutiful detail with the exception of his sexual life, which he pursued more vigorously than ever before, especially since Berlin allowed him to carry on enthusiastically, relieved of the guilt that hounded him back home. He even permitted himself discreet references to the notions that circulated in his new environment: "I think if it can be told from the

PHILIP, BERLIN, C. 1930

platform of a Berlin cabaret, it can be written in a letter to one's mother. How prudish I am getting, my, my! Recently in Berlin, it seems, the law against homosexual relations has been repealed, apropos of which the *conferencier* said that at Easter the law against relations with animals will also be repealed and the normal relation only will be prohibited. The audience thought it very funny, as I did myself, but then of course, I would not admit it." Such disingenuous restraint was meant for his family's ears; he did not bother with it in the company of the young men whom, by his later acknowledgment, he was happy to find in quantity among Berlin's best and most cultivated classes. "The Americans were the conquerors of old Germany," he once said, "and the young Germans were eager to accommodate them. Paris was never that *gastfreundlich*."

The personal relationships he struck up, nevertheless, were scrupulously kept independent of his professional life. He made a fast friend of a young German with architectural aspirations, Jan Ruhtenberg, who took him twice to nearby Dessau, where Philip had his first enraptured sight of the Bauhaus: "It is a magnificent building. I regard it as the most beautiful building we have ever seen, of the larger than house variety. Perhaps the

Hook [of Holland, the site of Oud's housing project, seen by Philip earlier in the summer] has what Hitchcock [architecture critic Henry-Russell Hitchcock] would call more lyric beauty, but the Bauhaus has beauty of *plan,* and great strength of design. It has a majesty and simplicity which are unequaled." With the help of Ruhtenberg, who worked as a public relations aide in the office of designer Bruno Paul, he met most of the faculty at the Bauhaus and made his first serious art acquisition, a painting by Paul Klee, "the greatest man there." Walter Gropius, who with Adolf Meyer designed the Bauhaus while serving as its first director, had meantime resigned. Philip caught up with him in his Berlin architectural office, where he judged him anew as "great," a label he never tired of pinning on heroes, whom, in turn, he never ran out of.

Hyperbole was catnip to Philip, but he wielded it with as much scorn as approbation. While his letters to Alfred Barr were overall more judicious in tone than those to his mother, he could write the former that "[Wassily] Kandinsky is a little fool who is completely dominated by his swell Russian Grande Dame of a wife. He has millions of his sometimes painful abstractions sitting around the house and thinks he is still the leader of a new movement. It is sometimes pathetic, sometimes amusing." Yet even such immoderate prose was not without perceptiveness; Kandinsky in 1929 was indeed neither the painter nor the influence he had been a decade and a half earlier. So much for scorn. The approbation followed, no less prophetically: "I like the things [Marcel Breuer] has done, and if he had only invented the now famous chair of pipes [the Wassily chair, named in fact for Kandinsky], he would be something at his age of 26."

Philip's romance with modern architecture came to full flower that summer in Berlin as he grew constantly hungrier, more excitable, and more ambitious. Encouraged by both McAndrew and Ruhtenberg, he tried his hand for the first time at designing, conceiving additions and renovations for Johnson family property at both the Townsend Farm and Pinehurst and writing home about them with tireless self-confidence. His suggestions for decor reflected an influence from the Dutch De Stijl movement: "The idea is the use of nothing but the purest primary colors. But there would be so much white (with gray, of course, for rugs) that the colors would only be bits."

Such a preference for lean over fat reflected the modernist canon. Yet he persisted in his love of the Baroque so steadfastly that he interrupted his Berlin stay with a trip to Dresden and Prague, at the time still two of the finest jewels of the Baroque in urban settings. "We must first look at Barock [the German spelling] architecture differently," he lectured Louise from Prague. "Get away from the idea that it is debased Greek architecture and realize that the former forms are now used for decorative purposes, purposes of light and shadow, and of elegant shape. I think of the comparison of the Zwinger and a fugue of Bach. Each is elaboration on a very simple theme. . . . See how [in the Zwinger pavilion, Matthäus Daniel Pöppelmann's masterpiece in Dresden] the plain pilasters with simple bases are put between equally simple windows and repeated many times. . . . It is about as dizzy a system as was ever invented, just as Bach frills up his fugues as much as possible."

If Philip's opinion of the Baroque was not shared by most of the modernists whom he was busy learning to admire, it was at least his own. He picked it up from no one in particular and it coexisted comfortably with his appreciation of the severities of Oud, Gropius, and their peers. There was in each of the two tastes, in fact, a certain extremity; he was never one to do things by halves. The modern had the virtue of newness for him as well as of rarefaction; it rewarded his most concentrated intellectual strivings. The Baroque, grandiloquent and unrestrained—in a favorite word of his, *gorgeous*—compensated for the purism of the modern and satisfied a more emotional appetite. He gravitated toward both the puritan and the sybaritic sensibilities, and at the end of his life he could look back to actions and accomplishments that were reflections of this psychic duality. The most obvious was his own architecture, which ranged from the most austerely abstract, or modernist, to the most exuberantly representational—that is to say, Baroque. (The difference may be cited between his Glass House of 1949, in New Canaan, Connecticut, and his Crescent complex of 1985, in Dallas.) Even on his way to Prague in 1929, only days after his mind had been braced by the spare geometries of Gropius at the Bauhaus, his emotions were swept up in the mystical thunder of Wagner at Bayreuth. (For the anecdotal record, Philip could exert a sensuous impact of his own. Seated one evening next to the sixty-year-old Siegfried Wagner, the composer's son, at dinner in the Festspielhaus, he was astonished to feel his neighbor's hand searching the length of his thigh. It was one Wagnerian movement he resisted.)

If there was a bridge that spanned the two shores of his nature, at least at the conscious level, it was a reverence for beauty, even an obsession with it—provided it was free of message and he of the obligation to reflect on the message. Thus he could enjoy equally the reductivist forms of the Weissenhofsiedlung and the opulent sounds of the *Ring of the Nibelungs*. Moreover, since his upbringing had confined him so narrowly to the study of beauty, he found it easy to make beauty the standard of goodness, to equate esthetics with morality. Thus he offered up his admiration, willingly and generously, to the fine things and the handsome minds he encountered throughout his life—even to those who opposed him—while conversely heaping ridicule on everything he viewed as esthetically beneath himself and them. There is no evidence that anyone in Prague in 1929 treated him meanly or discourteously, but he had the following to say, as he wrote his mother shortly before leaving the Czech capital: "I hope we get out alive. I don't trust any people that speak this awful language. There is no excuse for it, and here they are trying their best to propagate it. . . . Just so much spitting as far as we were concerned. At least when you were here everything was in German. And the stupid people, with their too broad mouths and blank expressions; Bohunks, I calls 'em."

On the seventh of November in 1929, The Museum of Modern Art opened formally in New York City. Philip remained in Europe for slightly less than two more months before returning home. It is not clear why he decided to forgo his expressly planned visit to the International Exposition in Barcelona, where he might have seen Mies van der Rohe's new German Pavilion, the building that by consensus ranks as the architect's masterpiece. Philip himself could not remember why, and his letters are no help. What is demonstrable is that he heeded one further piece of advice proffered him in Wellesley by Alfred Barr: Finish school. In January, he returned to Harvard for his final semester, moving into an apartment in the Hotel Continental in Cambridge, and in the spring of 1930 he received his bachelor of arts degree—cum laude, in fact, in spite of all the pitfalls he found his way into in the course of a seven-year college career.

Needing only a course to graduate, Philip chose one in Greek that he had begun and dropped the previous year. It is not likely that he worked overhard at it or anything else at Harvard until exam time. The real measure of his ambition was the dozen-odd visits he paid Alfred Barr in New York.

There, he was invited into the circle of precocious intellectuals, nearly all of them still in their twenties, who gathered around Alfred in the shadows of The Museum of Modern Art. He was at last introduced personally to Henry-Russell Hitchcock, Jr., author of the article on J. J. P. Oud that had so drawn him to modern architecture two years earlier. The introduction was negotiated by Margaret Scolari-Fitzmaurice, a gifted graduate student in art history at New York University who was a close friend of Hitchcock's from Vassar days and most recently a still-closer friend—the fiancée, in fact—of Alfred Barr.

The tight little cadre also included the art dealer J. B. Neumann, the émigré Austrian art dealer, and Jere Abbott, a former Princeton Graduate Scholar with multiple talents in the arts and sciences who had earlier shared an apartment in Cambridge with Barr and traveled with him through Europe in the winter of 1928–1929. Abbott had been installed as associate director of the museum. Rounding out the company was Cary Ross, out of Yale and Johns Hopkins, an elegant idler, aspiring poet, and, one heard, friend of Ernest Hemingway and the Fitzgeralds in Paris during the 1920s. Ross also was on the museum staff but unsalaried and unclassified, a factotum to Barr, who, it seemed, greatly prized him.

The group met together constantly, in particular at a Chinese restaurant close by the Heckscher Building at 730 Fifth Avenue, where, on the twelfth floor, the museum had its first home. Talk was nimble and smart, almost always about art, artists, and related gossip. Philip thrived in this atmosphere. He was good at persiflage; it was another way of imitating his father's natural conviviality. Margaret Scolari—Marga (sometimes Daisy) —found him entrancing, recalling later that "he was handsome, always cheerful, pulsating with new ideas and hopes, as if he had stored up in Cambridge and come to New York to unload what meant most to him while he still had to submit to academic drudgery. Those early months of the Museum were volcanic. Sometime in the spring I had to go to Boston and Cambridge. I saw Philip in his rooms (I think he lived in an apartment, not in one of the houses. . . .). He was wildly impatient, he could not sit down, he had a high lectern for his books, another . . . for his typewriter. He was . . . rearing to race." (Almost constitutionally incapable of sitting down, he did all his reading and writing while standing upright.)

Then, in an altered tone reflective of Philip's own still-habitual violent shifts of mood, she added: "At the same time he was desperate . . . he didn't see how he could finish and graduate. . . . I remember having written him . . . begging him to finish. . . ." Elsewhere she adds, "Twice while I was chatting with him, he called his analyst."

Philip's frenzy, short-lived but intense, was brought on by the stress of a round of comprehensive examinations and exacerbated by a sudden, impassioned, painful affair with Cary Ross. Late in April, he wrote Marga:

"You are the only one who knows about Cary and me, and to whom I can talk now. As you know the only reason it came about was because he is good-looking and identified with that group down there in my emotional life. Well it seems now that it was merely a passing whim with him, and he was too weak to tell me, and let me go on thinking more. He came up the other day, and naturally I soon found out where the land lay, and am now in a species of hell which I heartily dislike. My exams are next week and there is no alternative, I must get to work.

"If you have time won't you write some advice saying all the usual things about him. . . . there are complications like other people, that make me so jealous I am almost sick to my stomach. . . ."

Marga's reply to Philip is apparently lost, but it must have encouraged his successful negotiation of the examinations that amounted to his last academic hurdle at Harvard. He wrote her back, lavishing his gratitude on her in a letter typed in the all-lowercase alphabet that he had picked up from his visits to the Bauhaus, where such "progressive" usage was standard: "you really are wonderful. i hope you don't mind my saying so when you are going off to marry someone else, but what i would have done without that letter to read, i have[n't] the faintest idea. . . . i sleep pretty well and everything is going splendidly. i have been an awful mollycoddle all my life and i do hope this means turning over a new leaf."

It was still too early for that, yet in his own freakish way and however painfully, he was gradually focusing his scattered mind and mapping a professional route for himself. He had the ear of Alfred Barr, with whom he carried on his most earnest discussions in New York. More and more, these talks included Hitchcock, a shaggy, thickset bear of a man, short on the graces but long on intellect and formal education, who found himself as taken by Philip's quickness as Barr had been. In turn, Philip's respect for Hitchcock had only deepened with his reading of the latter's book of 1929, *Modern Architecture: Romanticism and Reintegration,* one of the first large-scale formal efforts by an American scholar to analyze and assess the development of the building art from the eighteenth century to contemporary times.

Within a matter of weeks, Barr, Hitchcock, and Johnson formed a bond of companionship based on a concordance of taste that eventually exerted a profound effect on the course of American art and architecture. Their alliance moved toward active collaboration in the summer of 1930 when each of them made his own trip to Europe and Philip and Russell joined forces in a project of their own. In May, Alfred, following Marga's trail by only a few days, met her in Paris and married her there, with Hitchcock and Cary Ross as witnesses. Philip arrived a month later in Cherbourg, landing in the arms of Cary, with whom he resumed his earlier dalliance, although on a less affecting basis. Proceeding to the French capital, they were reunited with the Barrs and Hitchcock, who in turn had fallen in with yet another company of cosmopolitans, chief among them the composer Virgil Thomson, J. B. Neumann, and the Hollywood executive George Kates.

After a few hectic days with that crowd, Johnson and Hitchcock settled down to the business that had brought them to Europe in the first place, a study tour that Philip thought might lead to a book similar to the one he and McAndrew had envisioned a year earlier. "But the book," he wrote home on June 20, "I cannot put it off any longer although we just got the idea [the] day before yesterday. It had been in mind for a year as you know, but I didn't really want to take the risk of alone carrying through such an ambitious plan when I knew so little about architecture really. And Russell has had the idea because he realized that his book was badly illustrated. So what the plan is now is to rewrite in a more popular way paying close attention to the buildings illustrated, parts of his book and incorporate about 150 full page half-tones. The text will be first and then the pictures in a bunch. Of course one disadvantage perhaps will be that the book will be in German. . . . The text will practically be a translation of Russell's big book. . . ."

In fact, the finished product, which took nearly two years to complete, proved to be more and of greater consequence than the popularized translation of a book already in print. Published in 1932 as *The International Style: Architecture Since 1922*, it went on to exert a tremendous impact on architecture worldwide. Nonetheless, if neither of the authors could foresee the fate of what they conceived in the summer of 1930, they could be fairly certain of their respective roles. Hitchcock was clearly senior in all professional respects and Philip functioned very nearly as his research assistant ("somewhat . . . of an apprentice"), which is not to say he was without advantages of his own. He had already seen more modern architecture and met more people in Europe who knew about it than nearly any other American, and probably as much as Hitchcock. Moreover, he was *salonfähig*—more presentable, that is, to the sophisticated company of the art world. While Hitchcock spoke French, German was the language they were likely to use most, and Philip had grown virtually fluent in it. "I learned it the best way," he often said. "The horizontal method." His wealth was no small factor either, especially insofar as it took the form of a sleek new Cord convertible that furnished the travelers with first-class transportation and access to places reachable best by car. And cars in Europe in the new Depression were becoming scarce.

Philip was quick to find Russell both an inspiring and maddening companion, as his letters attest:

"[He is] tenderhearted, enthusiastic and brilliant intellectually . . . his mind works like mine in discontinuous jumps, but he really knows a lot and can synthesize his knowledge. . . . He knows everything there is to know about traveling . . . does not fit in America, and does not feel at home there. He is much too strange, with his great Socrates face under a great messy red beard. But he is terribly sensitive. A great many people dislike him, but real people are always eminently dislikable, and he has many warm friends."

From another: "Russell and I live and eat and sleep architecture, which is wonderful for me. And he is only slightly disgusting. Only last night when I had a little fever, he asked me to bring him a glass of water because he was too lazy to get out of bed. . . . He is deaf, he talks too loud and smacks his food and cleans his teeth with his napkin and loses his temper at officials and doesn't bathe frequently nor even wash nor even pick up his clothes. . . . He is wearing on me in that he never lets down and doesn't expect me to. . . . His conceit is boundless, but then mine, by all reports, is considerable, so that doesn't really bother me. . . .

"Russell is a genius."

He was also a homosexual who had shown more than passing interest in Cary Ross before Philip turned up in New York. How he reacted to

HENRY–RUSSELL HITCHCOCK,
C. 1935

Philip's attachment to Cary, fitful as it was, is not certain, but a passage in a letter written by Alfred to Marga later in the summer suggests that the Johnson-Ross-Hitchcock relationship in Europe was essentially casual and unproprietary, surely more so than Barr, despite the presence of so many homosexuals in his life, was accustomed to:

"Berlin buzzes—it's nicer than Paris. Cary, Phil, Russell all too affectionate to each other. Cary and Phil in Hamburg. Cary and Russell here.

"How funny.

"But Cary's marvelous to me and so is Phil, and Russell, like an affectionate elephant!

"But oh gosh!"

It is also worth remembering that the professional bond between Philip and Russell was too strong to be loosened by any easy sexual adventure, nor were they ever involved at that level with each other. In any case, Cary remained with the Barrs after Philip and Russell left Paris. All five travelers were briefly reunited in Hamburg (whence Alfred's letter to Marga) and later in Berlin, but by that time Philip claimed to be less taken

J. J. P. OUD

by Cary's charms than put off by his melancholy, depressive nature: "To see Cary wallowing in all the problems of finding life or rather Life not worth so much, and nothing really an end in itself, gives me mixed feelings of pity and remoteness . . . the mystery of his close connection with us all remains strange. Alfred is strangely dependent on him and naturally he on Alfred, but my relation with him has definitely become less close."

This was written from Hamburg early in July, by which time Philip had completed the following itinerary:

—From Paris to The Hague, where he finally met Oud ("now one of my very good friends") and dreamed that the esteemed Dutchman might be persuaded to build a residence for the Johnson family in the United States. "[His houses] are livable and simply magnificent in proportion and material," Philip enthused in a letter to his mother, adding that he could not say the same for Le Corbusier, whom he had met fleetingly in Paris but got on with badly: "an objectionable man but unquestionably a genius. I would not live in any of his houses but they are certainly exciting to see."

—From Holland to Antwerp, Hanover, and Hamburg, briefly, and then to Stockholm, where the two Americans were much impressed by a huge exposition hall in the modern manner and all designed by Sweden's preeminent architect Erik Gunnar Asplund. "A marvelous restaurant there [the Paradise]," wrote Philip, "done in steel and glass and nevertheless very elegant."

—Then to Copenhagen. Philip, evidently reacting to the city as he had to Prague, was again content to equate beauty and worth, or the lack of one with the lack of the other. He dismissed Denmark with a sneer: "flat and uninteresting . . . no modern architecture . . . the language is unbeautiful, the people stupid."

—Then to Hamburg again and at last, as in 1929, to Berlin, always and for a variety of reasons, the ultimate destination.

In his correspondence of mid-1930, Philip took notice, but only in passing, of the Depression, which by then had shaken all of the Western world. The fact is, neither his father's material comfort nor his own was ever seriously disturbed by it. Moreover, while the crisis affected Germany at least as much as it did the rest of Europe, the cultural momentum of Berlin had not yet slowed as much as it would several years later with the Nazi accession, and the capital remained the best place in the world to study the new architecture. How it got that way is worth recalling.

A decade earlier, the Wilhelmine German state, already economically and militarily beaten by the Allies, was culturally disowned in a massive revolt of the nation's intellectual avant-garde. The Kaiser's conservative order, widely associated with defeat and disgrace, was repudiated in all the liberal precincts of the arts, the politics, and the mores of the postwar period. Rebellion took alternate extreme forms of rage over the present and hope for the future, with the bitter nihilism of the Berlin Dada movement and the relentless pillorying of the bourgeoisie by painters George Grosz and Otto Dix contrasting sharply with the social utopianism of Walter Gropius's impassioned 1919 manifesto of the new Bauhaus.

Since the war-crippled economy brought new construction nearly to a halt, most architects had little option but to dream their designs, which they did with a will, conjuring some of the most untamed architectural visions of the modern age, their very extravagance inversely proportional to the likelihood of their ever being realized. Expressionism, the highly emotive movement that was virtually the native language of the advanced German arts prior to the war, reached a fever point in architecture just after it, in Bruno Taut's millenarian fantasies of alpine landscapes studded with structures of crystal and glass and Wassily Luckhardt's drawings of gargantuan faceted monoliths meant to advance the religious unification of humanity.

Effectively, the dreaming stopped when the building started, about 1924. The previous year's runaway inflation had been curbed and a moderately left-of-center national government in association with local cooperative building societies began to act upon the widespread need for housing that had not been met since prior to the war. This move co-incided with a shift in the character of German and, for that matter, European architecture. In Germany, Expressionism receded, its flights of fancy appearing more and more to have been a poor man's luxury. The crafts, closely identified with the "personal" nature of Expression-ism, similarly faded from view, their value surrendered to the new machine technology that held out unprecedented promise to the build-ing arts. Not unrelatedly, a cooler, more consciously detached and unsentimental approach to creativity and production settled over all the arts. The Germans gave it the name *Sachlichkeit*—objectivity or matter-of-factness—a mood reflected in the dry, impassive portraits of the painter Christian Schad, the studiously neutral reportage of the jour-nalist Egon Erwin Kisch, and the depersonalized utilitarianism of *Gebrauchsmusik*.

Influences from outside Germany abetted the whole process: the socially idealist content and minimalist geometric form of De Stijl from Holland and Constructivism from Russia and, above all, the work and thought of the French-Swiss Le Corbusier, not only an architect of exceptional force but a writer who, having promoted a *"rappel à l'ordre"* in the pages of his journal *L'Esprit nouveau,* gave the world of postwar architecture its most significant book, *Vers une architecture.*

The *Neues Bauen,* or "new architecture," that emerged in Germany during the second half of the 1920s was an outgrowth of these interlock-ing developments. In formal terms, its smooth, carefully tooled geomet-ric look was both a reflection of postwar abstract art and a metaphor for the machine. Yet it was also noteworthy for its collective response to the collective social needs of the Weimar Republic and the technological innovations available for the satisfaction of them. Thus it had a double identity of form and function, with both components urgent enough that a generation of talented architects—Gropius, Taut, Mies van der Rohe, Erich Mendelsohn, and Ernst May among them—rose to the occasion, each rationalizing his work according to the emphasis he placed on one or the other of the components.

These were chief among the reasons why the architecture of Weimar Germany, more than that of any other country, drew the global attention of engineers and sociologists as well as esthetes. Even so, much of the new building throughout Europe began to take on common qualities as if in reaction to common stimuli. Philip had seen the process most coherently manifest in the Weissenhofsiedlung, whose unity of purpose was achieved by designers from Austria, Belgium, France, Germany, and Holland. Now he would learn still more about the whole corporate phenomenon in Berlin, not only the capital of Germany but an international crossroads where the clamorous vanguards of nearly all European countries converged.

He rented an apartment at Achenbachstrasse 22, had stationery designed and printed, and got to work. He preferred living alone now; Russell's mind may have been magisterial, but his creature habits were something else again. His German friend Jan Ruhtenberg reentered the scene and began to take up as much of Philip's time as Russell did, although as a threesome they worked together congenially. The Barrs showed up, with Cary, staying long enough to examine the plans Philip and Russell had for their book and to applaud them.

Clearly the thesis of the work was an extension of one of Russell's principal arguments in his 1929 book: The esthetic of the new architecture was ultimately of greater consequence than its social, political, or technological significance. Form and style, Russell reasoned—and both Philip and Alfred agreed—are what make architecture art as distinct from something else, and art was what each of them had elevated to the level of a faith, replete with convictions that smacked of formal religions: If certain values are sacred, certain others are proportionately invalid and, if not wrong, surely not relevant. In one of his few references to the Depression in Berlin, Philip wrote: "The architects here are so concerned with cheap building, and are so sunk in whatever shape the modern movement happens to take in their community, that they cannot take aesthetic stock of their work." He pursued his argument relentlessly: "We have come to the conclusion that no building is done without expense and that even in the movement those architects are the best who build expensively . . . here in central Europe where architects are sociologues, it is hard to avoid propagandistic building."

Given his criteria, it was only a matter of time before Philip made contact with the architect who fulfilled them more than anyone in Europe: Mies van der Rohe. By early August, the two men had met, with predictable results. Mies cast so enveloping a spell over Philip that he was commissioned to design the interior of a New York apartment the younger man had rented prior to his trip to Europe.

Philip had not seen any of Mies's major works with the exception of Weissenhof, to which, as we earlier conjectured, he apparently did not react as affirmatively as he did now to Mies himself once he had heard about him and finally met him in Berlin. Only after offering Mies the apartment commission did he set out to study Mies's actual recent work. Since the German Pavilion at Barcelona had been razed a few months earlier, he elected to seek out a new and much discussed house in Brno, built for the wealthy industrialist Fritz Tugendhat and his wife, Grete.

The Tugendhat House and the German Pavilion had certain attributes in common. Both were striking chiefly for the generosity of their open, flowing interior spaces, for overall flawless proportioning of parts, and for the opulent materials—chrome-plated steel plus assorted marbles and colored or translucent glass—that Mies employed in their construction. Neither budgetary constraints nor "social significance" interested him. He was never comfortable translating his motives into words, but when he did, he claimed he wanted to impart "spiritual" meaning to his work. That argument seemed too private and too ethereal for many of his German contemporaries, who criticized him for his material extravagance and his indifference to social issues. As for Philip, form mattered, if spirituality did not, and extravagance was all to the good; he was completely enthralled by the patrician splendor of Mies's art. The house "has one room very low ceiled," he wrote, "one hundred feet long, toward the south all of glass from the ceiling to the very floor. Great sheets of glass that go into the floor electrically . . . one wall is of onyx. It has cost already a million marks, which in Europe is a frightful sum."

Mies, in fact, had joined him on the trip to the Tugendhat House, "which," Philip wrote, "he had never seen. He knew only the plan." The remark appears in a letter to Russell, who by late August was already back in the United States. Tarrying long enough to make a second visit to Brno, Philip only heaped more praise on Mies's house: "[It] is like the Parthenon. One cannot see anything from pictures. It is a three-dimensional thing which simply can't be seen in two. It is without question the best looking house in the world."

Such fervor notwithstanding, Philip's agenda for the coming season made room for considerably more than esthetic enthusiasms. "This next year in New York," he wrote as early as August 6, "is for several purposes dedicated. . . . I must see what Lewis Mumford knows and how he did it. [this to keep Philip abreast of the issue of the social importance of architecture, even though he regarded it as less vital to the art than did Mumford, the leading authority on the subject in the United States]. I must see the construction men and see where they got it and how much they are really worth and helpful to me [this with a similar end in mind, to learn what he needed to know about the technological element in the new architecture, however little he valued that attribute]. I must use my position on the committee in New York to start at least influencing people [this referring to the advisory committee of The Museum of Modern Art, to which he had been appointed in April, a group adjunct to the board of trustees]."

Such ambitions were consistent enough with Philip's desire to know more about the new architecture in its manifold aspects. Nonetheless, the emphasis in each of his remarks on questions of practicality that were of secondary importance to those of esthetics, in his own mind and surely in Hitchcock's, raises the suspicion that plans were already afoot for something more during the 1930–1931 season than the publication of a scholarly study with overtones of a style manifesto. Had they an exhibition in mind, as well? Indeed, the major exhibition that Philip organized for The Museum of Modern Art and mounted a year and a half later would find room for the expression not only of his fondest beliefs but for the views of Mumford and the "construction men." It would also call for "influencing people" beforehand who were vital to the staging of the event.

Lacking further evidence, however, we can only wonder whether such an idea was alive as early as the summer of 1930. Nothing more in Philip's correspondence or elsewhere advises us. Instead, in the last letter to his family from Berlin, dated September 1, he was content to deal out a final and typical superlative—to which he would remain true far longer than was customary for him. "Mies is the greatest man we or I have met. Oud I like better . . . but Mies is a great man. He keeps his distance . . . only letting down graciously once in a while, thus honoring you as the nod of a god would. . . . He is a pure architect.

"I must stop now and hie me down to Wannsee for lunch.

"The only answer to this letter is someone's presence at the Biltmore [the hotel in New York, where he expected to be met by his family]."

THE AMERICAN INVASION

Even before he moved into his new abode, which was, in fact, a joint effort of Mies and his gifted associate Lilly Reich, Philip foresaw it as "a show apartment to counteract the terrible wave of modernistic apartments that we now have." By "modernistic," he meant the Moderne or Art Deco style that, largely because of its identification with France, appealed more and earlier to Francophil America than did the sterner architecture that he and Hitchcock regarded as more advanced, based on their study of it mostly in the central and northern European countries. To Philip, Mies represented the very best kind of "counteraction," especially in this instance, since he was as distinguished a designer of furniture as he was an architect. Philip's apartment was probably the first space in the United States to accommodate the famous chairs and smaller pieces originally designed for the Weissenhofsiedlung, the Barcelona Pavilion, and the Tugendhat House.

At about the time he moved into his flat, Alfred and Marga Barr took a place of their own in the same building, at 424 East Fifty-second Street. On countless evenings, the three of them gathered in one or the other of their apartments for long and lively discussions of art and architecture. Occasionally, Henry-Russell Hitchcock was party to these conversations, in the course of which, sometime in the fall of 1930, the idea of a pioneering exhibition of architecture at The Museum of Modern Art was either born or carried significantly beyond the point reached—as we have only conjectured—a few months earlier. It would be the kind of event that Alfred Barr had envisioned even before the museum opened as evidence that "modern art" encompassed more forms of creative expression than the traditional genres of painting and sculpture. Indeed, it might strike an authentically revolutionary note, for it was conceived as a full-scale documentation of the first collective architectural effort in centuries to extract a consistent artistic style from a disciplined study of the technical possibilities and cultural needs of its time. To Alfred and his two friends, such an interpretation was thrilling unconditionally, moreover typical of the intellectual passions that were the hallmarks of the early modern period. There would be time enough later for the letdown, for the revisionist counterattacks that forced them to realize that the best modern architecture at the turn of the 1930s was neither so unified as they thought nor necessarily admirable on account of form and style alone. Yet on those evenings in late 1930, the fire of the new faith burned inextinguishably in their breasts.

In Philip's, it reached the highest temperatures. That was his way; life was a series of epiphanies. By the end of the year, he had submitted a statement to A. Conger Goodyear, president of the board of trustees of the museum, proposing "an exhibition of modern architecture" made up of three principal divisions. The first would be devoted to the work of "nine of the most prominent architects in the world." These were identified by country: "From America, Raymond Hood, Frank Lloyd Wright, Norman Bel-Geddes [sic], Howe & Lescaze, Bowman Brothers; from Germany, Mies van der Rohe, Walter Gropius; from France, Le Corbusier; from Holland, J. J. P. Oud." The second division would emphasize the relationship of the new architecture to "the industrial side," specifically to "theories of city buildings," "factory design," and "industrial housing," while the third would feature entries to a projected "world-wide competition open to students and architects under thirty-five years of age." The exhibition was set for February 1, 1932.

Between the fall of 1930 and the spring of 1931, Philip worked steadily for the museum, earning no salary but keeping a secretary, Ernestine Fantl—a gifted Wellesley alumna and former assistant to art dealer J. B. Neumann—whom he paid out of his own pocket. His schedule was taken up mostly by the book and the show, but he also found time to lay the groundwork for both in a series of proselytizing maneuvers. In "Built to Live In," a pamphlet published by the museum, he preceded an announcement of the forthcoming exhibition with his exposition of more of the functionalist rationale of the new building than he really believed in: the pertinence of "mass production," "low cost," and public service ("Communities, like buildings, are [to be] planned from the point

of view of serving function"). In several later essays, he was freer in
expressing his own hierarchy of values, even if most of these suggested
refinements picked up from Barr and Hitchcock. By habit a polemicist,
he tended to write with greater zest when he attacked than when he
explicated: Applied decoration of any kind was anathema to him,
whether rendered in historical styles or in the newer but to his eyes dis-
reputable Art Deco manner. Tall buildings were likewise dismissed nearly
en masse—as Barr had flogged them in an article several years earlier—
especially the New York skyscrapers of the 1920s, whose growth Philip
attributed to "American megalomania" and whose principal fault he
ascribed to the concealment of the modern steel frame behind "miles of
machine-made ornament" and other embellishments "unnecessary and
merely imitative." He might have added, though he did not, that his hostility toward virtually all skyscrapers derived also from the very fact of
their verticality, an American feature almost without counterpart in the
horizontally oriented European modern architecture that he admired.

Early in 1931, he carried the battle from the journals to the streets and
back again. In February, the Architectural League of New York staged its
annual exhibition, which included a group of modernist works, the most
striking of which was the Philadelphia Savings Fund Society Building by
George Howe and William Lescaze, a tall structure but one indebted in
its massing, details, and horizontal lineaments more to the new European
architecture than to the conventional American skyscraper. The show
thus offered proof that some American architects themselves were already
committed to the principles of the vanguard as Philip saw it. Yet what the
League turned down attracted more attention than what it accepted.
Howe and Lescaze themselves, Philip later reported, "came to the defense
of the younger and omitted men," and Johnson and Barr, eager to throw
down the gauntlet on their own, rented a Sixth Avenue storefront and
assembled a counterexhibition there, modeling it after the famed Paris
Salon des Refusés of 1863 and calling it "Rejected Architects." Press reaction was mixed but lively, as the whole issue of modern architecture was
taken up in the daily newspapers. Philip wrote his own review of the critics' reviews, pointedly praising several nonfunctional features in "the
Pinehurst House by Clauss and Daub," a project commissioned by Mrs.
Homer Johnson following her son's recommendation. He concluded his
piece with the contention that "it remained for the Rejected Architects
to give the International Style what might be called its first formal introduction to this country." In fact, this very remark was probably the first
publication in the United States of the name capitalized. Some months
later, he elevated it to headline level in "Two Houses in the International

Style," which featured the Pinehurst House and another, designed for Col. Charles A. Lindbergh by the same Philadelphia architects. (Neither residence was ever built.)

With the coming of summer, Barr, Hitchcock, and Johnson were all in Europe again, mostly working independently but in touch with one another by mail and together in person at least once. Alfred was preoccupied with matters other than architecture, notably the supervision of an Henri Matisse exhibition planned for November at the museum. He and Marga were encamped in Paris, close to but separated from Hitchcock, who was busy with the text of the Hitchcock-Johnson book and spending as much time as he could with the European architect he most admired, Le Corbusier.

Philip was back in Berlin, his calendar divided evenly between architecture by day and carousing at night. "He showed me," the art dealer Julien Levy later wrote, "a Berlin night life such as few could have imagined. The grotesque decadence I was to discover over and over again in Berlin those few short weeks [in 1931] could only be compared, one might suppose, to Paris during the last days of Louis XVI."

Meanwhile, Philip's professional priorities were given first to a visit to the Berlin Building Exposition and the composition of a pair of articles about it for the American press, in which he reiterated his admiration for Mies van der Rohe and his abiding belief in the primacy of the esthetic, as distinct from the social or technical, in judging the new architecture: "Although Mies was made director of only one section, it is by this section that the exposition will be remembered. Only here has architecture been handled as art."

Mies was clearly secure as the standard by which Philip judged the new architecture. Oud ran a distant second, with Gropius apparently fading. That Hitchcock saw things differently did not arrest the growing self-confidence Philip manifested in a letter to him that attacked his favorite architect: "Le Corbusier's Pavilion de la Suisse [sic] is bad in plan and frightfully exciting as sculpture. . . . He doesn't know materials. I'm afraid Oud was right. Le Corbusier is no architect. . . . Alfred thinks [he] is entering the Mannerist phase of architecture, God forbid."

Ever the critic, Philip in the same letter was hardly kinder to Erich Mendelsohn, or to a pair of men whom, like Le Corbusier, he earlier admired and now dismissed: "[Mendelsohn's house] is undoubtedly the best he has done but it is a poor imitation of the style. He obviously doesn't know the first thing about what it is all about and I think in his heart he knows he doesn't . . . to all he keeps up this boasting arrogant front. . . .

"Mies says of Gropius and hence it is true of Breuer, he does not and never has understood the technical and hence his worship of it."

The tasks that fell to Philip as the formally designated organizer of the forthcoming exhibition put him in close if reluctant touch with the realities of the Depression. It was hardly a good time for any major museum venture, especially one dealing with a subject still so unfamiliar to most Americans as avant-garde architecture, and Philip in his letters to Alfred worried constantly over money, wondering even if there was enough in the budget to pay Russell for his entries in the forthcoming catalogue.

Assembling works for the exhibition was hardly less vexing. His admiration of Mies was frequently turned to exasperation by the great man's habitual, not to say infuriating, slowness to respond to inquiries. Mies's outwardly Olympian mien disguised the shyness of an isolate who, it seemed at times, bestirred himself only reluctantly at the behest of others. It is certain that he did not take kindly in June to the sudden descent on his atelier of the Barrs, Hitchcock, and Johnson, all bright-eyed and garrulous in their obeisances. He called the occasion the "American invasion" and got even for it as the summer wore on by ignoring most of Philip's requests for visits and conversations. For a time, Philip clung to his expectation that Mies would install the show and perhaps even design a house specially for it, but with time it became evident that Mies detested travel as much as he shrank from the importunings of what seemed to him a presumptuous young foreigner with a temperament hopelessly opposite his own.

Officially titled "Modern Architecture: International Exhibition," the show opened on February 10, 1932, with Philip providing the closest thing to an anticlimax by missing the vernissage. The reason is lost to memory; most likely it was exhaustion severe enough to lay him up in the hospital. Of more lasting consequence to the occasion was the narrowing of some of his original curatorial ambitions. The starring roles still belonged to the individual "prominent" architects—nine of them, as proposed, but with Richard Neutra replacing Norman Bel Geddes. On the other hand, the subtopics earlier associated with the industrial division were funneled into a section called Housing, which included more photographs of work for the most part by other architects, notably the German Otto Haesler, who was also represented by a model of his housing colony at Rothenberg, near Celle. The "world-wide" competition was eliminated in favor of an ensemble of photographs of work by figures of lesser rank than the featured players, from Austria, Belgium, Czechoslovakia, England, Finland, France, Germany, Italy, Japan, the Netherlands, the Soviet Union, Spain, Sweden, Switzerland, and the United States. This was the third division, offered primarily as evidence of the global reach of the new architecture.

Only designers with a record of built works were meant to be included in the show. No space was allotted to purely visionary endeavors, which is the main reason relatively little attention was paid the provocative but largely unrealized work of the Russian Constructivists. Philip, who installed the show, organized its contents so that the most prestigious space at the rear of the exhibition was reserved for the four architects who stood for a consensus of the judgments of Johnson, Hitchcock, and Barr. Thus, models of the Villa Savoye of Le Corbusier and the Tugendhat House of Mies van der Rohe were shown alongside those of two projects, the "House on the Mesa" by Wright and a house by Oud commissioned for Pinehurst by Philip's mother (and meant to replace the earlier, afore-mentioned design by Clauss and Daub). Why the work of Gropius, which had been earlier regarded as crucial to the whole enterprise, was set up in a gallery apart from the honorific space has never been fully

"MODERN ARCHITECTURE: INTERNATIONAL EXHIBITION," THE MUSEUM OF MODERN ART, 1932. INSTALLATION OF LE CORBUSIER EXHIBIT

explained. It may be that the curators considered two Germans (Mies being the other) too many for such marquee display, or that the model of the Dessau Bauhaus—the piece representing Gropius—was inconsistent with the theme of residences common to the other four architects. It is at least as easy to believe Johnson's later recall that his esteem for Gropius as a designer had already begun to wane, which it surely and progressively did in succeeding years.

The rationale of the exhibition appeared in the catalogue, which con-tained a foreword by Barr; a "historical note" by Johnson; a statement, "The Extent of Modern Architecture," by Johnson and Hitchcock; biographical entries on the principals (on Mies by Johnson, on Wright, Gropius, Le Cor-busier, Oud, Hood, Howe & Lescaze, Neutra, and the Bowman Brothers by Hitchcock); and an essay by Lewis Mumford on housing.

Mumford left no doubt about his belief in the social significance of the new architecture: "The building of houses constitutes the major architectural work of any civilization . . . it is only during the last generation that we have begun to conceive of a new domestic environment which will utilize our technical and scientific achievements for the benefit of human living." The revolutionary tone of his statement was appropriate to a revolutionary show, but the emphasis was strictly his

LEWIS MUMFORD, C. 1938

own. Barr, Hitchcock, and Johnson, however much they regarded Mumford's view as relevant and even necessary to the exhibition and however much they paid it lip service in their own remarks, persisted in their shared belief that modern architecture was noteworthy primarily as a phenomenon in the history of art. Barr recalled the dark age of nineteenth-century historical revivalism, which "nearly stifled the one genuinely important tradition in American architecture, the thread which passed from Richardson to Sullivan, from Sullivan to Frank Lloyd Wright." Johnson, reflecting much of what he had learned from Hitchcock, then cited the contributions—"simplified and freed from crass imitation"—of such early twentieth-century European figures as Otto Wagner, Henry van de Velde, Peter Behrens, and Hendrik Petrus Berlage. But these "great individualists" were only "half-modern"; true modern architecture, he suggested, awaited the lead of such movements in painting as Neo-Plasticism in the Netherlands and Expressionism in Germany and the development by Le Corbusier of "a new technic and a new aesthetic."

It was Barr in his foreword who identified most instructively the evolved character of the new style, not by declaring it simply cleansed of the impurities of the past but by stating its mature attributes in predominantly affirmative terms. "[It] is as fundamentally original as the Greek or Byzantine or Gothic," he claimed, taking further note of its four main principles:

"First of all, the modern architect working in the new style conceives of his building not as a structure of brick or masonry with thick columns and supporting walls resting heavily on the earth but rather as a skeleton enclosed by a thin light shell. He thinks in terms of *volume*—of space enclosed by planes or surfaces—as opposed to *mass* and solidity." And then: "Two other principles which are both utilitarian and aesthetic may be called *regularity* and *flexibility*." Traditional axiality and bilateral symmetry, Barr wrote, have given way to the composition of freer plans and facades in which the architect can permit "the horizontal floors of his skyscraper and the rows of windows in his school to repeat themselves boldly without artificial accents or terminations."

"A fourth comprehensive principle," he continued, "is both positive and negative: positive quality or beauty in the International Style depends upon technically perfect use of materials . . . upon the fineness of proportions in units . . . and in the relationships between these units and the whole design. The negative or obverse aspect of this principle is the elimination of any kind of ornament or artificial pattern."

Like Johnson, Barr was largely indebted to Hitchcock for the formulation of his ideas, since the exhibition catalogue depended for its theoretical underpinnings on the book Russell and Philip had long been laboring on. *The International Style: Architecture Since 1922* was published concurrently with the show. Its fundamental message, while largely identical with that of the catalogue, was more frankly propagandistic in tone, more nearly uncompromising in its estheticism, and only qualified in its attention to social issues in architecture. The text was completely Hitchcock's, although Johnson edited it, seeking to bring a measure of simplicity and clarity to his colleague's frequently stilted prose. Among the principles of the International Style, volume, regularity, and the avoidance of applied decoration were explored in special detail. One chapter devoted to the *Siedlung,* or housing colony, amounted to a reconstitution of Lewis Mumford's catalogue essay, although with Hitchcock viewing the subject, predictably, against the backdrop of style rather than communitarian welfare. In another chapter but with much the same frame of mind, he came down hard on functionalism, the doctrine that in his view ill-advisedly regarded building more as a product of science than of art.

The book's title can be traced to several sources at least, each to some degree independent of the others. Clearly, it identified an architecture that developed not only in one place but in many, yet with a perceived unity of form and in response to uniquely modern conditions. Hitchcock later acknowledged that it was suggested by Gropius's publication of 1925, *Internationale Architektur,* and he himself had used it in several publications of 1928 and 1929. According to Marga Barr and Philip, Alfred on his own thought of the same name, taking it from a still-older model: the art of early fifteenth-century Europe, which had so many elements in common that scholars had called it the International Style. Even so, writing in an article of February 1929, he had likened the work of the Russian Moisei Ginsburg to "that international style of which Le Corbusier, Gropius and Oud are perhaps the finest masters." (The use of lowercase instead of capitals suggests a descriptive usage rather than a formal name. The earliest identifiable formalization of the term, older than Johnson's aforementioned use of it (see pp. 72–3), appears to have been a reference made by Otto Haesler in a letter of October 1930 to Philip. Haesler spoke of the working title of the Johnson–Hitchcock book as "The New International Style, 1922–32.")

Such small distinctions in the roles played by Hitchcock, Johnson, and Barr call attention to the somewhat larger ones that qualified their fundamentally shared approach to both the exhibition and the book. Hitchcock was clearly the most accomplished architectural scholar of the three and the fiercest ideologue, forever ready to take up the cudgel in defense of an estheticized architecture. Philip's underlying sympathy with that viewpoint was nonetheless modified by the way he coped with his own assets and liabilities. He appears to have compensated for his lesser knowledge of art history compared with that of either Hitchcock or Barr by learning to manage and accommodate the widely assorted and sometimes conflicting interests that were assembled in the show. In some respects, he looked more and more like Homer Johnson's son, showing a growing propensity for pragmatism, albeit of an unsentimental sort that owed more to his mother. During the planning stages of the exhibition, he wrote several in-house statements in which he acknowledged a measure of the functionalist rationale of the new architecture. He discussed the "problems of urban building," relating them, however, less to the criteria of social welfare that Mumford would have emphasized than to the needs of industry dear to the heart of a good technocrat. Whatever his other motives, he was as determined to ensure the practical success of both exhibition and book as he was eager to argue the case for pure art in either. He was nothing if not the impresario of the event. (This was evident enough in 1931 when in a letter to Hitchcock he chastised him for indolence: "I am horrified about the book. You know very well that you have spent insufficient time in rewriting. . . . I am sorry but my name goes on the book too and it must be good.") Alfred Barr, in turn, as the director of the museum, was more removed from the front lines than Hitchcock or Johnson and overall more evenhanded—willing, that is, to see in the social dimension greater architectural relevance than Hitchcock, more humanistic implications than Johnson.

Given the reputation of the exhibition and the book as seminal events in the history of twentieth-century architecture, it is worth noting that reaction to both in 1932 was unexceptional among the public and impassioned—though no more nearly unanimous than that—only within the profession. The very sponsorship of the show by The Museum of Modern Art, already an important public institution in New York, guaranteed an engaged audience of culture enthusiasts. On the other hand, as an art, architecture was practiced conservatively in the United States (and at a reduced rate in the midst of the Depression), and the 33,000 people who attended the show, a number average by contemporaneous standards, suggested only a modest interest on the part of the public at large. Predictably, the majority were resistant to what they perceived as an architecture devoid of elements, mostly ornamental, that they associated with beauty and propriety in building. Some observers, despite the pains the organizers had taken to argue otherwise, blamed the overplainness on the "functionalism" they had so often heard identified with all new architecture.

The journalists, better informed than the public and more alert to the potential importance of the event, responded to it vigorously, from positions staked out well along the critical spectrum.

Ralph Flint in *The Art News,* while qualified in his praise, came closest among the critics to perceiving the characteristics of the new architecture that had most moved Johnson, Barr, and Hitchcock: "No matter how monotonous or repetitious or otherwise uninspiring the new style may appear to be in its lesser manifestations—there can be no doubt about its magnificent simplicities and structural logic for large-scale work—it is probably the most powerful lever in getting us away from our jumbled aesthetic inheritances that could have been devised. After continued contemplation of the new modes, even the work of such moderns as Frank Lloyd Wright begins to look overloaded and fussy, and we begin to eye our surroundings with a fresh severity."

On the other hand, H. I. Brock, in *The New York Times,* treated the new architecture with only faintly disguised disdain: "In practice, the windows are either glass sides to certain rooms or horizontal slits at about eye-level of a standing person in other rooms. Out of this simple combination must be extracted whatever interest fenestration may give to a facade which must, by rigid rule, have no other ornament and which, by strict dogma, should be flat and white wherever it is not glass." Brock's quarrel was as much with the catalogue as with the work it documented. " 'Within this style,' " he quoted Hitchcock, " 'there are no subsidiary manners which are ecclesiastical or domestic or industrial. The symbolic expression of function by allusion to the past, which the half-modern architects at the beginning of the century developed, has ceased to be necessary.' " Brock chafed at that—as postmodernists would a half century later—and retorted: ". . . there is suggested in the quotation above a mental slavery to the machine idea. . . ."

A position somewhat midway between Brock and the believers was struck by Douglas Haskell in *The Nation.* Haskell was prepared to give the International Style the esthetic credit the museum sought for it, but he had doubts about its place at the end of any deterministic line of historical development. "Considering events," he wrote, "we can be sure that houses more or less like these are what the man about town will build. . . . Elegant, recherché, the new forms appeal to the aristocrat of modern taste." That the strands of early twentieth-century architecture had converged to form the International Style in the course of the previous ten years seemed a persuasive interpretation to Haskell, but it led him to ask, "Will they all stay together? Are the paths to constitute a highway? . . . I believe . . . the paths will diverge. . . . We are at the beginning, not the end, of modern imagination."

Philip was not much moved by any of these judgments, as he testified in a letter written to J. J. P. Oud only a little more than a month after the show opened: "I may safely say that there was not one really critical review of the Exhibition. For the most part the critics make excerpts from the catalogue, or if they are constitutionally opposed to modern architecture, they merely remark that the Exhibition displeases them."

Meanwhile, the response of the professional press was scarcely more encouraging. The most provocative passages of it appeared in the magazine *Shelter,* especially the April 1932 issue (for which Hitchcock, Barr, George Howe, and Philip himself served as associate editors). There, Kurt Lonberg-Holm, echoing the old European *sachlich* arguments, attacked the elevation of the concept of "style" as applied to the architecture shown in the exhibition, contrasting it with Mies van der Rohe's sober manifesto of 1923, published in the journal G, which rejected "all esthetic speculation" and "all formalism." To this, Arthur T. North added that the new architecture with its dependence on repetitious formal devices (e.g., "the flat roof . . . [the] gaspipe railing for parapets . . . [the] outside ramp similar to hog runs at the Chicago stockyards") wasn't functional at all. Even Raymond Hood, one of the major exhibitors, questioned the validity of the curators' decision to identify him with the "internationalists." Hitchcock returned all this fire—in dubious grammar—from a clearly embattled position:

"Appalled by the arguments and above all by the lack of aesthetic sensibility of those supposedly trained critics who defend 'beauty' from the unexpected ramparts of the feeblest exhibition of the New York Architectural League in years, it is sobering to find that in one's turn one must defend 'beauty' in modern architecture against others by whom the entire existence of aesthetic categories is denied with the vehemence of propagandists of atheism."

Ironically, the most vituperative attacks on the exhibition were launched by one of its most honored players, a designer who from the standpoint of public relations might have had more to gain than anyone from his inclusion in it. Frank Lloyd Wright was widely regarded as America's greatest living architect, a judgment with which he had not the slightest quarrel, but he was sixty-five years old and commissions had been eluding him since even before the Depression. The shadows of a career arguably in its twilight seemed to be lengthening. Barr, Hitchcock, and Johnson knew this; moreover, they were uneasily aware when they asked him to participate in the show that he did not represent the International Style as they conceived it. He was the wrong generation and his work revealed too few of the characteristics they had associated with the output of the European leaders. Nor had they any assurance that his unbridled arrogance and self-love would permit him a role in any sort of group exhibition.

At the same time, they suspected that a survey of radical architecture featuring only figures from abroad would not sit well with an American public that harbored few if any feelings of inferiority about American building in the first place. Clearly, a native designer of first magnitude would be a counterweight to the Europeans, and in that single respect there seemed to be no alternative to Wright.

One can sense the strain Alfred Barr was under in rationalizing Wright's role in a catalogue that was otherwise so steadfast in the enunciation of its thesis. "One very great architect," he wrote, "is included who is not intimately related to the Style, although his early work was one of the Style's most important sources. But Wright while he does not precisely disown these architectural nephews remains, what he has always been, a passionately independent genius whose career is a history of original discovery and contradiction. While he is much older than the other architects, his role is not that of 'pioneer ancestor.' As the embodiment of the romantic principle of individualism, his work, complex and abundant, remains a challenge to the classic austerity of the style of his best younger contemporaries."

Wright was willing to accept the praise, not the association. He most enthusiastically disowned several of those "nephews," above all Neutra and Hood and even the redoubtable Le Corbusier. By his lights, the International Stylists were all, or nearly all, apostles of architectural sterility marching in lockstep, latter-day eclectics poorly disguised as revolutionary saviors of the art, enemies of freedom and democracy who were now being sold to America by "a self-advertising amateur and a high-powered salesman" identified, implicitly but unmistakably, as Johnson and Hitchcock.

Between the time he was invited to participate and the formal opening of the show, he threatened over and over to remove himself from it, agreeing to stay only when the curators persuaded *Shelter* to publish his essay "Of Thee I Sing." There, he visited more of his contempt on the International Style and its *Geist der Kleinlichkeit* (spirit of paltriness), which he equated with "senility in the guise of invention."

Even with these sentiments, his spleen was not exhausted. *Shelter* had made a botch of things after all, he decided, and he unloaded on it with scattershot in a letter to Philip. His article had been published "with objectionable editorial comment under an objectionable pirated photograph of the damaged model of the House on the Mesa taken from an objectionable angle that best serves your objectionable propaganda." Moreover, Wright found himself sharing magazine space with North— "a horse's ass but not clever enough to even choose a good horse"—and with Russell, whose "editorial is essentially Hitchcock. Sincerity is one of his limitations I am bound to respect."

On and on he went, summing up with no loss of zest: "In short, Philip my King, a strange undignified crowd you are, all pissing through the same quill or pissing on each other. I am heartily ashamed to be caught with my flap open in the circumstances."

Wright received two letters in reply—one from Hitchcock, the other from Johnson—that resembled his own, if only in revealing as much about the writers as about their topics. Russell first:

Dear Mr. Wright:

I am sorry that in this question of whether your exhibits are or are not to remain in the Show you should descend to unanswerable vulgarity. The decisions are not mine as to what will be done. But I must say that at last I am convinced that there is no further reason for attempting to remain on working terms with you. My "sincerity" which you find a limitation makes it impossible to alter my opinions of your work and your career. But I think it fair to say that there is not another architect in the world who would act as you have done in relation to this exhibition. If you represent the right path and we the wrong, which is conceivable, you should be delighted that the bad influences that we are supposed to be maliciously propagandizing through this Show are counteracted by the presence of your own work. . . .

I suppose you can comfort yourself with the consolation, and a proud one it is, that Michelangelo was impossible to get on with, and posterity has forgiven him. In so far as we are posterity doubtless we already forgive you. . . .

I regret now that we have ever begun to know you personally. But knowing you, I realize we could not otherwise have had dealings with you at all.

Believe, dear master, in the expression of my warmest and most respectful sentiments.

Henry-Russell Hitchcock, Jr.

By contrast, Philip, now practiced in his newly adopted pragmatism, made a reply of pure balm, remote from his normal aggressive hauteur and even touched with a hint of servility:

I feel more than badly that you have misunderstood my intentions and actions to such an extent, and I am writing in the hope of clearing up as much as possible the reasons for your complaints. . . . Please believe that I have appreciated your efforts to remain friends despite the many misunderstandings which I sincerely regret.

I feel as strongly as ever that I have a great deal to learn, much more so after the experience of trying to make an exhibition.

I still hope that we can have a good visit when I come West this spring. . . .

Yours [etc.]

Unsurprisingly, the last word, for the time being, belonged to Wright: "Of course you will be welcome at Taliesin any time. Any feeling I have in this whole matter is directly personal toward no one."

Wright had hardly invited Philip to his home in Wisconsin before Philip was there, in the late spring of 1932, with Russell Hitchcock at his side. The unpleasantness of a few weeks earlier was past, as all three men recognized—without fundamentally altering their judgments of one another—that there was more to be gained by restoring professional relations than by dwelling on personal pique. The excitement the exhibition had stirred up in the architecture world seemed only to be growing, since the museum decided for the first time in its short history, and largely to defray costs, to send the whole package on tour. Thus to audiences in thirteen cities outside New York, modern architecture was raised from rumor to reality.

It was destined for a substantially higher elevation. What must eventually have surprised even Barr, Hitchcock, and Johnson was the ultimate impact of their exhibition—and especially the name the International Style—upon world architecture. The full force of both was not felt until later. On account of the Depression and World War II, avant-garde building was retarded everywhere while the Western democracies as well as the totalitarian regimes took a measure of stylistic refuge in a form of neo-classicist revivalism that reflected nationalist intentions more than internationalist ideals. But once the radicals of 1932, notably Le Corbusier, Gropius, and Mies, were free to work again following the war, they found themselves in a climate unprecedentedly hospitable in both Europe and the United States to modernist expression in all the arts. The media and the profession itself were so awed by the resurrection of these gods that several noteworthy architectural developments of the intervening decades tended to be overshadowed. To Philip's satisfaction, the decorative schemes of Art Deco faded from sight nearly as quickly as the classicist revival, and for nearly a generation, from about 1945 to 1960, the architectural world was dominated by values and ideas that appeared at the time traceable most directly to the book and exhibition that appeared in New York in 1932. Certainly *International Style* had name appeal. It seemed a better label than the colorless and unspecific *modern* to pin on the steel-and-glass or ferroconcrete abstractions that had won the postwar day. Only in the late 1960s did it become apparent on a broader scale that the identification had been often carelessly applied, as if the term were not only more attractive than *modern* but effectively synonymous with it.

In fact, some architecture included in *The International Style* did not exhibit the properties Barr, Hitchcock, and Johnson had claimed for it. The great Barcelona Pavilion, for example, the masterpiece of Mies's early career, was conceived as an unenclosed space defined by freestanding walls; in no instructive sense was it a volume. Furthermore, Le Corbusier's de Mandrot Villa near Hyères in the south of France was built in large part with masonry walls that conveyed far less sense of the membranous thinness associated with the volumetric than the more customarily used stucco did. Both of these works suggested, as Philip himself later admitted, that the International Style had been codified too hastily from Le Corbusier's theories as interpreted by Hitchcock.

In his foreword to the 1966 edition of *The International Style,* Hitchcock himself felt obliged to acknowledge that world architecture from his cherished standpoint of style alone had not followed the deterministic path he and his colleagues had earlier set for it. Several of the movements they had called "half-modern," implying imperfect versions of a perfection waiting to be reached, did not rest so submissively in their assigned pigeonholes: ". . . some of these strands also retained independence and continued, with varying degrees of vitality, alongside the International Style: the 'organic architecture' of Wright, the Amsterdam School, German Expressionism, Scandinavian Empiricism, even others."

Moreover, the criticisms of the International Style as noted by Hitchcock do not begin to touch on the question of the social responsibility of the architect as distinct from his role as an artist. Lewis Mumford would never stop nagging either Philip or Russell on that point as all three of them grew older. Critic Peter Blake has further recalled that more than a few people central to the modern movement "loathed the term [International Style] and found it insulting, just as they loathed the term 'modernist.' They were *modern* architects. . . ." For that matter, Frank Lloyd Wright, his vitriolic conceit notwithstanding, had been perceptive enough in 1932 to apply the word *propaganda* to an exhibition that could have been composed quite differently with a quite different ultimate effect. When it has luck on its side, propaganda is transformed into history by a process of rhetorical alchemy. Wright knew that, too. So did Philip, well enough to make the knowledge ever more nearly central to his outlook on life.

Satisfied with their momentum, Johnson and Hitchcock went ahead with plans for a second exhibition at the museum, this one on the architecture of Chicago between 1870 and 1910, a phenomenon they saw as vital to the development of early modern building but still insufficiently recognized by the public and the profession alike. Hence the visit to Wright, whose role in the Chicago story had been comparable in importance with that of the other major players designated in the show, Henry Hobson Richardson, Louis Sullivan, William LeBaron Jenney, Daniel Burnham, and John Wellborn Root.

Now suddenly, the two young champions of an architecture of today and tomorrow showed themselves committed no less to an architecture of yesterday. And while the exhibition of the latter was inspired by the cause of the former, each legitimized the other. Modernism, that is, had a pedigree in building as well as in painting and sculpture; The Museum of Modern Art certified itself not merely as a *Kunsthalle*—a marketplace for the new and untried—but as an institution rooted in history as surely as any conventional art museum. That concept, in fact more culturally conservative than the views of the radical, more antihistorical modernists, had been integral to Alfred Barr's plan. Appropriately, following several weeks of research in Chicago during June, Philip and Russell were back in New York, where, on July 2, the formal establishment of a Department of Architecture at the museum was announced by the press, with Philip, described by the *New York American* as "the brilliant young authority on the history of architecture," named as its chairman.

Brilliance notwithstanding, he made it easy on the museum by continuing his unsalaried status and the freedom of his own schedule. It was
time for the yearly summer in Europe, which in 1932 he began with his
mother and Theodate in the first family trip abroad since his ill-fated tour
of 1928. He was psychologically stronger now, at least more fortified.
Ever since his meeting with Barr in 1929, his life had moved in a recog-
nizably straight line. Yet he was still capable of drift, and the first major
project he set for himself aborted, largely because he seized upon another
distraction that prefigured a still-unrulier, more portentous one later on.

Shortly after arriving in Europe, he left his mother and Theodate and
headed back to Berlin with intentions firm to carry out in depth a study

THEODATE JOHNSON, JAN
RUHTENBERG, AND PHILIP
JOHNSON, POTSDAM, 1932

of the architecture of Ludwig Persius, the disciple of the great nineteenth-century romantic classicist Karl Friedrich Schinkel. Philip had
come to know Schinkel's building from his previous stays in the German
capital, and along the way he was drawn especially to Persius. Once settled, he had an expensive camera made for himself, a splendid contraption
in wood lined with velvet, painstakingly crafted by a local artisan hurt by
the hard times and needful of business. Philip loved it as an object as much
as he prized it as a device that would document his researches.

Now, however, an aspect of German life to which he had earlier been
indifferent to the point of active derision began to intrude upon his attentions. The Depression had deepened, its impact by now more devastating

in Germany than anywhere in Europe, and the bonds that held the already-fragile political body of the Weimar Republic buckled as extremists of the right and left raged against the center as much as against each other. The number of unemployed rose to over 4 million nationally, 600,000 in Berlin alone. Strikes and street fights were daily occurrences. With the central government reduced to impotence, elections called in July produced a majority of voters opposed to the very idea of the continuation of the Republic.

Next to all of this, the measured classicism of Ludwig Persius's architecture grew pale and indistinct. Nor did it brighten when Philip one day encountered Paul Ortwin Rave, the architectural historian renowned for his exhaustive and meticulous scholarship on Schinkel. "You need a doctorate for such a study," Rave told him stiffly, "not a fancy camera." Wounded, Philip put Persius aside.

Fatefully at this time, a friend from New York, Helen Appleton Read, the art critic of the *Brooklyn Daily Eagle* and an avowed supporter of modernism, appeared in Berlin and called upon Philip with politics, not art, on her mind. She had become fascinated with one of the central figures in the gathering crisis, the leader of the right-wing National Socialist German Workers' party, Adolf Hitler. The Nazis had made capital of Germany's resentment over the Versailles Treaty by heaping the blame for the nation's current grief on its mistreatment by its old enemies France and England and no less on the Jews. Hitler's message of sustained execration was effectively linked with a call for national resurgence, which he promised through a radical, if simplistically expressed, program of economic reform. Liberals saw him as a menace, conservatives and the disadvantaged as a riveting figure of hope. Either way, he was more and more to be reckoned with.

Read lectured Philip, whose knowledge of matters at issue was vague, on the justifications of Hitler's cause and especially on what she regarded as the stunning charisma of the man. "You really ought to see him in action," she said. "And if you're interested, I can arrange it. There is a rally coming up shortly here. I have a friend [Ernst "Putzi" Hanfstaengl, heir to the fortune of a Munich publishing house and one of Hitler's early supporters] who can get us an invitation."

Philip remembered the atmosphere of the event, which took place in a field outside Potsdam, as "totally febrile. You simply could not fail to be caught up in the excitement of it, by the marching songs, by the crescendo and climax of the whole thing, as Hitler came on at last to harangue the crowd."

Philip's attention was arrested at several levels of his consciousness. Most immediately, he felt a sexual thrill, in his own words, at the sight of "all those blond boys in black leather" who seemed an exalted collective crystallization of the liaisons that had both dominated and liberated him already in Germany. Yet the occasion had an esthetic dimension, as well. The sheer physical drama of the rally, indeed of the whole German political situation, seemed to him to have taken on the character of high art in its scope and seriousness and was even more viscerally compelling. He could afford such a reaction, safe in his personal wealth and American citizenship from the reality of it. Thus he enjoyed the luxury of an interpretation: For while Hitler was plainly enough a vulgarian and as such presumably beneath Philip's educated contempt, he claimed to stand for an extreme and revolutionary ideal. He meant to lift a demoralized nation from the depths to the heights, a goal Germany's other politicians seemed incapable of, but one he, Hitler, proposed to achieve himself, like the warrior king Philip recalled—again from his own private, idiosyncratic reading of Nietzsche. Such a quest and such an accomplishment even reminded him of his personal experience with modern architecture. That, too, was a mission, no mere task. Power and art were somehow inextricably linked. Insofar as the 1932 International Style show was a professional success, he could attribute it to the efforts of himself, Barr, and Hitchcock, singular fellows, above the herd. To the degree, on the other hand, that he had been both irritated and frustrated by critical reactions to it, he could identify with the institutionalized aggrievance he now saw—from a secure distance—acted out on the fields of Potsdam.

Meanwhile, Theodate and her mother traveled through Europe mostly by themselves, reconvening with Philip and the Barrs in Switzerland in late September and driving with them into Italy as far as Rome. A recurrence of Theodate's ear miseries forced the two women to return home earlier than planned, while Philip remained until October, rounding out his stay with a sojourn in Paris, where he renewed his earlier acquaintance with the composer Virgil Thomson. In Thomson's autobiography, he recalls that his indigence was relieved by a loan from Philip that helped him to pay for his passage back to the States. Once in New York, Philip offered Thomson temporary sanctuary in his own flat and threw himself back into his old Manhattan life.

For the following two years, from the fall of 1932 until the early winter of 1934, Philip typically played as hard as he worked, belying the complaints he continued to register to family and friends about his purportedly weak constitution. "I was in a dinner jacket at least four times a week," he later remembered. Several distinct subcultures claimed his attentions, all but one of them—dubious and anomalous enough to be left to later discussion—comfortably unaffected by the Depression. His own social station made him welcome in the society of the rich, especially in the homes of Mrs. W. Murray Crane and families like the

ALFRED H. BARR, JR., PHILIP JOHNSON, AND MARGARET (MARGA) SCOLARI BARR, CORTONA, 1932

PHILIP, NEW YORK CITY, 1933

Browns, Warburgs, and Whitneys, who were among the principal patrons of The Museum of Modern Art. He was the perfect extra man in this set, a role he played without betraying his sexual inclinations. He loved parties and he performed flawlessly at them, his manner ever debonair and appropriately dégagé.

Still, while at home with these social aristocracies, he felt a deeper loyalty to the wide-ranging contingent of intellectuals, artists, and esthetes whose existences were bound together by a common devotion to modern thought and modernist expression. Central to this community were

the people directly or indirectly associated with The Museum of Modern
Art: Alfred and Marga Barr, of course; Philip's friend and mentor Henry-
Russell Hitchcock; members of the advisory committee, who, in addi-
tion to Philip, included the art historian–critic James Johnson Sweeney
and veterans of the Harvard Society for Contemporary Art Edward M.
M. Warburg and Lincoln Kirstein; and, more recently, the compelling
Englishwoman Iris Barry, newly installed in 1933 as librarian of the
museum, where she also founded the world's first film library. It was
Philip who, having discovered her at a cocktail party, persuaded her to
join the museum staff. He also paid her salary.

Musicians joined the circle, too, notably Virgil Thomson and John
Cage (more marginally, George Gershwin and Aaron Copland), and
artists: the Surrealists Pavel Tchelitchew and Eugene Berman and Thomson's companion, Maurice Grosser. Film and dance were represented by
Kirstein, who founded the journal *Films* in 1930 and the School of the
American Ballet in 1934, one year after persuading the great Russian
choreographer George Balanchine to immigrate to the United States.
With Philip's professional reputation securing itself, Kirstein turned from
the fearsome force he had seemed to be at Harvard into a friend whose
nervously intense personality and sexual orientation drew Philip because
both were like his own.

Nor was the group confined to New York; it extended to nearby
academe, where former students of Paul Sachs's famous Harvard museol-
ogy course were now professionals themselves and active in advancing the
modernist cause among their own students. Hitchcock, after all, made his
living as a regular on the faculty at Wesleyan, while Jere Abbott, having
left the museum in 1933, was in charge of the art collection at Smith. At
Vassar were Agnes Rindge and Philip's old traveling companion John
McAndrew, now an architectural historian himself, while A. Everett
"Chick" Austin divided his time between a teaching post at Trinity College and the directorship of the Wadsworth Atheneum in Hartford.

This uncommon company enjoyed a salon life on the Upper East Side
of Manhattan whose "centers of fraternity," as Thomson put it, were "the
house of Kirk and Constance Askew on Sixty-first Street, the sales-galleries
of Kirk Askew on Fifty-seventh (Durlacher Brothers), where Baroque
painting was a specialty, and of Julien Levy (importer of neo-Romantic
and surrealist painting) and a little bit that of Pierre Matisse (who sold
Modern Old Masters, including his father). The back offices of these galleries were open for gossiping every day and the Askews were at home at
six on Sundays. Also every day at five, when one could drop in on the
hostess for tea and be given cocktails later by the host."

It was a world whose very froth obscured its vision of the breadlines everywhere around it; yet for acuity of another kind, it had no collective equal in America. Some of the most perceptive sensibilities of the day consorted regularly with Philip and he with them, and their mutual gravitation was both cause and effect of a historic reordering of the priorities of the national cultural scene. These were the people who had been schooled early in their lives in the nineteenth-century Ruskinian worldview that identified culture with gentility and ennobling good taste—thus with values presumed to be lacking in the United States—but who grew impatient with that decorous tradition when they discovered the rambunctious modern European arts. They did more than give it up. They came to look upon their own native America not as a wasteland to escape but as a fertile field awaiting the nourishment they could provide as artists, scholars, teachers, and gallery and museum people. Collectively, they were as elitist as their forefathers, but the effect of their efforts was to proselytize culture by putting it literally on view. In identifying themselves less with literature than with the more immediately apprehensible visual, musical, and balletic arts, they helped to precipitate a shift to a "culture of the eye and the ear," as the historian Thomas Bender has characterized it. There is little doubt, moreover, that the plurality of homosexuals among them not only encouraged but reinforced the expression of their uncommon gravitation and receptivity to the sensuous arts. In any case, they remained elitist in their objectives. They meant to document and institutionalize culture, not to advance democracy.

Since the movement had already been started in the late 1920s by the likes of Alfred Barr, Lincoln Kirstein, and others, whom Philip got to know only later, there is no way of knowing whether his own abandonment of the classics and philosophy in favor of art and architecture was reflective of this shift in collective cultural priorities or only incidentally parallel to it. Nevertheless, it is certain that the older he grew, the more his silken antennae picked up the vibrations of change in the worlds of the intellect and the arts. No other figure of his time, in fact, surpassed him in this remarkable sensitivity.

Accordingly, he took his first serious lover in 1934. Jimmy Daniels was a black café singer whom Philip later called the first Mrs. Johnson. From all reports, he was an arresting stage presence, smoky-voiced, light-skinned, and delicately handsome. How Philip met him may be inferred from Thomson's reminiscences about the social habits of the Upper East Side crowd: "Often, toward midnight, some [of us] would decide for Harlem; but the Askews seldom went along, though Constance might be itching to. Russell, however, and Chick, always in town for just a day or so, loved making a night of it. It was on one of these trips uptown, at a small joint where Jimmy Daniels was just starting out as host and entertainer . . ."

Let the quotation be interrupted by Philip's own recall, which provided this much more with certainty: He met Jimmy on such an outing and was enchanted by him from the outset. He was gentle, endearing, and companionable, and Philip saw him frequently, usually in Harlem, rarely else-

PHILIP, 1933   JIMMY DANIELS, C. 1940

where, and solely at his own convenience. Toward the end of the year, Jimmy ran off with a more attentive man, leaving Philip more hurt than he expected to be.

That is all of the affair that Philip could summon up from his later memory, leaving us to speculate about his motives, especially in light of what we have already observed of the sharply critical attitudes, not to say bigotry, that he earlier displayed toward people he had written home about from Europe. He himself insisted that among the prejudices he picked up in his old Cleveland neighborhood, Roman Catholics were despised more than Jews, who were in turn thought to be at least more intelligent, while blacks were looked upon favorably, as an oppressed people waiting to be freed (albeit by a race, the whites, whose ability to carry out the liberation was an unstated measure of their superiority).

It strains credulity to suppose that Philip's crush on Jimmy had an iota of salvation about it. More likely, it was driven by the glands, together with a measure of the fascination many white intellectuals of the 1920s and 1930s felt toward the cultural movement known as the Harlem Renaissance. The preceding quotation from Thomson reinforces this when completed: ". . . realizing the impeccable enunciation of Jimmy's speech-in-song, [I] said, 'I think I'll have my opera sung by Negroes.' . . . next morning I was sure, remembering how proudly the Negroes enunciate and how the whites just hate to move their lips."

Thomson's opera was his celebrated *Four Saints in Three Acts,* written to a libretto by Gertrude Stein. If it proved a triumph for composer and author when it opened in 1934, it was a high-water mark for the whole Upper East Side salon as well, since almost all the people who figured in the world premiere of the work were part of that set or close to it. The performance took place at Chick Austin's Wadsworth Atheneum, specifically in the new Avery Memorial Wing, which was probably the first structure in the United States put up expressly to house activities related to modern art. The director was John Houseman; the conductor, Alexander Smallens. The sets were designed by Florine Stettheimer, with costumes by Maurice Grosser. Seed money came from Eddie Warburg and the very idea of staging the gala at an art center outside New York was that of Lincoln Kirstein. On February 8, 1934, when the curtain went up, Hartford was, in Philip's later words, "the omphalos, the navel of the world."

Philip's relationship with Thomson was never either a romance or even a deep friendship, but each admired the other's talents and both recognized a common bond. On one occasion, they put on a soiree of their own that not only reflected this reciprocity, profiting both, but worked to the advantage of Philip's younger sister, as well.

After her graduation from Wellesley, Theodate had turned the dramatic gifts Alfred Barr once noticed to the study of voice. She worked briefly in Boston before returning to Cleveland, where she secured a succession of assignments at the Playhouse, negotiating them well enough to animate her hope of a resumption of life on the East Coast.

Early in the spring of 1934, Philip welcomed her to his new Turtle Bay apartment on Forty-ninth Street, which he agreed to share with her, although as it turned out, not always comfortably. Thomson, whom Philip had offered brief refuge when the two men returned from Europe the previous fall, was still enjoying it, but he was grating more and more

on the nerves of his host, his host's sister, and, worst of all, his host's Ger-
man-born manservant, Rudolf, who threatened to resign if "the man
who came to dinner," as they later called him, came much longer. An
added awkwardness, at least for Theodate, grew out of Philip's sex life,

THEODATE,
C. 1932

which he carried on with zest and more than a few partners. So much
rough trade—Thomson's word for it—showed up at the apartment that
Theodate later claimed she could never be sure whom she would find
sharing breakfast with Philip on any given morning.

In the midst of this crowded domesticity, or rather shortly before
Thomson removed himself from it, he and the two Johnsons, the "Philo-
dates," as he called them, set about their soiree, which was meant to feature Virgil, with space for Theodate, too. "She was getting set to be a
singer," Thomson reported, "and as a brunette with blazing eyes and a
jacket of leopard skin, she was looking operatic absolutely. Her soprano
voice was warm, her presence commanding, her musicianship carefully

acquired. And she was about to move her studies to New York. Wanting to be of help to her, to me as well, Philip proposed a musical evening at his flat to which museum trustees would be asked. And he suggested we give my Second String Quartet, still unheard anywhere. . . .

"The party . . . accomplished exactly what had been desired. . . . Philip in fact was vastly content all around. I had been strikingly performed and handsomely received, Theodate had been heard to advantage and admired, and, to the benefit of his own projects, not only had divers influential trustees of the museum climbed his stairs, but Mrs. John D. Rockefeller, Jr., the most important of them [and one of the founders of The Museum of Modern Art], had left smiling."

By now, Philip's generosity had become an enduring feature of his behavior. If he could be hateful, as we have seen and will see again, he was exceptional among his professional peers for the way he put the money he possessed and the influence he accumulated to the service of people he cared for or believed in. He even gave each of his two sisters a hefty sum of money early in the 1930s, in recognition of the fortunes of the stock market that had made him substantially richer than they.

That he also knew the difference between munificence and charity may be inferred from his awareness that he had something to gain for himself at the Thomson soiree. For the most part, he maintained a reasoned balance between openhandedness and self-interest, although on one occasion he permitted the latter to get the better of the former, to his embarrassment. He usually made a point of keeping his lovers separate from both his professional life and the people he cultivated on Fifth and Park avenues. But Thomson introduced him in 1934 to the composer John Cage, with whom Philip had a brief but highly charged fling. It ended precisely because Philip neglected to invite Cage to a society party that John's own standing led him to assume he quite belonged at. To Philip, it had seemed a matter of little consequence. Cage found it enough of an insult to justify his calling an abrupt and angry end to their affair.

Philip did not let the efforts he put into the "Modern Architecture" show relax the pace of the department he now formally headed at the museum. Mindful of what he had seen at the Bauhaus, he turned his attentions to arts marginal as well as central to architecture and organized the first major exhibition of modern design and the decorative arts to appear in a major American museum. Following the "Early Modern Architecture, Chicago, 1870–1910" exhibition, which took up the midwinter months of 1932–1933, he supervised a display of American posters called "Typographic Competition." Two exhibitions followed directly, running for the most part simultaneously in the spring of 1933: "Objects: 1900 and Today" and "The Work of Young Architects of the Midwest." The former featured household objects in the Art Nouveau style juxtaposed with artifacts in the Bauhaus idiom. To document either genre was uncommon enough by itself, since the one was widely regarded at the time as old and outmoded, the other equally problematical because it was so very new. Showing them in comparison rather than contrast, moreover, as if each stood with equal dignity for the advanced taste of its day, was no less daring, yet another signal that he found more to like in the past than did the doctrinaire modernists.

This did not imply full-blown ecumenicism or neutrality. Of the young Midwest architects exhibition, which featured work by Robert W. McLaughlin and Howard T. Fisher, Philip wrote that it "consists mainly of projects . . . which show not only research into new problems but great strides away from the Beaux Arts classical (not to mention the Beaux Arts 'modernistic')." His parenthetical clause was meant to strike yet another blow at the Art Deco/Moderne manner much on his mind at the time because of its dominating presence at the national architectural event of the summer of 1933, the Century of Progress Exposition in Chicago. Philip visited the fair in August, dismissing it as "perfectly foul" except for a "semi-traditional house by [Ernest] Grunsfeld" and George Fred Keck's House of Tomorrow, the latter work pleasing to his eye because of its apparent proximity to the International Style.

Next to "Modern Architecture," Philip's most important museum achievement of the early Barr years was "Machine Art," an exhibition mounted in the spring of 1934 that consisted of an assemblage of manufactured objects, most of them standardized in type and all of them meant to demonstrate how that anonymous and presumably overarching force of modern times, the machine, could be made to produce utensils, instruments, appliances, and similar contrivances that were at once functional and beautiful. There had never been a show like it in any American fine arts museum. The galleries of the Department of Architecture shone with test tubes, paper cups, and even pea-sized wood screws, with an occasional motorboat propeller, circular saw, and porcelain insulator added, all of these chosen for their straightforwardness of design and clarity of form—that is to say, for their sculpturally abstract, undecorated elegance independent of function. The catalogue cover featured an arresting photograph of a ball bearing, cool, crisp, gleaming, exactingly fabricated. *The*

New Yorker likened the exhibit to "a hardware store . . . run by Brancusi and Fernand Léger."

Philip's friend Helen Appleton Read was more explicitly affirmative: ". . . Bauhaus technique," she wrote of the installation, "given, however, a personal and less doctrinaire interpretation. It is no exaggeration to say

JOHNSON INSTALLING
"MACHINE ART" EXHIBITION,
MUSEUM OF MODERN ART,
1934

that it is the finest example of exhibition technique that has been achieved in this country."

Philip was pleased enough by the reference to the Bauhaus, but he— more precisely, Alfred Barr, who worked steadily with him on the show—found justification for an art of pure form in another source, one much older. Barr based much of his foreword to the exhibition catalogue on a passage from Plato's *Philebus:* "By beauty of shapes I do not mean, as most people would suppose, the beauty of living figures or of pictures, but, to make my point clear, I mean straight lines and circles, and shapes, plane or solid, made from them by lathe, ruler and square. These are not, like other things, beautiful relatively, but always and absolutely."

Notwithstanding Philip's other doubts about Plato, it is safe to say he agreed with this declaration and with Barr's use of it. Nevertheless, the citation did not go unchallenged. The critic of the *New York Herald Tribune,* Royal Cortissoz, a rock-hard conservative but no illiterate, accused Barr of finding more in the philosopher's statement than the philosopher intended, and he fired back a citation of his own—from Whistler: "Art is Art and Mathematics is Mathematics." Cortissoz found nothing to like in the show, while C. J. Bulliet of the *Chicago Daily News* lodged a more far-ranging complaint. The Museum of Modern Art, which "started so brilliantly . . . in contemporary painting and sculpture . . . is drifting more and more in the direction of the crafts."

Other press reaction was emphatically more favorable, exceeding even that of Helen Appleton Read in approval. "Our best showman and probably the world's best," said the *New York Sun* of Philip. "Philip Johnson's high-water mark as an exhibition maestro," added *The New York Times.*

In the longer historic view, neither the praise nor the censure of "Machine Art" was as important an outgrowth of it as the consistency with which displays of modern utilitarian design have continued, down to the present day, at The Museum of Modern Art and elsewhere. Indeed no one has done more in the twentieth century than Philip Johnson did in four years at the museum to establish a connection between artistic creativity and utilitarian production, including activities with a consciously calibrated esthetic dimension, like architecture, and those not, like the design of electric lightbulbs. In less than half a decade during the early 1930s, he more than anyone anywhere established architecture and design as major museum disciplines. Until the 1980s, The Museum of Modern art was the only institution with a curatorial department devoted to them. None of his critics, neither a mossback like Cortissoz nor a genius like Frank Lloyd Wright, could take that from him.

Yet at the time that achievement was clearly secured, Philip had grown curiously close to not caring about it. Something else was eating at him; the ancient tide of distraction was rising. He continued his habit of presenting minor exhibitions in "The Architecture Room" on a variety of themes that included yet another project for a house on the Johnson family property in North Carolina, this one by a former student of Mies van der Rohe, William Priestley; the bold new Philadelphia Savings Fund Society Building of Howe & Lescaze; and "Early Museum Architecture" by Henry-Russell Hitchcock. The department's last major event of the year was an exhibition in the autumn, organized by Carol Aronovici: "Housing Exhibition of the City of New York." Philip was involved, but his heart was not in it. He was suffering another case of altered priorities, this one evolving from an earlier diversion into something approaching a rupture in his life, consciously calculated, existential in its implications.

PART TWO

THE INGLORIOUS DETOUR

1934–1946

ZARATHUSTRA AND THE KINGFISH

When Philip resigned from The Museum of Modern Art on December 4, 1934, he did more than surrender a job. He declared himself for another career, remote from anything he had ever done or seriously thought of doing: politics. Once committed, he brought to it all the missionary fervor he had earlier invested in philosophy and architecture—not, however, the gift, as matters turned out.

The question of aptitude did not occur to him at first, nor was he troubled that he had little theoretical understanding of the social sciences and less practical experience. Limited training had not stopped him from leaping into the arts, where he scored a stunning series of professional triumphs in a remarkably short time. Thus he took for granted that he had the intelligence equal to a new discipline and the money and social position that had always served him well in gaining entrée to realms he chose to invade.

If he was to make such a curious move into such unfamiliar territory, in one sense it is not surprising that he chose a politics of the right wing. He was a child of privilege, after all, with a record of disparaging the "sociologues" of the Weimar Republic and the Mumfords of this world, who he thought went on at prolix lengths about welfare. But why when he made his move did he attach himself to the populist faction of the right, which depended heavily on an expression of sympathy for the "common people," a class of humanity to whom he was normally indifferent except when he was sneering at them? And how could he square such a choice with the right wing's customary hostility to the modern arts he had worked so hard to advance?

Whatever the irreducible core of Philip's personality, it lay beneath multiple layers of motivations manifest in an almost unnatural facility at the intermingling of activities and interests, not all of them discernibly consonant with one another. Significant passages of his daily affairs between 1932 and 1934 were negotiated independent of the rigorous professional schedule he kept at the museum and the agenda he assigned his leisure time. In 1933, he arranged an exhibition of American modern architecture for the Milan Triennale, yet he was in Germany during the same year, watching with unconcealed fascination as the forces of the mostly antimodernist National Socialist party ascended to power. He worked earnestly if unsuccessfully to secure a teaching position at one of a number of American universities for J. J. P. Oud, with whom he continued the warm and spirited correspondence he had begun in 1930. His job-brokering efforts were of greater avail in the case of the German painter Josef Albers, a teacher at the Bauhaus. Thanks to a nonquota visa guaranteed by Philip and his friend Edward Warburg, Albers was able to emigrate to the United States when the Bauhaus came under attack in 1933 by the very Nazis who had caught Philip's eye.

Meanwhile, he kept his connections with Fifth Avenue society and the Askew salon, and continued a vigorous sexual life. Yet if his curve of fortune was rising and his public image growing proportionately brighter, the psyche at the root of it all did not change. This much we know about Philip: He yearned for success, thirsted for it, and was ever so good at achieving the look of it, if not always the substance. Yet he was given to growing bored, a reaction hardly consistent with the real mastery of whatever he undertook. Charmed by his own facility, he was not sure he could be more than facile, with the result that he would strive all the harder to succeed again, preferably in a new realm, taking up an unfamiliar challenge.

In the early 1930s, even as he amassed his various honors, he was seized with the melancholy suspicion that his two most important intellectual colleagues, Hitchcock and Barr, were not only more soundly educated than he but superior as scholars and historians. The cloud of dilettantism that hung over him at the turn of the 1930s only darkened when he recalled his failed Persius project of 1932 and Paul Rave's demeaning reaction to it. Similarly unsettling was the nagging sense that the 1932 "Modern Architecture" exhibition had not been met with as great or affirmative a public response as he had wished.

For a time, he nourished the hope that he might become an artist in his own right. In 1931, having done over a small bedroom in the Park Avenue flat of Mrs. Ray Slater Blakeman, he went on to design both of the apartments to which he moved, at 230 East Forty-ninth Street, in 1933, and 241 East Forty-ninth Street, in 1934, although in each instance he relied heavily for decor on the Mies furniture he brought with him from the flat at 424 East Fifty-second Street. For his friend Eddie Warburg, he designed an apartment in 1933 and a year later, for his sister Theodate, an evening gown and a custom-made wristwatch. In a letter to Oud, he claimed, "I am already building a house myself with my friend Jan Ruhtenberg," adding, "I discover that all my trys [sic] at designing my house come out looking much more like yours than like Mies'. It seems your style gives a better and more wholesome discipline than that of any of the other great moderns." Yet the house never materialized, and his creative efforts, all of them executed for friends or relatives, remained modest. "I just figured," he later recalled, "that I could never be a Mies or a Le Corbusier or a Wright."

If he could have expressed these insecurities to Alfred Barr on those occasions when he was most burdened by them, he might have recognized how irrational he was in both his manic grandiosity and his depressive self-criticism. Among his friends, Alfred and Marga were the ones clearly most willing and able to offer him spiritual counsel as well as social and intellectual sustenance. They believed in him. Between September of 1932 and July of 1933, however, Alfred was on a leave of absence from the museum, all of which he and Marga spent in Europe. Philip visited them twice on his own trips abroad, but each time there seemed to be other matters to discuss than any inner unease he may have been suffering. Indeed, the subject that took up most of their conversations was one of international consequence.

It was Adolf Hitler's *Machtübernahme* (assumption of power) in January of 1933. At the time, Alfred and Marga had taken quarters in Stuttgart, where they remained for much of the first half of the year. Alfred had psychic problems of his own, a severe case of insomnia, for which he sought help from a German physician. According to Marga, Philip joined the Barrs briefly in the spring at Ascona on Lake Maggiore and the two men argued about the Nazi regime, with more passion and violent disagreement than marked any previous exchanges between them.

Alfred deplored the takeover; Philip was exhilarated by it. Alfred foresaw a brutal repression of freedoms in all walks of German life, leading to an atrophy of national culture as a whole. Philip, remembering the Potsdam rally at which he found himself transfixed by the Nazi spectacle and transported by the charisma of Hitler, saw a *"nationale Erhebung"* (national resurgence), an amazing restoration of confidence among the German people, who only shortly before had seemed defeated by the Depression.

The friendship of the two men held fast, but so did their powerful difference of political opinion. On one point only did they concur: Like nearly everyone else in the Western world, they could not help but recognize that their lives were being affected more than ever before by developments in the global domains of politics and economics.

Philip, constitutionally alert to change, seems to have felt the force of this realization more than Alfred, in the sense that he began to give way to the belief that the Depression had already taken on a greater world significance than the arts. This shift of thought was gradual, but it was already under way when he wrote an article that was published late in 1933 in the literary quarterly *Hound and Horn,* edited by Lincoln Kirstein. Entitled "Architecture in the Third Reich," it signaled not only the new importance he accorded politics in his thinking about art but the respect he seemed willing to grant the new Nazi state even though he tacitly recognized the legitimacy of Alfred Barr's worries over Nazi attitudes toward the arts. *Die neue Sachlichkeit,* he wrote, appeared to be done for, a probability he implicitly applauded, since its products "all look too much alike, stifling individualism. . . ." Similarly, he seemed undisturbed by the disappearance of the Bauhaus style, since "it has irretrievably the stamp of Communism and Marxism . . . ," philosophies associated with the socialist esthetics he had long disdained. Yet he had little respect for the heavy-handed classicist form that the hard-core Nazis were determined to impose on most important new German building.

"Somewhere between the extremes is the key," he wrote, and after discussing the possible outcomes of the dispute current between conservative Nazi forces and "the young men of the party, the students and revolutionaries who are ready to fight for modern art," he offered up his own solution:

"Mies van der Rohe . . . has always kept out of politics . . . is respected by the conservatives . . . [and] has just won (with four others) a competition for the new building of the Reichsbank. . . .

"A good modern Reichsbank would satisfy the new craving for monumentality, but above all it would prove to the German intellectuals and to foreign countries that the new Germany is not bent on destroying all the splendid modern arts which have been built up in recent years. . . . Germany cannot deny her own progress. If in the arts she sets the clock back now, it will run all the faster in the future."

While the article sought to resolve the conflict between modernism and Nazi doctrine, it left unanswered several other questions pertinent to the latter. What were his feelings about the theories of German racial superiority that Hitler had candidly advanced well before he ever gained power? How did Philip rebut—if he did—Barr's contention that the Nazis were just as frank and serious in their promises to sacrifice individual freedoms to the greater glory of the state?

That Philip was already given during his student days to making degrading judgments of ethnic groups like the Czechs and the Danes is apparent from correspondence already quoted here. Moreover, in letters to Alfred Barr in 1931 when he was seeking financial assistance for the International Style show from wealthy Europeans, he wrote on one occasion that "the patrons of Mies are Jews and do we want them?" and on another, "you [Barr] don't seem to mind Jews so I will get the Tugendhats when I go to Bruenn."

Such bigotries so expressed were, in fact, indistinguishable from the hidden and not so hidden beliefs of many Americans—and Germans, Englishmen, Frenchmen, et al.—of the same period, nor is there evidence from any other source that Philip was a conscious follower of Nazi race theory, at least in 1933, so much as he was a garden-variety upper-middle-class American snob. The record has even less to suggest of any direct response to Barr on the latter's worries over the limits the Nazis meant to place on freedoms. Philip's thoughts on that issue would become apparent only later.

Nevertheless, events as they unfolded might already have given him pause on his own account. The hopes of the Nazi "students and revolutionaries" that the modern arts would endure in Germany dissolved when Hitler himself, siding with the conservatives, officially endorsed an architecture of monumental neoclassicism in 1934. In the same year, moreover, Hitler's chief challenger for authority within the party, Ernst Röhm, was shot to death in an act traceable by consensus to the Führer's orders. But Röhm was also a homosexual, and Berlin street wisdom had it that Nazi antagonism toward homosexuality, which had already hardened into official policy at some levels, was also behind the assassination. The implication of all these events, together with Hitler's inability to subdue the Depression so handily as he had promised earlier, was surely not lost on Philip. In any case, whatever his motivations, he appears to have pulled back from close contact with Germany by the end of 1934. He did not return there until 1937.

Yet it was just then, the end of 1934, that he quit The Museum of Modern Art, and his subsequent behavior suggests more a reorientation of his political outlook than a qualitative change in it. Indeed, he turned his face stateside, to the American scene, where influences sufficient to such a shift were ample enough, none of them more important than a fellow Harvard alumnus, Lawrence Dennis.

Thirteen years senior to Philip, Dennis had served in the American diplomatic corps before turning to a career in banking, which he gave up in 1930 to devote himself to writing. Philip read his book *Is Capitalism Doomed?* shortly after its publication in 1932, which was the same year he met the author. It is not clear whether the book led to the meeting or vice versa, but either way, the consequence was a deepening of Philip's interest in politics.

It is worth remembering here that the relationship began and grew at the very time Philip was carrying on his aforementioned frenetic and multifaceted life, moving from the Askew salon to the Fifth Avenue crowd to the haunts of Harlem; organizing "Modern Architecture" and "Machine Art" and the American entry to the Milan Triennale and writing a book with Henry-Russell Hitchcock; enjoying sex here and abroad; job hunting for J. J. P. Oud and Josef Albers; designing interiors and expensive baubles; thinking about Ludwig Persius and Adolf Hitler; brooding about his talent or the inadequacy of it—and more.

More included Dennis. In *Is Capitalism Doomed?* the author gave conditional answer to the title question. Capitalism, he contended, while he favored it in the abstract, was likely to be brought low in competition with the "living religions" of the new totalitarian states, Soviet Russia especially, unless it massively reconstrued and reconstituted itself. Dennis's argument was conducted mostly at the level of economic theory, in terms with which Philip had little prior acquaintance. Nonetheless, for all its technical verbiage, the book presented a point of view that was populist in its ends and salvationist in its means, easy enough, that is, for comprehension by an amateur reader with a history of fondness for bold solutions to formidable questions. One readily recalls his flirtation with the Buchmanites at Harvard.

Dennis recognized a potential convert in Philip, an affluent one at that. The capitalist system, he instructed his charge in numerous personal conversations, was being ruined by speculating financiers and big-credit bankers, and the people who were victimized in the process could look for help only to an exceptional and still-missing element in American life: great leaders. "The people must have a prophet," Dennis had written in his book, "and prophets have never come out of the world of profits."

The association with the leader of the German National Socialists was there to be made. Hitler rising up to save Germany in 1933: Was it not clearly that country's fulfillment of Dennis's call for a prophet emerging from a diseased capitalist milieu? Not rich himself, Hitler appeared to have co-opted the rich men of Germany. Whether Dennis's indictment of speculative wealth fed either a guilt Philip may have harbored about his

own money or a long-standing resentment of his moneyed father—or
both, or both and more—is beyond proof. Be that as it may, Philip had
long tended to surrender himself to authority figures, especially if they
offered him the attention and respect Homer Johnson had only given in
short supply. The prophet Dennis called for would be a fine extension in
fantasy of such a lordly man, and all the more beguiling if Philip found,
as he did, his own professional self-confidence in doubt. Thus even if
events in 1934 turned his attentions away from Germany, Dennis's argument about leadership seemed to him to have lost none of its theoretical
potency.

But it was not theory alone that had drawn Philip to Hitler in the first
place. He could have found just as much to admire in Marx, Lenin, or
even Stalin, as did so many American intellectuals of the 1930s who
looked left rather than right or center. But he had no personal contact
with Russia, neither with its contemporary culture nor with its people—
and he loved Germany. Besides, Hitler and the Nazis had color; the
Communists were gray, doctrinaire. There was dash to these Nazis: the
way they dressed and sang and marched and fought; their impudence,
their bravado, the sexuality Philip could not help but project on them.
How, on the other hand, could one be carried away by so stolid, sinister,
and secretive a piece of machinery as Stalin?

In short, for Philip the element of the esthetic could not be separated
from the new politics he sought. Nor was this just a vestige of his past. If
the ideal statesman must be a prophet, he would have also to be engaging
to the senses and the emotions as well as to the mind. He must be an
evoker, a sorcerer.

Philip's preoccupation with Dennis dovetailed with his continued reading of Nietzsche and his specific recall of the German's view of art as integral to politics. He concentrated his attentions on the Nietzschean text in
Der Wille zur Macht and its thesis that "the will to power" constitutes
man's fundamental motivating force. It is reasonable to presume that he
also responded to Nietzsche's corollary belief that there is more power in
art and philosophy than in the mere subjugation of people, although
Nietzsche's contempt for philistinism and his celebration of superior individual personalities like Zarathustra—a prophet, God knows—not to
mention his "revaluation of all values" (*Umwertung aller Werte*) that
reordered the whole moral hierarchy, must have appealed to the elitist
view in which Philip had been nurtured since birth. Indeed, it was not
just in the sphere of art that Nietzsche spoke to Philip but in that of
morality, as well. The way Philip had managed to turn his own personal
agonies into a workable, if complicated, existence had left him beyond

the reach of the prescriptions for the good life that Plato had put into the mouth of a pious and self-satisfied Socrates. Nietzsche hailed the willful soul, the man who had the audacity to create his own universe rather than abide by the strictures Socrates preached.

This much said, it is apparent that Philip was intellectually ready late in 1934 for his decision to resign from the museum, which became practically feasible through the agency of an old school chum, Alan Blackburn. In a sense, Blackburn is the figure most difficult to account for in this narrative, since in character he was so unlike any of the friends Philip had previously cared for. Yet that very dissimilarity may have been a complementarity that helped to create and sustain the alliance they formed, which lasted until 1937.

Blackburn was a year younger and one class behind Philip at Hackley and he had lived in one of the rooms of Philip's dormitory suite in Claverly at Harvard, where their friendship was cordial, if not close. Well schooled in the values and expectations of the middle class, Blackburn was heterosexual, athletic, and entrepreneurially ambitious, neither so complicated nor so engaging a personality as Philip but an overtly steadier one whose own considerable intelligence and self-confidence were for the most part more conventionally acted out. He reentered Philip's life in 1931, when he was appointed to the staff of The Museum of Modern Art, first as assistant treasurer and executive secretary and later, in 1933, as "executive director," the administrative counterpart to Alfred Barr. He had helped Philip edit Henry-Russell Hitchcock's text for *The International Style.*

Not long after Philip had reestablished his friendship with Blackburn, his restlessness grew acute. Blackburn, moreover, suffered from his own disaffection. He later recalled the frustrating efforts of the museum in 1933-1934 to raise the money needed to acquire the great collection of the late Lillie P. Bliss. One of the leading figures in the founding of the museum, Bliss had nonetheless been unsure of the stability of an institution less than two years old when she died, and her executors accordingly demanded a sum of $1 million for the collection. The trustees were unable to put together that much. Bliss's brother Cornelius, who took over her trusteeship himself, managed to persuade his coexecutors to accept a lesser amount. As Blackburn remembered the affair, it left him disenchanted with the museum administration for what he regarded as its impotence and distrustful of the ingrown power structure he saw running institutional culture in America. Such a reaction may say as much about immaturity in himself as about ineptitude and bad faith in higher places, but either way it became quickly apparent to both him and Philip that they had in common a growing conviction: The arts were at the mercy of an economic system whose catastrophic effect on the country as a whole was growing worse with each passing day.

If Lawrence Dennis had nurtured such suspicions in Philip, he had the same effect on Blackburn, who met him through Philip sometime between 1932 and 1934. Late in their lives, both Philip and Blackburn acknowledged that they had been drawn to Dennis and politics less by the ends of social betterment than by the means of achieving it, namely by power, especially the kind of power they found wanting in their lives but grandiosely affirmed in Dennis's philosophy. Blackburn, according to those who knew him, yearned to be politically active and believed himself capable of becoming a leader, a figure of major political consequence at the national level. "He had a Napoleon complex," said Theodate, who had little time for him or for Philip's new preoccupations. Philip and he spent evenings, "on the balcony of Philip's place," as Blackburn put it, analyzing Hitler's extraordinary ability to sway huge masses of people. With Dennis playing mentor and goad to both of them, they began late in the same year to think seriously about nothing less than the founding of a national political party. The following April, an initial planning session was convened in Philip's apartment, with sixteen people present, a miscellany of mostly unemployed young men whom Philip had somewhere and somehow rounded up—"riffraff," as Theodate scornfully recalled them. Several more meetings were called in the spring of 1934.

It would appear from everything thus far reported that the sponsors of the fledgling enterprise would stake out a position closer to fascism than to liberal democracy, socialism, or communism. Yet their early organizational efforts proved to be so naïve and clumsy that only the most vaguely definable program could be ascertained from them. The first meetings, which apparently did not include Dennis, produced little more than free-floating social and economic grievances from the people in attendance. In June, Philip and Blackburn, reasoning—or rationalizing—that they should be able to document whatever they stood for, decided on a measure that Philip had long associated with research—an automobile trip. It turned out to be a three-month, six-thousand-mile journey, the recollection of which, as later related by Philip, suggested more a tour than an expedition. Ostensibly, they meant to see backwoods America, the part of the country they knew nothing of except that the Depression had been especially hard on it; in fact, they rambled in Philip's new Auburn sedan through most of the southern states and the Oklahoma Dust Bowl. But old habits died hard. Philip kept his affair with John Cage alive by repeatedly phoning him along the way. At the Grand Canyon, he and Blackburn chanced to meet the famous couturier Gilbert Adrian, with whom Philip chatted amiably one night until nearly dawn—about design, not the Depression. Boulder Dam (later Hoover Dam) followed, in construction at the time, a gargantuan affair that they might have wanted to judge as economics but that Philip could not help seeing chiefly as a great architectural achievement. By the time he and Blackburn reached the West Coast, he had reverted largely to former social patterns, which included a visit in Hollywood with the actors Charles Laughton and Elsa Lanchester and another in Los Angeles with Richard Neutra, the Austrian immigrant architect earlier mentioned so unkindly by Frank Lloyd Wright.

It is not known what lessons the trip taught them that strengthened their cause, but the paucity of their later recollections suggested very little. Philip did recall being on the road when he heard—uneasily—of Röhm's assassination. He and Blackburn returned east in late summer, stopping briefly at Townsend Farm. Once in New York, they resumed their organizational chores and were heartened when, at one of their several public meetings, a hundred people turned out to hear Lawrence Dennis denounce the profit motive. In mid-December, both of them having tendered their resignations to the museum, they were ready to call a press conference to announce plans for a new political organization called the National Party and to review their proposals, or something roughly akin to them, for the deliverance of the American people.

The New York newspapers gave the event front-page coverage, evidently less for the urgency of its message than for its eccentricity, especially its resemblance to the scenarios of the escapist comedies that were common to the movies of the 1930s: Two privileged young men, purportedly idealists, had voluntarily forsaken their well-protected demesnes and plunged into a brutal real world for which, judging from most of their remarks, they seemed almost comically ill-prepared. The difference was that for this story, the predictably happy Hollywood ending was nowhere evident.

The *Herald Tribune* of December 18, 1934, in an article with no byline but written by Joseph Alsop and titled "Two Quit Modern Art Museum for Sur-Realist Political Venture," reported that "the party has Mr. Blackburn for leader, Mr. Johnson for co-founder, a flying wedge for its emblem and 'The Need Is for One Party' for its slogan. It is a home-made affair, for all the meetings which have been held since its foundation last April took place in Mr. Johnson's duplex apartment at 241 East Forty-ninth Street. Gray shirts are, or were, worn at meetings, but Mr. Blackburn and Mr. Johnson sternly deny any Fascist leanings. The party has about 100 members."

The New York Times of the same day reviewed the founders' motives: "Recently they became convinced that, after all, abstract art left some major political and economic problems unsolved. Consequently both have turned in their resignations [from The Museum of Modern Art] and will leave as soon as practicable for Louisiana to study the methods of Huey Long.

" 'We are entirely neutral about Huey Long,' Mr. Blackburn said last night. 'All we know about him is what we read in the newspapers. We may be disgusted with him when we learn more about him, but he is interesting and we want to know his methods.'

"It appears," the *Times* added dryly, "that the party is still in early stages of development."

Blackburn concurred, without intent of irony:

" 'We have no definite political program to offer. All we have is the strength of our convictions. You might say that our plan is something like the view that you get through an unfocused telescope.

" 'We know that we see something, but its outlines are not yet clear. We feel that there are 20,000,000 to 25,000,000 people in this country who are suffering at present from the inefficiency of government. We feel that there is too much emphasis on theory and intellectualism. There ought to be more emotionalism in politics. After all, life isn't intellectual. I think that what people want to do is eat, sleep and play.' "

If Blackburn's celebration of a politics of passion was a reflection—or a caricature—of Dennis's earlier contention that "states of feelings, not knowledge of facts or technique, determine choices, generate activity and, in short, shape human destiny," Philip carried the idea of the fiercely unified collective further—and just as grotesquely: "All you need is faith, courage and loyalty. If you have them, you'll get things done. That's the terrible thing today, why the Dillinger and Capone gangs are the only groups that have got courage and loyalty from their adherents. Beyond that nothing is needed, not even consistency. The only necessary consistency is consistency of feeling."

" 'We're adventurers,' he told the *Herald Tribune*, " 'with an intellectual overlay, so we're almost articulate, but not quite articulate.'

"The adventure begins on Saturday, after Mr. Blackburn and Mr. Johnson have left the museum, for which they expressed great admiration, and after they have collected necessary supplies. They were attacking the problem of firearms yesterday. Mr. Johnson favored a submachinegun, but Mr. Blackburn preferred one of the larger types of pistol. When such difficulties are settled, the baggage will be packed in Mr. Johnson's large Packard touring car and they will set off."

Assuming the newspaper accounts to be even roughly accurate, it is hard to believe that two intelligent and well-educated men in their late twenties could have conveyed so strong a public impression that they were, politically speaking, a pair of arrested adolescents. Philip's insistence that "the only necessary consistency is consistency of feeling" may contain a touch of Nietzsche, but it is hard to imagine Nietzsche sitting patiently through the press conference. The contrast between Philip's remarks about politics and nearly everything he had ever written about the arts, even in teenage letters to his mother, is so great that one must suspect the recurrence of some form of manic-depressive crisis. If this was the case, however, instead of dealing with his turmoil by collapsing, he seems to have coped with it by acting outrageously, thus at least staying on his feet.

Even so, no one among his circle of intimates aside from Blackburn and Dennis had anything good to say about his decision to go into politics, or about the way he publicized it. His family disapproved unanimously, although except for a letter (now lost) from his seventy-two-year-old father, which he claimed read more like a lament than a reproach, his parents made no effort to dissuade him from his purposes, and both Theodate and Jeannette maintained a discreet public silence. The trustees at The Museum of Modern Art were stunned and embarrassed. It is no longer certain how many of them were forewarned or how soon. Russell Lynes reports that Nelson Rockefeller was present when Philip told a third party, "I'm leaving in three weeks to be Huey Long's Minister of Fine Arts." If the frivolousness of the remark can be discounted, the conversation would appear to have taken place sometime in mid-November. Philip formally left the museum on December 4.

On the other hand, weeks, if not months, before Philip's resignation, Alfred Barr was glumly aware of its likelihood. The two men argued the matter, again, heatedly and repeatedly, with Barr chastising Philip for what he regarded as a politically repugnant as well as a personally foolish move. Philip stood fast.

The decision to seek out Huey Long in Louisiana was another sign that Philip by the beginning of 1935 regarded Hitler as a model to learn from and in some respects to emulate but not to follow directly. For the time being, he was done with Germany; America would be his arena of action. In fact, he was still too unsure of his theoretical underpinnings and unac-

customed to the ramparts to identify himself as a doctrinaire fascist or a
practical Nazi. His political program, such as it seemed to be then and
proved to be later, was closer to the American populist tradition than to
any other.

Power and populism would surely account for a fascination with Huey
Long, who was the most complete and dramatic embodiment of both factors in the United States at that time. He was a man of the people, even
though as a United States senator he had ascended to a place well above the
people. Born in 1893 and reared in the poor country of the upper parishes
of Louisiana, he learned early and easily to loathe the landowners and the
rich corporation men of New Orleans, whom he associated with the origins and perpetuation of the depressed communal life he had grown up in.
Appropriately, he gravitated to law and politics, showing immense talent in
both and an ambition to match. He was admitted to the bar at twenty-two
and won elective office three years later, his fame as the implacable foe of
big business spreading rapidly throughout the state. A spellbinding orator in
the Bible-thumping tradition of the Deep South, he parlayed his elocu-
tional skills and his natural sensitivity to the longings of his constituency
into a successful run for the governorship of the state in 1928.

He built roads, schools, and housing and strengthened state health programs, fulfilling his promise to lift up the people, all the while nurturing
their own virtually inborn hatred of big-city interests. Not least, with the
support of those he helped, he assembled an awesome political machine
that intimidated his adversaries as it secured itself through a dense network of patronage. Within a few years, he was able to seize near-total
control of the state legislature, and in 1930 he won a seat in the U.S. Sen-
ate. Huey was a political genius, an unexampled regional autocrat, a study
in raw natural charisma, the ruthless, willful, unchallenged Kingfish of
Louisiana.

On December 22, 1934, Philip and Blackburn climbed into the former's
big twelve-cylinder Packard and took off for Louisiana. The principal
political tools they carried were copies of Plutarch's *Lives,* the Bible, and
several volumes of Machiavelli, Nietzsche, and Shakespeare. Alan Blackburn, who would be financially supported by Philip for all of their coming time together, conveyed this farewell statement to the *New York Herald
Tribune:* "We are taking with us no arms of any sort. When we get down
there we will find out what the laws are and see about equipping ourselves. Of course we are interested in firearms, just as we are interested in
exercise and aviation, or any of the other things we are to do down there.

I don't think it will do any of us here in the United States any harm in the next few years to know how to shoot straight."

Having made no formal contact, even so much as an appointment, with Huey Long, they found him less accessible than they had anticipated. He chose not to see them at all. Abashed but only slightly, they decided to remain in Baton Rouge and follow him to Washington when he returned there late in January for the resumption of Congress.

In fact, they were obliged on arrival to contend with Earle Christenberry, Jr., the senator's protective secretary, who had already learned about them through newspaper accounts circulating nationally. His foreknowledge did Philip and Blackburn no good either, especially when a rumor sprang up among the Long faithful that the two Yankee boys, overdressed and overschooled but quoted several times in remarks about firearms, were in fact agents of Huey's numerous enemies. After some rigorous grilling, Philip and Blackburn succeeded in diverting suspicion from themselves, more likely than not because their interrogators decided they were as politically naïve and overall harmless as they looked. They had come to Louisiana, they told Christenberry, to volunteer their assistance to Senator Long in his various "researches," especially in the composition of his speeches, a proposal that must have seemed to the secretary like an altar boy offering counsel to the Pope. Christenberry disposed of them quickly enough, but they persisted with their plans. They put the Packard in storage and boarded the same train for Washington that carried Huey, who once again kept them at a distance. Arriving in the capital, they rented an apartment and renewed their efforts to meet the great man, now with a dash of success but no more than that. "We went up to his place," Philip recalled, "where he greeted us in his pajamas. We got nowhere with him." Several drafts of speeches were offered and rejected before Christenberry made them a proposal that got them out of Long's hair and his own. He told them to go back to Ohio and "organize it."

Huey was considering a run for the U.S. presidency. An early champion of Franklin Delano Roosevelt, he had broken with the New Deal in 1933 and by now, the spring of 1935, his power had grown to the point where he could conceivably challenge Roosevelt even if it required the formation of a third party. In April, he had spoken in Iowa, territory formerly unfamiliar to him, and done reasonably well there. Young Johnson, Christenberry had determined, was a native of Cleveland, with enough money to continue supporting himself and Blackburn in their current endeavor and apparently had no intention of returning to New York.

It was out of the question that they would live and work in Cleveland, so close to Philip's disconsolate family and friends, but Homer Johnson offered no objection to his son's taking over the old house he owned on Main Street in New London. By late spring, Philip and Blackburn were established there, determined to promote Huey Long's "Share-the-Wealth" plan with all possible vigor. Then Philip, victim of fate after foolishness, came down with a case of rheumatic fever.

The ailment was real, no mere reprise of his old hypochondria, except that he would tolerate only what he regarded as the best care. Thus he was bundled off to New York, where he spent most of the summer bedridden in Roosevelt Hospital. Meanwhile, Blackburn retrieved the Packard from Baton Rouge and went back by himself to New London.

Philip's return to Manhattan confirmed what he already presumed that virtually all ties with his career in the arts were severed. He heard nothing from Hitchcock and Hitchcock nothing from him; there was no contact with the other Askewites or the society people or anyone from

JOHNSON FAMILY HOUSE, MAIN STREET, NEW LONDON, OHIO, C. 1935

the museum—except Alfred Barr, who, predictably, visited him several times. Dennis saw him, too. So did Theodate. Otherwise, he was alone, rather as he preferred it. The hospital stay, aside from its therapeutic effect, reinforced the fact that his new life was wholly separated from and incompatible with his old one.

By mid-August of 1935, he had recovered and returned to New London. Now and then, he would drive to Cleveland to visit his family, with whom relations, if strained, were preserved. He was at the house on Overlook Road on Monday, September 9, when his mother appeared in the doorway of his room and breathlessly reported what she just heard on the radio: Huey Long had been shot in the Louisiana state capitol the previous night in what was described as an assassination attempt. On the following day, September 10, shortly before dawn, the Kingfish died.

Philip raced back to New London for a conference with Blackburn, who agreed they should pay their respects in person. They packed hurriedly, clambered into the Packard again, and headed south for the funeral in Baton Rouge. Miscalculating the distance, as they already had so much of their misadventure with politics, they arrived a day too late. The senator's body had already been laid to rest. In an appropriate, final, grim little irony, the tomb was installed in the new capitol building that Huey had built for himself—in the Art Deco manner Philip so cordially despised.

NEW LONDON AND THE RADIO PRIEST

New London in 1935 was a community of fifteen hundred. It had a bank, a high school, a weekly newspaper, *The Record,* a small public library, and a hospital made over from what had earlier been a house. A man could walk from one end of the town to the other in fifteen minutes.

There, Philip Johnson and Alan Blackburn, formerly of Harvard, The Museum of Modern Art, and sparkling Manhattan, set themselves down. Philip had known the place from childhood and was known there in turn as the son of the wealthy lawyer from Cleveland who owned the vast eighteen-hundred-acre Townsend Farm northwest of town. Nevertheless, he and his friend now seemed an odd pair, alien to the environment. They had materialized voluntarily and unannounced, two obviously citified bachelors with a big expensive automobile but no gainful employment. They divided their time between the farm and the Johnson house on Main Street, an ample and sturdy white frame structure that sat among stately trees on one of the town's best corner lots. There is no evidence that Philip and Blackburn had a relationship or that they were suspected of it by the townsfolk, who normally didn't think in such terms anyhow. But their purpose was unclear to all who encountered them locally.

It was not altogether clear to themselves. The sudden death of Huey Long had not only robbed them of the embodiment of the message they had sworn to evangelize. It had weakened the message, as well. They were as alone now as they had been at their December press conference, but they could no longer even get the attention of the New York papers. Dennis, of course, was still in Manhattan, five hundred miles away.

Attracted to power, they found precious little of it in the life available to them on the plains of northern Ohio.

Moreover, there were conflicts and contradictions in Philip's motives. Accustomed in all things to privilege based on hierarchy, he was now attempting to champion a cause to which he brought neither experience nor natural affinity. Even allowing for a massive change of character—an allowance not warranted by his record—how would he tame his constitutional impatience or achieve his ends from a staging area as remote as New London? What would he do for intellectual nourishment meanwhile? Or for diversion? Or sex?

One of his habitual ways of dealing with dilemma was to call upon his sociability and his flair for the dramatic. In this instance, he was true to form, although it took him several months to work things out. He and Blackburn elected to make the best of their new home, reasoning that they had the requisite brains on the one hand and no workable alternative on the other. According to historian Geoffrey Blodgett, Philip "was soon showing up at town council meetings to raise questions about procedure, forcing the town solicitor to defend traditional village practices. Then Johnson got himself appointed to the local park board. Next he tried to organize local dairy farmers in protest against low milk prices. . . ."

Cleveland was beginning to listen. The narrative is picked up by the journalist Omar Ranney, who wrote in the December 6 issue of the *Cleveland Press:*

> Young Philip Johnson, restless, temperamental son of a prominent Cleveland family, is about to embark on another venture in his in-and-out career that so far has taken him into the fields of modern architecture, the share-the-wealth movement and dairy farming.
>
> He is going to "raise a rumpus" in state politics, he says.
>
> Mr. Johnson, still listed among the wealthy socialites in the Cleveland blue book, despite his share-the-wealth activities as a devout follower of the late Huey Long, is the 29-year-old son of Homer Hosea Johnson, prominent Cleveland attorney.
>
> Once a leader in the new modern school of architecture in this country—a career he junked to fight for Huey—he came here to "settle down" on his father's 1800-acre dairy farm after Huey's death.
>
> But the peace and quiet of the farm could not stay his tempestuous thoughts.
>
> So today he said he was going to become a political figure.
>
> That he can command considerable attention is conceded.

Just as a beginning, he's going to run for state representative from Huron County.

Once he gets in the House, he plans to expose "the road graft, the liquor graft, the crooked politicians, the power interests" and everything else about our economic and political system he thinks runs contrary to the interests of "the people."

In fact, he says he's going to devote all his time and money to fighting the fight of the common people. He says it makes no difference to him that his family doesn't quite approve.

Right now he's warming up for the fray by battling the Cleveland milk dealers, because he doesn't think they are paying the farmers enough for their milk. He is agitating for a farmers' milk strike.

Also, he has been fighting the New London Power Company, which supplies New London with its electricity, and the Ohio Fuel & Gas Company, which supplies it with gas. And he's busy in the evenings talking up the Townsend Plan. . . .

Ranney's account did not name the party on whose ticket Philip planned to run. One is tempted to suppose that the prospective candidate himself wasn't sure. His own stated argument sounded too liberal for the Republicans, too close to Huey Long to suit the organization Democrats, but just vague enough to be associated with the populist movements of the day. Hence, presumably, his devotion to the Townsend plan. A pension program meant to help elderly Americans and conceived by one of their own, the sexagenarian California physician Francis Townsend, the plan was yet another in a number of extreme reform measures spawned in the desperation of the Depression. Most competent economists regarded it as crude and unworkable and it never made any real progress through Congress. Nevertheless, by late 1935, it still claimed a national legion of supporters, and Philip and Blackburn recognized it as a promising vehicle to which they could attach themselves and, so doing, gain a wider following.

An audience was already forming in New London, where they had gone on the offensive, making friends as well as enemies. One New Londoner, Mrs. Lee Ignat, later recalled that townspeople were nonplussed when Philip, late in the year, knocked a hole in the south wall of the seventy-year-old Johnson house and installed a startlingly large modernist window in it that smacked of modern architecture. But she added that the two men were "colorful characters, hippies before their time. A lot of people liked them." In fact, a big noisy crowd, young folks mostly, showed up for a lavish Christmas party that Philip and Blackburn staged at the former's expense in the local high school gymnasium, where the hosts laced the punch and shocked more than a few parents who remembered that Prohibition had been repealed just two years earlier.

Having broken through their local isolation, Philip and Blackburn promptly applied what they had learned to a wider canvas. They took to the radio, the new communications device that Franklin Roosevelt in the United States and Adolf Hitler in Germany were already using to reach unprecedented numbers of people. Just before Christmas, Philip went on the air from Cleveland to underscore his grievances about the milk-price situation in northern Ohio. "If the farmer does not get his just due," he warned, "then I shall certainly urge a 100 percent strike."

He never carried out his threat, largely because he shortly discovered something potentially grander: the prospect of an alliance with another major figure of power, comparable in viewpoint and stature with Huey Long. If Huey had been a personality type foreign to Philip's upbringing, this one was even more so: a Roman Catholic priest, the Rev. Charles E. Coughlin, who lived and worked less than 150 miles from New London, in the obscure Detroit suburb of Royal Oak, Michigan.

Coughlin himself, however, was hardly obscure, and he was immensely more than the simple proprietor of a parish who wore his collar backward. Simply put, he was the most sensational national radio personality of his day. Every Sunday afternoon, he settled in front of a microphone at the Shrine of the Little Flower in Royal Oak and broadcast a message that was heard by as many as 30 million Americans. No one in the entertainment industry or regulation political sphere—not Fred Allen, Jack Benny, Eddie Cantor, Major Bowes, or President Roosevelt himself—could match such numbers.

More to the point, so far as Philip and Blackburn were concerned, Coughlin talked politics as they liked to hear it in both form and content. He had a natural congeniality with the medium: a richly mellifluous voice shaded with a lilting brogue and a style of speaking in easily comprehensible sentences that were seductively loose in substance but enlivened with colorful imagery. His listeners responded so enthusiastically to him that in less than a year after his first broadcast in 1926, his office was inundated with as many as four thousand letters a week. In 1930, he signed a contract with the Columbia Broadcasting System that brought him within reach of audiences across the entire country. Cough-

lin's early pleas to the faithful tended to be religious in theme, but with
the onset of the Depression, politics crept into his speeches, beginning
with assaults on that most certifiable nemesis of Christianity, communism.

Like Huey Long, he had been an early supporter of Roosevelt, whose
1932 election he helped to promote from his radio pulpit. But he had
other traits in common with the Kingfish: a delight in the fame his abilities had earned him and a longing for more of it. He began to regard himself as an authority on secular subjects, notably those that ruled daily
discourse: politics and especially economics. In the course of arguing his
positions, he came to realize that his impact on the public was greater
when he attacked a target with passion than when he analyzed it with
probity, and greater still if the target was one the people in their own dis-
content could help him hate. His formulas grew ever more simplistic,
nearly in proportion with the increase in the sense of his own self-impor-
tance. Accordingly, his readiest enemies included those whom Huey
Long had so profitably singled out, the rich bankers and city businessmen, as well as some he made the object of his personal wrath: international capitalists whose material greed exceeded any loyalty they might,
or should, have felt toward America and Christ. He excoriated the
English banking houses and denounced America's commitment to the
gold standard.

Coughlin moved steadily closer to a break with Roosevelt. As early as
November of 1934, he had announced the birth of the National Union
for Social Justice, an organization based on sixteen "principles" that called
for measures as radical and antithetical to Roosevelt's views as the aboli-
tion of the Federal Reserve System and the creation of a government-
owned central bank.

In the eyes of Philip and Blackburn, Father Coughlin was something
close to heaven-sent. They secured a speaking engagement at a January
1936 meeting of the Legion for Social Justice, a Cleveland group organized around one of Coughlin's friends, Congressman Martin Sweeney.
There, Blackburn challenged the crowd with the unashamed admission
that he was "three times crazy, once because I believe in Huey Long and
his program, twice because I believe in Dr. Townsend and his program,
and the third time because I believe in Father Coughlin and his program.
But I've got lots of company!" Philip followed him, with a statement
notable less for its rhetoric than for his pitch to a crowd that was as loyal
to Catholicism, a religion he had been taught to despise, as it was opposed
to the Birth Control League of America, an organization he had never
had occasion to think twice about. "The big boys think there are too

many poor people," he said, adding, "I accuse these people of being the murderers of unborn people."

If there was opportunism in those sentiments, they are worth keeping in mind in view of the articles on race-oriented birth patterns in the United States that Philip wrote with more serious intent several years later (see p. 141).

In February of 1936, he and Blackburn made direct contact with Coughlin, offering him their services just as they had to Huey Long. This time, they were warmly received by the "radio priest," who even put them up briefly in his own residence at Royal Oak. Returning to New London, they assembled a local chapter of the NUSJ that met weekly to hear Philip inveigh against the sales tax and the money interests of Wall Street.

He had momentum now. Risen to the post of district organizing supervisor for the NUSJ, he fulfilled his promise of the previous December by formally announcing his candidacy for the office of state representative. Following the practice of other National Union members when running for elective office, he declared himself a Democrat. He had no sooner taken the nomination easily, by a 40 to 2 vote in the primary election of 1936, than he regretted it. For great things had transpired in Royal Oak during the first quarter of the year, events exciting enough to thrust the prospect of two seasons in the Ohio legislature, that tiresome body, into the shade. Coughlin had broken with Roosevelt, fully and in white heat, setting machinery in motion that would create a third national party—the ancient goal of Philip and Blackburn—and with it, their own close involvement with a campaign for the United States presidency in the forthcoming November elections.

The strategy was based on a coalition of the three major American populist constituencies of the day: Coughlin's NUSJ, the Townsend movement, and the remaining southern followers of Huey Long's Share-the-Wealth movement, now supervised by one of Long's most ambitious lieutenants, the Rev. Gerald L. K. Smith. The emergent political entity called itself the Union party and the presidential candidate it nominated at a Cleveland convention was the North Dakota congressman William Lemke, whose radical plans to help the nation's farmers added up roughly to the agricultural equivalent of Townsend's pension proposals for the elderly. Smith was as heart-stopping a stump speaker as Huey had been and as much a demagogue; in fact, he was commanding enough in person to ignite a smoldering jealousy in Coughlin, whose rhetoric was most effective when disembodied—on the radio. Measured against either of their allies, on the other hand, Townsend and Lemke were uninspiring, the latter an especially tedious orator with a glass eye and an earnest but leaden manner even in personal conversations. Philip met him in May ("a crashing bore") and provided him a night's stay in the New London house but saw little more of him during the campaign.

Mostly, his responsibility, and Blackburn's, lay with Coughlin. At first, they were assigned to the production of *Social Justice,* a weekly periodical the priest had begun early in the year, but as summer approached, they joined the national campaign entourage. In August, Philip infuriated the local Democrats by withdrawing his candidacy from the November race for state representative in Ohio.

His personal big moment lay ahead, together with its anticlimax, in Chicago, at a rally that attracted the largest crowd of the Coughlin campaign. At Riverview Park, an enormous amusement complex on the city's North Side, a throng estimated by the *Chicago Tribune* at between 80,000 and 100,000 heard Coughlin speak from a huge platform that Philip had taken special pains to design. It was modeled after the one he had seen used so effectively at the 1932 Nazi rally: "A special stand, bordering on the moderne," the *Tribune* reported, "had been created at one end of the field. It provided a glaring white background 50 feet wide and 20 feet high for the solitary figure of the priest." A brace of flagstaffs was mounted close to the platform, each bearing a large and colorful banner. Chicago's winds, however, were unrulier than Potsdam's; they punished the flags, which snapped so noisily that they had to be lowered to allow Coughlin to make himself heard.

The contretemps was an omen. The Union party as a whole never succeeded in catching the ear of the nation at large. Its three coalitional factions, at no time quite happy with one another, quarreled increasingly as summer turned to fall and the anticipated widespread disaffection with the Roosevelt administration never congealed. Yet at last, the election was not theirs to lose so much as Roosevelt's to win, which he did, in spectacular fashion, taking all but two of the forty-eight states and persuading the electorate that his policies had begun to restore the nation's economic vitality.

By the end of 1936, Philip Johnson had spent two years in overt pursuit of his political muse, who not only eluded him most of that time but mocked him more than a little. One of the salient facts of his life in the 1930s is the stunning dissimilarity between the success of his endeavors at The Museum of Modern Art and the virtually total failure and frustration of everything he undertook immediately thereafter. Yet the obviousness of that difference leads to a puzzlement: What prompted him to persist in his political quest, distractible as he was, after the death of Huey Long, the defeat of the Union party, and the apparently imminent end of the Depression?

For he did persist, some three years longer, accumulating more frustrations along the way. To be sure, he had largely blocked his own escape routes. There was no easy retracing his steps to New York, which had quite forgotten him by now. Cleveland was evidently out of the question, too, for much the same reason, plus the unattractiveness of the place and his parents in it. Finally, there was Germany, but homosexuals were hardly welcome there.

There is no ready answer to this. He himself late in life never offered a better explanation than a shrug that indicated he didn't know or hadn't the will to unravel the reasons that prompted him to persevere as he had. Even so, it is worth recognizing that his very distractibility had a reverse psychic aspect: He could, when so inclined, impose an immense concentration on whatever concept seized him. And in the late 1930s, he seems to have been impelled partly by the same willful, headlong drive to have things his way, despite all reason to the contrary, that had long identified him as Louise and Homer Johnson's spoiled, foot-stomping offspring. It is more speculative than demonstrable to suggest as much, but his behavior had about it the air of rebellion against a family that early on seemed to make him feel more privileged in isolation than comfortable in their company. Surely he had long since learned to invest his affective energies less in people than in causes, whether philosophy, art, politics, or the varied and intermingling symbols of them. Something had to fill the gap left by an estrangement from the formative figures of his life. And if he had forsaken friends as he himself had been forsaken, what better sustenance, even at the expense of frustration, than the unrelenting dedication to an outsize maverick idea?

On November 8, 1936, just five days after the election, Philip and Blackburn returned to the radio, apparently as unabashed as ever, with the first in a series of broadcasts over WSPD in Toledo. One of these was cited in *Social Justice* of December 14, 1936, under the title "Youth, Impatient with Excuses, Demands Action and Leadership." Philip and Blackburn had evidently chosen a new tactic: They would rely on their youthfulness to gain the momentum that had never developed while they were in service to older, more established figures. On March 22, 1937, *Social Justice* reported again: "Youth and the Nation held its first public meeting and formed an organization to bear the same name as the radio broadcast."

The "Gold Dust Twins," as they were called by the Coughlin group because of their apparent closeness and Philip's wealth, had in a sense turned full circle, back to 1934. As in New York, now in Ohio: Declaring themselves leaders of their own enterprise, they began recruiting followers, unemployed, idealistic, and/or restless young locals. According to one of these, Richard Bowers, who was nineteen at the time, most had backgrounds in the Ku Klux Klan, the German-American Bund, the Share-the-Wealth movement, and a right-wing outfit of the district, the Black Legion. "After the meetings," Bowers recollected, "we would occasionally march to the Communist party headquarters in Toledo and exchange insults with them through their windows.

"Sometime in 1937, we changed the name of the group to the Young Nationalists. Philip tried to organize us into a more disciplined bunch, like the National Socialists, but it didn't work too well with Americans, I guess. Once, he stationed two of the biggest guys in the group as guards at the door of our meeting hall. One was a former German amateur heavyweight boxer named Heinie Weiss. The other was a Black Legionnaire named Charley Capron. Heinie stood at that door for an hour without moving a muscle. Charley just kept fidgeting. It distressed Philip no end."

Bowers's recollection reinforces the presumption that Philip was still driven, however idiosyncratically, by his millenarian dream. "I couldn't help feeling he was a good guy," Bowers went on. "He would invite us all to dinner oftentimes at the New London house or Townsend Farm. He was really generous with us. But I always had the feeling he was looking for something, some philosophy. I think the museum didn't satisfy his philosophical cravings. And his impatience, mostly with people who weren't as quick as he was, sometimes drove us mad. He kept a speaker system on top of his big Lincoln Zephyr. He used it when we campaigned in small towns. Once when he was driving very fast—as he often did—the wind tore the whole apparatus off the top of the car."

There is no evidence that Homer Johnson ever saw his son careering across the Ohio landscape, flags with the flying wedge symbol proudly flapping on the fenders of his car. Homer was seventy-five now. It was a bit late to start the housebreaking; fate would have to take care of that.

Indeed, as 1937 wore on, the signs went up that the Johnson-Blackburn partnership was beginning to unravel. The national economy was steadily improving, which meant that the cause of the flying wedge was not. And Blackburn had taken up with a New London girl. In the summer, for the first time since 1934, Philip went abroad, back to Germany, although partly, it would seem, for recidivist reasons: he wanted to see Mies van der Rohe again.

Mies was surely the most nonpolitical—more exactly, apolitical—of architects. Philip late in life claimed that Mies would have been willing to

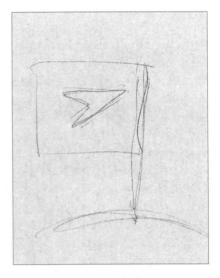

JOHNSON'S DRAWING (1988) OF THE FLYING WEDGE, THE SYMBOL OF THE YOUNG NATIONALISTS, THE POLITICAL GROUP HE FOUNDED WITH ALAN BLACKBURN IN OHIO DURING THE LATE 1930S

build for Hitler as readily as he had been for patrons of all political colorations, Communists as well as capitalists, during the period of the Weimar Republic. The supposition is credible, given Mies's utter absorption—and Philip's early discipleship—in the pure art of architecture to the exclusion of nearly any other attribute or dimension of the discipline. Ironically, it was the unshakable belief in the esthetic rightness of his designs more than any consciously adopted doctrinal stance that made Mies unacceptable to the Nazis, whose congealed antimodernism had turned Philip's *Hound and Horn* article of 1934 (see p. 107) into the wrongest prophecy.

Philip found Mies where he had left him, in his old atelier in Berlin, too exalted and remote a spirit to oppose the Nazis actively or even to think much about them. With hardly any work on his board, he remained stoic in his solitude and modest circumstances. Philip, isolated in his own way, may well have identified with him.

The two men kept their conversations to architecture. Philip wined and dined Mies in the best Berlin restaurants and drove him and his companion, the designer Lilly Reich, up to Lübeck and Stettin to see the great Gothic hall churches in brick that Mies especially cherished. Along the way, they passed one of the newer *Siedlungen*, erected by the Nazis.

Pitched roofs closer to the old German vernacular than to the new national monumentality had replaced the flat roofs of the modernists. To Philip's surprise, Mies liked it.

In the course of this 1937 journey to Germany, Philip happened upon a copy of a *Festschrift* that had just been published in honor of the sixtieth birthday of the famed German economist (and Adolf Hitler's Minister of Economics), Hjalmar Schacht. Among the scholars represented was another figure of renown in the field, Werner Sombart, whose earlier Marxist sympathies had given way to a position closer to that of German National Socialism. Impressed by Sombart's argument, Philip sought him out, found him, conversed at length with him, and offered to translate his essay into English.

Under the title *Weltanschauung, Science and Economy*, the translation was published two years later, in 1939. The quality of the prose is effortless and literate, reminiscent of Philip's previous writing on architecture and hard to reconcile with the image of ineptitude he had stamped on himself at the New York press conference of December 1935. In addition to reflecting his persistent interest in the new Germany, the text provided the first clear evidence that its translator had learned to handle political and economic concepts and terminology with understanding and authority.

Summer was nearly over. Philip, back in New London, took over the organization of the town's Labor Day celebration and personally donated a new Chevrolet sedan to a lottery he had set up. He passed the holiday easily and unpolitically, aware that any speech making would only have disturbed the communal mood, brightened as it was by the sense that the Depression was winding down.

With Blackburn increasingly taken up by his courtship, Philip was left with little more than time on his hands. Normally, sex might have diverted him, but since it had been less available to him in New London than in New York, he continued to seek it only occasionally, in nearby towns, with young men and once, in Sandusky, with a female prostitute. Otherwise, his evenings were more and more spent playing poker with local friends.

Even in headier times, he had been fond of that one game of cards, but now the idleness of the evenings seemed symptomatic of an imminent end to something. Appropriately, Blackburn announced his plans to marry and move back to New York. He would have to find employment there, since he could no longer count on Philip's support.

Their working relationship of three years, however little it had to show for their pains, seemed to both of them to call for a valedictory of sorts. Since Blackburn had decided that a job-hunting trip to Manhattan was in order, Philip proposed that they go east together and invite some of the Young Nationalists along who had never seen the big town. For reasons no one seems to recall in detail, the caravan headed first for Washington for a visit with Secretary of Labor Frances Perkins. How they secured an appointment with her is likewise no longer clear, nor for what purpose except perhaps a last lark, a final aggressive gesture: a demand that she press for the deportation of the left-wing labor leader Harry Bridges to his native Australia. Perkins rejected the proposal faster than it was made; the confrontation was over. In New York, the young troopers were left to have a good time by themselves, which they did, while Blackburn looked for work and Philip paid a visit to the Barrs. In November, after returning to New London, Philip, Blackburn, and his fiancée, Janette Emerson, were back in New York for the wedding. Philip was best man.

With the winter of 1937–1938 approaching and his parents in Pinehurst, Philip returned to Cleveland, where he had the family place on Overlook Road to himself. He made the season a time of convalescence, not unlike others he had known following other ordeals. He played. He threw a series of parties for the wealthy younger Cleveland set and took an actor from the Cleveland Playhouse as a lover. His daily affairs were kept pleasantly thoughtless, with conversations mostly unburdened by politics, architecture, or anything heavier than air. "I tried now and then to find some professor in Cleveland to talk with," he later recalled. "I didn't do too well. I had no place to go but back to New York."

TOMORROW THE WORLD

That Lawrence Dennis resumed his place in the forefront of Philip's consciousness is borne out by the close and steady contact the two men maintained in the spring of 1938. In fact, Philip saw only a little of Alfred Barr during that time and nothing of his other old friends. He claimed to have been even unaware that Barr had arranged a commission for Mies van der Rohe to design a house in Wyoming or that Mies had spent the late summer of 1937 in Jackson Hole and the whole subsequent winter in New York.

In short, Philip was back in politics to the exclusion of all else, but with a difference, traceable to Dennis's own approach to the subject, which had always been more theoretical than activist. Since Philip last saw him, Dennis had written a book, whose title, *The Coming American Fascism,* suggested the direction his sympathies had taken him. If populist causes had gone nowhere—and Philip with them—fascism and its associations with Mussolini's Italy and Hitler's Germany seemed more unlikely than ever to prosper in the American climate of the late 1930s.

That, however, was of little concern to Dennis, busy enough in his realm of thought and theory. Nor did it bother Philip, who had already shown himself capable of running against the current and liking it to the point of perversity. Moreover, as Richard Bowers observed, he had his own long-standing "philosophical cravings," which conversations with Dennis amply assuaged. Fascism as an ideal grew more appealing to him, until—and in this respect he was more impetuous and pragmatic than Dennis—he felt the urge to see it again in action. Having failed in his efforts at gaining power for himself in the United States, he sought it vicariously in a place where, whatever its faults, a brave new world had already gotten off to a blazing start.

As soon as the weather was warm, he was en route to Germany. The Depression was waning there as well as elsewhere, but Hitler took credit for vanquishing it. The Germans were quick to thank him, enabling him to seize upon their gratitude by declaring repeatedly that it was they who were superior to the peoples who had betrayed and humiliated them. It was an affirmation built upon negation, a message of hope rooted in hate, as effective as it was incendiary.

The Führer's fortunes were at the crest; between the spring and fall of 1938, he stirred up two international crises and resolved each to his advantage. In March, he annexed Austria to the Reich and in September at Munich he persuaded Britain, France, and Italy to surrender to his demands for the Sudetenland, Czechoslovakia's German-speaking western provinces.

Philip arrived in Berlin midway between those two fateful developments. He had prepared for his trip by first looking up an official of the German embassy in Washington, Ulrich von Gienanth, whom Dennis knew from a trip he had taken to Germany in 1936. Two goals were uppermost in Philip's mind: one, to attend the Nazi *Parteitag* in Nuremberg, a ceremony, as he recalled it, that marked the passing of five years since the *Machtübernahme;* the other, to sit in on a *Sommerkurs für Ausländer,* a series of lectures in Berlin designed to instruct foreigners on the ends and means of the National Socialist government. Von Gienanth provided him with information about the second of these events but no tickets to the first, which Philip obtained by other means once he was in Berlin and which he recollected far more vividly.

In fact, he retained no later memory of the *Sommerkurs,* except that it was calculated chiefly to disabuse non-Germans of the "errors" that had led to the poor reputation the Nazis knew they had in many quarters of the international community.

The *Parteitag* was another matter. Knowing that Nuremberg would be crowded to overflowing, he got there a day or two early and even so succeeded in finding lodgings only in the attic of the house of a local family. As with many Nazi affairs, this one was orchestrated for maximal cumulative psychological impact. Martial music was pumped through loudspeakers all over the city for several days, rising to a crescendo as Nuremberg itself filled with pilgrims. "You cannot imagine the atmosphere," Philip later said, likening the event to the 1932 Potsdam gathering, with the qualification that this one was in all ways vaster. "Like the [Wagner] *Ring,*" he added, "even if you were at first indifferent, you were at last overcome, and if you were a believer to begin with, the effect was even more staggering." At the rally itself, children marched, followed by legions of women and labor units and uniformed youths, these, in turn, preceding the perfectly executed formations and goose-stepping parades of soldiers, and SS and SA battalions. And at last came Hitler himself, his voice strident and challenging and growing only more so as he whipped the crowd to a climactic frenzy. "Even the Americans who were there—no special friends of the Nazis—were carried away by it all," Philip recalled.

His remarks leave no doubt that he was among those transported. He later claimed he was never active in the Nazi movement or more than an enthralled observer of it, or even in contact with any major German political figure. No evidence has come to light to contradict him. As an American homosexual with no connections at higher levels in the Nazi party, he knew he would never find ready acceptance in its ranks. And he surely had learned by 1938 how determined the Nazis were in their intention to strangle the modern arts, since their *"Entartete Kunst"* (Degenerate Art) exhibition in Munich the year before had been heavily publicized by the Nazis themselves.

Still, the romance of the thing overpowered him. He had no real taste for physical violence or overt racial brutality, but he learned about them vicariously during the 1930s, reading widely in a language he commanded and a literature rich in what he sought. Ferdinand Fried's defense of authoritarian rule, *Autarkie,* was already part of his library, while beyond political theory he found more than a little to stir his blood in the broad range of mystical-romantic German thought. He surrendered completely to the novels of Ernst Jünger, glorifications of war and violence that treated sacrifice as the highest form of mental and physical stimulus. *"Schwärmerei!"* he later described his response to Jünger—rapture, with overtones of fanaticism. He was similarly taken by the writings of Arthur Moeller van den Bruck, whose call for a regeneration of culture in Germany was founded on the imperative of a unified nationalist sentiment.

Yet since he seems to have admired the new fascism, like the new architecture, in the abstract, and since the very act of abstracting was a special way of editing the world, he could eliminate from his awareness all that interfered with a romantic image of the Nazis, while elevating whatever most accorded with it. Moreover, he could afford to be close enough to the movement to watch the new society it sponsored unfold—deliciously close to what Nietzsche called "living dangerously"—yet remaining distant enough to be safe from any real menace he might encounter in the process.

We know little more of his life in the fall and winter of 1938–1939, following his return to New York, than is touched upon in a letter of April 23, 1939, excerpted here:

> This winter has been a long series of lectures for me and I have enjoyed the experience immensely. Talking is always so flattering to the ego, don't you think? My plan to do something about the American Mercury fell through. The Jews bought the magazine and are ruining it, naturally. And now I am planning to go to Europe and cover the whole continent this time, Russia, Turkey, Spain, as well of course as Germany.
>
> What are your plans? Are you going over soon? I hope we are going to meet. I was so sorry not to get West this winter so I could visit you, but things have kept me here.
>
> Your brother was certainly right about everything, —what? And now what on the German horizon? Do you look for war? I do not, but that may only be because I am ignorant. I feel that England won't fight and that Hitler can take what he wants when he wants to. But I would give a good deal to hear from you before I jump into the cauldron maybe. What think?
>
> Maybe we can go over on the boat together. I leave about the first of June. Does that coincide with you? We had such fun that I should like to prolong the pleasure. Please give my very best to the mister.
>
> Here's hoping to see you soon.
>
> As ever,
>
> Philip Johnson.

The letter, which is included in a dossier on Philip assembled between the 1940s and the 1970s by the Federal Bureau of Investigation, was addressed most probably to Viola Bodenschatz. Her name is excised, but Philip remembered having written it to her. She was, he further recalled, an American journalist married to Maj. Gen. Karl Bodenschatz, a leading figure in the German Air Ministry (referred to by Philip, uncharacteristically, as "the mister"). The dossier, in a memo dated February 1, 1945, identifies her as a "convicted agent of the German government."

What Philip could not recollect when queried late in life was how he ever got to know her in the 1930s or what she was doing in the "West," or who her brother was, or what kind of "fun" he had enjoyed with her, or, for that matter what, aside from bigotry, might have persuaded him that Jews were "ruining" *The American Mercury,* a conservative periodical he had earlier thought of buying as a potential public conduit for his ideas and those of kindred spirits. The FBI dossier sheds no light on any of this.

Far more certain, on the other hand, was the sojourn that he took with her in the summer of 1939 as part of his last and surely most eventful trip to Europe prior to World War II. While most of that journey was spent with Theodate, beginning with stays in London and Paris, Philip pushed on by himself to Berlin. Somewhere along the way, he met Frau Bodenschatz. A motor trip followed that carried him and the lady first to Memel (now Klaipéda) in the north, then back into Poland, the locale of the latest international crisis, stemming this time from Hitler's territorial demands on the Polish Corridor. Their return route ran through the town of Maków, where Philip inadvertently wandered into a shtetl, whose narrow streets forced him to slow his car to a near halt. The local folk, unaccustomed to an automobile as grand as Philip's Lincoln Zephyr, promptly surrounded it and began to run their hands over its hood, windows, and trunk while shouting to Philip and one another about the extraordinary object in their midst.

Philip was terrified. "At first," he said, "I didn't seem to know who they were except that they looked so disconcerting, so totally foreign. They were a different breed of humanity, flitting about like locusts. Soon enough I realized they were Jews, with their long black coats, everyone in black, and their yarmulkes. Something about them . . . desperate, as if they were pleading about something . . . maybe because we were Americans, with our American license plates. You know how in your dreams your world sometimes drops from under you? I felt out of my depth. . . ."

Emerging without harm, Philip and Frau Bodenschatz proceeded to Warsaw, which he described as Baroque and beautiful, then to industrial Lodz, for which he had little praise: "Worse than Gary . . . covered with black . . ." That much done, they made their way back to Berlin after taking note of the trench-digging preparations, hasty and primitive as Philip saw them, that the Poles were making in anticipation of war with Germany.

The Polish tour only reinforced Philip's preconceptions of backwardness among the Poles and the Jews, while reminding him of the superiority of German society and the German military force. Even so, if the war had grown close enough to nourish his sense of adventure, it also jostled it, as an incident in Czechoslovakia shortly proved.

Returning to Berlin with Frau Bodenschatz, he bade her good-bye and, joined by Theodate, began the planned journey southeast toward Turkey. They stopped overnight in Brno, where Philip decided to pay an impromptu visit to Otto Eisler, who lived there.

Eisler was one of the architects Philip had invited to participate in his "Modern Architecture" exhibition at The Museum of Modern Art in 1932. Calling on him now seemed a gesture of courtesy mixed with pleasant nostalgia. What Philip failed to consider, as he later remembered it, was that Eisler was a Jew and a homosexual, and this was 1939. Eisler answered his phone call in a perceptibly faltering voice.

"May I see you?" asked Philip.

"What do you want to see me for?" replied Eisler.

"Well, you remember we put you in the book [*The International Style*], and I wondered how you are and how things are going."

"They are not going well. But I'll see you."

Greeting Philip at his home, Eisler could keep his head up only at a distorted, evidently painful angle. "Obviously you don't know," he said, "but I've been in the hands of the gestapo, and they let me out just the other day. I don't know how long I can talk to you."

It was the kind of occurrence for which Philip in the ebullition of his mission was quite unprepared. It shook him. He wrote for help to Oud, who was powerless to do anything. Finally, he had nothing but his sympathies to offer Eisler, whose extremity in any case did not divert Philip from the purpose of his adventure. He pressed forward with it.

The report of the German-Soviet nonaggression treaty of August 23 came to Theodate and Philip as they were crossing the Bosporus by boat on their way back to the continent from Istanbul. The news was stunning; the two colossal experiments of modern times in state government, each implacable in its opposition to parliamentary democracy yet no less hostile to each other, had suddenly signed a compact capable of either foreclosing the likelihood of world war or of hastening it.

Once on land Philip threw the Lincoln Zephyr into high gear and sped back in the direction of central Europe. But the car had given its all to its demanding master and it collapsed in Cluj, Romania, forcing driver and passenger to abandon it and make their way to Vienna by train. There they parted, Theodate heading for Zurich, away from the war zone, Philip for Berlin, in hot pursuit of it.

Hitler's army marched into Poland on September 1, 1939. Within three days, Great Britain and France had declared war on Germany and World War II was under way. The Germans struck quickly in the east, meeting earnest but ineffectual resistance from the Poles, who were prostrate within three weeks. In fact, the Polish campaign was negotiated so swiftly that Philip barely had time to prepare for the most exciting episode of his summer: The German Propaganda Ministry had formally invited him to follow the Wehrmacht to the front.

He had Father Coughlin to thank for the opportunity. Despite having lost touch with the priest since 1937, Philip had had the presence of mind early enough to remember that Coughlin's loathing of Roosevelt and growing anti-Semitism had turned *Social Justice* into a sheet frequently apologetic of Hitler and the Nazis. Even before he arrived in Germany in July, Philip had written Royal Oak to ask if he might file dispatches to *Social Justice* from his advantageous position on a continent boiling over with talk of impending war. Coughlin agreed.

In the course of the summer and fall of 1939, five articles appeared in *Social Justice* under Philip's byline. The first, published July 24, attacked Britain and "aliens" for turning France into "an English colony": "Lack of leadership and direction in the [French] state has let the one group get control who always gain power in a nation's time of weakness—the Jews."

The second, published September 11, after the war had started, recounted Philip's experience in Poland with Frau Bodenschatz: "The boundaries of Europe seem to the traveller to the most part arbitrary lines. But here was a real boundary. Once on the Polish side, I thought at first that I must be in the region of some awful plague. The fields were nothing but stone, there were no trees, mere paths instead of roads. In the towns there were no shops, no automobiles, no pavements and again no trees. There were not even any Poles to be seen in the streets, only Jews!"

The third article, written from Munich on September 2 for the October 16 *Social Justice,* recorded Philip's understanding of Germany's wartime rationale: ". . . the German position is that a minor war in Poland is no more England's business than England's countless minor wars in India were Germany's business. The Germans think in terms of spheres of influence and '*Macht politik*' [*sic*], whereas we think in terms of international law, international justice and the rights of smaller peoples (except sometimes, the Nicaraguans)."

Philip's fourth piece, titled "This 'Sitdown' War," written after the defeat of Poland and published on November 6, chided Britain again: "In the moral war, then, unlike the economic war, Germany has a slight edge over England. Her war aims are already attained, which is consistent with her inaction in the military sphere and her peace offensive in the 'talk' sphere. England's war aim, on the other hand, is the destruction of Hitlerism—a large order requiring an extremely aggressive war against the best armed nation in the world; an aggressive war which she is not waging."

The last of the five, also published on November 6, claimed that the war was being unfairly covered by the American press: "America is the best misinformed nation in the world." Philip went on to report his trip to the front, which had taken him close enough to Gdynia to see the sky lit up by distant gunfire. The Germans, however, had not been marauders: ". . . 99% of the towns I visited since the war are not only intact but full of Polish peasants and Jewish shopkeepers."

This report, insofar as it dealt with the Jewish population, was not altogether in accord with the recollections he offered in a second letter to Frau Bodenschatz, who must have returned stateside meanwhile. Included in the FBI dossier and written in the United States probably in December of 1939, it is excerpted here:

"Everything was fine and dandy in Berlin when I left about October 6. They were just putting in food rationing with cards and the Bristol had no more coffee so you see you got out in time. Everyone was taking the war very well indeed. I was lucky enough to get to be a correspondent so that I could go to the front when I wanted to and so it was that I came again to the country that we had motored through, the towns north of Warsaw. Do you remember Markow [*sic*]? I went through that same square where we got gas and it was unrecognizable. The German green uniforms made the place look gay and happy. There were not many Jews to be seen. We saw Warsaw burn and Modlin being bombed. It was a stirring spectacle."

In its very offhandedness, this last sentence may be the most unsettling statement that Philip ever put into writing. It had the sound of heartlessness; did it have the substance, as well? When he reread it himself late in life, he appeared not only embarrassed by it but haunted, adding after reflection that, as he recalled, the experience of watching the bombing reminded him of William James's recollection of the emotions he experienced during the forty-eight seconds of the 1906 earthquake in San Francisco: "pure delight and welcome," James described his feelings, which sprang, he said, from "the vividness of the manner in which such an 'abstract idea' as 'earthquake' could verify itself into sensible reality."

R. W. B. Lewis's explanation of James's remarks, that he "at last underwent his personal battlefield experience," may apply in some sense to Philip, but in view of all we have recounted here, it may be more to the point to regard his letter to Frau Bodenschatz—written when he was already thirty-three years old—as a further manifestation of a man and child whose life of privilege not only never encouraged him in compassion but never offered him much of it. Thrills would have to do.

Besides, he appears to have meant what he said when he said it, a suspicion that hardens into conviction when one reads several of the essays he wrote and published at about the same time he was corresponding with Frau Bodenschatz. These are all in all more scholarly than the *Social Justice* articles, more educated and skillfully shaped in their arguments. None is more arresting than "*Mein Kampf* and the Business Man," which appeared in the Summer 1939 issue of *The Examiner*. It is probably the most studied summary of the political views he held on the eve of World War II, a mixture of gleanings of the philosophers with whom he was most familiar at the time. It began on a Dennisian note, with Philip attacking "Liberals" and insisting "that the values of Liberals are merely the values of business men, of money, that democracy is plutocracy. . . ." He continued:

> Plutocrats and business men, owing to the nature of their power, tend to be doctrinal pacifists. If in the past business men were often in favor of small wars, it was because these wars did not vitally affect the social fabric in which they held their place; war was, to ring a change on Clausewitz's celebrated phrase, only the extension of commerce by other means. But war today appears not as ancillary to business, but in opposition to it and, so far as National Socialism is concerned, in opposition to the two most lucrative forms of business—international trade and international banking.
>
> Hitler, it hardly needs saying, is not a doctrinal pacifist; the name of his book, after all, is *Mein Kampf.* But his point of view is not a novel, Hitler-invented barbarism, but is part of the stream of German thought . . . German thinkers, since Nietzsche, have not denied their "barbarism," if civilization as the opposite of barbarism is to be equated with Liberal democracy. They have thought of themselves as standing for "culture" against civilization, to use Spengler's terminology. To such Germans, Liberal ideals are centered on comfort, not on heroism. The comfort pursued in the name of "freedom" cancels out true freedom, which is not a matter of happiness but of effort, and effort is, in the nature of things, quite likely to include war.

If Philip still saw Hitler as more an inspired crowd-lasher than a thinker, he was eager by now to grant him spiritual stature:

> Hitler's accomplishment has not been to apply the ideas of various thinkers from Heraclitus to Moeller van den Bruck with full doctrinal purity, but to bring these ideas into the market place by uniting them with the tremendous powers of moral and national feelings. . . .
> At the basis of the Hitlerian *mystique* is the notion of "race." . . . If . . . we overlook the terminology that Hitler inherits from Gobineau

and Houston Stewart Chamberlain—and that has become so repugnant to Americans because it has been made to appear primarily anti-Semitic—we shall find a different picture from what we had been led to expect by reading excerpts from the more lurid German "anthropologists." Reduced to plain terms, Hitler's "racism" is a perfectly simple though far-reaching idea. It is the myth of "we, the best," which we find, more or less fully developed, in all vigorous cultures. Thus Plato constructing the ideal state in his *Republic* assumed that it would be Greek: apparently even in the realm of Ideas nationality occurs, and one's own takes precedence over all others.

Having given up on Alan Blackburn and on the radio and milk-strike agenda of his populist years, Philip intensified his search for the "philosophy" that young Richard Bowers had already seen him at pains to define in New London. One can discern the concept of "we, the best" taking form in the essay "Are We a Dying People?" published in the Summer 1938 issue of *The Examiner.* There he seemed to enlarge on the interpretation he assigned to Hitler's use of "race" in "*Mein Kampf* and the Business Man." Expressing himself with only slightly more indirection than was common among the eugenicists of Nazi Germany, Philip lamented what he perceived as a contemporary "decline in fertility . . . unique in the history of the white race." He invoked the specter of "ghost cities and race suicide" before fixing the blame for such imminent disasters on the American philosophy of "Individualism and Materialism," which "is eugenically bad." "Population growth brings prosperity," he added, sounding not a little like Hitler even as he sought above all to issue an appeal to patriotism: "If we will to live and grow, we shall be fitter than the Japanese. If we sit back and look at the situation purely 'objectively,' the Japanese are likely, with their strong will to live, to become fitter to survive than we."

This essay was reprinted in the June-July 1939 issue of *Today's Challenge,* the house organ of the American Fellowship Forum. It was with this periodical and its staff, as well as with Dennis, that Philip busied himself after he returned from Europe in October. In later years, he didn't remember his life that way. Instead, he attached singular importance to a conversation with Joseph Barnes, a foreign correspondent with the *New York Herald Tribune,* that took place when both men, together with other American journalists, made the trip to the Polish front that had been organized by the German Propaganda Ministry. Barnes, Philip said, having recognized him for his radical rightist views, offered him Dutch uncle counsel: Get out of fascism and do it now. It's a bad cause and a losing one; Germany will one day be at war with the United States, and where will that leave you? Philip recollected being sufficiently chastened by the advice that he spent a desolate winter in New York wondering what to do with himself next.

This account of the order of things is only partly believable. Certainly within a year of his return, he had given his life a new direction and begun a new career. Nonetheless, the record shows that among the many conversions he underwent, this one occurred less suddenly than he intimated in his old age.

Credibly enough, the FBI dossier reports that he helped found the American Fellowship Forum in Newark in the fall of 1939. The editor of *Today's Challenge,* whom Philip befriended, was Friedrich Ernst Auhagen, a handsome and personable cosmopolite who claimed to have defected from the National Socialist party before emigrating from Germany earlier in the 1930s but who was eventually prosecuted by the U.S. government and convicted as a Nazi agent. A similar legal fate was in store for the assistant editor, George Sylvester Viereck, a naturalized citizen of the United States, whose sedition trial, as we shall see, intruded upon Philip's later personal life.

Thus, during the fall and winter of 1939–1940, Philip's circle of associates was composed of more of the same fascist sympathizers whom he had cultivated before his conversation with Joseph Barnes. He was occupied with at least several lectures, delivered under the auspices of the Forum, each covering subjects he had already written about: on December 13, 1939, for instance, in Philadelphia, he spoke of "Facts and Fiction in the Present War," and late the next month in Springfield, Massachusetts, at the local *Turnverein,* on "America and the War." The printed program for the latter event promised that Philip would provide "both a vivid picture and an entirely new perspective on the great struggle in Europe." Sometime in 1939, his translation of Werner Sombart's *Weltanschauung, Science and Economy* was published in New York, with the help of one Oskar Piest, whom Philip later remembered as "a German agent of some sort."

Yet the more he publicized his cause, the more he brought publicity to himself. In May of 1940, the FBI began to assemble its dossier on his allegedly dubious activities, an entry recording that the Office of Naval Intelligence suspected him as early as June of 1940 of being a spy. By the beginning of September, the October issue of *Harper's* magazine was on the streets with an article by Dale Kramer, "The American Fascists," that traced, for the most part accurately, the chronology of Philip's major affiliations, beginning with the Huey Long affair and proceeding to the fall of

1939, when "he accompanied the German army in Poland as correspondent for *Social Justice.*"

To all appearances, it was not until late in the summer of 1940 that he began perceptibly to reverse the direction of his six-year-long political fling, and even then, his actions seem cloaked in a shadow of uncertainty that his own later memory was unable to lift. The FBI dossier contains the following entry, dated April 27, 1942:

"From a strictly confidential source it was learned that on September 17, 1940, one Philip Johnson attempted to contact [name excised] at the German Embassy, and left information as to where he, Johnson, could be reached. This source also advised that on September 20, 1940, one Johnson made an appointment to meet [name excised] at the German Embassy."

The "strictly confidential source" remains unidentified, leaving us uneasy in our only certainty—namely that three days after the alleged appointment at the embassy in Washington, Philip was back at Harvard, enrolled as a student in the school of architecture.

Until the late 1980s, most accounts of Philip's life and career glossed over the period 1934–1940. People who like him or whose interest in his achievements is primarily professional have been for the most part unexpressive on the subject, either because they know little about it or because they seem willing to accept the judgment of Abby Aldrich Rockefeller, one of the founders of The Museum of Modern Art. Apropos of Philip's political indiscretions, she is reported to have said—in words to this effect—that "every young man should be allowed to make one large mistake."

Some critics have been far less charitable. Writing in *Spy* magazine of October 1988, when Philip at age eighty-two was probably the most famous figure in the American architectural world, Michael Sorkin posed a question: ". . . it's true, nobody has produced any pictures of the elegant tastemaker sporting in the Balkans in SS drag. Still, to coin a phrase, *where was Philip?*"

Sorkin's own answer began: "Sucking up to the revolting anti-Semites and right-wingers William Lemke and Father Charles Coughlin." Quoting some of the more damaging excerpts from Philip's articles in *Social Justice* and *Today's Challenge,* Sorkin went on to a summation: "And what about some sort of apology? Some version of the [Kurt] Waldheim grovel? There never has been one from Johnson—not publicly, at any rate. However, apology or no, he has been forgiven."

In fact, more people than Sorkin have not forgiven him; their resentment smolders to this day. But the implicit bitterness of Sorkin's conclusion, like the explicit vituperation of his prose, only underscores the fact that Philip's political odyssey has all in all attracted little close scrutiny over the years and less public outrage, even when documented, albeit unmercifully, as in Sorkin's article.

A number of reasons have been proposed for the inattentiveness, including the argument that Philip's eventual amassment of heaps of power in the architectural profession in general and at The Museum of Modern Art in particular has discouraged everyone in both environments from making a major issue of a matter by now more than a half-century old. Moreover, unlike Martin Heidegger, Paul de Man, and T. S. Eliot, all of them charged, during the late 1980s and amidst fanfare, with anti-Semitic behavior or fascist sympathies, Philip was still alive at the time, a moving target far more agile than those dead men and especially adept at calling attention to his other, later activities—his close interaction with Jewish colleagues, his work on behalf of causes identified with Judaism—that could be reasonably interpreted as efforts at atonement.

Only in the 1990s, when confronted by reporters drawn by his fame to the potential of a lively story, did he feel compelled publicly to issue the apologies Sorkin demanded. In several television and magazine interviews, he admitted he felt shamed by his early foolishness. Yet he did not document his generalities with details and he was never pressed to do so. There remains no ready way of determining with certainty how complete his later recollections were, how sincere or how contrived his confessions or other apparently expiatory gestures that remain to be discussed here.

The debate over his political activities of the later 1930s tends to overshadow a major irony: The amount of power he yearned for was inversely proportional to the amount he actually attained. In politics, he proved to be a trifler, the dilettante he earlier feared himself to be, a model of futility who sought to find a messiah or to pursue messianic ends but whose most lasting following turned out to be the agents of the FBI—who themselves finally grew bored with him. In short, he was never much of a political threat to anyone, still less an effective doer of either political good or political evil. The audience to which his writings appealed proved small and inconsequential, and if he was involved in anything approaching espionage—which is altogether unproved—it most probably took the form of donating money to people whose own roles are indeterminate. In any case, to the extent that his actions can be made out, they were decidedly unheroic, meriting little more substantial attention than they have gained.

Far worthier of examination, on the other hand, especially as they illuminate his later life, are the ideas that lay behind his populist-fascist dabblings, of which his failed political career was but the outward trapping. These concepts and the way he gave them practical force would prove pertinent not only to his later spiritual development but to his eventual role—not trifling at all but very large—in the world of culture, not politics.

Remarkably, it was he who drew the attention of this writer to an article he claimed came closer than anything we have so far cited to explicating the worldview he espoused in the 1930s. Written by John Carey and titled "Revolted by the Masses," it appeared in the *Times Literary Supplement* of January 12–18, 1990.

It begins: "English writers and intellectuals in the first half of the century were alarmed by what was for them the new phenomenon of mass culture." Carey credits the "classical intellectual account" of the subject to José Ortega y Gasset's *The Revolt of the Masses*. Remarking the rise in European population between 1800 and 1914 from 180 to 460 million, Carey quotes Ortega: "Europe has produced a gigantic mass of humanity, which, launched like a torrent over the historic area, has inundated it."

Carey goes on to discuss the various expressions of "alarm" among the intellectuals cited: "H. G. Wells, for example, refers to 'the extravagant swarm of new births' as 'the essential disaster of the nineteenth century.' "

None of Carey's complainants proves to be more crucial to the argument he reviews than Friedrich Nietzsche, "who declares in *Also sprach Zarathustra* that 'far too many live and they hang on their branches.' A great storm is needed to shake all this rottenness from the tree. Where the 'rabble' drink, all fountains are poisoned.' Nietzsche, too, denounces the State 'machine.' . . . The State was brought into being, he says, for the sake of the mass; 'for the superfluous ones was the State devised. . . . The State, where the slow suicide of all is called "life." ' Nietzsche's message in *The Will to Power* is that 'A declaration of war on the masses by higher men is needed.' The conclusion of this 'tyranny of the least and the dumbest' will, he warns, be Socialism—a 'hopeless and sour affair' which 'negates life.' "

That Nietzsche's contempt for the state was inconsistent with any support of fascism—as well as of socialism—was canceled out in Philip's mind by the conviction he held during the 1930s, namely, that the state was the only device available in the modern world to the prophet/messiah who seemed to him the sole instrumentality by which an ideal world could be achieved. Philip envisioned the "great man"—how many times had he initiated the use of the term or its synonym in letters to his mother—as the personification of Nietzsche's "great storm," a force strong enough not only to combat the rottenness but to exercise power over the state itself and keep it in line. Thus the vague ideology of populism finally meant less to Philip than the clear outlines of the iconic Huey Long, just as National Socialism was identified with the demonstrably charismatic figure of Hitler.

Philip identified this view as a moral belief, in the sense that it stood for the preservation and the enhancement of better things. To be sure, this was no commonplace morality: He had retained no passage more faithfully from his readings in moral philosophy that Nietzsche's elevation of the question "*Was ist vornehm?*" (What is noble, refined, elegant, of high rank?) above the question "*Was ist gut?*" (What is good?). Morality was bound up with superiority and inferiority rather than with rightness and wrongness.

Philip's politics, then, were driven as much by an unconquerable esthetic impulse as by fascist philosophy or playboy adventurism—just as he himself was an esthete now and forevermore, in the arts or out of them. This truth about himself he took to heart in the course of the 1940s, realizing no less vitally that if the realization of political authority had proved a fantasy, power of a different sort was no less real, a worthy substitute and attainable in a world more in line with his aptitudes. That world, however, would be the antithesis of the one he had once, as a teenager, learned so gratefully from Plato. It would not be without rules, but the rules would be fashioned, like a work of art, not discovered, like a scientific finding. Art was more trustworthy than science or metaphysics, since in its capacity to persuade, it did not need to prove, and proof, in any case, was unattainable by the mind. It cost Philip a good deal to come to these conclusions, all of which reflected his interpretation of Nietzsche and the Sophists; he also turned them to an immense eventual profit, by an intricate chemistry that governed the composition of the rest of his life.

BACK TO HARVARD

When Philip entered it, the Harvard Graduate School of Design was in the process of a massive shift in educational theory from the Beaux-Arts tradition to modernism. Due largely to the efforts of Dean Joseph Hudnut, who had become persuaded of modernism's imminent takeover of the profession, the directorship of the school passed in 1938 from George H. Edgell to none other than Walter Gropius. Accompanying Gropius to the Harvard faculty at the same time were two other pioneers of the great German period that by now was only a memory, albeit a living memory, of the pre-Nazi past: Marcel Breuer, whom Philip had earlier praised as a designer of furniture and later criticized as an idolator of the machine, and Martin Wagner, former chief of city planning for Berlin. These three men and hundreds of other artists, scientists, and intellectuals of similarly liberal viewpoint, all of them driven from Germany by the Nazis, constituted a collective living gift of immeasurable magnitude that Hitler made during the 1930s to the United States in an ironic twist and grotesque perversion of his intentions to cleanse and elevate German culture.

Only somewhat less ironic was the presence of a student at the Graduate School of Design, Philip Johnson, who, despite his fledgling academic status, had a broader, if not more intimate, knowledge of the modernist revolution than did any of his teachers, Gropius, Breuer, and Wagner included. While he had not designed any of the now-famous buildings of the 1920s, he had studied them in depth and detail. *The International Style,* the book he and Henry-Russell Hitchcock had published in 1932, was already a text in a history of architecture course from which, reasonably enough, the professor excused him.

He was thirty-four. The good looks he enjoyed as a youth were even more pronounced now, the hazel eyes clear as ever but the jawline firmer and more angular, the striking cleft in his chin more proportionately suited to it. He stood five feet ten, weighed 150 pounds, and carried himself briskly, erectly. His hair was graying and already thinning somewhat, but this only granted his appearance more authority, a quality still further transmitted by a refined but naturally easy sociability. Thus his presence as well as his age and reputation quickly won him a special place among his younger colleagues. He earned it in the studios, too, where the students, already respectful of the new modernism but inarticulate in it, were impressed by how easily Philip was able to call upon it in his designs. He could do so because he had committed to memory all he knew about the work of Mies van der Rohe and also, ironically again, because the Beaux-Arts teaching method, not altogether dead yet at Harvard, permitted students to design entire works at the very beginning of their studio courses.

Had he chosen to study with Mies, a sterner taskmaster than any of the Beaux-Arts men or Gropius or Breuer, he would hardly have exercised any such privilege. Indeed, he had had the opportunity to work with Mies, himself now one of the legion of accomplished refugees from Germany. Mies was living in Chicago, where he had been installed in 1938 as head of the architectural program at Armour Institute of Technology, later Illinois Institute of Technology. Quite consciously, Philip had declined to study with him, partly because he could not bear the thought of returning to the Midwest. Even Chicago, its singular architectural tradition notwithstanding, was a hinterland that would have reminded him too much of Cleveland, New London, and all he had striven to escape both early and late. Moreover, he knew that Mies's students, who came mostly from public high schools in Chicago and environs, were less worldly and less interesting to him than their counterparts at Mother Harvard. Finally, he was sufficiently familiar with Mies's program to find it too constraining for his temperament. With Mies, you learned first to sharpen a pencil by hand, then to draw perfectly straight lines with it, then to plot a single course of bricks, and so on. Before actual architectural design assignments began, months, even years of the most painstaking, hierarchically conceived steps would have to be negotiated. It was not Philip's cup of tea.

Besides, the one skill he could never master, drawing, was something Mies did dazzlingly well. Philip worried about his clumsiness with a pencil even before entering architecture school, but he had been put at ease in a prematriculation interview with Breuer, a straightforward, unfinicky sort who said to him simply, "Let me see your hands. Move them. Move the fingers."

Philip complied. "They work all right," said Breuer. "I don't see any problem."

Much of what is known about Philip's fortunes at the Graduate School of Design, especially his first year, we owe to the letters that passed between him and Carter H. Manny, Jr., and between Manny and his family. Later one of the principals in the architectural firm of C. F. Murphy Associates in Chicago and director of the Graham Foundation for Advanced Studies in the Fine Arts, Manny was an undergraduate at the time he met Philip, who responded to him and his considerable promise much the way he was normally well disposed to all people of discernible ability. While the ensuing relationship was purely platonic, Manny was even more struck by Philip, by his uncommonness and, of course, by traits with which we are already familiar. In these several excerpts of letters to his family, he wrote:

"Tuesday noon I had lunch with Johnson . . . at J's house. He has rented a cute little two-floor house [at 995 Memorial Drive in Cambridge]. Has a maid and the whole works . . . beautiful china and silverware, etc. He's quite a guy. I have learned much from him . . . (also am now reading his book), but he is too much an aristocrat architect, caring nothing for practicality or cost."

"Johnson has been a great help. He's a rather eccentric bird, but he knows what he's talking about. In fact he knows more about architectural design than the professor, who is an older man [and] who just hasn't quite caught on to the true meaning of modern architecture." (The professor was Walter Bogner, a native Swiss and former Beaux-Arts man now endeavoring, with some difficulty, to adjust to Gropius's increasingly modernist curriculum.)

"This guy Johnson must be made of money, for he spends it like a drunken sailor."

Manny also documents the first assignments he and Philip, who were members of the same first-year design class, undertook: an architect's lodge, a nursery school, and a beach pavilion, the last, as done by Philip, bearing a striking similarity in plan to Mies's Barcelona Pavilion. Philip scored high marks in each of these efforts, with special praise coming from Gropius himself, in a jury critique.

The chairman's affirmation made only a slight impression on Philip, who, despite having chosen to study in Gropius's program at Harvard, had found his opinion of the creative abilities of the once-"great" founder of the Bauhaus steadily declining over the years. Gropius, Philip was now convinced, was an uninspired designer, a man of fine appearance and mediocre talents—"the Warren G. Harding of architecture," as he later called him. His 1938 house in Lincoln, Massachusetts, which Philip had visited, was poorly planned and insensitively proportioned, or so the latter thought. It was hardly a match for another abode in the same town done a year later, by Breuer, for whom Philip had begun to recover a large measure of his earlier respect. Even the Dessau Bauhaus, which had impressed Philip deeply when he first saw it in 1929, now seemed to him less certainly attributable to Gropius than to his partner Adolf Meyer. And now, at the end of 1940, he was obliged to attend sessions in which Gropius went on and on about the value to the new architecture of socialist philosophy in general, prefabrication and low-cost housing in particular—and teamwork. What a bore, thought Philip, same old stuff I used to hear in Berlin, not to mention from Mumford.

As time passed, Gropius returned the hostility. He recognized Philip as an unashamed admirer of Mies van der Rohe, with whom he, Gropius, had maintained a long and chilly rivalry throughout their careers in Germany and whom he had lately beaten in a competition for the chair at Harvard. Philip was also on good terms with Hudnut, the dean who had offered Gropius the chair, only later to find his own relationship with him gone sour.

The Manny letters are also full of talk about other teachers at the school. Since he and Philip were still in the first year of the program, they were not eligible for Gropius's or Breuer's advanced classes, but they shared a high regard for Manny's tutor, G. Holmes Perkins (later dean of the School of Architecture at the University of Pennsylvania) and for Henry Atherton Frost, a Beaux-Arts veteran described by both as unfailingly helpful and *sympathique*. The two students socialized together at length, their time given largely to shoptalk. Manny was Philip's eager protégé, and his correspondence records in detail the progress of a house Philip began to design for himself in the late winter of 1941.

While it is mentioned among a number of projects Philip busied himself with during the academic year, it proved unique in that he actually saw it through to completion, his first realized full-scale, freestanding architectural work. He waited until May to purchase a lot for it, at 9 Ash Street in Cambridge. Certainly he was not the only student at the GSD rich enough to build his own residence, but probably none of his classmates matched him in the boldness and self-assurance needed to persuade the faculty to regard the house as the constructed equivalent of the normally conceptualized senior thesis project. With equally characteristic extravagance, he hired draftsmen in Holmes Perkins's office to execute the working drawings and to help him with a model, which, when completed in late May, guaranteed him a place in Breuer's advanced class, scheduled for the fall. "He is the only real designer in the school," Manny wrote at the close of the school year, with hyperbole worthy of Philip himself. "None of the profs can touch him."

However extreme such praise may have been, it reflected accurately enough the success Philip enjoyed in his first year of architectural study at Harvard. Riding a psychological crest for most of the first half of 1941, he worked briefly on several house projects meant for locations in New England, but he gave more of his time with more profit to the design of the Ash Street house, the plan of which was far enough along by late July to show up in a sketch in one of Manny's letters. Conceived as an ell, it consisted in its long tract of a living and a dining room, side by side, that surveyed a lawn with a small pool from behind a long four-paneled glass wall. The main interior space extended from a fireplace to a kitchen, the latter paralleling a short hall that led to the arm of the ell, where a bathroom separated a study from the single bedroom. Philip envisioned reddish brown Roman brick for the exterior of the house and for a fence that was meant to run along two sides of the sixty-by-eighty-foot lot. He knew he had Mies to thank for the look of what he had done, but he was, as Manny observed, "a strong advocate of copying during one's training. . . . Gropius . . . however, favors each student expressing himself differently." Evidently sharing Philip's opinion of the chairman, his young colleague added, "The work looks like it too. No discipline whatsoever."

By late September, the plan of the Johnson house was in its final and more simplified form, a long rectangle, with kitchen and dining room flanked by a single bedroom at one end (and no study), the living room at the other. The glass wall now extended the full length of the side that faced outward—to a court, however, not a lawn, surrounded by a high wall that pointed even more unashamedly to the example of the court houses Mies had designed in the early 1930s but never realized. Philip also had his building permit by now. The house, Manny wrote, "is progressing nicely."

In the midst of this new sanguinity, Philip was rocked by the first of a series of events that exacted retribution for much of his political past. This one took the form of a book, *Berlin Diary*, by William Shirer, a correspondent of the Columbia Broadcasting System and one of the pioneering radio journalists of the early phase of World War II in Europe. It was published in May of 1941. A report of Shirer's tour of duty in the German capital between 1938 and 1940, it became a best-seller within weeks of its appearance. At the time, there was no more engrossing subject to the public at large than the events leading up to and including the outbreak of the monumental international conflict now unfolding, and millions of readers throughout the English-speaking world were riveted by Shirer's account.

Philip, albeit reluctantly, was one of them, his attention drawn especially to a passage in which the author, writing from Zoppot, near Danzig, on September 18, 1939, remembered driving "all day long from Berlin through Pomerania and the [Polish] Corridor to here . . . we watched tonight the battle raging around Gdynia. . . .

"Dr. Boehmer, press chief of the [German] Propaganda Ministry in charge of this trip, insisted that I share a double room in the hotel here with Phillip [sic] Johnson, an American fascist who says he represents Father Coughlin's *Social Justice*. None of us can stand the fellow and suspect he is spying on us for the Nazis. For the last hour in our room here he has been posing as anti-Nazi and trying to pump me for my attitude. I have given him no more than a few bored grunts."

It is reasonable to suppose that Philip should have been prepared for such a blow, given his unshrinking, altogether public pursuit of political adventure just a few years earlier. In fact, as soon as he got to Harvard in the autumn of 1940, he had attempted to organize something called the Committee to Defend America by Aiding the Allies, clearly a device for presenting a new face to the world, that of an antifascist patriot. He attracted at most two or three respondents, proof that he was no more skilled at politics in Cambridge than he had been in New London. He gave up the notion quickly enough and threw himself into his architectural studies, presuming—or hoping—that his safest course would be the avoidance of any kind of overt political display.

The Shirer indictment, however, left him no option. Approached in the fall by a former friendly professor of philosophy, Ralph Barton Perry, in the meantime emeritus, who had lately assembled a civilian defense unit at the university, Philip eagerly agreed to join it, confident that his experience in New London with Alan Blackburn would qualify him to work with the radio committee of the group. "He has now become publicly interventionist," wrote Manny, ". . . he is doing this to save his shirt. His long experience in Germany and his naturally dogmatic manner have given him unsavory fascist reputations. Shirer in 'Berlin Diary,' I understand, is none too kind to him."

He had only begun to feel the effect of the unkindness. Manny again, writing on October 30, 1941: ". . . people are constantly calling up the Harvard Defense Group to inform it that one of its heads is a fascist. [Philip has] had to be relieved of his office, though [he is] still on good terms with them all." One of "them all" was Arthur Schlesinger, Jr., later a distinguished historian of liberal sympathies, to whom the responsibility fell to dismiss Philip. Years afterward, Schlesinger recalled his reluctance at carrying out the assignment, since in his frequent debates on politics with Johnson at Harvard, he had found him a reasonable, altogether likable adversary.

In the same October letter, Manny continues: "Also [Philip] says that he has reason to believe that the FBI has been watching him . . . and says that he is certain that they know the truth and that he is no more a fascist than Earl Browder [then head of the American Communist party]."

An FBI report filed on December 8, 1941, makes it clear that the bureau was indeed already watching him but that it knew no such "truth." Instead, it withheld judgment: "In some quarters," it said, "[it is] believed that [Johnson] has reformed and is attempting to convince people of his sincerity while others feel that his present position is covering up his real feelings."

Manny's further remarks, about World War II, are more to the point: "Phil thinks that Russia [which was invaded by Germany in June 1941] will hold out and [he] is becoming more and more interventionist. The reason: we have already discarded neutrality and isolation and now should go in whole hog. Though he opposed going in in the first place, if we go, we must go the whole way."

If Philip as thus reported is to be believed, it would seem obvious that his sympathies had shifted, but less certain whether he was motivated by the love of country or the saving of his skin. In any case, slightly more than a month after these last sentiments had been recorded by Manny, the United States entered the war, and four weeks after that, in early January 1942, Philip's hopes of enlisting in U.S. Naval Intelligence were dashed. The navy had gotten word of his dubious past and decided it could live without him.

Other setbacks of a similar kind were imminent, and more embarrassments. Late in February, he learned that he had been recommended by a Harvard professor (name lost to memory) for a post in the Federal Office of Facts and Figures in Washington, where men competent in foreign languages, especially German, were being sought. Assuming his appointment was certain, he impulsively withdrew from Harvard and caught the next night train to the capital. The favorable impression he made on the interviewing officer in the morning only reinforced his confidence, and he began to prepare himself for a form of patriotic service to which he appeared uniquely suited. Later the same day, the officer, in a routine check of his record, discovered some facts the navy had earlier found in what the FBI was now building into a dossier. Philip was excused from his assignment. Two days after he left Cambridge, he was back again, readmitted to the GSD but chastened in the process. The FBI, however, had only just begun. They had picked up a trail that led to Lawrence Dennis.

After the war started, Philip lost contact with his erstwhile mentor, who had meanwhile gone on to attract a considerable amount of negative attention to himself. He was, in fact, one of several dozen Americans under serious suspicion of espionage at the time. Another was George Sylvester Viereck, whom Philip had also known earlier, in the councils of the American Fellowship Forum, and who was indicted for sedition in the spring of 1942 and eventually convicted. On May 13 and 14, Philip was summoned to Washington to testify to a grand jury about his knowledge of Viereck and a month later he was interviewed on the subject of Dennis by an FBI agent in Boston. In July, an indictment drawn on twenty-eight Americans was the first formal action preliminary to what came to be known as the Great Sedition Trial, a legal complexity that lasted from April until November of 1944. Philip, as we will see, became embroiled in that action, and while he was never officially accused or convicted of any wrongdoing pertinent to it, it cost him long and substantial mental anguish.

In a letter of March 8, 1942, written shortly after Philip had been turned down for the position at the Office of Facts and Figures, Manny reported that his friend "was quite depressed." He explained this with a reference to Philip's manic-depressive history, but he went on to another observation that cannot be accounted for simply in clinical terms:

"Phil is a brilliant man. It is too bad that he is so cynical—and worse, that he is resigned to doing nothing about it. I am going to make an effort to see more of him and try to restore in him some of the ideals that he once had, but lost."

So noble an end was more than the twenty-three-year-old Carter Manny, or probably anyone known to Philip, could have reached on the latter's behalf. On the brink of middle age, Philip had already endured the collapse of two careers, each begun in high hopes and given up in disappointment and frustration. The world was plunged in blood, the pattern of national alliances and enmities nearly the exact opposite of what he had personally worked for. Nearer home, the future of the Harvard architectural school was in doubt as its students began to leave for military service. It was easy for Manny to talk of ideals, harder for Philip to see the point of them.

Obviously, he had made his own bed; most of his distress could be traced to decisions he had enacted by himself and voluntarily. But he was on the one hand a narcissist unwilling to wear sackcloth for his mistakes and on the other, by now a skeptic as well, sufficiently disenchanted by his experiences to expect penitence to have any effect upon a world that had never promised in its own right to be fair. Moreover, he had had his share of purely private emotional misery, none of which had profited him much. Consolation could at last be had only in his return to that great universe of illusion, the arts, where the good really could be safely differentiated from the bad—the high from the low, that is—and rewarded accordingly. To art, he would be faithful by day. By night, he would pursue the more palpably sensual pleasures. There would be no need for regret or any other sadness along the way.

For he was able, in fact, to prosper as well as suffer—after his increasingly hardened intellectual fashion. Liberals, and not just Arthur Schlesinger, Jr., could like him as easily as detest him, nor did he necessarily resort to dissimulation to earn their appreciation. The author Freda Utley, well known in the late 1930s and early 1940s as a champion of socialist causes, recalled a dinner party of these years at which the philosopher Bertrand Russell was seated next to Philip: "Next day Bertie told me how much he liked him. 'Your friend Philip,' he remarked with a chuckle, 'is a diabolist, which is a strange thing for a friend of yours to be, but how much pleasanter it is to spend an evening with a gentleman you disagree with than with a cad you agree with.' "

Distractions aside, Philip's academic performance during 1941–1942 was overall equal to that of his first year. He actually failed one course, Mechanical Plant of Buildings, but recorded A's, B's, and credit grades in all the others. Perhaps more importantly, he continued to be regarded by teachers and fellow students alike as a superior talent or at least a singular force in their midst. He got on especially well with Breuer, whom he had come to regard as the best architect on the faculty, while friction increased steadily between himself and the group around Gropius and Wagner. He was powerfully impressed by the students in the class ahead of him, now approaching graduation. Among these were John M. Johansen, Edward Larrabee Barnes, and Landis Gores, each of them destined for distinction in the profession. Carter Manny, having switched late in 1941, and temporarily, from architecture to business, receded somewhat in Philip's social life, a portion of his place taken by Gores and Johansen. Johansen proved especially supportive not only during the Shirer crisis but following several of Philip's subsequent, all in all preordained misadventures. Philip's antipathy toward Barnes appears to have been due to jealousy over Barnes's own disarming social adroitness qualified by the fact that he was disconcertingly good-looking but heterosexual. Gores seemed to Philip by far the best educated and most intellectually substantial of an uncommonly promising Harvard class. He took over much of the role of chum and protégé that Manny previously had to Philip.

While these various relationships were being formed, Philip moved into an apartment in the Hotel Continental, where he kept an English butler. He renewed his friendship with Raphael Demos, now back at Harvard, and pursued affairs with a pair of lovers, Karl Schlubach, a Wall Street broker, and John Wisner, an interior decorator, both of whom he had met in New York before he reentered Harvard. In the course of these two liaisons, Wisner and Schlubach got to know each other, and one day Wisner told Philip, "I hate to say this, but I have met my life." It was Schlubach, of course. There followed "tears, the works—*my* tears," as Philip later recalled. But Wisner knew his own mind. He and Schlubach became lifelong companions, and Philip, drying his eyes soon enough, found a new partner, a Harvard undergraduate named Ed Boysen, whom he would later have special reason to return to—during the time, soon coming, when the fruits of love were not easily won.

During the spring of 1942, having failed several times to cleanse himself politically, Philip elected to devote an increasing amount of his energies to the completion of the Ash Street house. Shortages of resources occasioned by the onset of the war, together with pressure from the faculty to utilize prefabrication, required not only changes in materials (striated plywood replaced brick on the exterior and on the court wall) but delays in the schedule, as well. Once construction began in mid-April, it proceeded quickly, but not without still another complication that took the form of a complaint by a neighbor who had detected two legal violations in the design. Philip had erected one side of the house several feet beyond the boundary of his lot and raised the wall to nine feet, two feet above the lawful limit. The neighbor took his case to court and lost it when it was decided that neither he nor anyone else had been seriously discommoded by Philip's actions. Manny reported further that most of the other neighbors were fascinated with the daring new structure in their midst, highlighted as it was by "65 feet of glass along the garden expanse." Philip had, in fact, built the first Miesian court house anywhere. Late in May, Louise Johnson, now seventy-three, was the guest of honor at a "prehouse-warming," and in August of 1942, with details on the house completed and furniture in place, her son moved into it.

In the following academic year, 9 Ash Street became a conversation piece among the local architectural community as well as the neighborhood. Accomplished host that he was, and advantaged further by the services of a Filipino houseboy, Philip invited a steady train of teachers and fellow students to his new digs. One of the first dinner guests was a gifted Chinese immigrant architectural student with an illustrious future of his own ahead of him, Ieoh Ming Pei, eleven years younger than Philip but already well reputed at both Massachusetts Institute of Technology, where he had earned his bachelor's degree, and at Harvard, where he was now pursuing a master's. The new American Society of Architectural Historians, a scholarly group organized just two years earlier, convened at least once at the house—to hear the critic and historian Emil Kaufmann dis-

PHILIP JOHNSON HOUSE, CAMBRIDGE, MASSACHUSETTS, 1942, INTERIOR LOOKING
TOWARD COURT; "BARCELONA" CHAIRS, OTTOMAN, AND LOUNGE
BY LUDWIG MIES VAN DER ROHE IN COLLABORATION WITH LILLY REICH

cuss his book *Von Ledoux bis Le Corbusier: Ursprung und Entwicklung der Autonomen-Architektur,* a historical study of architectural form that interested Philip because of his own background in history and his friends because of the increasing urgency with which Le Corbusier seemed to be speaking to them. Henry-Russell Hitchcock, now teaching at Wesleyan and once again close to Philip, made his way to the Ash Street place. Even Gropius accepted an invitation. So did old friends Alfred Barr and George Howe. The house became a bachelor's salon—private enough for lovers and public enough for colleagues to meet in scheduled weekly séances on a variety of architectural issues.

Quite evidently, Philip remained as much a critical as a creative intelligence, producing his first writing on architecture since his brief aforementioned article of 1933, "Architecture in the Third Reich." One of the new pieces, "Architecture of Harvard Revival and Modern: The New Houghton Library," was published in a student periodical, the *Harvard Advocate* of April 1942, while the other, "Architecture in 1941," intended for an encyclopedia, did not appear in print until an anthology of Philip's writings was brought out almost four decades later, in 1979. Despite the obscurity of these wartime essays, in retrospect they prove to be vitally important to any account of his career. It is not only that the keenness of the observations and insights he demonstrated in them proved the rightness of his return to architecture. Rather, his outlook had quite evidently matured since the old days at The Museum of Modern Art; he now wrote with a critical independence and sobriety that reinforced both the accuracy of his reporting and the persuasiveness of his judgments, the latter including a precocious view of the architectural history of the previous hundred years that was uncommon, not to say virtually unique for its time, surely among writers with a sympathy for the modern.

"Architecture in 1941" was a review of the building art in America on the eve of this country's entry into the war. While acknowledging the impact on design and education of the great European émigrés whom he had helped to make famous, he did not lose sight of the increasingly important role played by public housing and community planning, activities of little personal interest to him in the past. He even had kind words for a project in Pennsylvania done (together with Breuer) by Gropius. The name of the International Style never appeared in his text as he took note of the dominance of public commissions over private ones, moreover of the growth of lively regional schools in California and the Midwest.

The article on Harvard architecture, a more ambitious and original effort in criticism, is chiefly noteworthy for its articulation of opinions well in advance even of those held at the time by the vanguard, moreover for viewpoints associated with Philip's own much later buildings and writings. Since the late nineteenth century, he claimed, "we have had two histories of architecture: one, the history of Revivalism, the other, the history of what we shall have to call, for want of a more specific term, modern architecture." Instead of savaging the former, as he might have in 1932, he now found more than a little to say in behalf of the best of it: "... the fact that the Romantics used strange, copycat names for their architecture can no longer blind us to the excellence of their work, or to the inherent unity of the design of the period." Having taken note as early as the late 1920s of the growing force of modernism, by the early 1940s—even as modernism was gaining a foothold in the United States—he foresaw the still-later triumph of historical eclecticism. Thus he emphasized the virtues of the past that he had only adumbrated during his directorship of the Department of Architecture at The Museum of Modern Art. Doubtless his association with Hitchcock and Barr, not to mention his education in the classics at Harvard, left him with more respect for history than he might have had if he had listened only to the more rabid modernists. Still, the profound restlessness of his temperament, not to mention his voracious mental appetite, kept him exceptionally alert to change, even prescient in detecting it. Moreover, by emphasizing that "appreciation of architecture is, at least in part, kinetic," he expressed for the first time in print his preoccupation with the act of moving in and around a building, the processional element, as he put it, a factor he would eventually admit he considered more important than any other in the making and understanding of architecture.

THE PENITENTIAL PRIVATE

By the end of 1942, it was clear that World War II would last longer than most Americans had anticipated when the United States joined the conflict. The tide of battle had begun to turn in favor of the Allies, but the price of eventual victory promised to be high enough to warrant the widening of the national conscription net. On March 12, 1943, four months shy of his thirty-seventh birthday, Philip was drafted into the army. In view of wartime exigencies and especially of the valedictorian award he had recently won from the Graduate School of Design, the School Medal of the American Institute of Architects for the class of 1943, Harvard decided that he had satisfactorily completed the labors requisite to the bachelor of architecture degree. It was granted him in May.

By that time, with six weeks of basic training at Camp Devens in Massachusetts behind him, he was stationed at Fort Belvoir, Virginia. Reminiscing late in life on the year and a half that he spent in military service, Philip allowed that he felt pride more than any other emotion—qualified, however, by a residual mixture of surprise and relief. It was not that he had done the job well but that he did it at all, that he managed to see an experience through for which he might reasonably have thought himself incapable before he ever got into it. For he never secured the position he earlier sought: an officer's commission, or a post calling for intellectual rather than physical strength. He managed to get just one desk job, and it was short-lived. He went into the army a buck private, spent most of his time cleaning kitchens and latrines, and came out a buck private. Hence his pride, which was free of the vanity pride usually meant for him. It amounted instead to the simple appreciation that in proving himself equal to his enforced responsibility he had gotten out of the army alive. Even so, he had reason to be more grateful to the foot soldiers he was obliged to share the barracks with than to most of the military and civilian higher-ups he encountered, whom he would normally have assumed to be his peers.

". . . since I can hardly lift the rifle," he wrote his family, "much less aim the dratted thing, I don't quite know what to do. They say I am not supple enough, only they call it 'soopel.' "

"They" were his campmates, who perceived quickly enough that he was not only an oaf but an aging oaf, more pitiable in his tanglefooted-ness than recognizable by the standards of the Nietzschean *Übermensch.* They called him "Pop" and more than once relieved him, gently, of the shovel he was so patently inept at digging ditches with. In a burst of uncharacteristically fraternal sentimentality, he wrote home of "the robust Whitmanian Americans of Belvoir, with their fine character, military bearing and strict discipline."

Within several months of his induction, his luck changed twice—first for the better, then emphatically for the worse. In June, he learned that he was being shipped to Camp Ritchie in Maryland for an assignment in prisoner interrogation. The position required a superior knowledge of German and it opened up the further prospects of Officer Candidate School.

For a short time, he was lyrical: ". . . here languages, intellect, travel experience count for much, and physical prowess and military spit and polish for next to nothing . . . my interviewer said my German was more correct than that of many who were born and brought up there." And then, as if to show how much his thinking about things had changed, he added, "My companions are all ex-Germans, to put it euphemisti-cally . . . my old nativism gets aroused again once in a while, but if we talk German, it is O.K. It is just the German accent that is so annoying. . . ."

If we give Philip the benefit of the doubt that he had sincerely given up his Germanophilia and been seized with a renewed love of his homeland, the shift was not enough to mollify fate—or the compilers of the FBI dossier. His problem was politics again, particularly, in mid-1943, his per-sonal bad penny Lawrence Dennis. The investigation leading to the Great Sedition Trial of 1944 had impinged upon Philip already in 1942, most tellingly in the testimony he was required to give at the Viereck trial and in the questions asked of him about Dennis in a later personal interview by the FBI in Boston. Shortly after he arrived at Ritchie, the authorities there learned of these prior events, which included yet another FBI inter-view that occurred in New York early in 1943.

Now a brisker ill wind blew in from Washington. Philip was formally advised that the sedition trial was scheduled to begin in April of 1944 and that Lawrence Dennis was one of the defendants (now numbering thirty in all). In due course, he would be called to the capital to reveal his previous dealings with Dennis, specifically how much money he had given him and to what ends. Philip had indeed contributed materially toward the publication of Dennis's book of 1940, *The Dynamics of War and Revolution*. Had he also provided money for purposes demonstrably seditious? In letters to his family, he insisted he had not: "The reason why I am so important in that trial is because I did *not* give him a lot of cash that he says I gave him. And by circumstantial evidence, they [the prosecution] say that he got it from the Germans. . . . The prosecutor, John Rogge, says he will write a letter of recommendation for me, whatever that may mean."

His responsibilities at Ritchie were brought to a summary halt and he was returned to Belvoir, where the routine of kitchen and latrine duty imposed upon him proved to be the least of his miseries. All hopes for a commission vanished. The liberal organization Friends of Democracy, led by its president, the mystery writer Rex Stout, got wind of Philip's predicament and worsened it with an investigation of its own that resulted in only more unfavorable accusations. People Philip had seen socially in Washington on his earlier tour at Belvoir were now made sharply conscious of his humiliation. "The situation there," he wrote later, "with all my old friends looking on me with suspicion was the hardest thing I have gone through in years." Dennis, meanwhile, had his own reasons for feeling darkly about Philip's imminent testimony and he did not shy from reminding his former pupil of the things he could tell the court about him.

Given its inflammatory ingredients, the drama worked itself down to an anticlimax, with the trial dragging on for seven months, until November of 1944, at which time the presiding judge died. A mistrial was declared and the matter at issue was formally dropped.

By then, the FBI had wearied of its own investigation of Philip. A memo of February 13, 1943, had this to say: "He [Philip] repeatedly explained that he has never been in need of money; [he] has always spent a great deal of it on theories and projects to which he took a special liking and he admitted that he spent most of his money foolishly without keeping any record, not even to the extent of preparing check stubs at the time he drew checks against his bank accounts. He stated that he never knew at any time what his bank balances were and that he often dropped in at the bank and drew a counter check to obtain cash for himself or for his many friends to whom he gave much money."

The FBI, not to mention the principals of the aborted sedition trial, was never able to determine whether Philip's money aided seditious activity by Dennis or anyone else. Very likely, it did not. While he was as irresponsible with his resources as his own testimony reflected, there is no reason to doubt that he knew the difference between propagandizing on behalf of radical causes and participating in genuinely treasonable acts. Contempt for the system was one thing, breaking its laws another. Besides, he lacked the grit of the committed revolutionary. An FBI memo written on August 22, 1944, even before the sedition trial ended, declared that ". . . this case [Philip's] is being closed upon the authority of the Special Agent in Charge."*

Formal conclusions notwithstanding, the odor of Philip's past clung to him over time and space. On September 24, 1943, once he had slunk back to Belvoir, Alfred Barr wrote the following to Rex Stout about the Friends of Democracy:

> I can easily understand why Friends of Democracy should investigate Mr. Johnson, who, during the thirties, was active in politics with what might well be called Fascist leanings. Consequently he may have been classed with those, who, like the Communists, are lacking in loyalty to democratic institutions. However, unlike the Communists, he never, I believe, put the interests of another power above those of his own country. I have also heard him deplore the antisemitic excesses of Hitler, as well as the anticultural activities of the Nazis. But like many Americans whose loyalty is now unquestioned he felt that democratic government was not effective during the depression of the thirties. . . .
>
> I can understand the zeal of those who for reasons of precaution or resentment feel that it is necessary to harass Mr. Johnson, even in his efforts to be of service to his country. Nevertheless, believing as I do in Mr. Johnson's change of heart and genuine patriotism, I would like to ask you to reconsider his case. I do not suggest that you call off your investigation, but simply that you think twice before you take action.

Whether due to this entreaty or not, no further action was taken by the Friends of Democracy. More certainly, the letter stands as a testament to

---

*The FBI kept its file intact, adding to it as late as 1974. Representatives of Presidents John F. Kennedy, Lyndon B. Johnson, and Richard M. Nixon saw fit to initiate security checks on Philip, and in fact in 1966, after a review of the dossier and its less inspiriting passages, President Johnson's White House was reported in a memo to have "advised that . . . no further consideration would be given to the appointment of [Philip Johnson] to the [National] Fine Arts Commission."

a personal affection deep and durable enough to survive Philip's protracted affronts to the principles Barr held dear. Friendship, in fact, did a
lot to save the apostate's skin, if not his soul. A letter of January 5, 1944,
addressed "to whom it may concern" endorsed Philip's repentance more
resoundingly than Barr's statement had, for the very reason that it contained an implicitly different and more accurate recollection of Philip's
attitude toward ethnicity:

> I, Pvt. Lincoln Kirstein, have known Pvt. Philip Johnson for fifteen
> years. When he left the Museum of Modern Art to join Huey Long,
> I did not speak to him again until a few months prior to my induction
> into the Army, February, 1943.
>
> In his most rabidly facist [sic] days, he told me that I was number
> one on his list for elimination in the coming revolution. I felt bitterly
> towards him, and towards what he represented.
>
> Since being in the Army, I have seen Pvt. Johnson frequently, both
> of us having been stationed at the Engineer Replacement Training
> Center, Fort Belvoir, Va. I am convinced that he has sincerely
> repented of his former facist beliefs, that he understands the nature of
> his great mistake and is a loyal American. . . .
>
> I am a United States Citizen, born Rochester, N.Y. May 4th, 1907.
> I am of Jewish origin. . . .
>
> This statement was not solicited by any person, and is made
> unknown to Pvt. Johnson.
>
> Pvt. Lincoln Kirstein [etc.]

During the months of military duty in which Philip waited for the Damo-
clean summons from Washington, he took pains not to languish. Daily
chores were discouraging enough: mostly washing dishes and polishing
urinals. His only relief from such menialities consisted of an interlude with
a mapmaking group at Belvoir that ended, army style, abruptly and without explanation before he ever became acclimated to it. On the other
hand, consolation was available to him in his spare time, especially fur-
loughs, which he spent both resourcefully and, true to form, comfortably.
He was allowed to keep an automobile of his own—another big new Lincoln Zephyr—which he drove frequently to Washington. There he found
nesting places substantially more accommodating than his barracks space,
notably in the Carlton Hotel and the apartment of old friend George
Howe. Lately appointed supervising architect of the Federal Public Buildings Administration, Howe was now living in the capital but was out of

town often enough to permit Philip the use of his flat from time to time as a personal pied-à-terre. Once the shock of banishment from Ritchie wore off, Philip was Philip again. He consorted cordially with other former friends and people in professional and government circles, who invariably found him winning and companionable. He got to know his brilliant contemporary Eero Saarinen, with whom he spent time in the cherished game of architectural debate. He met an officer in the British diplomatic corps, Isaiah Berlin, an exceptionally trenchant and erudite mind possessed of a worldview that would later shape and sharpen Philip's own. Howe, meanwhile, endeavoring to help him clear his name with the FBI, introduced him to Attorney General Francis Biddle—the effect of the effort apparently negligible—while career diplomat John Wiley put him in touch with a Washington lawyer. In fact, Wiley liked Philip well enough to nominate him for the design of a U.S. embassy building in Bogotá.

Typically, Philip took longer trips whenever the opportunity arose. He made several visits to his family in Ohio and at least one to Minneapolis to reunite with his old lover Ed Boysen, whom he had seen at Harvard and on occasion at Ritchie when Boysen's visits relieved an otherwise-barren love life. He also spent enough time in New York during 1944 to help in the organization and design of "Built in U.S.A.: 1932–1944," the architecture section of The Museum of Modern Art's fifteenth anniversary show. During his brief stay in Manhattan, he was called upon to offer solace to Alfred Barr, who the previous October, just a month after writing the Friends of Democracy on Philip's behalf, suffered a blow at least as demoralizing as anything visited upon Philip. He was dismissed as director of the museum following a protracted conflict with the institution's president and chairman of the board, Stephen C. Clark. While Barr had no choice but to accept the decision, he refused to leave the museum. A black depression descended on him. He took over a cubicle in the library and stayed there, in adamant and unassailable solitude, until the trustees in 1944 created a title for him, advisory director, soon changing that to director of research in painting and sculpture. The appointment left him in a demoted position overall, but his personal authority was enough to enable him to continue for several decades as the de facto soul of the institution. It also provided greatly for the eventual full-scale professional rehabilitation of his friend Johnson.

Philip made further use of his spare time at Belvoir by studying and in a limited but remarkable way even practicing architecture. As a student at

the Harvard GSD, he had already visited Mies in Chicago in the spring of
1941, and he did so several times more while he was in the army. The
clearest evidence of the effect of this discipleship could be read in the
pages of *Architectural Forum,* where the first publication of any of his
works, 9 Ash Street in Cambridge, appeared in December 1943.

"One of the most obvious and consistent trends in modern architecture," the text related, "has been the tendency to simplify, through stan-
dardization and repetition, and through elimination of every element
which might be left out. Described in this manner the process sounds
more negative than constructive, but in the hand of an accomplished artist
and technician, such as Mies van der Rohe, the approach has produced
buildings of remarkable quality. . . . This little house in Cambridge is
probably the best example in America of the same attitude toward
design."

The work Philip did while still in service is of little consequence except
that he packed into a few designs the attitudinal elements of his later,
stylistically quite varied career. His preoccupation with Mies was evident
in a tool-storage shed, completed in 1944 on the western edge of the
Johnson family's Townsend Farm, and a hospital project intended as an
addition to the aforementioned (see p. 120) medical facility of New London. Both efforts featured unarticulated brick walls with ribbon cleresto-
ries, rather similar in elevation to some of Mies's early works at Illinois
Institute of Technology. Two other projects, contrarily, were premonitory
of his endeavors a decade and a half hence. The first was a residence
intended for Ambassador John Wiley, the extravagance of the design
together with the absence of any specific site suggesting that neither client
nor architect really expected it to be realized. It consisted of five pavilions
arranged in a rambling rectilinear configuration around a pair of tree-
studded courts. One of its three bedroom wings was constructed on *pilotis* sunk in a long serpentine lagoon. Only the plan of the house survives,
but Philip later recalled that he had in mind low pitched roofs with wide
eaves: "The house was part Wright, part Chinese, part Mies. It had lots
of glass." He might have added to his list of influences Marcel Breuer,
whose habit of separating his house plans into two more or less independent units—"binuclear houses," as he called them—inspired his student
not only in this instance but in a school project of 1942 and in several of
his later, post–World War II residential designs.

No less worthy of note, especially since it prefigured Philip's later shift
from International Style modernism to a form of neoclassicism and still
later to postmodernism, is a house mentioned and illustrated in a letter to
Carter Manny dated August 3, 1944. It is probably identical with an

unbuilt project commissioned by his friends Julius and Cleome Wadsworth of Hartford, Connecticut, for a site in Virginia. "You will be very surprised," Philip wrote, ". . . at my later work. One formal house (*piano nobile* and all) which has arches on both facades and is completely symmetrical. The entrance hall is 2-storeyed with a *double* flanking stairway. All my modern friends hate it. George Howe likes it and the clients like it, but you should hear the moderns!!" A drawing in the letter to Manny shows a flat-roofed facade with a rank of seven arched windows, just the sort of thing Philip would have sniffed at at the time he and Hitchcock wrote *The International Style.*

Late in 1944, with victory in the war close enough to foresee, the military decided Philip was at last fuller in years than in usefulness. Moreover, he was suffering from an almost unbearable skin itch that was probably related to his nervous constitution. At thirty-eight, he was honorably discharged at Camp Atterbury in Indiana. He returned to Cleveland. A letter written on January 2, 1945, to Carter Manny contains the following passages:

> When I got home I was restless so I hiked off to Chicago to see Mies. . . . He is building *the* great modern monumental building, the administration and library of the I.I.T. [In fact, the work was never realized.] The bays are 24′ by 64′ so you get some idea . . . the effect of such staggering simplicity, I can, for one, scarcely imagine. Drawings give no idea, naturally. . . .
>
> Went to Racine to see the *Meister's* work [Frank Lloyd Wright's Johnson Wax buildings, which *were* completed, in 1939]. Very exciting. Details execrable. Structurally falling down. Lolly columns put in after to hold up too ambitious a span, rain coming in so badly that a new *plate glass* roof has to be built over whole thing. Color and shapes very good. Entrance geared too low and too 'in behind' for me.

Late in his life, Philip remembered this visit to Racine as the occasion when he realized for the first time how unqualifiedly great an architect Wright was. The claim, however, was a reflection of hindsight; his letter to Manny suggests that in 1945 the ambivalence he had felt toward Wright ever since the old man had made life so difficult at the time of the 1932 exhibition was still with him. It kept him from forming as clear and integrated an image of Wright as he had of Mies, who stood, for the time being, for unalloyed excellence. Indeed, Philip, on the brink of a career in architecture, would make Mies the model of most of what he did for the next ten years of his life.

Yet complex as he was and given almost naturally to love-hate relationships, he would never be able to resist gravitating toward the comparably convoluted Wright. For that matter, as early as 1946, writing further about the Wadsworth House, on which he was still working at the time, he called it "one-half Wright, one-half Persius." No Mies. Whatever else had happened to him during the stormy ten-year odyssey that ended with his release from the army in 1944, he had lost none of his ability to live several lives at once, on the drawing board and in the salons of the town he now made haste in returning to: New York.

PART THREE

REBIRTH AND RENEWAL

1946–1953

BARR AGAIN, MOMA AGAIN,

MIES AGAIN

With the beginning of the second half of his life, Philip Johnson made a pact with fate and kept it. If luck had been good to him in his earlier museum days, and equally contrary during his political and military *Wanderjahre,* it was at least consistent in the lessons it taught. Thus, when he had the good sense to return to his natural realm, the arts, they rewarded his devotions. He moved in a single year from relative obscurity back to the center of the American cultural stage.

Events unfolded rapidly on all fronts. At the outset of 1945, the war was still raging in Europe and the Pacific as Philip took over just enough space at 205 East Forty-second Street to begin a one-man practice. The surrender of Germany followed in May, that of Japan in September. By the end of December, Philip had not only hired an associate but established, more exactly reestablished, himself as the de facto head of the Department of Architecture at The Museum of Modern Art.

He had not consciously intended such a professional double track, even if it was altogether in character. Yet little architectural design work was available to him with the national economy still geared more to wartime production than to consumer needs. He knew that well enough when he invited his old chum of Harvard GSD days, Landis Gores, to join him in his office. There were a few projects already in hand, such as the Wadsworth and Wiley houses, enough perhaps to keep two people busy. Neither project was ever built, but a competition design of a house for *Ladies' Home Journal* was published in the July 1945 issue of that magazine.

Remarkably, it was a deep bow to the functionalism Philip had so long abhorred. It "could be assembled," Richard Pratt wrote in the *Journal,* "in

a single day with a mere few hundred fully finished panels, parts and units."
As he had proved in organizing the 1932 "Modern Architecture" show,
Philip could, when it seemed appropriate, be as practical as he had to be.

More important in the long run, however, a model of the house was
exhibited concurrently at The Museum of Modern Art. The implications
of that fact were irresistible. By midyear, notwithstanding the practice he
was trying to build with Gores, Philip was back in close touch with Alfred
Barr, their ancient colleagueship completely rekindled.

Barr lost no time setting the table for Philip, just as he had in 1930. The
most obvious difference in their roles now was that Barr was no longer
director of the museum. For several years, the museum was run by a committee of the trustees, leaving a power vacuum on the staff that Barr, with
his refusal to leave the institution, had gradually filled by his stolid and
unwavering presence. With his help and the added support of trustee
Nelson Rockefeller, Philip encountered no serious opposition in resum-
ing a place in the Department of Architecture, whereupon his high-voltage
personality and breadth of experience enabled him to take command of
the office quickly and easily enough.

Except for a passage in the late 1930s, the department had operated
without a strong leader since Philip's earlier tenure. Following his 1934
resignation, the trustees placed the Department of Architecture under the
formal direction of Philip Goodwin, a trustee himself and an architect,
but a man more of manners than of ambition. Goodwin had left most of
the substantive responsibilities of the department to his assistants. Ernestine Fantl, earlier Philip's secretary, was named curator of Architecture
and Industrial Design in 1935, relinquishing that position two years later
to Philip's old traveling companion John McAndrew, newly hired away
from Vassar College.

Exactly when and why Philip's intense and unyielding dislike of
McAndrew developed is beyond anyone's recall. The two men saw a lit-
tle of each other at the Askew salon during the early 1930s, but they lost
all contact during McAndrew's 1937–1940 stay at the museum, when
Philip was off on his political escapade. Yet through correspondence with
Alfred Barr, Philip kept abreast of McAndrew's record, which featured as
one of its major entries his assembly of the Bauhaus show in 1938,
mounted with the cooperation of Herbert Bayer and Walter and Ise
Gropius. Confined to the years of Gropius's leadership, 1919 to 1928, with
Mies van der Rohe's 1930–1933 directorship omitted, the exhibition was
greeted by the press less hospitably than McAndrew anticipated. The fact
was not lost on Philip, whose decision to leave the museum had never
precluded his interest in the way it was run. McAndrew was also curator

at the time, 1936, when the trustees appointed Goodwin as the architect of a new building for the museum and Nelson Rockefeller proposed that young Edward Durell Stone work together with him. The structure was completed and opened, likewise on McAndrew's watch, in 1939. Principally the work of Stone, as matters turned out, and by consensus of little more than average merit—albeit in the International Style—it was never much appreciated by Alfred Barr, whose original hopes of giving the commission to Mies had been dashed by the trustees. McAndrew had played a marginal role in Stone's design, having proposed the Art Moderne round holes that were carved into the parapet cornice of the building. He also laid out, in collaboration with Barr, a garden space behind the new museum.

In short, he did much of the sort of thing that might have reminded Philip of his own erstwhile ambitions and achievements at the museum, moreover in a way that could easily have earned Philip's jealousy. Philip never admitted as much, contenting himself with the criticism that McAndrew was simply a mediocrity with an inferior eye.

McAndrew was gone by 1941, dismissed at about the same time the Department of Architecture fell under the trustees' suspicion that its exhibitions were not fiscally profitable. In 1939, Nelson Rockefeller was appointed president of the museum and Stephen Clark chairman of the board. Neither much liked McAndrew's personal style, reportedly lacking in the deference to which trustees as a species tend to grow accustomed.

Barr, who respected McAndrew, regretted his loss, yet the signs of his own eventual deposition were already up and there was no stopping the subsequent reduction in emphasis on architecture as a museum-worthy discipline. In 1940, the Department of Architecture and Industrial Art, so named in 1935, was divided into two parts. Architect Eliot F. Noyes was brought in to head the latter section, now called Industrial Design, while Goodwin retained Architecture, leaving its handling for the most part to a brace of successively hired young people, all of them women and intelligent enough, but all inevitably obliged to make do with a minimum of authority.

It is little wonder, then, that Barr, himself already officially stripped of the directorship but retrenched at an estimable level, welcomed the sight of Philip Johnson, who he felt had the talent, drive, and grace necessary to restore architecture to its former status at the museum.

Formally the director of the Department of Architecture was Elizabeth B. Mock, who had held the position since 1942 and made something of a name for herself as an expert on housing. She was also the organizer of the exhibition "Built in U.S.A.: 1932–44" earlier reported here (see p. 165) as an event about which Philip, in touch with the museum solely through Alfred Barr, had offered advice. Now, a year later and whether she liked it or not, Mock was about to be gentled into the departmental shade. Philip recalled a luncheon he had with her and Barr at which, by his own admission, he so pointedly ignored her that she was nearly reduced to tears. She evidently never had a chance.

As there were no objections from Barr to Philip's return, neither were any expressed by René d'Harnoncourt, the gifted Viennese who at the time occupied a vice presidential post at the museum but, more to the point, had functioned as the nearest thing to a director ever since Barr was fired. Less a scholar than an administrator, d'Harnoncourt possessed a quick intelligence, flawless taste, and a genius for diplomacy, traits collectively manifest in his repeated counsel to the trustees during the mid-1940s that Barr was too precious a commodity ever to be dropped entirely from the museum rolls. Thus in the fall of 1945, with such direct and indirect forces working on his behalf, Philip was showing up every afternoon at the museum, as usual collecting no salary and no less typically getting ready to supervise a major architectural exhibition of his own devising.

As matters developed, he needed two years to do it, and only following an endeavor whose failure was traceable to a conflict he was unable to resolve between one of his great devotions of the 1930s, modernism, and another he had learned to cultivate in the meantime, history.

This much seemed apparent to him, to begin with: If World War II had brought a virtual end to all new building everywhere, it had only quickened a desire in the United States for a lucid, uncluttered manner of architecture that would suit the country's victorious and forward-looking mood. Surely that must be modernism. He had, of course, long since identified himself with that point of view, but lately he had begun to realize how much the age-old elements of symbolic meaning and monumental form had been lost to the lean, sentiment-free abstraction of modernism.

Thus he hoped to promote a reconciliation of these two architectural effects by organizing a show of twentieth-century memorial buildings— better still, in view of the recently ended global conflagration, of war memorials. He argued his case in an article in the September 1945 issue of *Art News* magazine:

> Ever since the mound builders of Ohio and the artisans of the grand monoliths of Stonehenge, monuments have been considered the highest form of architecture . . . the monumental buildings and sculp-

tures of the Acropolis . . . are for the most part memorials to the Persian wars. . . .

We have, however, only to look at the monuments in this country built in the last hundred years to understand one of the causes of their unpopularity. They are very ugly.

But there is a deeper cause, rooted in our current philosophy of life. . . . The functionalists of our day have applied the philosophy of utilitarianism to the field of design; according to them what is useful is beautiful. . . . [But] "form follows function" has no application in the design of a *baldacchino.*

The obvious answer is to commission better artists and architects.

Philip finally got nowhere with his plans, which are nonetheless worth remarking as symbolic of the bridge he sought to build between his political ambitions of the 1930s and his esthetic renewal in the 1940s. Monumentality might stand for heroic sentiment, yet it might—or so he hoped—be conveyed in modernist form. Raising little professional interest in his project and less money for it, he fought on, in the hope of a publication, if not a show.

"It will be a book," he wrote in a letter of October 18, "of the ideas of the best artists of the world on War Memorials. I hope to get Le Corbusier, Oud, Frank Lloyd Wright, Henry Moore, Calder, Picasso to do drawings for us."

It was one of "the best artists" to whom he addressed the letter, which began:

Dear Mies:

Since my very delightful visit with you I have been trying strenuously to put across the idea that you should build in our garden [at the museum] a pavilion to house "Guernica" [Pablo Picasso's huge canvas, done in 1937 in outraged response to the brutal air raid on a Basque town during the Spanish Civil War]. Unfortunately I can not get any money. . . . We shall therefore have to think of something else to do.

My hope is this, that you can design a pavilion for, let us say, Lincoln Park or some appropriate site in Chicago to contain "Guernica." In this way there would be no limits of money to stop us and you could let your fancy free rein.

I would like to show these designs by means of your perspectives, with "Guernica" montaged on them. This could be of large scale . . . and would be beautifully reproduced in the book which we expect to put out.

Since Mies did not answer, one can only guess at his reasons for shying from Philip's project. Wright was more forthcoming. "I do not believe in monuments," he wrote Philip flatly. "Memorials are better if they are useful to those who live in the memories they memorialize. . . .

"Symbols are out."

So was Philip's project.

Early in 1946, several months after his decision to abandon the memorials project, Philip issued another invitation to Mies, this time that he be the subject of a monograph and a major retrospective exhibition at the museum. The idea, if unexceptional in retrospect, was more than a little daring at the time. Not only had Mies never been featured in a full-scale review of his work and career, either here or abroad; he was in some respects a difficult topic of research. Most of his personal and professional records from the prewar years were still in Germany, worse still, locked in a farmhouse in Thuringia, a province of one of Europe's postwar Communist states, the vehemently anti-Western German Democratic Republic. For all purposes, those papers were irretrievable. Philip had no choice but to rely on Mies's memory together with the material he had managed somewhat hastily to carry with him when he emigrated in 1938. Moreover, Mies was hardly an expansive conversationalist, and he could not be counted on to provide more than a minimum of information in any interview process.

Everything so far reported here thus might suggest that Philip's admiration of the man was so encompassing that it alone inspired him to pursue the twin objectives of book and show. Yet writing on New Year's Day of 1946 to J. J. P. Oud (who was still in Holland), he called that supposition into question and, in a few casually constructed sentences, suggested how his earlier attitudes had grown less assured, more searching:

I am very impressed by your analysis of national and international. I suppose being in America now where we have had so little Berlage [Hendrik Berlage, the early twentieth-century Dutch modernist] and where Wright has been such an individualist, we have taken too hard to the International Style. But there seems little attraction for me in a more traditional approach. I agree with you the accent on domestic architecture is unfortunate. We all long to build larger more monumental building of the size of your SHELL [Oud's Shell Building of 1938–1942 in The Hague]. But I still cling to the hope that the home can be a little monumental, like a Blondel or Gabriel Chateau or pavilion. As for Mies, his school [I.I.T.] is less interesting than that Barcelona Pavilion and the windows were changed in their propor-tions at the last minute by the builders to make them cheaper. But I like the purity, the careful brick work . . . and I like the proportion, except for the changed windows. Wright I admit is the greatest archi-tect in this country or maybe in the world, though I find him difficult to adopt as an example. He is so romantic and so little interested in the monumental as such.

Anyhow I am working on a new house for myself which will be high ceiling and very monumental (like LeDoux [*sic*] whom I like very much).

Clearly, monumentality had come to occupy a high place in his hierar-chy of architectural values. The term eludes easy definition, but Philip, once he consciously acknowledged his devotion to it, never stopped iden-tifying it with the classical, lasting, eloquent and large-spirited in archi-tectural form. Hence not only his recent fascination with memorials and the work of the French neoclassicist Claude-Nicolas Ledoux but his life-long love of the Baroque and his ambivalence about the Gothic (his ado-ration of Chartres the surpassing exception he made to *that* generalization). Hence, too, apparently, a growing shadow over his image of Mies, about whose reductivist tendencies he expressed doubts even as he was putting the Mies retrospective together. Late in April, he wrote Oud again:

Most architects and critics think that [Mies's] slogan of "beinahe nichts" [almost nothing] has gone so far that there is really nichts. I don't know. . . . History will tell us and tell us no doubt very soon.

The qualification of his former unqualified reverence for Mies notwith-standing, he proceeded with the exhibition. It is uncertain whether he really believed Wright the greater architect, since in all his later profes-sional life he never gave up the habit of shifting the object of his superla-tives from Mies to Wright to Le Corbusier. Surely he had more reason in 1946 to show Mies than either of the others. He never found Le Corbu-sier other than sour and contemptuous as a person, and while he was already redressing the poor opinion of Corb's work that he had expressed to Russell Hitchcock in 1931, he never freed himself fully of an ambiva-lence about the work of the great Swiss. Wright, by contrast, could be vastly more engaging than Le Corbusier but no less impossible to work with, certainly at the level of an exhibition. Moreover, Philip meant it when he wrote Oud that Wright was "difficult to adopt as an example." The fact that he was starting his own architectural career in 1946—and finding Mies a model more easily emulable than Wright—likely helped to make Mies the best choice for the retrospective that he came increasingly to regard as The Museum of Modern Art's first major postwar acknowledgment of the worldwide victory of modernism.

In a sense, the exhibition, which opened in September of 1947, proved at once a debut and a resurrection, for both Philip and Mies. For the former, it stood for the unarguable restoration of his personal authority in the American architectural world. For Mies, it represented equally certain formal recognition in the same sphere following the near obliteration of his international name during the Nazi period.

The preface to Philip's monograph began: "Of all the great modern architects, Mies van der Rohe is least known." Two hundred pages later, any such ignorance in the reader would have been dispelled, for good. Despite the lost papers in Germany, Philip filled most of the lacunae in the life and work of the architect, who in turn, give or take an occasional and typically exasperating fit of unresponsiveness, was as cooperative as he needed to be. The book was the first serious summary of its subject in any language and it remains today one of the central works in the Miesian bibliography. Combing diligently through yellowing architectural periodicals and depending as much on Mies's students and assistants in Chicago, chiefly George Danforth, as upon Mies himself, Philip discovered far more about Mies than he had ever known, most notably about the architect's early, premodernist work, his designs of exhibitions and furniture, and his little-known published writings and lectures.

Having failed in 1932 to persuade Mies to come to New York and supervise the design of the "Modern Architecture" show, Philip now made a similar overture, which was accepted. Mies's installation, in fact, proved to be as integral to the striking success of the event as either the work displayed or Philip's published discussion of it. Driven by his reductivist impulse, Mies created the impression of a nearly column-free space in the museum's galleries by obscuring some of the pillars behind floor-to-ceiling photo murals that were sizable enough by themselves to amplify the force of the works they depicted. The resultant dynamic flow of interior space recalled an effect Philip had so admired in 1930 at the Tugendhat House. Edwin Alden Jewell in *The New York Times* extolled the "almost breath-taking largeness of effect" the installation lent the exhibition as a whole.

Philip, meanwhile, was as dutiful in his hospitality to Mies as he was in his curatorial responsibilities. He extended his welcome to the entourage

JOHNSON AND MIES VAN DER ROHE IN THE GALLERIES OF THE MIES RETROSPECTIVE
EXHIBITION CURATED BY JOHNSON AND INSTALLED BY MIES AT THE MUSEUM OF
MODERN ART, 1947

of I.I.T. alumni who accompanied the master from Chicago, and he made
a special point of introducing Mies to his close friend the sculptor Mary
Callery, a woman of striking good looks who was quickly drawn to Mies
and he to her. Their ensuing liaison was brief but intense. She was on
Mies's arm at the opening, which, since it was a major event of the
1947–1948 season, attracted none other than Frank Lloyd Wright, who
made sure to do what he could to divert attention from Mies to himself.
The two men had been closer in the late 1930s than might be expected of
a pair of certifiably prodigious egos. When Mies visited the United States
for the first time in 1937, he made a special pilgrimage to Taliesin in Wisconsin, where Wright received him with comradely warmth and respect.
In the meantime, however, a distance had developed between them as
Mies's way of designing moved closer—Philip bearing witness already
cited here—to a state of "*beinahe nichts.*"

"Much ado about almost nothing," Wright was heard to say, archly,
as he toured the exhibition, thus straining what little civility remained

between himself and the proud but stoic Mies, who made light of the incident but withdrew for the remainder of his life from all further voluntary contact with Wright.

One of the notable differences in the positions Philip occupied at the museum in the early 1930s and immediately following the war was the result of the 1940 change in institutional structure that created a Department of Industrial Design, close enough in its interests to the Department of Architecture but formally independent. Its curator, Eliot Noyes, enjoyed little of Philip's affections, since Philip could not bring himself to forget that it was he, Philip, who had pioneered several major design shows in his pre–Huey Long days. Besides, Noyes was not the sort who could be picked up and put aside quite so easily as Betty Mock. Worse still, he had studied at Harvard with the disesteemed Gropius and later even worked for him in his office, reason enough to reinforce Philip's judgment that Noyes was a second-rate architect and possessor, like John McAndrew before him, of the worst of professional liabilities, a tin eye. In daily routine around the museum, Philip and Noyes did what they could to avoid open confrontation. Nevertheless, the tension was palpable at times and it was Philip who released it more often than Noyes, behaving as often as not "outrageously," in the recall of Mary Barnes, who joined the curatorial staff in Philip's department in 1947, shortly after Noyes's last exhibition, "Printed Textiles for the Home," opened at the museum.

Barnes was not alone in her assessment. The consensus among those old enough to remember is that Philip's air of authority was more than occasionally thickened by his own imperiousness. Despite a certain mellowing—he was forty in 1946—he could still carry on like the most resolute snob. Mrs. John D. Rockefeller III—the former Blanchette Hooker—phoned him one day to say she had an extra ticket to the ballet. Philip inquired of his staff who might like it. One of the secretaries allowed she would. "I hope you know how to behave," said Philip. "What have you to wear?"

"I have something nice."

"Well, do not converse with Mrs. Rockefeller. *No* conversation."

"Naughty, very naughty" is how another of his curators—Peter Blake—summed it up. Blake, Berlin-born and London-educated, went on to establish a solid reputation as a critic after working at the museum from 1949 to 1950 (alongside an assistant curator with a golden future of her own as a writer on architecture, Ada Louise Huxtable). Nonetheless, while Blake acknowledged Philip's supercilious deportment around the museum, he also claimed his boss was hard not to like, harder still not to admire for the demonstrable depth of his knowledge, the keenness of his insights, and the inventiveness of most of his curatorial endeavors.

Philip did encounter a genuinely pugnacious adversary during the early postwar years. He was Edgar Kaufmann, Jr., Noyes's successor in Industrial Design and a man capable of matching Philip insult for insult with a few left over for anyone else in the museum he didn't care for. Kaufmann was the son of the Pittsburgh department store executive who had commissioned Frank Lloyd Wright to design the spectacular house Fallingwater, completed in 1937, that had virtually by itself restored the architect's then-sagging career. Thus young Edgar, as financially comfortable as Philip and similarly unsalaried on the staff, was on cozy terms with a formidable figure of the profession whom Philip had already engaged in jousts that cost him blood. In his personal tastes, moreover, Kaufmann was as devoted to the early modernism of the Vienna school—chiefly Josef Hoffmann and Otto Wagner—as Philip had been to the sterner, less decorative German International Stylists.

In short, there was ample room for bile to build up between the two of them. Kaufmann was the one person at the museum, at least in Philip's recall, who not only knew of his political past but saw no reason to forgive him for it. In fact, he went so far as to initiate a private investigation of Philip's earlier anti-Semitic sentiments and activities. Nothing much came of it (see pp. 238–39), either to narrow the gap between them or to prevent the museum in 1949 from merging Architecture and Industrial Design into a single Department of Architecture and Design, with Philip officially designated its director.

In a sense, the act was only a formality, as one much like it had been in 1932. Then and now, he had become clearly the major mover behind all events pertaining to architecture and design at the museum, and he had lately restored to both disciplines the importance they lacked in the years of his absence. Kaufmann, his only rival for power during the later 1940s, was bright enough, and well schooled, but surely no more so—probably less—than Philip in both respects. Nor was he as professionally aggressive or, most important, as comfortable in maneuvering in the circles of museum high society. In the latter regard, too, it was 1932 all over again. Philip got on handsomely with the Blisses and the Burdens and the Whitneys and the first family of the museum, the Rockefellers. Nelson Rockefeller, who succeeded Conger Goodyear as president of the museum in 1939 when Philip was deep in his personal exile, yielded that post in 1941 to John Hay Whitney but resumed it in 1946, shortly after Philip was escorted back to his former place by Alfred Barr. Yet it was Barr, always more at ease with pictures than practicalities, who had a consistently hard time winning the approval of the power-conscious Nelson, while Philip, simply because he was cannier and more overtly charming than Barr, experienced no such problem. He was equally at home with René d'Harnoncourt, who took over formal directorship of the museum at the same time, 1949, that Philip was made head of the new Department of Architecture and Design.

Between the 1947 Mies van der Rohe exhibition and the end of 1950, Philip supervised exhibitions with subjects as various as Louis Sullivan (for whom he actually harbored a low opinion at the time, and eternally); "From Le Corbusier to Niemeyer, 1929–49"; a new design by Frank Lloyd Wright for a theater near Hartford; textiles by Anni Albers; "New Posters from 16 Countries"; several new apartment towers in Chicago by Mies van der Rohe; the recent work of Skidmore, Owings & Merrill; Matthew Nowicki (a gifted American architect who had only recently died); and "Architecture of the City Plan."

At least as significant as any of these exhibitions were several events that extended the reach of the Architecture and Design Department beyond standard limits. Two of them were the displays of actual houses, one by Marcel Breuer in 1949, the other by the West Coast architect Gregory Ain in 1950, each specially built and set up in the garden space that John McAndrew and Alfred Barr had jointly laid out behind the museum between Fifty-third and Fifty-fourth streets. The others were a pair of panel discussions, carefully orchestrated by Philip to feature his adversaries as well as his friends. The first, which mixed memories of 1932 with the desires of 1948, was titled "What Is Happening to Modern Architecture?" It was moderated by Philip's old bête noire Lewis Mumford, who faced no fewer than nineteen strong-minded colleagues on the dais, including most notably Henry-Russell Hitchcock, Alfred Barr, Walter Gropius, John McAndrew, Marcel Breuer, Peter Blake, Edgar Kaufmann, and, of course, Philip Johnson. In 1950, a second round table under Philip's own moderating guidance had fewer speakers (Raymond Loewy and George Nelson among them) but a topic, "Aesthetics of Automobile Design," that was anything but customary fare by international museum standards of the day.

While the chief motive of these occasions was to add to the variety of offerings of the museum and its Department of Architecture and Design, they proved of equal consequence to Philip's own later career. There had been no precedent in the United States for the design, construction, and presentation of an actual building as part of a museum display. Moreover, the lackluster character of the McAndrew-Barr garden site where the two houses went up alerted everyone to the need for an improvement, which eventually took the form of a sculpture garden designed by Philip, one of his most successful early architectural efforts. The symposia were no less prefigurative. Philip loved nothing more about the art of architecture than discussing it and hearing it discussed by the best and most widely assorted of his peers, friend and foe alike, all admissible so long as they were intelligent. Drawn as he was to salon conversation, he became the first curator to make panel discussions a regular part of his departmental fare.

DOMESTICITY

In the early months of 1945, at a vernissage, Philip had his first encounter with Jon Stroup. It was a meeting of sudden impact for both men, and within several weeks they were living together in Philip's place, known to all his friends as Hidden House. Theodate had given the name to the little house at 751 Third Avenue that stood behind the row of apartment buildings fronting the street. As early as 1939 Philip had rented it, turning it over to Theodate in the fall of the following year, when he went off to the Graduate School of Design at Harvard. She kept it meanwhile, enjoying her own free and easy bachelor life. On occasion, Philip would show up, especially for his trysts with John Wisner and Karl Schlubach, and now he was moving back again, establishing his first primary personal abode since Cambridge. He thought it only fitting to indulge himself by taking along the twenty-eight-year-old Stroup, ten years younger than he, and Stroup became the first live-in lover of any duration in his life.

Theodate of course stayed on; there was no reason for her to leave. Brother and sister were properly civilized about the way each of them lived, and Stroup assumed his place without fuss. Theo, whose marriage in 1935 (to a Belgian hotel manager, Paul Blancpain) lasted only two years, had never lost her ferocious attachment to Philip, but she was old enough to know they both had lives of their own, unconventional by bourgeois standards but acceptable to each other. Stroup, meanwhile, continued to work as a freelance writer on art and culinary affairs and as an editor at *Town & Country*. Arresting neither as an intellect nor in his physical appearance—indeed rather "waiflike," in Philip's own words— he lasted as long as he did with Philip, until 1950, because he was unfailingly affectionate, comfortably passive, and forever appreciative of his lover's material generosity. And convenient: He did nothing to keep Philip from carrying on with other partners as the urgency of the moment dictated. After a while, Philip tired of him, thus encouraging him to play the field himself well before the two of them broke up, amid

JON STROUP,
C. 1949

tears—all of them Stroup's. He never got too close to Philip's professional life, which in any case and at all times was kept scrupulously separated from affairs of the heart. Even so, for five years he was witness to Philip's major activities not only at the museum but in the latter's slowly unfolding architectural practice.

The routine was steady: afternoons at the museum, mornings with Landis Gores in an office that was Philip's to control in all significant respects. Senior in age and experience, Philip made himself the chief designer and took on full responsibility for seeking clients. With the national economy only gradually adjusting to a peacetime condition, commissions were not easily secured, especially by a neophyte architect who had not yet obtained a license to practice in New York. Matters did not improve when Philip sat the state license examinations late in 1945 and flunked them cold.

This state of affairs only made his return to the museum more worth treasuring, but it did not diminish his creative ambitions. He needed no license to work outside New York, say in nearby Connecticut—provided his projects were houses, not institutional buildings—but he was willing anyway to take his chances on New York clients by persuading a licensed friend to sign any working drawings he might do for them. The prospect of adhering to legalities until he passed the exams seemed less tolerable to him than bending the rules a little. Certainly, he told himself when approached by Richard and Olga Booth, a young couple who wanted a suburban place, he knew enough to satisfy them. Early in 1946, in Bedford Village, New York, he completed his first building done for someone outside his family.

He later remembered the Booth House as an architectural stillbirth. Gores, whose memoirs provide one of the best summaries of the architecture Philip and he worked on during the late 1940s and early 1950s, was more detailed and less judgmental. The house, he wrote, was a "cross-breed in concrete block between [Philip's] Lincoln project for [Professor] Bogner and [Le Corbusier's] De Mandrot house from which it had taken its origin: a raised podium." There was also at least as much of Mies in the austerely rectangular volumes, and of Breuer's binuclear efforts as well, which evolved here into a "studio block" fully separated from the main rectangular tract, with both sitting on a raised terrace. The smaller component was never finished.

Thus, unsurprisingly, the Booth House was more a pastiche of the work of Philip's mentors than an invention of his own. The same was true of a second, more coherent residence, finished within weeks of the first, for Mr. and Mrs. Eugene Farney, at Sagaponack, Long Island. It was a beach house, perched on a ridge of sand dunes along the Atlantic shore. Gores recalled its debt to "Mies's unexecuted project for a summer house across a stream in Jackson Hole [Wyoming] commissioned by . . . Stanley Resor."

The latter house, which influenced several of Philip's early designs, was notable for a rectangular plan with a midsection occupied by a large living-dining room flanked in turn by service quarters at one end, bedrooms at the other. Philip followed the idea faithfully in the Farney House, varying the foundations just enough to fit the sandy ground it rose from and even mounting it on piles that reminded Gores of the *pilotis* associated with the man Philip had earlier found so easy to criticize, Le Corbusier.

No further finished work emerged from the office during the remainder of 1946. Hopes of designing an entertainment pavilion for the Connecticut estate of the Wall Street broker Gerald Loeb went nowhere at roughly the same time Lincoln Kirstein's sister Mina Curtiss was making noises, ever less audible, about a house for herself in Massachusetts.

Kirstein himself, now an impresario of the ballet, wanted Philip to turn a space he had found in New York into a theater that could be put at the disposal of his greatest single discovery—dancer, choreographer, and Russian émigré George Balanchine. Philip made a few preliminary studies, but the prospect died with the collapse of a leasehold transaction.

At last these frustrations were put to rest by a project Philip had been working on since the Booth House, for a client he could count on.

He had in mind a country place for himself. Having long since sold the Ash Street bandbox in Cambridge, he decided that his next abode should be designed at an appropriately more ambitious level. Hence his interest in New Canaan, a handsome Connecticut town suburban to New York, dominated by well-heeled Establishment types, socially of his own kind though culturally far more conservative. Two architects of his acquaintance, Marcel Breuer and Eliot Noyes, had recently moved there, and while he felt no special closeness with Noyes, he had learned to like Breuer, and besides, both Noyes and Breuer were fellow professionals, fundamentally modernist in their tastes. Philip reckoned that if New Canaan was big enough to abide a few art pioneers in the midst of a majority of tories, it could tolerate him and vice versa. He had only to see to it that he found enough property to ensure his own privacy. In fact, the parcel of five acres on Ponus Ridge to which a local realtor directed him was a nearly impenetrable tangle of woods, mostly of second and third growth relieved by an occasional stretch of field grass and some older trees. It was most certainly private. He and Stroup poked about it for a time, following the gentle slope it took downward from the road. Stroup was the first to reach an open space on the edge of a tumble of boulders, beyond which lay a declivity deep enough to disclose a startling view of the Rippowam Valley. "You can see almost to New York!" he shouted to Philip, who made his way to the spot, intently studying all he saw. An hour later, he had bought the place.

Three years were required for the completion of the house on the space that had arrested Jon Stroup's attention. It is the Glass House, one of the most famous residences of the twentieth century, a work of architecture that at first glance is not only simplicity itself but to some eyes egregious simplicity. It consists of a floor and a roof and four walls of floor-to-ceiling glass, held together by steel piers at its corners and two more on each of the long sides, all of them framing the glass. Inside, a cylindrical volume of brick, situated close to the northeast corner, contains a bathroom on one side and a fireplace on the other. It protrudes through and slightly above the flat roof. A head-high closet-cabinet and a table-high counter that serves as a kitchen facility are the only other fixed interior partitions, and they do not enclose any space. Thus the building is a single room, fifty-six by thirty-two feet, almost totally transparent, a house more in name than in fulfillment of the functions most people regard as requisite to fundamental domesticity.

On the other hand, Philip made it a home for himself that satisfied his needs as he defined and ordered them. The sensation of existing in an environment separated from nature by only a vitreous membrane was, for him, uplifting enough by itself to compensate for the lack of customary household devices and amenities. Some years later, lecturing to a group of architecture students at Yale University, he declared that he would be more than happy to make his home in the nave of the cathedral at Chartres, with the nearest comfort station well removed down the street: that's how much the sheer esthetic transport provided by such a setting meant to him. When one of the many tourists who visited the Glass

PHILIP JOHNSON RESIDENCE, NEW CANAAN, CONNECTICUT: THE GLASS HOUSE, 1949

House told him she would never want to live there and he responded saying, Madam, I haven't invited you, he was affirming the same thing: This
was a piece of art first and a "house" second, thus built to *his* desires and
priorities, none of which made room for children he didn't have or for
utility machinery he could place in another building—and did, later on—
or even for guests' casually tossed jackets, which he would forever pointedly pick up and stow in a closet so that the visual equipoise of the space
would not be disturbed. He who had sweated and sighed in the arms of
lovers hastily picked up on the streets of Weimar Berlin, who consorted
with some of the grubbier American right-wing flotsam of the 1930s—
he could be the most fastidiously self-abnegating puritan in his glass
palace in Connecticut. For he did not exempt himself from the house
rules. Once the place was finished, only the merest changes were ever
permitted in the number or location of the objects inside it, nor did he
allow himself, when reading or woolgathering, so much as a pillow to
prop up his head. The dining table remained where it was when he first
entertained at it; the writing desk, too, and the bed, and the large figure
sculpture and the painting mounted on the easel adjacent to a white car-

Richard Payne

JOHNSON RESIDENCE, NEW CANAAN: THE GLASS HOUSE, INTERIOR.
CHAIRS, OTTOMAN, AND LOUNGE BY MIES VAN DER ROHE WITH LILLY REICH;
PAINTING, *THE FUNERAL OF PHOCION,* ATTRIBUTED TO NICOLAS POUSSIN

PLAN, THE GLASS HOUSE, LATE 1960S

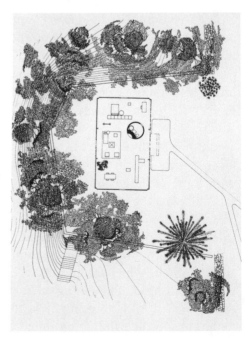

pet, the last of these meant to accommodate two chairs, a chaise, and a coffee table, all by Mies van der Rohe, judiciously selected and punctiliously put in place.

The Glass House was so spare in form that it gave little outward hint of the amount of labor that went into it, still less to the variety of ideas brought to bear on it. Landis Gores recalled that he drew up as many as seventy-nine schemes and variations, nearly all of Philip's devising, with twenty-seven clearly distinguishable approaches among them. Such a claim is reinforced by the ninety-five drawings Philip gave in 1976 to The Museum of Modern Art, the best-known record of the progress—more precisely, the play—of forms in which he indulged himself.

The earliest of these sketches suggest that the house might, in fact, be composed of several rooms, and that one or more of them would contain the necessaries kept at so obvious a distance from the built solution. Living and service elements, however, would be separated; the whole enterprise, that is, was conceived as a grouping of autonomous parts. These drawings appear to have been done about the end of 1945 or the start of 1946. They look Miesian, which seems at odds with the remarks Philip made in his letter of January 1, 1946, to J. J. P. Oud, reporting his wish to emulate the monumentality he associated with the neoclassicist Ledoux. It may be that he was seeking to imbue the lightness of Miesian volumes with the largeness of space suggested by the "high ceiling[s]" he said he wanted for his house. Yet in view of a subsequent shift in his drawings from thin Miesian rectilinearities to heavy masonry forms with round arches—the latter anathema to most modernists of the day—one may be justified in accepting a recollection of his old age that his first sketches were even more overtly Ledolcian, but that they may since have been lost.

What is more demonstrable is his further claim, which Gores confirms, that from the very start he was fascinated by the idea of a house with walls all of glass. It would have been a splendid vessel through which the view from the New Canaan prow on which he planned to build could be enjoyed. Yet he didn't believe such a plan feasible—until he visited Chicago in 1946, when he was organizing the Mies retrospective for the museum. Mies, he was thrilled to discover, was designing exactly such a house.

It was a weekend country retreat commissioned by a Chicago physician, Dr. Edith Farnsworth, and intended for a site on the banks of the Fox River near Plano, a town fifty miles west of the city. On paper as early as mid-1946, when Philip first studied it, it was not completed until 1951, later than the Johnson Glass House. But Philip always acknowledged that it was the model, more than any other, for the character and appearance of his own residence.

The Farnsworth House was also a single rectangular room, its roof and floor slab secured by wide-flange columns, four to a side. The apparitional quality produced by the glass walls framed in steel painted bone white was enhanced by the suspension of the house some five feet above the ground so that it would stand clear of the occasional flooding of the river, which ran a few yards from the long south facade.

Philip was moved by the exquisiteness of the design but just as instructed by Mies's simple decision to consolidate all interior elements—kitchen, closets, a pair of bathrooms—in a core, no part of which abutted the outer walls. The walls could thus be composed of a material as fragile as glass; the only cost would be an unpartitioned interior, a condition Philip found less a defect than a boon.

Yet however much he may have been impressed by the lessons of the Farnsworth House as an object unto itself, they did not keep him in his ruminations from exploring issues more pertinent to the site he would build on. The historian Kenneth Frampton has argued that while Philip was inspired by the prospect of a glass box, he wanted no less to take full advantage of his grassy shelf by creating a house that looked both outward, like a belvedere, to the freedom of the distant landscape and at the same time inward, to an entry court that ensured intimacy and privacy. Gores put it another way: ". . . would we build a light and airy contemporary skeleton edifice of glass and other paneling, or a mighty fortress of brick, or field stone, or even cut stone brought in to order in neo-classic mold?"

Gores's formulation implied something of a dilemma, while offering an insight into the variety of proposals Philip pondered over more than two years of work. The aforesaid Miesian first sketches must have been done before he saw the Farnsworth studies, since they revealed the use of the paneling mentioned by Gores. They also featured two structures, one a fully equipped house, the other a smaller building nearby that contained a pair of bedrooms and a garage. The schemes recalled Breuer's binuclear-ities and, even more immediately, the preliminary stage of Philip's Booth House. A solution to the belvedere-court problem was also implicit, based on a pergola that joined the two right-angled structures, enclosing a courtlike space while simultaneously providing a view from it.

Several later plans seem drawn from a wide assortment of sources, most of them Miesian: an elevation fronted by a battered wall, reminiscent of the master's 1934 mountain house project; a plan suggesting interlocking volumes and another pergola and bringing to mind a still earlier Mies project, the 1912 Kröller-Müller House (which Philip greatly admired).

Toward the end of 1946, the newly discovered glass house solution took command. In several drawings, it appeared by itself, encouraging one to suppose that he thought a transparent chamber might be enough in its very address forward to the valley landscape and backward to the entry forespace to achieve a balance in the extroverted-introverted ends he sought. Drawing at once from ancient and modern history, he set the house down on a Greek two-step stereobate. He then organized the interior around Suprematist circular shapes that translated in elevation into cylinders, first a pair joined by a serpentine wall, then three independent of one another, then two—one containing a kitchen and bathroom; the other, a fireplace.

He was, however, still not married to the idea of either a single unit or a house sheathed totally in glass. He tried several more variations on Miesian devices, including the use of walls as exterior dividers or girdles—in one instance as an interface between two houses; in another, almost identical to Mies's 1946 Cantor House project, as a three-sided enclosure of a courtyard. One of his proposals, clearly a reference to the plan of Mies's 1935 Hubbe House project, showed the living area open to a view in front and an entry in back but flanked by two closed areas—for dining and sleeping, respectively. And in the midst of all this shopping around, sometime in 1947, he turned from glass to masonry, sketching several elevations of images—Gores's "mighty fortress"—that are punctuated by round arches, very likely in salute to such nineteenth-century figures as Richardson or Persius, or to both of them plus others, Ledoux included.

In short, he darted restlessly through several overtly dissimilar phases of architectural history rather as he had tooled his big Lincoln Zephyr around all corners of the Ohio landscape in 1937, when he was trying to synthesize political rather than architectural ideals. At the same time, he labored concentratedly, as if perseverance were yet another habit he had learned from Mies, until he produced a solution that by historical consensus is one of the several most successful works of his architectural career. Derivative it may have been, and one more sign of a constitutionally eclectic temperament, but the Glass House in final form is not only the best of the dozens of schemes he proposed but a good deal more than the Son of Farnsworth. The roof slab of Mies's effort is cantilevered longitudinally from its piers, which in turn are hung visibly in front of the glass wall. Four piers of the Glass House, on the other hand, are located exactly at its four corners and all eight are suppressed behind the glass and joined by a thin horizontal handrail. The Farnsworth House is thus, as Frampton pointed out, conceived tectonically, the Glass House scenographically. Unlike the former, moreover, the Glass House has neither a terrace landing nor a single entry, but four doors, each fixed exactly midway in each of the four walls, a treatment by itself more implicitly classical than the one employed by the great classicist Mies. Nor does the Glass House hover above the ground. It sits on it, in keeping with the fortress metaphor, and so doing it secures its site, which itself is raised. Philip even dropped his earlier notion of a granite stereobate, contenting himself instead with a simple, less conspicuous platform of brick that rises nearly flush with the glass, slightly more than a foot off the ground. The several cylinders earlier proposed have been reduced to one. The grassy prow has been flattened and a long, low stone rail runs along the edge of a rather precipitous drop, thus engendering the sensation that a green-carpeted "room" extends, if only visually, beyond the glass walls.

Gores remembered March 18, 1948, as the date of groundbreaking, which included a site for a second house, set back from the shelf some fifty yards east of the Glass House. It "had long since been 'frozen' [with] working documents prepared for it," he added. While preliminary versions of such an auxiliary structure appeared in Philip's early drawings but not the late ones, it had apparently not been abandoned but was instead, by the time plans for the Glass House had reached their approved final stage, a fixed and foregone conclusion. The Guest House, as it came to be called, would be as rectilineally prismatic as the Glass House but smaller, made of brick and almost totally opaque, in form exactly opposite the latter's delicate transparency. It would accommodate the services and amenities from which the Glass House had been freed: three bedrooms and a bath, as well as utility space for the heating, electrical, and water systems that served itself and its larger neighbor.

Thus the dull necessities had been provided for after all, at a distance figuratively akin to the one Philip later admitted willingness to endure at Chartres. Yet there appeared to be a motive for the separation of the two buildings that went beyond establishing the priority of an all-glass, one-room, functionally unburdened enclosure. Reenter Ledoux.

As always, Philip was alert to the lessons of literature as well as those of the plastic arts and, equally typically, he could regenerate enthusiasm for ideas previously forgotten or even rejected. Gores reported as much, noting that in all of Philip's proposals for the Glass House, "a few points of reference seemed to emerge; only simple blocks, *prismes purs,* in Le Corbusier's phrase . . . no variations in roof lines, no interlocking or intersection of volumes.

"At the top of Philip's reading pile of the moment was the small but crucial tract by Emil Kaufmann, *Von Ledoux bis Le Corbusier: Die Entwick-*

JOHNSON RESIDENCE, NEW CANAAN: THE GUEST HOUSE, 1949
(ON THE LEFT, THE GLASS HOUSE)

lung der Autonomen-Architektur." Gores paraphrased the author's argument, which Philip had heard at his Ash Street house in Cambridge when Kaufmann spoke there in 1942: "From the Hellenistic Era . . . until the two cited Frenchmen, basic composition had ever been '*pyramide,*' massed toward a climax usually more or less central, with smaller lateral elements expanding both in plan and in elevation to empower a focal dominance. But Ledoux. . . . had had another vision, another sense of sculpture not really appreciated until the evangelizing services of Le Corbusier: now clarity was all, volume was all, independence was all, anything less pure was a fudge. And here on Philip's prow unsurpassed were the components and opportunities for a truly crystalline statement of the newly promulgated esthetic."

Philip was at least as conscious of what he had done as Gores was. He knew he had at last designed and erected a building that would persuade the American profession that he was a figure of consequence as an architect, not merely as a critical commentator on the art. For if Mies had conceived the image of a glass house before he did, Philip had given it material form before Mies did. In fact, the Glass House was at once architecture and architectural history, and Philip proved he knew that, too, when he published an article that documented the genesis of the Glass House, the Guest House, and the grounds around them. Written slightly more than a year after he completed the ensemble, the piece was a uniquely perceptive recognition of the closeness of modern architecture to the very past from which so many modern architects wanted to distance themselves.

In "House in New Canaan, Connecticut," which appeared in the September 1950 issue of *Architectural Review,* Philip acknowledged his debt to the Farnsworth House but laid claim to a striking variety of other sources, as well. If Mies was crucial among these, Ledoux proved hardly less so: "The cubic, 'absolute' form of my glass house," he wrote, "and the separation of functional units into two absolute shapes rather than a major and minor massing of parts comes directly from Ledoux, the Eighteenth Century father of modern architecture. The cube and the sphere, the pure mathematical shapes, were dear to the hearts of those intellectual revolutionaries from the Baroque, and we are their descendants."

Thus the image of Ledoux had been shifted from celebrant of historical monumentality to precursor of modern abstraction. But Philip was in full cry. Considering the features of the Guest House, he cited the "Baroque plan central corridor and three symmetrically placed rooms . . . derived [also] from Mies's designs," and claimed the trio of round windows in the rear facade were "a Renaissance approach to a Miesian motif." He recognized the origins of the setting of the houses as well, not only tracing the position of the Glass House on a shelf to Schinkel's Casino in Glienicke Park near Potsdam but finding in the asymmetrical relationship of house to house to long entryway another merging of the ancient and the modern, the components of the Athenian Acropolis on the one hand and the "sliding rectangles" of the Dutch De Stijl movement on the other. Even the layout of his pathways was affected, he added, by the plan of a farm village by Le Corbusier, whom he apparently now found emulable enough, if not as the master maker of great buildings, then as the form-giver Gores remembered from Emil Kaufmann's tribute, or as a planner working at a small rural scale. Philip's two houses were part of an encompassing project in landscape architecture.

One formal attribution and another distinctly more personal were given the principal solid form of the interior, the brick cylinder—in Philip's words, "the main *motif* of the house." In plan, it read like a circle, taken, he said, not from Mies, since its relationship to the cabinets was "more 'painterly' than Mies would sanction," but rather from a Suprematist painting by Kasimir Malevich. In elevation, on the other hand, it reminded him, remarkably, of "a burnt wooden village I saw once where nothing was left but foundations and chimneys of brick."

It is highly unlikely that anyone reading this last citation at the time the article was published would have identified it with the insensate rapture Philip felt a decade earlier when he toured the countryside of Poland, an eager witness to that nation's destruction. The association, which he acknowledged, is disquieting, viewed alongside the virtuoso gush of his other attributions. All of them are art-historical; it alone is so private, it cannot be argued, only wondered at. Is it to be interpreted as a confession of the guilt he felt about his youthful foolishness? Or, contrarily, does it suggest that he could, unfeelingly, with no affective association, translate an object of misery into an object of pure artistic form? No reliable answer is forthcoming, but another question persists: Was he challenging himself to find and identify, in some cases after the fact, more influences than were there, so as to impress the reader with the breadth of his knowledge and his quickness in summoning it up, rather than recording what indeed had moved him to do what he did when he did it?

In later conversations, he vacillated on this, sometimes insisting he had been genuinely and consciously moved by all the sources he named, sometimes admitting he may only have read some of them like a Rorschach blot. The two procedures, of course, are not mutually exclusive. Besides, if he conjured some free-associationally, he apparently repressed others, or at least one. The Museum of Modern Art owns two drawings of preliminary versions of the Farnsworth House that show a cylinder and cabinets arranged in a manner very like the plan that Philip claimed Mies would never tolerate. It is as likely Philip had seen these sketches as that he took greater delight in noticing how much the circle brought to mind the work of another historic figure, Malevich, whom he could add to his stylistic genealogy.

In any event, if Gores's memoirs and Philip's own letter of January 1, 1946, to Oud confirm the importance of Ledoux in the development of the Glass House, and if Jon Stroup further remembered Philip's constant talk in 1946 and 1947 about Schinkel and shelf siting and the Acropolis and asymmetrical planning, then surely Philip's major argument holds fast—namely that the Glass House, so apparently pure an example of distilled modernism, was, in fact, a mixture of many elements, modernism only one among them. As the destiny of later twentieth-century building would prove, this was no small realization.

While construction proceeded at the New Canaan property, Philip, Stroup, and Theo kept a weekend place on the outskirts of East Hampton. Philip would drive regularly to the building site, not only to check the progress of the two structures going up but to initiate the tailoring of the surrounding terrain. Negative landscaping, he called the process, chiefly because it consisted of the ruthless removal of so many trees that his neighbors grumbled about the apparent destruction. This hardly stopped him, partly because he believed the woods he left were evidence that he was taming and organizing them, not ravaging them, and partly because he basked in the attention his new enterprise was already attracting. He moved into it on New Year's Eve of 1949, spending the night in the Guest House. His guest for the holiday was Mary Callery, whom he had asked to prepare a piece of sculpture for the area between the Glass House and the Guest House. She was at work on it.

"By the following spring," Landis Gores wrote, "every architecture editor in New York had been brought out to visit. Sunday traffic [led to] parking jams up on Ponus Ridge Road where the inadequate degree of protection offered by the low farmer's wall had caused special police patrols and warning signs to be posted, and Philip was a public figure as never before. *Life* magazine promoted an article in the regular series feature '*Life* Goes to a Party,' to which some two dozen of us were invited to 'come and be a scale figure.' All the professional magazines were vying and jockeying. For the most part it was all taken very seriously, thus occasioning amusement on my part one weekend afternoon at the house when in conversation with Lincoln Kirstein I heard his summary wonderment: 'How absolute can you get?' "

If Philip rode boldly into the 1950s on the strength chiefly of his Glass House, he went on to a series of buildings less bold, which dutifully abided by the Miesian example. They were handsome objects, most of them, and never lackluster, but notable all in all less for originality than for a consistently decorous, tasteful, and well-behaved look. Even as he labored on them, he sensed that the energy of the modern movement as a whole was winding down. Moreover, while he did at last break free of Mies, he entered almost simultaneously—1954—into an actual business partnership with him that lasted five years, delaying his efforts to establish a viable personal position. When fully free to pursue the new way he had been brooding on for more than a decade, his work split into a multiplicity of ends and a near-compulsive variability of manners, as if he was, in one of his favorite metaphors, galloping off in all directions. Controversy hounded him more than ever, with his champions applauding the vivid assortment of his inventions, his critics chiding him for what they regarded as an affected polymorphism of style.

Meanwhile, his appetite for the whole menu abated not at all. He became a teacher, too, whose influence on several generations of students was more coherently expressed in the words he uttered than in the architecture he designed. For he did not give up writing either, sometimes working his lectures up into published essays and in the process preserving his reputation as one of America's leading architectural critics.

The many-headed Johnson: The image hardly started with the 1950s, nor did it end there. Even so, he was not as focused as he had been earlier or would be later. And the reason had more to do with the state of world architecture at the time than with any other factor.

The International Style, defined by Philip, Hitchcock, and Barr as the phalanx of the global architectural avant-garde at the turn of the 1930s, reached its climax about that time and was never quite the same thereafter. The successive disasters of the Depression and World War II not only brought building everywhere to a halt but relocated several stalwarts of the movement, notably Gropius and Mies, both of whom emigrated to the United States. Moreover, in the ensuing decades, those seminal figures, together with Le Corbusier and, less dramatically, Oud, began to develop more individual manners in their work, compromising the unity earlier perceptible in the International Style, fragmenting the direction of the phalanx, and raising a question as to its very identifiability.

All of this suggests, accurately enough, the victory of modernism— surely in ascendant America, if not in exhausted Europe—over the traditional styles the pioneers had rebelled against. Nonetheless, the triumph led to its natural consequences, a period, the 1950s, in which some architects made a mere recipe of International Style modernism while others strained to create forms whose very exoticism seemed to prove the same point—that modern architecture was locked in a late phase and collectively uncertain of a way out. Philip was part of both camps.

Early in May of 1951, Peter Blake, Philip's onetime assistant, now on the staff of *Architectural Forum,* addressed his former boss with a "questionnaire on future developments in American architecture." The first three questions were:

> 1. In your opinion, which one of the current leaders in modern architecture (e.g., Wright, Mies, Gropius, etc.) has given the younger generation the most to go forward on? Please explain.
> 2. In what way do you think modern U.S. architecture differs from contemporary work in Europe and Latin America?
> 3. What factors (architectural or other) do you believe to be the chief obstacles to the architectural renascence currently under way in the U.S.?

In a letter dated May 10 Philip replied point for point:

> 1. Mies has given the most for the younger generation since he is easiest to copy *well.* Frank Lloyd Wright is the most difficult because he is the Michelangelo of our time and invents a new style every time he designs.

2. It is hard to compare European work with the United States since so little is done over there. Latin America has one half of one per cent Corbusier label and then nothing.

3. There are no obstacles to an architectural renascence except the various theories of functionalism which keep people's eyes turned away from the *art* of architecture.

There is no more succinct or comprehensive statement of Philip's position on things early in the 1950s. If anything, he showed himself firmer in certain of his beliefs than has often been supposed of him, while remaining typically flexible in his perceptions. Surely he had not changed his mind about the falseness of his favorite false god, functionalism, even as he rightly observed, along with Blake, that the "renascence" of the day was led by America, with Europe languishing.

LEFT TO RIGHT: PHILIP JOHNSON, FRANK LLOYD WRIGHT, ALFRED BARR, C. 1950

Most to the point, he explained why he took Mies van der Rohe more than anyone else as the model he wanted—more exactly, could manage—to follow in his own work. Wright would likelier drown than nourish him, and Le Corbusier was worth no more than an oblique reference. Yet instead of following the alternatives he said he invoked in the Glass House—instead, that is, of giving freer rein to a Ledoux or a Schinkel, or to Baroque planning, or at least of retreating somewhat from Mies—whose limitations he had already told Oud he knew—he did just the opposite: relied more on Mies, less on all others. Exceptions to this generalization do nothing to diminish it. Assuming that Philip could be truer to his love of history—a devotion unmatched by any of his architectural contemporaries—if he worked for himself than if he labored for a less compatible client, one recalls Henry-Russell Hitchcock's comment about his work of the late 1940s: "In those years, because of, rather than despite, his age—and thanks also, doubtless, to the fact that he had so long been an observer rather than a maker of buildings—Philip Johnson was a timid designer."

Yet if he was timid, or perhaps because he was, Philip knew himself well enough to know whom to follow and why. Mies's way of arriving at a design was as rational and clearheaded as it was uncapricious. Moreover, he was a classicist. All of this was true of Philip, too, who realized moreover that he could neither emulate nor learn from a nature so restive, so romantic as Wright's. In this respect, Landis Gores's taste ran opposite to Philip's. He worshiped Wright and styled himself accordingly. Since he had a substantial respect for Mies as well, he was able enough, at least for a time, to help Philip carry forward his work of the early postwar years.

Several of Philip's built pieces from the turn of the 1950s might better have died on paper, while several others unbuilt deserved happier fates. Philip himself remembered the G.E. Paine House of 1948 in Willsboro, New York, as a work of little distinction and the Benjamin Wolf House of the same year, in Newburgh, New York, as "the worst house I ever built." On the other hand, a 1948 project for his earlier and at the time still-occasional lover Ed Boysen disclosed an engaging combination of Miesian parts. With its open midsection flanked by service and sleeping quarters—the latter looking out on a walled court—and a single round window in the elevation, it was inspired mostly by the Resor House and several other items in Mies's catalogue of the 1930s. It was never built. Neither was a 1947 house meant for Mr. and Mrs. John E. Abbott of Mt. Desert Island, Maine, or another of 1950 for Henry and Anne Ford in Southampton, New York.

Philip had far better luck with two other families high in the ranks of the American elite, a subculture he was normally very good at impressing. The Schlumbergers and the Rockefellers, in fact, were crucial to the launching of his postwar architectural career. Both clans had in common oil as the source of their worldly gain and art patronage as a favored means of disposing of it. Shortly after Mary Callery introduced Philip to Dominique de Menil, née Schlumberger, in the social circles of The Museum of Modern Art, Mrs. de Menil commissioned him to design a house for her in her adopted city of Houston. Preoccupied as he was with the Glass House, he took his time about the assignment, completing it as late as 1949. His reliance on dependable Miesian devices produced a one-story structure with a flat roof, a single walled court, and floor-to-ceiling windows and doors that left enough wall space for what Gores called "a fabulous collection of largely late nineteenth century French painting." Happy with the result, the de Menils if anything were happier still with Philip, whom they eventually remunerated far beyond his fee for the house itself. With an entrée provided originally by Dominique, he went on to put up no fewer than twelve buildings in Houston, where it is now nearly impossible to walk more than a few blocks downtown without running into a piece of Johnson's work. Via the same networking route, meanwhile—mostly during the 1950s—he completed several of his most important houses for friends and other members of the de Menil–Schlumberger family.

His relations with the Rockefellers were just as fruitful and long-lasting, if considerably more complicated, not least because of the steady proximity of him and them—so many of them—over decades in the councils of The Museum of Modern Art.

Philip was not above recalling—or claiming—that the marriage of Blanchette and John D. Rockefeller III was "nominal," not firm enough to keep the lady in the late 1940s from developing a crush on him. That, as he related it, was the source of her request in 1949 that he design a sculpture pavilion for her and her husband in the garden of the family compound in Pocantico, New York. His recollection that Blanchette liked his proposal and John did not is confirmed by Gores's words: "Our primary client was delighted, keeping the model to show off to the family; the rest of the story was kept for my part at least classified, only the negative decision coming through firm and clear."

The incident, however, was more the beginning than the end of something. Blanchette quickly concocted another notion, which did materialize, even within months of the loss of her pavilion. Encountering Philip one day at the museum, she told him of hopes she was nursing for a piece of property she had acquired in the city. It was a sliver of land on East Fifty-second Street, just wide enough, she reckoned, for a town house that might do nicely as an adjunct space to her apartment on nearby Beekman Place. She would show a portion of her sculpture collection there, serve tea and host receptions and parties, and even put up guests. The commission was Philip's if he wanted it.

He leapt at the prospect of a building for the Rockefellers in Manhattan. By mid-autumn of 1950, the new house—tolerated by John D. III, if not blessed—was up and ready for use. Its composition grew expectably out of Miesian example, which Philip employed, nonetheless, more inventively than obediently. The facade, brick-paneled on the ground floor, with a Mondrianesque pattern of steel and glass upstairs, was the first piece of International Style modernism on the city's East Side, exceptional to behold in the tight little slot it held down between two traditional building fronts. The interior was more arresting still. Almost totally opaque on account of its short front and back and the long party walls on its sides, it was, in Philip's words, an "inside building," as necessarily introverted as the Glass House, an "outside building," had been willfully extroverted. Rather than disguising its tunnel-like length—25 by 125 feet—Philip exploited it, leaving the distance between the living room up front and the sleeping area to the rear unimpeded except by two floor-to-ceiling glass walls that enclosed a court open to the sky. The court, which punctuated the space without interrupting its long visual reach, was filled with a shallow pool that the retiring guest could traverse on the way to his bed only by walking, carefully, over three small islands of stone—and possibly shaking off whatever sleepiness may have prompted his passage in the first place. Pool and court, liquid and light, provided an elegant contrast to the material density of the walls, whose expanse was an ideal backdrop to the Rockefeller sculpture.

Blanchette enjoyed the place enough to entertain there for eight years, giving it in 1958 to The Museum of Modern Art, which used it as a guest house before selling it in 1964. Philip himself leased it for a while in the 1970s, reporting to an interviewer at the time that he had put a second story on the house (accessible by stair from the living room) only to provide height to the facade. "I only added it," he said, "because there is no point to doing a one-story house in New York."

"It's a house built for giving parties and magical moments," remarked one of its later owners, Robin Symes. "One day the doorbell rang and it was Greta Garbo—looking for Philip Johnson."

At the time of the completion of the Rockefeller Guest House, Philip was still unlicensed in New York. Several times, he sat the necessary examination and each time failed it. It was a small nuisance and a smaller embarrassment—little more than that. Since he was able to persuade one or another of his licensed colleagues to sign his working drawings, his illegal status seemed worth bearing in view of the growing prospects of the practice he shared with Gores in the office on Forty-second Street. For the commissions coming to him now were not only from the suburban bourgeoisie but from people whose connections with major corporate institutions might lead before long to large-scaled work, the kind of building that would broaden his repertory even as it brought him closer to the achievement of his cherished monumentality of form.

MRS. JOHN D.
ROCKEFELLER III GUEST
HOUSE, NEW YORK CITY,
1950: INTERIOR

Indeed on the heels of Blanchette's Guest House came two commissions from The Museum of Modern Art itself, both bearing in differing degrees the imprint of the Rockefellers, with one of them initiated in part by members of another famous New York family name, the Whitneys. The first assignment was an annex to the original Stone-Goodwin museum building and as such the first major material testimony to the popularity and place the institution had gathered to itself in its twenty years of existence.

Two decades in the other direction, at the turn of the 1970s, a respect for the conscious harmonization of a new building with its immediate surrounding would become a matter of high priority in American architecture. In 1949, however, with the ascendant religion of modernism demanding its own kind of compliance, Gores reported of Philip's new annex that it "would be . . . the first all-glass building front in Manhattan, utilizing Miesian methodology in a purity so complete that it needed show no specific rapport to its neighbor on either side."

Thus, while Philip's facade design was clearly indifferent to the French Renaissance town house directly to the west, it was not in full accord even with the museum building to the east, to which it was attached. The walls of the latter were partly faced with marble, a material more traditionally institutional than Philip's stark steel and glass. Moreover, while the heights of the two structures matched, Philip was obliged by the program assigned him to allot seven stories to the annex, as distinct from the five in the museum proper. By later standards, the difference might have been judged ill-fitting. At the time, on the other hand, the sudden emergence on Fifty-third Street of a glistening piece of modern architecture connected to an institution devoted to modern art seemed, if not visually consonant, symbolically forward-looking, a sign of good things to come.

In preliminary planning, Philip's facade was meant to be repeated on the rear of the annex. From there, the museum garden, where the Breuer house had been displayed, could have been seen at an oblique angle, while the parcel of land visible directly below was the back lot left from the building the annex replaced. It was a patchwork landscape clearly in

THE MUSEUM OF
MODERN ART ANNEX
(THE "21" BUILDING),
NEW YORK CITY, 1950;
ON THE RIGHT, THE
MAIN BUILDING BY
EDWARD DURELL STONE
AND PHILIP GOODWIN,
1939

need of integration, and it prompted discussions about the advisability of an altogether-new garden.

More far-reaching changes, meanwhile, were afoot. The Whitney Museum of American Art, a historic New York institution long ensconced in a downtown location, was eager to expand its quarters and move uptown, where the growing symbiosis of commerce and culture was rapidly turning New York into the leading metropolis of the postwar Western world. Having acquired several old town houses on Fifty-fourth Street, west of The Museum of Modern Art garden, the Whitney meant to put up its new building on axis with Philip's new annex. Presently, both institutions realized that the two structures could be joined, with a passage from one to the other that would profit both. While the Whitney people had hired their own architect, further conversations with The Museum of Modern Art led to the decision—an indication by itself of Philip's influence in the matter—that he would design one portion of the new Whitney building, its eastern flank, which overlooked the garden area and which he proceeded to treat as a vast wall of brick interrupted only by Miesian ribbons of glass on the bottom and top stories.

The scenario now moved toward its climax. The Rockefellers did decide to build a new garden, meaning to dedicate it to the memory of Abby Aldrich Rockefeller (Mrs. John D., Jr.), matriarch of the clan, who had died just a year earlier, in 1948. That Philip was granted this commission, too, was no surprise. Even so, what he did with the assignment was by consensus a major leap forward in his accelerating career as a designer.

Quite aside from personal motives, he had long held a poor opinion of the garden as it existed. The original notion of an outdoor space for sculpture and the leisurely enjoyment of it is traceable to the period of the construction of the Stone-Goodwin building. Mostly, its design is credited to John McAndrew, with Alfred Barr working at his side. Neither man had had any experience with garden design, not least because outdoor exhibition space had little precedent in American art museums of the time. But McAndrew felt justified in relying on his earlier experience as an architecture student at Harvard and Barr not only knew how to install sculpture but welcomed the prospect of showing it in daylight. In such a setting, he reasoned further, each piece could be seen at a distance and comfortably by itself, so that the promenader could study it without being distracted by other works behind it. He and McAndrew decided on a flowing, asymmetrical plan, punctuated by trees and freestanding walls, some straight, others curved or T-shaped, but all further reflective of the pervasive influence of Mies van der Rohe on the museum in those days.

Since McAndrew and Barr were confined to a narrow budget, the interior walls and the enclosure along Fifty-fourth Street were constructed of
plywood and woven wood on frames. The ground was subdivided into
organically shaped areas and covered with multicolored pebbles originally
meant to be tamped into a mixture with sand and cement, the latter
materials arriving too late for the opening on May 5, 1939. The pebbles
remained, all too easily scattered and disagreeable underfoot.

If photographs certify that the McAndrew-Barr garden was unusual for
its time, they also suggest a design of little conspicuous merit. The plan
seems arbitrary, the trees meager, the inner and outer walls casual bordering on tacky. Nor do the photo records of Philip Goodwin's 1942 alteration show much improvement. Principally, Goodwin added refectory
facilities, centered in a pavilion where food, wine, and beer were served.
It looks a spindly affair, with a modernoid slope to its roof and a grove of
trees nearby whose formal organization seems out of keeping with its
informal placement and the irregular pathway around it.

In his own design for the new garden, Philip retained nothing of the
McAndrew-Barr-Goodwin plan. Instead, he laid out a rectangular area 175
feet deep and 200 feet long, lined by two-and-a-half-by-four-and-a-half-
foot slabs of Vermont marble. This space was articulated mainly by two long,
shallow pools—canals, he called them—that ran parallel to the longitudinal
axis, the long one slightly ajog and to the north of the shorter. A footbridge
crossed each channel, slightly off center. In a model built in 1952, he proposed a pair of huge boulders for the space where the pools parted. He also
had in mind a floor that ran up to low retaining walls in front of the north
edge of The Museum of Modern Art and the east wall of the Whitney
Museum, with a tall rampart to the east (in front of the west side of a house
owned by Mrs. E. Parmelee Prentice, a sister of John D. Rockefeller, Jr.) and
another, eighteen feet high, to the north along Fifty-fourth Street. This last
was notable for the insertion of several grilles that relieved the monotony of
the expanse of masonry while providing a tempting view of the garden to
pedestrians passing in the street. By the time the garden was opened in 1953,
he had replaced the boulders with cryptomeria trees, adding them to others
he originally planned for that spot. The retaining walls gave way to planted
earth banks. The patio space outside MoMA was left free for exit and entry,
while the dining terrace before the Whitney was protected from the sun by
a double row of hornbeams and European white weeping birches. Several
other species of trees enriched the whole area.

Having been drilled in botany at the knee of his mother in New London, Philip was versed in the subject; even so, he relied heavily on the
landscape architect James Fanning of New Canaan, whom he already

ABBY ALDRICH ROCKEFELLER SCULPTURE GARDEN, THE MUSEUM OF MODERN ART, 1953

knew well enough to trust with all aspects of the planting. The rest of the project belonged to him, or in a sense to all those other makers and thinkers of gardens, past and present, known and unknown, to whom he was beholden for his ideas. And while he did not record his debts in essay form, he had typically much to say about all of them anyhow. Irrepressibly the critic as well as the historian, he saw the garden as "a roofless room" with a sunken court, the latter so planned that the garden could not be seen as a whole at any time or from any place. "What I did," he said, "was to make a processional, using canals to block circulation and preserve vision, greenery to block circulation and block vision too, and bridges to establish the route. Always the sense of turning to see something. The garden became a place to wander, but not on a rigidly defined path. Because the ground is paved, as it would not be in a Japanese garden, one is free to find one's own winding path. . . . By cutting down space, you create space. Frank Lloyd Wright understood that, but Mies didn't. Mies [who never designed a large garden] would probably have designed it symmetrically."

Philip clearly had the Mies of 1950 in mind, who had lately drifted from the subjective organization of his European spaces to a classical rectitude of planning and massing. But Philip invoked both Europe and classicism anyhow, after his fashion: "I have always loved the Square of St. Mark's, in Venice. I showed the model to Sigfried Giedion, the Swiss architectural critic, when he was here recently, and he said, 'At last, a piazza in New York!' "

All of Philip's free associations, delivered as if from the analyst's couch, admitted of their equally credible opposites. A classical piazza with trees, even in informal composition? "Japan, don't you think?" he offered. "Nature encroaching as an asymmetric imposition upon a regular, rectilinear pattern system. There had been something of this in the courtyard of my Cambridge house, but in that case the trees were already there and all I did was push the pavement up to them. Then there's Tenniel's drawing of the chessboard landscape in *Through the Looking Glass.* Strong, direct lines and squares, but nature pushing through. Or it could be a dream of that drawing. Or possibly Dali."

The garden was well received by the press when it was opened and it is still commonly considered one of Philip's best efforts, varied in the roles it plays and successful in playing each of them. On a summer day, it encourages the visitor to serious study or luxurious lazing or both at the same time. It is ideal for outdoor museum receptions, formal and informal. Even in the winter, it functions well, as a panorama visible through the museum's north glass wall. And it has aged gracefully, serving up its pleasantries as comfortably in the 1990s as it did forty years earlier. More than a few critics, reflecting on the garden while remembering the grounds of the New Canaan compound, have regarded landscape architecture as Philip's foremost creative accomplishment. There is no record that he ever disputed their judgment.

With the completion of the Rockefeller Guest House, the museum annex (known by its address as the "21 Building"), and the Rockefeller Sculpture Garden, Philip was nearly as much a moving force in the architectural circles of New York City as in the American museum world. Ironically, he had closed his office in Manhattan and opened another forty miles away, at 89 Main Street in New Canaan. The move was not voluntary. The law was after him.

Early in 1950, the Manhattan Building Department had discovered the identity of one of the licensed architects who had been illegally signing Philip's name to the latter's working drawings. This seemed enough of a news item to turn up in a gossip column in *The World-Telegram and The Sun,* with names appended. At about the same time,

Philip received a phone call from an acquaintance informing him that he "had enemies around town," left unidentified, who knew of his little fraudulence and meant to bring it to the attention of the appropriate authority. He never learned who they were. He had enough enemies not to bother speculating.

Having several times failed the license examination, he promptly enrolled in an evening cram course organized to help people who, like himself, had had trouble with the complicated technicalities of the exam. It was likely to last several months. His ongoing assignments, especially those for The Museum of Modern Art, made the prospect of any enforced idleness, however temporary, unbearable to contemplate. Gores remembered the moment: "Shortly after a last Christmas eve lunch at our habitual spa, Tim Costello's on Third Avenue at 44th Street, we packed up the tables and stools and moved to the more tranquil and accommodating environment of New Canaan."

Here and there, the residential work Philip completed in the first half of the 1950s revealed a hint of the independence of Mies van der Rohe that had been implicit in Philip's approach to the design of the Rockefeller Sculpture Garden. Overall, however, the old indebtedness was palpable, not only in stylistic features but in the measured, patrician Miesian mood with which he endowed nearly all his works of the period, sometimes quite convincingly. Mies van der Johnson, the critics called him.

The house he finished in 1951 for Mr. and Mrs. George C. Oneto in Irvington-on-Hudson is one more evidence of the impact Mies's 1938 Resor House had made upon him. The formula is simple enough: three-part rectangular plan, with living room in the center, open on both long sides; bedroom wing to the north and dining area to the south, both more conspicuously enclosed. His earlier Farney House was derived from the same idea, although in the Oneto House the presence of a freestanding L-shaped wall sheltering a terrace behind it and, even more strikingly, the view addressing the Hudson through the living room glass wall suggest that the formative germ is the same one that grew into the Resor House: Mies's Hubbe House project of 1935. There, on a site overlooking the Elbe River at Magdeburg, Mies had clamped two sheltering courts around a central tract that opened itself to a comfortable view of the river.

Like the Oneto House, the Richard Hodgson House in New Canaan, also completed in 1951, followed the three-part Resor-Hubbe plan, as well as Mies's trusted brick wall/glass wall/brick wall elevational rhythm capped by a shallow steel cornice and flat roof.

MR. AND MRS. GEORGE C. ONETO HOUSE, IRVINGTON-ON-HUDSON, NEW YORK, 1951
(LANDIS GORES, PARTNER)

In the Hodgson House, however, Philip was clearly less responsive to one of the master's more pronounced recent habits. Not only in Mies's Farnsworth House but in other works, from later in the 1950s, compactness of form and severe simplification of volume took on the status of major, if not primary, expressive ends. (The Glass House is the only work by Philip driven by a similar motive, and it, too, is not so self-sufficient that it does without the counterpart of the Guest House.) In the Hodgson House, the interior spaces grow more, not less, complex in organization. The main axis carrying from the entry foyer through a glazed central court open to the sky is countered by a cross-axial corridor that leads to living areas flanking the court. However much of Mies there is in the plan, the layout of an ancient Roman house is equally perceptible.

Nonetheless, the development of the court into the atrium, which occurred in two buildings Philip finished a year later, in 1952, pointed more to Mies than to any other source—specifically to the 1944 project for the Library and Administration Building of I.I.T., a work about which

MR. AND MRS. RICHARD HODGSON HOUSE, NEW CANAAN, CONNECTICUT, 1951
(LANDIS GORES, PARTNER)

MR. AND MRS. ROBERT C. WILEY HOUSE, NEW CANAAN, CONNECTICUT, 1953

Philip had earlier written enthusiastically to Carter Manny. There, a garden surrounded by four walls relieved the volumetric density of the structure. Philip employed the same device, quite obediently in fact, in another design he executed for the Schlumberger family, an administrative headquarters in Ridgefield, Connecticut. He treated the atrium more imaginatively in the largest of the houses he built during the early 1950s, one for Mr. and Mrs. Richard Davis in Wayzata, Minnesota. The Davis plan recalled his own Glass House turned inside out, since a glazed atrium was set in the middle of the main tract, which was largely walled—a concession to the client's wish for space on which to hang a substantial collection of art. Further homage to Mies appeared in the podium, which is articulated on the rear elevation by a staircase running up its side—an unmistakable reference to the famous Barcelona Pavilion.

Otherwise in the Davis House, Philip was again free in his compartmentalization of the interior spaces, going so far as to join a second tract to the main house by the slenderest isthmus, thus recalling another model he had called upon before: the binuclear plans of Marcel Breuer. A similar reliance on those twin sources is more obvious still in the Robert Leonhardt House, completed as late as 1956 in Lloyd's Neck, Long Island. There, a bedroom wing has been joined by a narrow passage to a parallel living room that projects outward as if to seize a spectacular view of Long Island Sound. The latter wing is as fully glazed as the Glass House, but it harks back, almost to the point of plagiarism, to Mies's 1934 project for a so-called Glass House on a Hillside. Somewhat more original, if only in the audacity of Philip's crossbreeding of components, is the 1953 Robert Wiley House in New Canaan. There, a tall transparent Miesian cage has been perched athwart a ruggedly solid masonry base, the latter indebted a little to Breuer, a lot to Le Corbusier. Forever aware of his own compulsion to gnaw at the bones of the past—and to chide middle-class domesticity—Philip rationalized the Wiley House: "One more attempt to reconcile the (perhaps) irreconcilable. Modern architectural purity and the requirements of living American families. Why can't people learn to live in the windowless spheres of Ledoux or the pure glass prisms of Mies van der Rohe? No, they need a place for Junior to practice the piano while Mother plays bridge with her neighbors. . . . The Wiley House 'solution' of putting private functions below in a sort of podium to the 15-foot ceilinged public pavilion gives the architect great freedom. The client can design downstairs as he pleases. . . . The architect can design the pavilion above."

Two of Philip's most provocative projects of the 1950s were never built. The William A. M. Burden House of 1955, more fully defined in drawings than the Walter Chrysler House of 1952, may stand for both of them.

MR. AND MRS. ROBERT C. LEONHARDT HOUSE, LLOYD'S NECK, LONG ISLAND, NEW YORK, 1956: VIEW OF LIVING AREA

LUDWIG MIES VAN DER ROHE: PROJECT, GLASS HOUSE ON A HILLSIDE, ELEVATION, 1934. INK ON PAPER. (COURTESY OF THE MIES VAN DER ROHE ARCHIVE, THE MUSEUM OF MODERN ART.)

It consisted of three separate one-story cubic pavilions mounted on a high podium and sheltered by a huge column-free steel-and-glass canopy-frame open on all four sides. The pavilions accommodated differing functions: one, the living-dining space; another, the family bedrooms; a third, a guest bedroom suite. Breuer's binuclear houses may have been an antecedent, but no Breueresque connections were used. There is, in fact, more evidence of the two architects Philip mentioned in his remarks about the Wiley House. The podium surely represented Mies, as did the great canopy, its roof supported on long trusses in emulation of Mies's stupendous Convention Hall project of 1953–1954, meant for Chicago. The pavilions themselves were further suggestive of Mies in their rectilineally abstract elevations, but as a group of separate units, they harked back to Emil Kaufmann's reading of Ledoux's "Autonomen-Architektur." Trees and sculpture pools would have shared the podium with the pavilions, the whole ensemble a massive study of parts within parts within a whole—Philip's tendency to compartmentalize convincingly united with Mies's drive for simplicity. If completed, the Burden House would have been an unsurpassed fulfillment of its architect's dream to achieve monumentality in the modernist idiom.

Saturday mornings were the best time for gallery hopping, especially by 1950, when the New York art scene was steadily brightened by an ascendant postwar generation of American and European painters and sculptors. The samplings came in a variety of forms. On one occasion, Blanchette Rockefeller joined Philip for a walkabout of midtown. At one of the stops along the way, the Buchholz Gallery, each of them found a prize and took it home: Blanchette, an equestrian bronze by Marino Marini; Philip, a twenty-four-year-old gallery assistant named John Hohnsbeen.

That is Hohnsbeen's memory of the first event in a stormy but affecting affair of ten years' duration, which earned him a place in Philip's personal history as the third Mrs. Johnson. Philip, whom Hohnsbeen found "terrifically handsome," confirmed the force of their initial attraction, not to mention the eventual importance of Hohnsbeen in his life. Within a few weeks of their first night together, the two of them met with Jon Stroup for dinner, after which Philip advised Stroup that *their* liaison, by then five years old, was over. The scene, according to Hohnsbeen, was "terrible," but "Philip and I loved each other," and there was no turning away from that. Hohnsbeen added that he canceled a relationship he had at the time with the writer Christopher Isherwood. He promptly moved in with Philip and Theodate at Hidden House.

PROJECT, HOUSE FOR WILLIAM A. M. BURDEN, MT. KISCO, NEW YORK, 1956

Hohnsbeen was no carbon copy of Stroup. Blue-eyed, fair, and well put together, he had the bearing and the manner of a colt, not nearly so pliable or passive as his predecessor. He was, in fact, "fiercely promiscuous" throughout much of his time with Philip, who he said was, by comparison, "pretty faithful." The terms are relative, of course. Philip often described himself as a "chicken hawk," with an enduring fancy for young men that, even as he lived with Hohnsbeen, he indulged episodically enough.

Among the bonds that sustained the relationship over the years were a taste for luxury and a craving for glamorous company that came naturally to Hohnsbeen and easily enough to Philip, provided he first got his daily chores out of the way. His habit of keeping professional duties separate from personal pleasures was observed with Hohnsbeen as it had always been with everyone else. They took their ease at the Glass House, often with men from Philip's community, like Kirstein and Hitchcock, who gathered there from time to time for "boy talk."

Even so, the weekends at New Canaan belonged more to Philip's colleagues than to anyone else. The Barrs were constant guests, and Philip would regularly invite students and aspiring architects, offering them, with the assistance of his inevitable houseboy, the most unsparing hospitality. Sunday lunches would turn into discussions that frequently went on for hours. Philip adored them. Hohnsbeen, with a low threshold of tolerance for professional palaver, did not.

By his own admission, he was happiest when unconstrained by either intellectual or practical responsibility. Among the remarkable number of people to whom Philip at one time or another gave financial support, none enjoyed it more thoroughly than Hohnsbeen. "I hated working," he freely confessed. "I *lived* for the summers, when Valentin [Curt Valentin, who owned Buchholz] would close. He would take me to Europe. I'd see Picasso at work, and Giacometti.

"But I was bored. Valentin finally gave up on me and fired me. Later I joined forces with Lou Pollock; we opened Peridot Gallery around 1953

JOHN HOHNSBEEN,
C. 1955

or 1954, in a space designed by Arthur Drexler [by that time the new director of the Department of Architecture and Design at The Museum of Modern Art]. Philip helped us with money.

"I was halfhearted at this, too. I loved chatting up people, not selling." Indeed it was Hohnsbeen's fluency, manifest in a caustic wit born of a dis-abused attitude toward the world—qualities to which Philip was invari-ably drawn—that made him even more irresistible as a lover. Moreover, he introduced Philip to his own circle of homosexual friends, thus adding another lively subculture to Philip's already-numerous haunts.

For a while Theodate was part of their life, her devotions directed to her brother, inordinately, as they always had been. "There was no intimacy between them," Hohnsbeen reported, "but she did love him more than he loved her." At the same time she was constantly in the company of Virgil Thomson, who had known and liked her ever since their idyll with other expatriate Americans in Paris during the 1930s. It was still a genuine affec-tion, independent of their shared connections with the world of music. Theo's voice, a fragile instrument even during her best years, had never fully recovered from the stress of an illness brought on by overwork in 1940 in Bordeaux, where she had labored to help Americans stranded by the war to return home. She and Thomson later resumed their friendship stateside; the postwar gossip that they might in fact marry came to an end in 1953 when instead she succumbed to the allure of Tony Kloman, a man remembered by the Johnson family as long on looks and charm, short on a commitment to any definable career. He trafficked a little in antiques, painted an occasional portrait of somebody who could afford it, and idled much of the rest of the time, content to survive on Theo's money. Theirs was a divorce made in heaven, filed and settled in 1956.

Somewhat before Theo married Kloman, Philip and John Hohnsbeen moved to their own apartment on East Fifty-fifth Street. There in 1955, Hohnsbeen was diagnosed with tuberculosis, "the perfect psychosomatic illness," as he identified it. The protracted period of bed rest recovery called for in those days led Hohnsbeen to a state hospital near Bedford Village, New York, not far from New Canaan and the Glass House. Philip had the means to send him to a more expensive private facility, but Hohnsbeen knew the resident physician at the state hospital and liked him; that was enough to recommend the place. Philip was more manifestly generous in his faithful semiweekly visits to the hospital, where by cozying up to a German nurse, he managed to smuggle martinis to the patient and keep up sexual contacts with him. After a half year's sequesterment, Hohnsbeen returned to New York for a similar period of convalescence. "Philip had done the apartment up grandly, all in white," he said. "I was *at home,* not cruising. It was our happiest time together."

Philip's rejoinder to a friend who complained that he could not do justice to any one of a lot of different activities on his schedule because he was slowed by the shifting of mental gears each required was: "That is exactly what brings out the best in me." He was in his eighties when he said it. With nearly a lifetime of labor behind him, he knew his working habits well enough. Thus, it was fully in character, in the late 1940s, when he was rebuilding a department at the museum and launching a private practice, that he added teaching to his agenda. He was a natural at it. Never at a loss for words, which he couched in an engaging, cunningly self-deprecating sense of humor, he lectured to large groups of students as easily as he undertook face-to-face studio critiques. Following adjunct appointments at Pratt Institute in the late 1940s and Cornell University early in 1950, he accepted an offer late in 1950 from old friend George Howe, who had just taken over the chair at Yale University, to join him in the Yale School of

Architecture as a visiting critic. He continued at Yale on a more or less steady part-time basis until the early 1960s.

Howe had been hired to provide the leadership the university saw lacking in the department for much of the late 1940s. He arrived within a few months of the elevation of another major figure, Josef Albers, to head the art department, also perceived to be in need of fresh blood. Unlike Albers, who had been schooled at the Bauhaus, Howe had little of ideology in him and less of revolution. His vision of architectural education, while informed by a belief in modernism, was hardly as single-minded as that of Gropius at Harvard or, especially, that of Mies at I.I.T. In fact, his view of the world was fundamentally skeptical—an attitude high among the qualities Philip had long found most winning about him. He was also, again to Philip's liking, cut to the mold of a gentleman, whose amiably aristocratic manner contributed greatly to his success in infusing the Yale department with a sense of itself that it had not possessed since its old Beaux-Arts days of the 1930s. During Howe's tenure, which lasted only until his retirement in 1954, there was room for argument within the department and controversy between the department and other parts of the university. But he was the kind of ringmaster who inspired his players collectively, thus turning Yale into one of the most spirited architectural schools in the country. While he was there, such highly regarded professionals as Louis Kahn, Christopher Tunnard, and King-Lui Wu were among his regular faculty, while a broad spectrum of viewpoints was reflected in his roster of visiting critics, which included, in addition to Philip, Pietro Belluschi, R. Buckminster Fuller, Harwell Hamilton Harris, Frederick Kiesler, and Paul Schweikher.

Howe's educational strategy was to strive for a balance of opposites in both practical and theoretical contexts. He talked at length about the equal and preeminent value of imagination and intellect in the training of architects. At the same time, one of the teachers he most prized was Eugene Nalle, who was no moderate at all but, rather, a passionate, inarticulate man whose admiration for Frank Lloyd Wright was matched by an obsession with the smallest details of pure constructive technique. Yet if Howe liked Nalle, he was no less satisfied with Philip, who represented an exact and bracing opposite image. Strikingly more urbane and verbally adroit than Nalle, Philip was also more devoted to style and history than to the details of structural discipline, and he continued to harbor mixed feelings about the lord of Taliesin. His own biases were evident in the assignments he gave his students, such as the design of a house in the personal manners of Mies, Le Corbusier, or Wright. "Johnson," wrote Robert A. M. Stern in his essay on architecture at Yale, "brought to Yale a concern for classicism in design and an impulse to reintegrate the compositional theories of the International Style within the tradition of western classicism." Elsewhere on the campus at New Haven, the young historian Vincent Scully viewed architecture from yet another perspective, laying greater stress on social and environmental issues than on Philip's formalist outlook. The expression of these various positions was encouraged further by Howe, who in 1952, with Philip's endorsement and assistance, established *Perspecta, the Yale Architectural Journal,* a periodical in which several major statements by or about Philip appeared. One of the most important was "Whence and Whither," an article of 1965 in which he affirmed, apodictically, his view of the fundamental order of things in the art of building: "Architecture is surely *not* the design of space, certainly not the massing or organizing of volumes. These are auxiliary to the main point, which is the organization of procession. Architecture exists only in *time.*"

His own verbal procession took him and the reader through the Propylaea to the Parthenon, from Park Avenue across the plaza to the entry of the Seagram Building, and through the "tiny door" at the Guggenheim Museum to rejoice in "the jump into the hundred-foot-high hall."

"Whence and whither," he concluded, "is primary. . . . What we should do is to proceed on foot again and again through our imagined buildings. Then after months of approaching and reapproaching, and looking and turning, then only draw them up for the builder."

Philip's personal relationship with the creator of the Guggenheim, Frank Lloyd Wright, lasted almost three decades, from 1931 when planning for the "Modern Architecture" exhibition threw them together until Wright died in 1959. During that period, except for Philip's political exile and subsequent army stint, the two men were in more or less steady contact by mail or in person. Such shoulder rubbing was inevitable, given their respective positions in the architectural world. Equally unavoidable, in view of their personalities and philosophies, was the constant, if irregular, rhythm of civility and strain that marked their interaction over the years.

Since Wright was the more aggressive but also the more capricious personality, he was quicker than Philip to extend the hand of friendship or withdraw it, either way abruptly. For he had also the shorter fuse by far, vain, testy, and arrogant as he was, and if he could admire Philip's excellence of mind, he could just as easily argue that it was Philip's wrongheaded opinions and high-handed actions that brought out the righteously offended beast in himself. Philip, younger and less distinguished in the profession, was necessarily more often on the defensive toward, not to say downright intimidated by, a man whose singular talent and monumental reputation he could not help but recognize. Yet he also had little reason in his own right to be modest or to shrink from either the generous gesture or the withering remark.

Moreover, as we have already suggested, he and Wright had in common not only surpassing critical intelligence but a penchant for the canniest kind of salesmanship. Philip, of course, as architect, museum curator, and university teacher, knew that he should not and even could not ignore Wright,

FRANK LLOYD WRIGHT
AND PHILIP JOHNSON,
C. 1953

and he would summon all the charm and social skills he had learned from his father when cottoning up to Wright was called for. Wright was just as conscious of the need to retain the goodwill of one of the most important architectural tastemakers in the country, even if he consistently sought to disguise that dependence by a belligerent display of independence. And each knew that he was in major respects a mirror image of the other, a realization that made it only easier to like, and to distrust, each other.

Wright had made life nearly unbearable for both Philip and Hitchcock back in the early 1930s, and while Philip, as earlier recorded here, reacted more placatively than Hitchcock (see p. 84), he never forgot Wright's contemptuous dismissals of him as a propagandist. Late in life, he claimed that his famous slighting identification of Wright as "the greatest architect of the 19th century," delivered formally in his "Seven Crutches" lecture of 1954 (see p. 233), had been conceived in a retaliatory frame of mind and passed around his circle of New York friends as early as 1932 or 1933.

Yet something approaching a mutual warmth appears to have developed after the war, with Philip making several pilgrimages to Taliesin East and West, on which he was invariably well received. "You are always a welcome inmate," Wright wrote him in 1948 before one such visit, following up with "Nice to see you again, and the sooner the better. We don't have to see eye to eye to love each other do we." Landis Gores in his memoirs recalled Philip's account of an occasion at Taliesin West: "the vivid first evening when [Philip] dined with the Master and Olgivanna [Wright's third wife] on their raised platform alongside the main dining space under the canvas: Mr. Wright, after introducing his guest to the assembled lower orders, leaned across the private table to say in a stage whisper, 'The prince visits the king!' "

The king's hospitality was made easier by the prince's publication in the August 1949 issue of *Architectural Review* of an encomium, "The Frontiersman," in which he called Wright "the greatest living architect, and . . . the founder of modern architecture as we know it in the West, the originator of so many styles that his emulators are invariably a decade or two behind."

It is worth noting, nevertheless, that the *Review* was the same British periodical in which a year later Philip's summation of the influences on the "House at New Canaan" included nothing about Wright and a whole lot about Mies.

Wright, in fact, found nothing more disagreeable in Philip than his willingness to admire, worse still to take as a model, anyone other than himself. "Dear Philip," a 1949 telegram from the old man began, "If you think I'm such a great architect, why doesn't your work look more like mine?" It was a multiple insult, belittling Philip as a mere epigone, moreover one with the bad taste to imitate bad architecture—the International Style as a whole and Mies van der Rohe in particular.

Surely Wright meant what he said; did he not always mean what he said when he said it? Yet as with Philip's habit of gearing his remarks to an audience to accord with what he thought it wanted to hear—and ever so cagily changing his meaning as his audiences changed—Wright's thrusts were also not always reliable. At times they seemed meant more to strike out than to demolish, more to affirm his own strength than to take advantage of his opponent's weakness. Philip, in turn, while less inclined to pick fights, had the nimbleness to rob nearly any attack of its effectiveness by appearing to praise the cleverness of the attacker. Both men, when they chose to be, were expert players at charade.

When Wright was asked by Selden Rodman in the mid-1950s for his opinions of Philip's Glass House, he replied, "Is it Philip? And is it architecture?" Relaying the comment to Philip, Rodman recorded the reaction: "He put his head in his hand and smiled with his eyes half closed. 'Isn't that *wonderful* . . . "Is it Philip? . . . And is it architecture?" . . . Who else can say things like that—with such perfect spontaneity and phrasing that even the spiteful becomes lovable? Wonderful, wonderful . . .' "

If Wright concealed his vulnerability behind a show of vainglory, Philip relied on lighthearted self-deflation. To Rodman again: "You know what he said to the maid when he arrived at my house in New Canaan?"

"What?"

"He walked in flourishing his cane, looked around, and said to her: 'I don't know whether I'm supposed to take my hat off or leave it on!' [In other versions of this anecdote, Wright is said to have added at this point, "Am I indoors or outdoors?"] The maid asked who he was and what she could do for him. 'Oh,' he said airily, 'just another client. I want Mr. Johnson to build me a house—a house of glass.' "

If many of the apothegms Wright aimed at Philip seemed more akin to war games than to warfare, he remained as capable as ever of the kind of outright assault that had earlier drawn Hitchcock's full-scale counterattack (see p. 84). The Glass House really annoyed him, although it seems certain that if he had been simply contemptuous of it as architecture, he would have dismissed it from his mind. Instead, it ate at his guts, symbol of the false gods—Philip's "foreign legion," as he called them—who had been raised up in the temple of postwar American architecture. On a scratch pad imprinted "Don't Say It—Write It," Wright wrote it:

"Philip: We are all monkeys less or more. I have always maintained that in front of the monkey house at the zoo was the best place to study human nature. You made yours a little more available for that purpose. That is all. Don't you feel just a little ashamed of yourself? F. Ll. W."

Wright's pique sometimes coupled with pique, begetting fury. One evening in 1955, having been invited to lecture at Yale, he arrived in New Haven, to find no one waiting for him at the railroad station. Interpreting as an affront what had been a student oversight, he worked up a full head of rage that had dissipated only a little by the time he was finally picked up and spirited to the Taft Hotel. It was the ill luck of Philip, who happened to be on assignment at Yale at the time, to encounter him a little later in the middle of a knot of students and faculty. Wright made the most of the moment. "Why, little Phil," he roared, his voice equal parts unguent and acid, "I thought you were dead! Are you still putting up all those little houses and leaving them out in the rain?"

While the incident became quickly and permanently fixed in contemporary architectural lore, the kind of item architectural students made a point of recounting to their girlfriends, it proved of less ultimate consequence to Philip than another of Wright's hostile offerings to him.

Or so he said. Rodman wrote of another meeting of the two men that took place about two years prior to Wright's invasion of Yale: "Wright had once said to him: 'The reason I hate you is that you carry water on both shoulders. You practice when you feel like it, and the rest of the time you sit in a protected position from which you criticize all of us.' This, Johnson said, more than any one thing had made him decide to practice architecture seriously."

In his later years, Philip repeatedly gave Wright's scolding as the event that persuaded him in 1954 to resign the directorship of the Architecture and Design Department of The Museum of Modern Art. The claim must have been in large part a rationalization. During the early 1950s, he organized no exhibition at the museum so ambitious as the 1947 Mies retrospective, nor did he produce any large-scale publications. His architectural practice together with the time he spent at Yale apparently put such achievements beyond the grasp even of someone with a reach as long as his. Moreover, the choice between making his own architecture and promoting someone else's—while not easy, because he was so good at both—was at last easy enough. It is likely he simply decided he wanted to be one more than he did the other.

In any case, by the time he did quit his post, it was already reasonable to judge him the most important architectural museum figure of his time, an assessment that stands even at the end of the century. Nor did his exertions on behalf of the museum end with the record we have so far set down here. Alfred Barr forever had reason to treasure the special and unstinting generosity that Philip showed in all his dealings with the museum, not least his attitude toward the permanent collection. On those occasions, and there were more than a few, when the trustees disapproved a purchase Barr wanted to make, Philip could almost always be counted on to buy the questioned piece, then donate it to the museum. Some of the most valuable objects in the collection, not just architectural drawings and models or design artifacts, were assembled that way. Philip in his lifetime made more contributions to the museum than all but one or two other benefactors.

Moreover, he made the most important single appointment of his MoMA career in 1951 when he filled the curatorial post vacated by Peter Blake with the twenty-five-year-old Arthur Drexler, who didn't even have a college degree. Philip knew hardly anything about him except that he had read articles Drexler had written for *Interiors* magazine. One of them, an essay on the Glass House, was obviously interesting to Philip, who was, however, impressed less by its admiring tone than by the exhaustiveness and sensitivity of Drexler's observations.

For all his experience with academics, Philip suspected them of collectively suffering the occupational disease of pedantry and intellectual orthodoxy. Drexler was not so infected, having spent only a year in the architecture program at New York's Cooper Union before being drafted at seventeen into the U.S. Army Corps of Engineers. After the war, he worked in the office of designer George Nelson and did some freelance writing before being appointed in 1948 as architecture editor of *Interiors*. Not only free of academic taint, he was also a classic autodidact and quick study who read a lot and retained it all. Since Philip himself answered to the same description to some extent—and knew it—he was rapidly drawn to Drexler, mostly to the younger man's natural gift for writing. For the rest of his life, in fact, Philip delighted in reciting to friends the sentence, "Automobiles are hollow rolling sculpture," with which Drexler began his essay in the catalogue of the 1951 "Eight Automobiles" exhibition that he and Philip organized for MoMA. It was not only the neatness of the simile that struck Philip's fancy but the clear-cut evidence that Drexler possessed the crucial element of sensibility as Philip saw it—the will to reduce a utilitarian object to its esthetically formal essence. He was also drawn to Drexler sexually, and he even tried on one occasion—or so Drexler later reported—to seduce him. The attempt was turned down.

Once hired, Drexler proved handsomely suited to the role of Philip's assistant in the Architecture and Design Department, encouraging as well as helping him with the automobile show and its 1953 sequel, "Ten Automobiles," both typically pioneering efforts at MoMA in widening the compass of artistic expression in modern design. Drexler was also assigned several other writing chores, each growing out of a museum exhibition that Philip oversaw. Chief among these and probably the most important of Philip's museum exercises of the early 1950s was a 1952 show titled "Built in U.S.A.: Post-War Architecture." An earlier exhibition with a similar title, "Built in U.S.A.: 1932–44," had been organized (see p. 165) by Elizabeth Mock for the museum's fifteenth anniversary, which occurred when Philip was still in the army. This second review was thus his to do with as he and his trusted deputies saw fit. Henry-Russell Hitchcock was made responsible for selecting the contents of the show and writing an essay on the contemporaneous state of the art, while Drexler added descriptive texts about each of the entries. Dominating the roster of forty-three works were Wright with four and Mies with three. Included among the Europeans of the older generation were Alvar Aalto, Walter Gropius, Eric (formerly Erich) Mendelsohn, Richard Neutra, and Marcel Breuer, while younger men born or bred in the United States like Edward Larrabee Barnes, John M. Johansen, Eero Saarinen, Charles Eames, Harwell Hamilton Harris, Wallace K. Harrison and his partner, Max Abramovitz, Ralph Twitchell and his partner, Paul Rudolph, the firm of Skidmore, Owings & Merrill, and Philip Johnson himself provided proof that they had learned the lessons of their elders well.

Beginning his own preface with the remark, "The battle of modern architecture has long been won," and ending it by saying, "With mid-century modern architecture has come of age," Philip affirmed in a museum context what he found other ways of saying in his teaching at the same time—indeed what he would shortly be obliged to confront head-on in his own work. It was time, for him personally and for building globally, to take a new step forward. He supervised several smaller shows at MoMA and put together a few panel discussions. At last, after seeing to the construction of another house in the museum garden, this one a Japanese confection based on sixteenth- and seventeenth-century prototypes and designed and built by Junzo Yoshimura, he delivered his department into the manifestly capable hands of his young curator.

PART FOUR

BREAK WITH MODERNISM

1953 - 1967

Among Philip's recorded utterances, his contribution to a symposium at Smith College in 1953 has attracted relatively little attention, perhaps because it contained more references to his personal past and fewer observations about the more public subject of architecture. Yet on that very account it is worth noting, since it revealed that he had only modified but not fundamentally altered the worldview he had carried with him into politics two decades earlier. Now it was a safer, more disinfected outlook and even above reproach. But it grew from the same old root.

The occasion was an informal symposium in which he was one of the speakers. The majority were literary people, while he was a lone representative of architecture. That ratio seems to have put him on the defensive from the outset, and he responded with his customary impudence in the service of showmanship. Yet there was more than a little seriousness even in his mock contradictions. He—the purebred rational animal—began with this jab at rationalism and the rational attitude:

"I find myself at a great disadvantage at a gathering like this one, the only non-word-minded speaker among the word experts of America." It was surely a disingenuous remark. But he had a point to make:

"To add to the difficulty of 'words' on 'art,' the fact is that I have always been a poor sort of intellectual. I failed Alfred North Whitehead's course at Harvard, thereby snuffing out one of my deepest ambitions, and Lord [Bertrand] Russell once called me, in an unmistakable tone of derogation, a Dostoevskian. The worst of that is that I do not even now know what he meant."

Of course he knew, and he knew his audience knew he knew, which made his feigned puzzlement only more calculatedly winsome. And if there were any doubt it was feigned, he could switch back to the book-learning mode at will:

> However, it is precisely Lord Russell whom I wish to take as my intellectual guide this afternoon, since there is no one I regard more highly among systematic philosophers living today. There is none more conscious of mathematical achievement [or] of the limitations of mathematics, science, knowledge and even of the intellect. Scientific knowledge, he tells us, can be of no help in the realm of ultimate values. There is no real objectivity possible on questions of ethical or moral standards. Although he dislikes admitting *de gustibus* [*non est disputandum*] as a rule, Whitehead, I remember, went so far as to say that "Rationalism," itself a word which one feels these men capitalize even in private conversations, is in the first instance an act of blind faith— a most unrational or irrational act indeed.
>
> Now I have no particular dislike of the Rational faith. It seems to add to the pleasures of scientists and even . . . to their effectiveness. I enjoy science; and I use automobiles. What I find unfortunate is that Rationalists tend to find what cannot be reasoned about either nonexistent or unimportant. Bertrand Russell might go so far as to call you a Romantic-Subjectivist and . . . it [would then be] easy for a word magician like Russell to show step by step how you really enjoy cruelty and war, and love totalitarian government. These dialectics I find frightening but then Socrates frightened me the same way years ago when I was in college. I used to be able to feel his argument making fun of my feelings in front of friends and strangers. The only answer I dared make was rudeness, but this merely served to increase my inferiority feeling.

In no other public pronouncement of the 1950s did Philip discuss quite so candidly the loss of faith in Socrates (read Plato) that he had undergone during his undergraduate years. Nor did he allude elsewhere to the psychological vulnerability ("inferiority feeling") that attended it or to one of the defenses ("rudeness") he mounted against it. Moreover, while his references to cruelty, war, and totalitarian government were meant to allege Bertrand Russell's capacity for verbal gamesmanship, they resonate more privately, as if Philip was as eager—still—to rationalize them as to forsake them. Indeed, he spent much of the lecture invoking the spirit he had much earlier chosen to replace Plato as the thinker closest to his heart: "Nietzsche, being a poet as well as a philosopher, said some wonderful things along these lines. In reading them today one must remember his love of shocking the bourgeois and of making paradoxes, but the statements themselves still titillate: 'Our religion, morality and philosophy are decadent human institutions. Counter agency: Art.' " [Or:] " 'Truth is ugly. Art is with us in order that we may not perish through truth.' "

Overt invocation even turned briefly, almost inconspicuously, to covert identification, as if Philip was still wrestling in his mind with the memory of himself in the 1930s: "Mr. Nietzsche was an extremist, and said a great many strange, as well as a great many silly things. But as he himself says, he is the only philosopher, at least up to his time, who took the side of the artist.

"We in our generation, however, are in no position to express ourselves so violently."

Quite so: Art was safer than politics, but common to both was the centrality of the individual, the great man, in Lawrence Dennis's terms, the prophet, in Nietzsche's, the artist, both of them freed from subjugation in a world of rules, reason, science, technology—or of egalitarian democracy.

Philip now felt free to extend his attack on rationalism to its applications in his own field. To his old bugbear functionalism, he added several more, each related to it:

"For the good of art (or should I more modestly say architecture?) can we not, please, reduce a few degrees at least the high temperature of four contemporary values? In small doses they are all good puritan virtues, and all come down to us with clear pedigree papers from the English seventeenth century and the rise of capitalist culture. It is only in large doses, and only in the field of art, that they have such baleful effects. The four are utility, progress, economy, and hard work."

Perfect Johnson nemeses, these, as intact in 1953 as he found them twenty years earlier. Of utility, he now went on to say: "Of course it is a social technique, of course it is structural engineering as well, and one cannot practice the art without mastering the craft. But I contend that *art* is nevertheless the cause for the sake of which the other elements exist."

On progress, which "breeds contempt for history as a source of inspiration," he quoted Picasso: " 'To me there is no past or future in art. The art of other times is not an art of the past; perhaps it is more alive than it ever was.' "

And of economy and hard work: ". . . only in this country . . . [must] the artist . . . talk of research or some word that will have a 'business' ring. And we would all like to ask, if we dared, 'How much did you make last year?' because that would be a measure of the man's inner worth as well as his outer."

Philip concluded the Smith lecture with an indictment and a tribute: "Maybe it is all Socrates's fault: the Philosopher of the West, who felt that salvation was by knowledge and by the knowledge that could be communicated by arguable communicable points. How much clearer the Greek message comes through the plays of Aeschylus or the Parthenon or the Acropolis. Tragedy and sculpture talk to us directly."

Delivered at roughly the halfway point in his life, the Smith talk underscored Philip's ongoing low opinion of the dialectically derived systems of Western epistemology. If his personal, private, even solipsistic outlook seemed at odds with his patent and unfailing sociability, it was nonetheless the foundation of the power-oriented defenses he had built into his personality.

Far more widely publicized than the Smith statement was the lecture it grew into, pithier, less autobiographical, and more professional, but touched in the opening phrases with a similar sentiment:

"Art has nothing to do with intellectual pursuit—it shouldn't be in a university at all. Art should be practiced in gutters—pardon me, in attics.

"You can't learn architecture any more than you can learn a sense of music or of painting. You shouldn't talk about art, you should do it.

"If I seem to go into words it's because . . . we have to use words to put the 'word' people back where they belong."

Thus he began a talk delivered at Harvard in 1954 and titled "The Seven Crutches of Modern Architecture," which he identified as essentially the same unprofitable "values" cited at Smith, but now increased to include the Crutch of Pretty Drawing ("the illusion that you are creating architecture"), the Crutch of Comfort ("a habit that we come by, the same as utility"), the Crutch of Serving the Client ("when do the client's demands permit you to shoot him and when do you give in gracefully?"), and the Crutch of Structure ("I have nothing against [Buckminster Fuller's] discontinuous domes, but for goodness sake, let's not call it architecture").

The last "crutch," structure, Philip admitted, "gets awfully near home because, of course, I use it all the time myself." Mies, that is to say, was still inside his head; the houses he was building at the time were evidence enough of that. Yet despite such a specific loyalty and the consistency with which he maintained his passionate estheticism over the years, it was clear he had curbed his commitment to the radical modernism that had inspired him, Barr, and Hitchcock when they staged the "Modern Architecture" exhibition at The Museum of Modern Art in 1932. Indeed, both his Smith and Harvard lectures amounted to attacks on the very concept of formula, of doctrine, of architectural theory. He was feeling a renewed response to the message of a book that had long occupied a place in his library. The thesis of *The Architecture of Humanism,* published in 1924 by the English critic Geoffrey Scott, came uncannily close to all Philip believed and promoted in the 1950s. Scott argued that a "mechanical fallacy" in architectural criticism was the wrongheaded identification of quality with functionalism. In turn, an "ethical fallacy" equated excellence, irrelevantly, with moral purpose, while the "romantic fallacy" idealized "the curious and the extreme"—anathema to a classicist like Philip—and the "biological fallacy" forced on the reading of architectural history a notion, taken from evolutionary theory, of the rise, peak, and fall of ages and species. Scott saw theory itself more enslaving to the architect than instructive. For him, and for Philip, the crucial element in creating and judging buildings was taste. And taste, like truth, was beyond measurement or proof.

Philip's first serious attempt to escape the strictures of orthodox modernism began modestly and inconspicuously, with himself as his own client, at his own place in New Canaan. There, in 1953, he undertook the remodeling of the interior space of the secondary structure on the grounds, the Guest House.

Since 1949, when the two buildings were completed, he had made only the smallest changes in either of them. The artworks he installed in the Glass House were limited to two large objects and a smaller one. A near-life-size sculpture of two rotund embracing women, done in papier-mâché by Elie Nadelman and recommended to Philip by Lincoln Kirstein, stood near the south end of the large room, between the kitchen counter and the dining area, facing north. Counterposed against it from its perch on an easel at the north edge of the living area carpet, facing south, was a neoclassical landscape depicting the funeral of Phocion, as sober an image as the Nadelman was mannered and slyly unchaste. Alfred Barr and Walter Friedlaender believed that the painting was by Nicolas Poussin; Anthony Blunt contended it was a copy. A small Alberto Giacometti sculpture in plaster of a striding man on a blocklike base sat on the Mies van der Rohe Tugendhat coffee table. Between the carpet and the brick cylinder stood a tall floor candelabra, which, together with a fire burning in the fireplace, afforded the only indoor illumination. (Spotlights on the roof scattered light externally on the lawn and trees.) Having rejected the sculpture Mary Callery had proposed for the lawn, Philip acquired in its stead a bronze figure by Jacques Lipchitz. The latter piece was positioned between the Glass House and the Guest House, at a place

Philip claimed worked as a pivot around which the two structures revolved.

He later removed the candelabra in favor of a low floor lamp, one of the few articles of furniture he ever designed, in this instance collaborating with Richard Kelly, who also added canister lamps at the baselines of the glass walls. The Poussin came down and went up again when Philip found that its replacement by several modern paintings, most notably a canvas by Franz Kline, did not supplement so much as overload the abstractness of the environment.

PHILIP JOHNSON RESIDENCE, NEW CANAAN: THE GLASS HOUSE, C. 1990; INTERIOR.
VISIBLE THROUGH GLASS WALLS ARE THE GUEST HOUSE, LEFT, THE LIBRARY/STUDY, RIGHT

All of these changes, however, with the exception of the Lipchitz, were decorative rather than structural or compositional. The major architectural move was made when he took a sledgehammer to the interior of the Guest House, reducing its three rooms to two. One became a study; the other, a bedroom.

It was the latter that Philip executed in a manner previously unexampled in his personal catalogue. He fitted sliding panels along the long walls of the markedly narrow space so that the door and the two circular windows could be covered and the room made as dark as a tomb. That is how he preferred it when he slept there himself or with someone, on a low double bed stationed on the longitudinal axis at one end of the room, just below an abstract wall sculpture by Ibram Lassaw. The walls and the panels were lined from floor to ceiling with rich, duskily shimmering Fortuny fabric.

JOHNSON RESIDENCE, NEW CANAAN:
THE GUEST HOUSE.
REMODELED IN 1953.
WALL SCULPTURE BY IBRAM LASSAW

While these devices were enough to turn the atmosphere of the room away from the wholesomely spare simplicity common to many modernist interiors, what contributed most to the air of mystery, sensuality, and exoticism was the vaulted structure Philip mounted inside the room. It became a room within a room, its roof suspended below the ceiling, its supporting columns mounted inside the walls. Lights inserted between roof and ceiling produced an indirect, almost sacral glow. If the Guest House as a whole was the opaque counterpart of the transparent Glass House, the bedroom in its introversion only emphasized that quality of oppositeness.

Typically, Philip identified the ancestry of the piece: the vaults of John Soane, the neoclassical British architect who specialized in highly individualized variations on classical domes. The most intimate of these, and the specific inspiration for the bedroom, was the thin masonry canopy that Soane made the ceiling of the breakfast room of his house in London, completed in 1813. (One may recall, too, that the screen walls of the main chamber of Soane's most famous work, the Bank of England [1788–833], were constructed without windows.)

A generation younger than Ledoux and a generation older than Schinkel, Soane was another of the great eighteenth- to nineteenth-century classicists Philip had made a special point of admiring. He was also the most idiosyncratic of the three. In the past, Philip had preferred the soberer formality of Ledoux and Schinkel, but now, perhaps in consequence of his search for new forms, he found Soane's eccentricity especially appropriate to the faintly decadent mood he wished to evoke in the Guest House bedroom. Yet what made that remodeled space appear most radical by the standards of 1953 was Philip's candid use of arch and dome, historical forms that had been nearly universally discarded by the modernists, especially by those close to the International Style.

Philip employed the concept of the interior canopy in several other designs of the same period. It appeared in pronounced form in one of the versions of an unbuilt private art gallery drawn up in 1954 for the critic Thomas B. Hess. That project, moreover, featured a central plan, another deviation from the rectilinear norm of the International Style.

Meanwhile, the first institutional work in which he departed from straitlaced modernism was notable not only for that reason but for its very identity. It was a synagogue.

Philip had been reflecting at leisure on the question of his politically moral redress well before he began work on the Kneses Tifereth Israel Synagogue in Port Chester, New York. His thoughts in detail are impossible to reconstruct at this late date, but one may wonder whether they consisted of the heartfelt yearning to atone for the sins of his profascist years as they may have directly or indirectly affected Jews. Old and young, Philip seems to have had little place in his mind for heartfelt yearning unless it involved the pleasures of the flesh. As he had lost faith in the alleged verities of classical philosophy, he was impatient with either religious or romantic views of the world, believing rather that power and persuasion—certainly not truth—were the instruments by which historical moral positions have been rationalized. Aware of his failed mission of the 1930s, he recognized, too, that it had left him with a burden of guilt, but it is less certain that he felt the guilt personally and more that he saw it as a measure of the need in post–World War II America to be free of public perception of his kind of political taint. Late in life, he argued that he had long been sensible of a personal guilt, and he cited a visit he paid shortly after World War II to the New York offices of the Anti-Defamation League of B'nai B'rith, where he delivered a formal apology for his past sins. The call was made, however, directly after Edgar Kaufmann, Jr.'s private investigation of his prewar political activities (see p. 181). Thus his apology appears to have been prompted as much by practicality as by shame. It is worth recalling, moreover, his aforementioned claim of 1953 that "it is easy for a word magician like [Bertrand] Russell to show step by step how you really enjoy cruelty and war, and love totalitarian government"; he seemed, in fact, to be suggesting he may have been misunderstood rather than guilty. Whatever his motives at the time, and however complex, the raising of a temple to a faith profoundly aggrieved by the very forces with which he had allied himself seemed an irreproachably good thing to do (notwithstanding, of course, Geoffrey Scott's admonitions against mixing art and morals).

Philip already had some experience with the uses of art and architecture in the service of compensation for Jewish loss. Several years earlier, the architect Percival Goodman, a Jew, had won a competition for the design of a memorial to the 6 million Jews killed by the Nazis. A dispute had later flared between Goodman and the New York City Parks Department, which held that the actual construction of the memorial was impractical. Philip, in his own right fascinated as ever with memorials, leapt at the chance to show Goodman's model at The Museum of Modern Art, calling it "probably one of the best monuments of this kind to have been developed in this country in recent years."

The prospect of designing a synagogue, then, can be traced to an architectural ambition as well as to a perceived ethical imperative. A religious building would be an ideal vehicle for the achievement of the monumentality he so wanted for his own architecture yet had found relatively little opportunity to pursue. In fact, at about the same time he was at work on the bedroom of his Guest House, he had produced a design for a church he hoped to build in Greenwich, Connecticut. It was conceived with a dome over a central plan, the altar in the middle of circular rows of seats. An elliptical foyer would have been nearly independent of the main mass of the building, connected to it by only a short, narrow corridor, an isthmus.

Shortly after he failed to win the Greenwich assignment, he learned that a Jewish congregation in Port Chester was in the early phases of planning for a new temple. His proposal to design it without fee was hard for the potential clients to resist, coming as it did from an architect, and a New Canaan neighbor, whose professional reputation was growing at about the same rate his political past seemed to be receding in most people's minds.

How the synagogue followed from the form of the Greenwich church is apparent in the nearly complete separation of the foyer, elliptical in plan, from the main building housing the sanctuary. Hitchcock traced

Philip's oval to the Baroque, a period that used the shape fondly and often. On the other hand, the independence of the foyer from the main building tempts one once again to recall Ledoux, at least Philip's admiration of the Frenchman's autonomous geometric volumes.

The sanctuary, actually more indebted than not to strict modernism, was a large steel-framed rectangular prism, basilican in plan, with structural supports visible along the sides. The white precast concrete walls were punctured by rows of vertical slit windows filled with variegated glass panes in five tiers of alternating rhythms. The structure suggested Mies, while Philip may—or may not—have designed the colored glass before he knew of Le Corbusier's similar treatment in the fenestration of his chapel at Ronchamp, finished in 1955, but begun several years earlier.

On the bema at Kneses Tifereth Israel stood the ark, also designed by Philip, and behind it a screen twelve by thirty-four feet, featuring an abstract relief sculpture by Ibram Lassaw, the same artist whose sculpture decorated the wall in Philip's Guest House bedroom.

The only other reminder of the latter space was the huge canopy, a veritable velarium, that hung beneath the ceiling and extended in seven sections the full length of the auditorium. It was the most visually arresting component of the interior and the chief prefiguration of the drift away from Mies that was set into motion in Philip's secondary structure at New Canaan. He denied that it was symbolic of anything, but the congregants could not help associating it and its black wall supports with the portable worship tents of an ancient past. In fact, it is hard to believe Philip was indifferent to the numerological significance of the number seven in Judaic tradition. But it was the mid-1950s, a time in the history of twentieth-century art and architecture when the cognoscenti commonly regarded symbolism as a layman's game and iconography as the province of pedants. Content bowed low to form, and Philip, as he long had been, was among the most unashamed of formalists.

One day in the spring of 1954, Phyllis Bronfman Lambert paid a visit to Alfred Barr at The Museum of Modern Art. The recently divorced daughter of Samuel Bronfman, chief executive officer of the Joseph E. Seagram and Sons Corporation, she was wealthy, well placed, bright, and accustomed to having her own way. All these attributes bore on her visit to Barr. The Seagram Corporation, she informed him, was preparing to build an office building in New York City as part of the observance of its one hundredth anniversary in 1958. An occasion of such importance called for a structure of major architectural significance. She had recently

KNESES TIFERETH ISRAEL SYNAGOGUE, PORT CHESTER, NEW YORK, 1956

KNESES TIFERETH ISRAEL SYNAGOGUE: INTERIOR

been in Paris, she said, where she happened to see in the press the photo of the model of a design her father had solicited and received from the California firm of Luckman & Pereira. She emphatically did not like it. Hence her visit to Barr; she wanted some informed professional counsel.

By the standards most familiar to him, Sam Bronfman had been well advised in approaching Luckman & Pereira. They had ample experience with large commercial structures that were normally neither very expensive to build nor troublesome to maintain. Bronfman was a businessman, no esthete. He had risen from humble beginnings, for a time living from bootlegging before liquor went legitimate, and he with it, following Prohibition. He was now a rich, comfortable man who could afford to send his children to the best schools. Phyllis went to Vassar, where she learned more than a little about the arts, enough surely, together with her natural gumption, to prompt her to tell her father in no uncertain terms that she thought the Luckman & Pereira design was a mediocrity, hardly equal to the ambition the company had set for itself. Bronfman acquiesced to her judgment, requesting only that she assume control of the search for an architect who could confer historic stature on the Seagram enterprise.

Barr advised her to discuss the matter with Philip Johnson, and lose no time about it, since Johnson was scheduled to leave the museum to devote himself to his own practice. Lambert was delighted to find that Philip gave her all the time she asked for and then some. The likelihood that the Seagram commission would enjoy a generous budget was enough to capture his attention, but he was equally conscious of the relationship the Seagram Building might have with the construction boom that as early as 1954 was qualitatively altering the appearance of the American cityscape—with consequences both good and ill. While modernism had become the standard language of urban architecture since the war, more often than not the buildings going up in Manhattan looked like meretricious knockoffs of one another. An architecture whose clean undecorated forms had once reflected the hopes of the early modernists to achieve a better society by uniting art and the machine under the banner of abstraction was finding large-scaled expression at last, but one all too often hasty in design, cheap in craftsmanship, and motivated by quick corporate profits that left little place in its agenda for the elegance and invention Philip associated with modern building at its best. The major exception in New York was the Lever House, a lofty shaft of steel and glass completed in 1952 by the most prolific—likewise the most Mies-influenced—of the postwar American corporate offices, Skidmore, Owings & Merrill.

Lever House, it happened, stood on the west side of Park Avenue, at Fifty-third Street, diagonally across from the site the Seagram Building was intended to occupy. Philip could not help but hope that Lambert would choose an architect capable of producing a work that would equal, if not surpass, Lever House as a standard the American profession might follow.

Together, she and he devised an initial strategy for the selection and evaluation of candidates. "We listed those," she recalled, "who should, but couldn't—Paul Rudolph, Eero Saarinen, Marcel Breuer, Louis Kahn—all good but with insufficient experience—then those who could, but shouldn't: the big firms, including Skidmore, all competent enough but indebted in every case to someone more original.

"Lastly, those who could and should. On that list were Wright, Le Corbusier, and Mies."

Philip, no more experienced than any of the first group and in all events still unlicensed in New York, took pains to dismiss himself from contention in order to work more freely with Lambert. Together, they set aside their should/could/shouldn't/couldn't distinctions long enough to talk to Saarinen, Breuer, and I. M. Pei—at least to those three—and to George Howe, whom they regarded more as a consultant than as a candidate. Eventually, the issue narrowed down to Le Corbusier and Mies. As Lambert later wrote: "One is fascinated by [Le Corbusier's] spaces, his sculptural forms, but are not people likely to be blinded by these and skip over the surface only? Mies forces you in. You have to go deeper. You might think this austere strength, this ugly beauty, is terribly severe. It is, and yet all the more beauty in it."

Manifestly, Mies was as nearly ideal a candidate as Seagram could hope for; still, he won the commission partly because his competition lost it. Le Corbusier was too distant from the project, not only ensconced in Paris but imperious as ever, hardly the sort of man to put himself willingly within the reach and secure control of a client a continent away. Wright was rejected on the grounds of a comparably unmanageable temperament. Mies appeared the most trustworthy—the most neutral, that is, in both personal manner and expressive style.

Even so, he posed a problem from the outset that prompted a suggestion from the chairman of the designated construction company. Lou Crandall of the Fuller Company reminded Lambert and Sam Bronfman that Mies was already sixty-eight years old, with a worsening case of arthritis. He would most likely have to shuttle back and forth by train from Chicago to New York to carry out his assignment. Was he up to it? Shouldn't he have someone to back him up, someone local?

Mies had already hired Kahn & Jacobs of New York as his associate architects, but that is not what Crandall had in mind. He meant a partner.

Apprised of this, Mies not only saw the point of it but foresaw a multiple advantage in naming Philip Johnson. So doing, he would gain the services of a major New York architectural figure and a disciple at that. And Mies could use the occasion to repay Philip for the inestimable favors Philip had done him in the past.

According to Lambert, Philip was astonished and moved by the gesture. The prospect of working on something close to an equal footing with so seigneurial a figure as Mies was more than he had thought about or hoped for, and far more than he could turn down. He would not only enjoy ample reflected glory but profit from the experience that even the best of the "should but couldn't" group would be deprived of.

PHILIP JOHNSON,
MIES VAN DER ROHE,
PHYLLIS LAMBERT,
C. 1955

Mies's presumptions about Philip were mostly accurate. He miscalculated only the depth of Philip's discipleship. Like so many great teacher figures— like his archrival Frank Lloyd Wright above all—Mies regarded loyalty as an absolute and permanent, not a qualified or temporary, condition. He did not yet know of the restlessness Philip had felt toward Miesian modernism ever since his 1946 correspondence with J. J. P. Oud. When Mies finally began to realize that Philip was capable of the blasphemy of contrary thought, their relationship began a slow unraveling, the most dramatic premonitory evidence of which exploded early in the course of the Seagram project—in the winter of 1954–1955 and in the Glass House, of all places, for whose form Philip was so heavily in debt to his distinguished guest.

The occasion was a small dinner for Mies and Lambert, following which it was understood that Mies would spend the night in the Guest House. Philip's hospitality, typically unstinting, provided Mies with all he wanted to drink. His capacity was legendary, which meant, in fact, that he more often than not got as sodden as any lesser man. As the evening wore on and all three tongues loosened, Mies, in his cups, could not keep from complaining about the design of the house. He commenced to belabor Philip, not for having copied him but for trying to and failing. The corner, he complained, pointing to one of the four supporting piers, was badly understood and miserably detailed. Obviously, Mies concluded, the designer did not know how to turn a corner.

Philip, no longer the breathless acolyte he once had been, reacted coolly and unflappably, but the urge to get even would not be suppressed. He came back at Mies, indirectly rather than head-on: "I've been meaning to ask you about Berlage and the Stock Exchange he put up in Amsterdam. All that decoration mixed up with masonry and metal . . . in view of your love of pure structure, I am at a loss to comprehend what you see in him or in it."

Thus the gauntlet was flung. There were few architects Mies revered as much as the Dutchman Hendrik Berlage, with whom he had competed for the Kröller-Müller House commission—and lost it—in 1912, when he was twenty-six (see p. 192). Berlage's work in Mies's eyes was *built,* and he could think of no more salient architectural virtue, especially if the building was carried out, as the Stock Exchange was, in his cherished brick.

With more exertion than control, he hoisted himself unsteadily to his feet, announcing he was finished with the evening and any intention of passing the night on the premises. Philip had no choice but to find another place for him nearby. It turned out to be the New Canaan home of Robert C. Wiley, designed by Philip in 1953. While Mies knew the house from previous visits—signaling disapproval of it as surely as of the Glass House ("Philip, why do you build the ceiling so high?")—it is just as well he overnighted there. More likely than not, amid the liquescent forms and perfumed atmosphere of the Guest House bedroom, he would have felt himself the victim of Philip's recent architectural apostasy.

Superficially at least, the dinner incident came and went with little immediate consequence and no interruption of a routine that was already fixed. Philip had managed finally to pass the state examination qualifying him for a New York license. Thus he moved his office back to Manhattan, where Mies opened up his own quarters, the two of them deciding to share space on Third Avenue between Forty-third and Forty-fourth streets. Each brought his staff with him, Mies's headed by Gene Summers, Philip's by Richard Foster.

Landis Gores was now out of the picture, and had been since 1951, when he and Philip fell out over their plans for the Hodgson House and the "21 Building." In retrospect, the split seems to have been inevitable. Too intelligent and gifted to remain forever subordinate to Philip, Gores had presumed to propose to the Hodgsons a design of his own that was clearly alternative to Philip's. The clients' expression of displeasure over the confusion coincided with grumbling from the museum over Gores's field management of the annex project. Philip suggested pointedly that he and Gores break up, which was tantamount to the latter's dismissal. By the time the Seagram project began, Richard Foster had become Philip's chief assistant.

Foster had been hired as early as 1950, directly after his graduation from Pratt Institute, where he had been Philip's prize student in the late 1940s. He brought to the Seagram project enough authority in the Johnson office to feel some discomfort over the new two-headed arrangement. Unable to understand Miesspeak as the master employed it ("Responsibility is not given here; it is taken"), Foster resigned, only to be coaxed back by Mies himself, who took him and his wife to dinner, "equal," Foster later said, "to asking me not to leave."

While Philip never shied from taking credit for his role as partner in the creation of the Seagram Building, he consistently acknowledged that the design belonged to Mies in all significant respects. It was Mies who took the step, virtually unprecedented for the time, of setting the building back one hundred feet from the apron of Park Avenue, thus opening a plaza before it and enabling passersby to view the finished thirty-nine-story structure from a unique and comprehensively revealing point of view. The very spaciousness of the approach, which was as precisely defined as it was open, was integral to the total impact of the work. A rise of three low stairs from the Park Avenue sidewalk followed the model of a Greek stereobate, while an equally rigorous classicism was apparent in the frontal symmetry of the building, with two shallow pools flanking the pink granite-clad terrace that led on axis to a canopied entrance under the middle of five bays. While the curtain-walled tower itself was a standard Miesian rectangular prism, the lavish Seagram budget—another provision traceable to Phyllis Lambert—granted Mies license to clad the facade in

LUDWIG MIES VAN DER ROHE: SEAGRAM BUILDING, NEW YORK CITY, 1954–1958
(PHILIP JOHNSON, PARTNER)

bronze, a substance whose historic association with elegance and durability not only softened but palpably enriched Mies's modernist severities. A cluster of volumetric elements varying in height and cubic capacity according to programmatic requirements was marshaled to the rear of the tower. The effect of this grouping was to preserve the simple silhouette of the great slab. Thus Mies endowed the Seagram Building with a dominant central form whose siting, patrician materials, and secure proportions yielded up one of the most enduring iconic images in the Manhattan cityscape.

Philip's own contributions to the design, while fundamentally dependent on the master plan, were worthy of the trust Mies placed in him. Most impressive was the interior treatment of two Four Seasons bar-restaurants in the twin wings that extended north and south from the tower slightly to the rear of its base. Both rooms, comfortably ample unitary spaces, had been conceived by Mies but built—in defiance of his own fabled structural honesty—by the concealment of massive transfer girders in their ceilings. Philip made the most of the high, wide dimensions Mies gave him by introducing a walled large pool in one of the restaurants, an outsize bar in the other, and by organizing both in carefully proportioned parallel/perpendicular arrangements of tables and walkways. The faithful addition of Mies's furniture throughout only added consistency to the overall effect.

Elsewhere, Philip's completed assignments consisted of the design of the elevators, the lighting, and a pair of glass canopies that covered the entranceways leading up to the building from Fifty-second and Fifty-third

FOUR SEASONS RESTAURANT,
SEAGRAM BUILDING,
NEW YORK CITY,
1959

streets. All of these efforts materialized following Mies's approval; the one offering that went nowhere was Philip's proposal to turn the entire plaza into an enormous pool that would have been contained by a marble wall rising on all sides to a curious razor-sharp edge. Access would have been gained by a bridge extending from Park Avenue to the building's entrance. The idea took shape in Philip's head when he was briefly in charge of the office, Mies having suddenly and angrily walked away from the whole project. Ironically, in the course of the building's construction, the master architect had been advised of his own lack of a license to practice in New York State, a condition that required his sitting an examination, just as Philip had. Such a prospect was intolerable to Mies, who returned to Chicago in an absorbing sulk that did not lift until Gene Summers came up with boyhood school records that somehow satisfied the New York Board of Registration. Once back in New York, Mies simply ignored Philip's aqueous plaza scheme in favor of his own. The Seagram Building, including the Four Seasons restaurants, was in operation by the end of 1959.

HISTOROPHILIA AND MONUMENTALITY

If Philip Johnson's self-liberation from Miesian authority effectively began with the suspended vault of his Guest House bedroom and the velarium at Kneses Tifereth Israel Synagogue, both reminiscent of the work of the neoclassicist John Soane, it continued—expanded, one might say exploded—in other forms traceable to historical sources beyond that of Soane. An almost compulsive waywardness of idea, form, and style, united only by an overall modern look, marked the work that came off Philip's drawing boards in the mid- to late 1950s and all of the 1960s. During this period, it pleased him to call himself a functional eclectic, by which he meant that he had enough common sense to keep the buildings he designed practical and usable, but that the form he gave them might be drawn freely from any number of models ancient or contemporary. And at will: It is next to impossible to discern any overall development, evolutionary or otherwise, in his use of these forms. Stylistically, they are scattered through the years, looking sometimes quite conservative, sometimes idiosyncratic and potentially revolutionary, but in any lasting sense neither one nor the other. Some ideas appear once and no more, while others are followed briefly, for as much as several seasons, but with interruptions and deviations along the way. He seems to have taken pleasure in shopping rather than buying, in adding rather than subtracting, in elaborating rather than distilling. Thus he became progressively more unlike Mies, and, one might add, at last truer to his own character, his own ravenous sensibility.

In this regard, he was not alone. With the passing of time, more and more American architects seemed bent on inventing an assortment of forms and shapes demonstrably modernist but consciously alternative to what they perceived as the aging and constricting canon of the International Style. None of his colleagues, however, tried on as many costumes as Philip, who looked elegant in some, considerably less so in others.

One of his must successful efforts was the house he built for Mr. and Mrs. Eric Boissonas in New Canaan in 1956. This work was surely derivative, although he was never comfortable about admitting it. He found it easier to acknowledge his debt to Mies in the Glass House than to trace the Boissonas House to the Adler and the DeVore house projects (both c. 1954–1955) of Louis Kahn. Mies, after all, was generationally distant enough to warrant homage; Kahn, just five years older than Philip, apparently was not. Besides, while Philip and Kahn saw a lot of each other at Yale in the mid-1950s when the latter was drawing up the Adler and DeVore schemes, Philip was little attracted to Kahn personally and not at all to what he regarded as Kahn's woolly metaphysics ("What does a brick want to be?"). Moreover, neither the Adler House nor the DeVore House was ever built; their impact on Philip's memory faded readily, if conveniently.

MR. AND MRS. ERIC BOISSONAS HOUSE, NEW CANAAN, CONNECTICUT, 1956

Nevertheless, the Boissonas House followed Kahn's remarkable treatment of the interior plan in both those projects, notable for so firm a differentiation of spaces that rooms became distinct compartments, separated from or set ajog of one another, with pillars mounted in the four corners of each space. Philip did something very similar in Boissonas, although his plan was developed from the rigorous use of a square module. Thus the living room consisted of four such modules stacked atop another four, creating a two-story-high space that accommodated a pipe organ. Exterior articulation took the form of sturdy piers and spandrels that gained in apparent substance through their contrast with the great panes of glass they enclosed. If the module was the one Miesian device Philip kept alive in the Boissonas House, the pronounced division of interior volumes, echoed, as it were, by pergolas based on the same module, was in total—one might say pointed—opposition to the open, unimpeded plan so definitively associated with Mies both in Europe and in the United States.

Mies would never again take full command of Philip's expressive inclinations, although like a virus in sporadic remission, he would return from time to time to affect them. In 1957, Philip completed a design for the campus of the University of St. Thomas in Houston, a complex that looks on first glance like a near copy of Mies's buildings at Illinois Institute of Technology. Further attention, however, discloses that the copy was a mannerist reworking that so overstressed the linearity of Mies's structure that some of its beams and columns resembled sticks more than steel. The plan, moreover, bore no relation whatever to I.I.T., where the buildings had been encouraged by Mies to slide past one another in an arrangement that recalled the compositions of the De Stijl movement. Philip, on the other hand, organized the St. Thomas group in the form of a bilateral central mall that he acknowledged had been conceived with Thomas Jefferson's campus of the University of Virginia in mind.

At the time the St. Thomas campus was nearing its completed form, Philip had begun work on an art museum whose surface kinship with buildings by Mies tended to deflect attention from its several distinctly

CLASSROOM BUILDING,
UNIVERSITY OF ST. THOMAS,
HOUSTON, 1957

non-Miesian features. The Munson–Williams–Proctor Institute in Utica, New York, was a large box whose roof was hung from two pairs of powerfully visible crossing girders mounted on piers that rose from the ground outside the plane of the main mass. That very description recalls Mies's use of overhead girders to secure the large unitary space of S. R. Crown Hall at I.I.T., finished just a year before Philip began his Utica design. The handling of structure at Crown Hall, however, is emphatically more straightforward than Philip's at Utica, where the box and even the girders were dressed in masonry. Yet ironically, this very concealment harked back to another Miesian source, the Electricity Pavilion at the 1929 Barcelona Exposition, a building so overshadowed in time by the legendary German Pavilion that reference to it in 1957 could have occurred only to an architect as devoted to history as Philip.

Curiously, then, and altogether eclectically, Philip had used one Mies idea to subvert another. Nor did his mannerist gestures end there: The masonry block, though supported by the piers, rose above a ground floor whose exterior was totally glazed, creating the illusion that an encompassing sheath of glass at the base of the building was supporting the stone wall above it. Finally, and more important than all these quasi-Miesianisms, was the square, severely symmetrical classical plan of the museum, notable on the exterior for a grand staircase leading across a dry moat to a central entrance, and on the interior for two more stairs flanking a column-free central space.

Classicism had shown up in Philip's earlier work, but in the St. Thomas mall and the Utica museum he applied it more academically than he had in any previous built projects. It was evident elsewhere, too, in a group of even more reactive, not to say reactionary, designs that together represented one of his few stylistically definable directions of the period.

There is little doubt that the nagging quest for monumentality accounted for much of the look of these works, since the monumentalizing impulse was satisfied more readily by historical than by modernist forms. Thus, the buildings that have come to be associated with Philip's "ballet classicist" period, a term meant as much in derogation as in description by the British critics who invented it. Common to these efforts was the use of the podium and the arcade, clearly classicizing devices, while Philip's standard materials, sleekly molded concrete or stone, reminded some viewers of epicene gestures they associated with the dance.

Philip had experimented with the arch in some of the preliminary designs for his Glass House. He returned to it in an early proposal for Asia House in New York City (1959), where he placed it atop a modernist

glass facade before abandoning it in favor of a final scheme more consistently Miesian. It is most pronounced in two works substantially different
in function but similar in their suavely expressive tone: a little pavilion he
built on his New Canaan property in 1962 and the Sheldon Memorial Art
Gallery of 1963 in Lincoln, Nebraska.

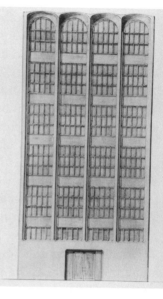

ASIA HOUSE, NEW YORK CITY, 1960:
PRELIMINARY SCHEME

JOHNSON RESIDENCE, NEW CANAAN:
PAVILION AND FOUNTAIN, 1962

   The pavilion was the first structure Philip added to his country place
following completion of the Glass House and the Guest House more than
a decade earlier. In the course of the 1950s, he bought more neighboring
land and trimmed it further, removing hundreds of trees to produce a play
of clearings framed by woods. He also added earth and rocks around the
eminence on which the Glass House stood, so that a more emphatic
declivity led downward to the base, where, at the turn of the 1960s, he
elected to put a pond with a structure of some sort riding on it.
   When finished, the pavilion was, in fact, a little island, roughly thirty by
thirty feet. It was sited close enough to the south edge of the lagoon that

one could—or was obliged to—leap onto it, and only by taking careful aim, since it was easy enough for a woman in a straight skirt to misstep and find herself standing in a foot of water. "There is something attractive about making some part of a building precarious," Philip once said, reflecting further, "It is titillating. I sometimes get an erection when I jump over that little stretch of water."

The remark was as casual as it was appropriate to the vibrations of hedonism resonating from the pavilion, which was above all a plaything, as Philip further intimated when he likened his motives in building it to "a girl's desire for a doll's house or a boy's for a tree house." A union of wit and idleness, it was constructed to a scale slightly too small for adults; most males could not stand full height in it. Philip even played the game of giving functional names to its palpably abstract spaces: entrance hall, library, living room, boudoir. Modeled after the dwarfs' chambers in the Ducal Palace at Mantua, it became Philip's private retreat, his personal Cythera, an eighteenth-century *folie* updated.

The plan also featured a pair of "patios" based on a square module extending outward in pinwheel, vaguely Mondrianesque fashion from a little basin to which rainwater was guided by a pair of channels incised in the floor. A tall jet of water was installed a bit farther out in the pond. The quality of "ballet classicism," with its implications of effeminacy, was most apparent in the elevation, where three-feet-on-center bays separated by molded concrete columns concavely diamond-shaped in section and topped by elliptical arches produced an effect of mannered, superfine softness that recalled the bedroom of the Guest House. "The 'toeing' of the columns," as Philip referred to their thinned midsections, a kind of entasis in reverse, "I derived from [Robert] Delaunay's famous painting of the Gothic church of St. Séverin."

The Sheldon Art Gallery was in all customary technical respects a more formal piece of work, especially in its unswerving symmetry. A long front elevation was composed of a nine-bay arcade, including three open central bays that provided access to the building and two trios of blind bays flanking them. An outer foyer reached through the entry was separated by a glass wall from an inner foyer where a pair of matching staircases could be seen from as far away as the street. This visibility at a distance, together with the long colonnade, prompted comparisons with similar treatments in the fabled Altes Museum of 1824–1828, built in Berlin by one of the heroes of Philip's youth, Karl Friedrich Schinkel.

The indisputable marks of classicism notwithstanding, the Sheldon Art Gallery conveyed to the viewer a feeling quite at odds with the stern masculinity of Schinkel's museum or of the ancient classical stoa. The arches

SHELDON MEMORIAL ART GALLERY, UNIVERSITY OF NEBRASKA,
LINCOLN, NEBRASKA, 1963

SHELDON MEMORIAL ART GALLERY: INTERIOR

were smoothly elliptical, as in the New Canaan pavilion, and the columns—pilasters, actually, in the blind bays—were molded again, and "toed," the whole producing an effect more satiny than substantial.

Philip's design for the Amon Carter Museum of Western Art (later the Amon Carter Museum) in Fort Worth, Texas, was completed in 1961, before either his own pavilion or the Sheldon Art Gallery, but in one significant respect it was a clearer prefiguration of an issue, urbanism—the relation of individual buildings to their urban settings—that took on increasing importance as the new decade wore on. The museum was constructed to overlook a long, generously proportioned, podium-mounted terrace that descended to a high retaining wall where a panoramic view could be had of the city beyond and slightly below. Thus the Carter Museum posed a more striking contextual problem—more precisely, contextual opportunity—than most of the other major commissions Philip busied himself with at the turn of the decade. Siting, in fact, was its most impressive asset. Since it crowned the long hill, he made it optimally readable from a distance, organizing its front elevation into five open bays separated by columns. This was indeed a classical stoa, its plan interpreted with almost academic fidelity: A glass wall was the only

AMON CARTER MUSEUM OF WESTERN ART (LATER AMON CARTER MUSEUM OF ART), FORT WORTH, 1961

physical divider between the columns and a single large gallery inside that ran the length of the building. Behind that space, five smaller ones, originally meant as offices, followed the dimensions of the outer bays. Only the molded travertine of the arcade, with its segmented arches and ever so chicly tapered columns, disclosed a similarity with the other works of Philip's ballet classicist period.

The Amon Carter Museum was hardly Philip's first urbanistic assignment. As early as 1955, at the calling of the Canadian uranium magnate Joseph Hirshhorn, he had designed the plan of an entire town meant for a site in Ontario. While that project never materialized, several efforts comparably contextual in their implications did. Surely the garden at The Museum of Modern Art was executed with a sensitivity to its surrounding cityscape, while the several years spent with Mies on the Seagram Building enabled Philip to study the problem of fitting a large building into a dense urban milieu.

Indeed, an awareness of urbanism and the discipline it implied, city planning, was a further sign of a mounting dissatisfaction with the rationale of International Style modernism, which had emphasized the primacy of the individual architectural object. Such self-referentiality had been justified by the presumed superiority of the new modern building to its old and outmoded environment. But with the multiplication of triumphantly modernist buildings in the city cores of the 1950s—higgledy-piggledy, all too often—it became ever more apparent that the environment itself, as a problem in design, required the serious application of design intelligence. Traditional ideas, ignored or discredited outright by radical modernism, were explored anew. Philip himself, alert as ever to the change of direction in the architectural air currents, was impelled to look past the outlines of the individual building to the context of which it was a part. None of the enterprises in which he was involved was as urbanistically ambitious—or filled, as it turned out, with as many frustrations—as the conception, design, and construction of the huge Manhattan complex that came to be known as Lincoln Center.

The project began in the mid-1950s as the outgrowth of an exercise in urban renewal, that nationwide impulse to tear down threadbare neighborhoods and replace them with bold, glistening new complexes rendered in the modernist idiom. A Committee on Slum Clearance, headed by New York's Mayor Robert Wagner and the politically powerful builder-planner-developer Robert Moses, had decided to redevelop a tattered portion of the city's West Side. From that primary vision, a secondary dream emerged: the north end of the area, between Sixty-second and Sixty-fifth streets along the west edge of Broadway and Amsterdam Avenue, would be turned into a mighty, all-encompassing center for the performing arts, potentially the artistic counterpart of an earlier New York urbanistic commercial triumph, Rockefeller Center. The anchoring institutions were the Metropolitan Opera and the New York Philharmonic Orchestra, both of them touched by the magic dust of modernity and eager for a bright new physical facility. Soon enough, other institutions with comparable motives became involved, and by the beginning of 1958, plans were projected for an opera house, a concert hall, a dance theater, a drama theater, an education building, and a library-museum building.

It was in the nature of such a mammoth enterprise that planning became its most important architectural priority, and the several years of vexations that followed may be ascribed as much to faltering organizational leadership as to any failures of the individual designers. The overall directorship was given early on to John D. Rockefeller III, largely on account of the cachet attached to his family name. But Rockefeller had neither a talent for administration nor any special sympathy for the arts, as Philip already had reason to believe, given the indifference, not to say coldness, of Rockefeller's reaction to designs Philip had done earlier for his wife, Blanchette (see pp. 203–04). Further, Rockefeller neglected to provide sustained or consistent support to Wallace K. Harrison, the architect entrusted with the physical planning of the project. Harrison in his own right showed little appetite for authority and less for the toughness required to maintain order among the five gifted but rambunctious architects who together with himself were at last assigned the task of carrying out the individual buildings.

Rockefeller had presumed that Harrison would designate and take charge of the architectural team in the same way he had some years earlier coordinated the designers who organized and built the United Nations complex on Manhattan's East Side. But Harrison remembered that endeavor with more pain than pride, and he preferred to play the referee rather than the manager at Lincoln Center. He did choose an advisory group of architects, including such stellar figures as Alvar Aalto of Finland, Sven Markelius of Sweden, Marcel Breuer, and Pietro Belluschi, but he left the directors of the center with the responsibility of selecting the final lineup of designers of the individual structures. By the end of 1956, the advisory group had reached agreement on a perceptibly neoclassical plan that placed the opera house at the head of a grand forecourt, to be flanked by a concert hall on the north and a dance theater on the south. The other buildings would be sited to the north of this main trio.

The selection of architects followed, with the directors retaining only one of the advisory group, Belluschi. Harrison was awarded the opera

house and his partner, Max Abramovitz, the concert hall. The dance
theater went to Philip Johnson, largely on account of his close relationship with Lincoln Kirstein, who was not just the head of the New York
City Ballet but a good friend of yet another figure of consequence, John
D. Rockefeller III's brother Nelson. As governor of New York, Nelson
Rockefeller could affect the amount of state funding the center would
receive—depending, as Philip remembered it, on whether Philip was
given the dance theater. Commissions were also forthcoming for the
buildings outside the forecourt periphery. Eero Saarinen was granted
the drama theater, sited north of the opera house, and Gordon Bunshaft
the library-museum, west of the opera house. The education building,
with the Juilliard School of Music as its tenant, would be designed by
Pietro Belluschi and constructed on a separate city block above Sixty-
fifth Street, just north of the main complex.

Yet even with this much apparently definite, a good deal was not definite at all. Writing early in 1959, Harold Schonberg, music critic of *The
New York Times,* compared the architects to "six great pianists . . . all
mighty executants, all overpowering personalities . . . locked in a room
and ordered not to come out until they had decided on the correct interpretation of Beethoven's 'Hammerklavier' Sonata. How many eons
would pass? How many wounds would be inflicted? How much blood
would be shed?"

It was an apt, if brutal, simile. The advisory group's plan notwithstanding, each designer had his own idea of how the center as a whole should
be laid out, and the inevitable wrangling with his colleagues canceled out
many of his notions and theirs. Bunshaft and Saarinen were especially
resentful of being consigned to a space outside the forecourt complex,
and Bunshaft even argued that all the arts and the institutions representing them ought to be brought together in a single structure.

But who would be chief architect of such a colossus, or of any other
device, say a colonnade or an arcade, that might weave its way around or
through the individually designed buildings and thus bring a semblance of
unity to them? Philip's initial design for a dance theater provided the
germ of his own proposal of a tall arcade that would girdle the forecourt,
even running along the Amsterdam Avenue front. He had not been happy
with the original site proposal for his building, chiefly because he didn't
relish accommodating his design to those of Harrison and Abramovitz.
He preferred to build north of Sixty-fifth Street, where, in fact, Belluschi's Juilliard was eventually erected. Since the entrance to his proposed
building would have faced the acute angle of Sixty-fifth and Broadway, he
conceived a semicylindrical front elevation that consisted of slender steel

pillars rising to a rank of trusses whose surface industrial look was softened into lissome curves reminiscent of his ballet classicist manner. Since the arcade, which was based on that configuration, would, of course, stand in front of the other facades—to that extent upstaging them—it found no takers. Philip was finally given no choice but to jettison his designs for both the arcade and the building and to resume his place in the original plan.

LINCOLN CENTER PLAZA, 1958:
STUDY FOR ENTRANCE ARCADE
(REJECTED)

The structure that materialized as the New York State Theater opened in April of 1964, six years after Philip and Richard Foster had begun work on it and two years after Foster had opened his own office. Not quite two decades had passed since the failed first attempt of Philip and Kirstein to provide a theater for George Balanchine (see p. 187). Now they handed him a space equal in scale and glamour to the formidable reputation the celebrated Russian expatriate had meanwhile made for himself in the United States.

Philip's building on the exterior was a piece of standard modernist white geometry, classical in form but freed from all trace of ballet classicism except the diagonally set columns he had used in his own New Canaan pavilion to facilitate, as he often said, "a coherent turning of the corner" (the very thing Mies had said he failed at in the Glass House). The most memorable passage of the interior was not the theater to the rear but the promenade up front, a five-story volume of space reached from the ground-level foyer by a pair of stately staircases that recalled

NEW YORK STATE THEATER, LINCOLN CENTER, NEW YORK CITY, 1964
(RICHARD FOSTER, PARTNER)

NEW YORK STATE THEATER, LINCOLN CENTER: INTERIOR
(RICHARD FOSTER, PARTNER)

Philip's lifelong love of Baroque movement. Its most arresting embellishments were two massive figure sculptures by Elie Nadelman, one of them an enlargement of the pneumatic ladies Kirstein had earlier persuaded Philip to put in his Glass House. In this public setting, they were less successful than in that private one. Not only enormously, even grotesquely, bovine, they also shone overmuch, like billiard balls. The decor, moreover, turned out to be glitzier than one would have associated with Johnson, whose refinement of taste in such matters was normally taken for granted.

If his earlier efforts at unifying the forecourt had failed, later, less ambitious proposals did not. He managed to persuade Harrison and Abramovitz to join him in the use of travertine for the cladding of the Metropolitan Opera House, Philharmonic Hall, and the State Theater, and to agree on common balcony-level heights that made the milling crowds inside those structures attractively visible through the great glass walls mounted on each front. He also insisted on a uniform twenty-foot bay system for the forecourt buildings, further securing for himself the design of the plaza floor and of the fountain that rose from its concentric center.

Nonetheless, neither his efforts nor those of the other major players in the scenario altered the critics' consensus: Given so much struggling among so many people, Lincoln Center, buildings and planning, the whole and its parts, added up to little more than a middling achievement. Philip's various contributions to it are seldom counted among his most distinguished endeavors. The five tall arches of the facade of the Metropolitan Opera House suggest that Harrison himself had retreated to a safer stylistic position, choosing to "modernize" traditional forms rather than venture into uncharted territory. And if the works of the other four architects were, like Philip's, executed in an unarguably modernist manner, it follows that they hardly broke important new ground in their own right. Lincoln Center was neither a summing up nor a reconciliation of the various directions into which American architecture at the turn of the 1960s had found its way. Nor did it point toward a promising alternative.

Equally noteworthy was Philip's personal recollection of the venture, which only confirmed for him that a modern democracy with its built-in reliance on committee-driven action was decidedly less effective in organizing a vast human environment like a city or a large part of a city than a king, or even a dictator, with taste.

When Philip turned fifty, in 1956, he felt himself materially well off and all in all satisfied with his day-to-day existence. Worldly goods, of course, had never been a problem; moreover, the ease with which he negotiated social encounters, from faculty critiques at Yale, where he continued part-time teaching, to the most rarefied uptown dinner party, now approached a form of mastery. The good looks were still intact. His hair had grown thin, but the well-crafted face was as notable as ever for its firm jawline and clefted chin. In middle age, it had settled into an expression of steady, critical alertness. Philip was forever on the mental qui vive and it showed not only in his features but in the quickness of his movements, the near double time of his walking gait. And he dressed very well, in expertly tailored Bernard Weatherill suits and French-cuffed shirts, his manner *sportif* but flawless.

If pleased with himself and his life, however, Philip could never be called comfortable. Chronic impatience and a short attention span were attributes picked up early in life, probably in reaction to the intellectual prodding of his mother. Now they showed up more and more in the variability of his architecture and even affected his love life, especially the relationship with John Hohnsbeen as it neared its tenth anniversary.

Halcyon enough in its early stages, that affair turned sour as the 1950s ended, symbolic, if not symptomatic, of a shift in Philip's fortunes that left him gradually less certain of things than he had been on his fiftieth birthday. Hohnsbeen's convalescence from tuberculosis had required him for several years to stay closer to the fireside of the Fifty-fifth Street apartment and the country place in New Canaan than was customary for him.

That, however, did not prevent Philip from pursuing extramural opportunities on his own, one of them taking the form, in either 1958 or 1959,
of Peter Vranic, a Yugoslav immigrant described by both Philip and
Hohnsbeen as one of the most beautiful lovers Philip was ever drawn to.
Neither Hohnsbeen nor Philip could later recollect what Vranic did for a
living. He was not a whore; they agreed on that, and on the abandon
with which Philip gave himself to his new passion.

PHILIP JOHNSON, WITH PHOTOGRAPH OF THE GLASS HOUSE
IN THE BACKGROUND, EARLY 1950S

Hohnsbeen hated all of it: "I was insanely jealous. Philip broke off our
relationship. There were terrible, *appalling* scenes between us. I threatened several times to kill him."

Instead, Hohnsbeen took off for Paris, where a friend had offered him
the loan of an apartment for a year. There, he reported, Philip paid him a
visit that evidently had little more to it than a confirmation of farewell.
But Hohnsbeen added quickly, "When Philip got back to New York, he
phoned me to say that the Yugoslav had walked out on him. Left him a
note saying, 'You never told me I wasn't in your will!' Philip was crushed.

I was delighted. Sweet revenge. He asked me to hang on a bit with him, until the hurt of the other affair was over. I refused."

Hohnsbeen moved on to Italy, taking a position at last on the staff of Peggy Guggenheim's private museum in Venice. With the passage of the years, a restoration of good feelings with Philip set in, permanently but at a lower temperature and a substantial distance.

Meanwhile, recovery from the turbulence of the Vranic and Hohnsbeen affairs was hastened by the appearance of yet another lover in Philip's life, one whom he met before the other two relationships had worked themselves out. This liaison started rather as many another had, quickly and casually, with a man much younger than Philip, in this case by thirty-five years.

As time passed, however, the affair did not. When David Whitney showed up one day in 1960 at the Glass House in New Canaan, he was still a student at the Rhode Island School of Design in Providence, and he did not move into Philip's New York digs until several years later. What prompted him and Philip to remain together for more than three decades, the remainder of Philip's life, is complex enough to be left to later chapters.

In the course of his labors on the Seagram Building, Philip was approached by a consortium of businessmen in Havana who asked him to design a hotel for them in the Cuban capital. If realized, which it never was, it would have been his first independent high-rise structure, and he seized the opportunity. The spokesman of the group was Meyer Lansky, one of the panjandrums of organized crime in America and, pertinent to this assignment, a kingpin in the gambling rackets of Havana, where the Hotel Monaco would have been as much a casino as a hostelry. Philip's claim that he had no idea who Lansky was at the time of the commission may or may not be believed, but late in life he did not shrink from warm praise for Lansky's wit, charm, and perceptiveness: "Yes, he was unschooled. 'Dese and dose' and all that, but with a natural sparkle. He caught on immediately to what we planned to do in the design. Everybody in the office who knew who he was was scared to death of him, but he was actually a great schmoozer. 'How's old Sam?' he would ask me of Sam Bronfman, whom he knew in the old bootlegging days and knew I knew from the Seagram project."

The design that Lansky apparently understood so readily was unique in Philip's personal catalogue. Even as he was at work on Seagram, he was paying close attention, along with most of the rest of the architectural world, to the inventions in rough-cast concrete that Le Corbusier had produced during the 1950s. Philip conceived the Monaco in similar vein, as a tall building supported on sculpted concrete stilts, one of the few works in which he paid conscious homage to Le Corbusier. It was never built. The Cuban civil war that led to Fidel Castro's overthrow of the Fulgencio Batista regime got in the way.

Philip was as eclectic in forming friendships as in making architecture. Sibyl Moholy-Nagy, whom he saw steadily during the 1950s and 1960s, is remembered by many, especially by admirers of Mies van der Rohe, as much for her unqualified personal loathing of Mies as for any of her more affirmative accomplishments. When she was not assailing Mies, and sometimes when she was, she taught and wrote about architecture, insightfully, but with a tartness that said more about the chronic grouch in her than about the failings of any subject that piqued her.

Her bile, however, was also proportionate with her passion for the arts. A native of Dresden, she had been married earlier to the painter-designer-photographer László Moholy-Nagy, whom she met during the heady days of the 1920s in Germany, at the Bauhaus, where he was one of the most influential members of the faculty and a trusted lieutenant of the school's director, Walter Gropius. Since the rivalry between Gropius and Mies grew during that period into a personal enmity, Sibyl's loyalty to her husband was readily translated into a distaste for Mies and rationalized further by what she, Moholy, and Gropius interpreted—not altogether fairly—as Mies's effort to accommodate himself to Nazi art policy in the early days of the Hitler regime.

Thus the Johnson–Moholy-Nagy bond was not without its ironies, since Philip had once been closer to the Nazi movement than Mies ever was—to whom, in any case, he was infinitely more devoted than to Gropius. He was, to be sure, eager as always to rid himself of bad political odor and, lately, to be free of his former stylistic indebtedness to Mies. Yet it was hardly any change of political or esthetic sympathies that led him to cultivate Sibyl. Besides, it was she, not he, who was the aggressor in their relationship. At the heart of it was the fact that each of them was attracted to the other's intellect strongly enough to allow for the occasional expression of a sharp difference of opinion. And both of them were elitists, as she did not shy from suggesting in one of her many letters to him: "Coming out to see you, or our rare meetings in the city, have never failed to restore me to a feeling of superiority over the 'democratic' drudgery of feeding architecture to the multitude." Philip must have liked that attitude, even if he did not share the romantic urge that moved her in the same letter to add: "Although I have regretfully resigned myself to the fact that I shall never be a friend of yours as Earthly Bliss (lacking the 3 essential qualities of being asexual, equanimous, and socially predictable), I am most grateful for our mutual admiration society which has been the most enriching and humanizing experience of the last 10 years."

Among the many traits ascribed to Philip by writers over the years, "humanizing" may have been cited by Sibyl alone. She worshiped him, and while his affection for her was indeed strictly intellectual, and even then not so requited as she wished (". . . I can no longer bring myself to make those one-way telephone calls asking humbly whether you might have a free evening"), he had an uncanny knack in his letters to her of leavening substance with solicitude, leaving her feeling petted as well as challenged:

"Your points on Moholy are extremely well taken. I did not mean to jibe [sic] you for your admiration of him since I also admire his work, and indeed purchase the same! I merely regret that you do not like the younger painters as well as I do. [Philip is speaking of the Abstract Expressionists, at the time the dominant spirits of the New York art world.] However, you are very logical in pointing out their break with architecture and their moods. I suppose I rather enjoy the difference from architectural tonics which I practice and see around me constantly. I think I enjoy the 'barbaric' seeming chaos. I say seeming because I think the order is merely of a different kind from what it was in the post-cubist abstract period."

The statement was one of the few instances of an address, by Philip or anyone, of the issue of the striking dissimilarity between the aggressive confidence of New York painting in the 1950s and the increasingly ambivalent state of the architecture of the same period. He had nothing more to say on the subject to Sibyl, in part because he didn't know as much about the new painters as he implied. (For his opinions on painting and sculpture, he relied mostly on Alfred Barr.) About architecture, he could be surer, and more pungent: "I am sorry that I can't agree about Carson Pirie [Louis Sullivan's Carson, Pirie, Scott & Co. store in Chicago]. I think it stinks. The same for the Bank [his National Farmers' Bank in Owatonna, Minnesota]."

Another difference of view between Philip and Sibyl ran deeper than any caviling over a single work and was, in fact, responsible for driving them gradually and finally out of each other's orbit. Evidence of it emerged in her response to a letter Philip wrote late in 1961 to the German critic Jürgen Joedicke. He had taken issue with Joedicke's criticism of the history-based eclecticism that, with Philip's own help, had begun to undermine modernist orthodoxies at the turn of the 1960s. "I am old enough," Philip wrote, "to have enjoyed the International Style immensely and worked in it with the greatest pleasure. . . . But now the age is changing so fast. Old values are swept away by new with dizzying but thrilling speed. Long live Change!"

It was vintage Johnson, who showed himself alert as ever to shifts in the action and ready not only to accept what he could not alter but to make the most of it. Sibyl, on the other hand, clung to a faith she too had learned early on: "My main reaction to your letter is regret that you have wasted such . . . carefully considered formulations on a philistine like Joedicke who . . . hardly deserves being taken so seriously. . . . I most emphatically agree with you that the 'modern movement' is 'winding down its days' but again I am puzzled by your statement—made often before—that today the only absolute is change. . . .

"I see the revolutionary aspect of our time, I mean right now, in the breathtaking fact that structure *is* the basic absolute, around which the virtuosity of the designer spins forms of unlimited variety."

Philip had earlier let Sibyl know that he did not share her tough-minded view: "Hope you won't be too hard on those of us today who don't always use structure expressively." It was his way of saying he was no longer loyal to one of the central articles of the modernist canon, which took structure as the fundamental source of architectural form. Sibyl continued to believe it was. (So did Mies, of course.) Their disagreement was not enough to close out their friendship, but it did little to nourish it. Slowly in the passing course of the 1960s, the correspondence between them faded. Sibyl died in 1971.

Philip maintained his adjunct status at Yale through the 1950s and into the early 1960s, dividing his time there between studio critiques and occasional public lectures. Students in the School of Architecture enjoyed the luxury of two exceptional speakers in their midst. Vincent Scully, a member of the permanent faculty in art history, was renowned for his elegantly literate flights through history, usually delivered at breathtaking pace, while Philip's equally educated commentaries were flavored with an extemporaneous wit unmatched by any practicing architect—for that matter, any architectural historian—of his day. It was at Yale on May 9, 1958, in a talk titled "Retreat from the International Style to the Present Scene," that he nominated the dozen architects

whose work he believed most compellingly illustrated the flux of the
moment. They were Marcel Breuer, Gordon Bunshaft, Bruce Goff, Wallace Harrison, John Johansen, Philip himself, Louis Kahn, Frederick
Kiesler, the lately deceased Matthew Nowicki, Paul Rudolph, Eero
Saarinen, and Edward Durell Stone.

He admitted his list was biased: "I am not going to try to keep it objective in any way." He mentioned I. M. Pei but did not feature him, and he
ignored Edward Larrabee Barnes, Ulrich Franzen, Hugh Stubbins, and
Minoru Yamasaki. Victim, furthermore, of that special provincialism of
New Yorkers whose horizons are often blocked by the lofty walls of the
great city they live in, he omitted all the major figures of the West Coast
(e.g., Craig Ellwood, William Wilson Wurster) and Chicago (e.g., Bruce
Graham, Harry Weese). Even so, he made his point, not only that he had
named most of the major up-and-comers of American architecture but
that as a group they were free of the International Style orthodoxy and
their work describable only in disparate terms. Breuer became a "peasant
mannerist"; Goff a "Wrightian romantic" who "uses things that are lying
around the house"; Kahn a "neo-functionalist"; Nowicki a "pioneer
wavy-roof boy"; Rudolph a "decorative structuralist"; Saarinen another
romantic who, like so many contemporaries, seemed party to the view
that "we will build the building and then see how we can hold it up."
Those were Philip's words, not Saarinen's, meant to encapsulate an attitude he attributed to Saarinen and others, like himself, who no longer
felt any binding allegiance to Mies/Moholy-Nagy's beloved structure as
genesis.

Philip enjoyed the podium too much to restrict himself to American
audiences. No better summary of his outlook in the early 1960s is on
record than the untitled informal talk he gave in London, at the Architectural Association, where he faced a group of listeners who knew him
and his growing tendency to shift stylistic positions well enough to be
more than a little skeptical of both. But he relished his adversarial position, summoning a defense that bristled with the assorted ironies he knew
so well how to offer up. There was a technique to this. Tongue firmly in
cheek, he would parry criticism with the most affable self-deprecation,
then riposte: "Today I am ashamed for the terribly scattered work that I
do, and its lack of direction. I am perfectly willing to admit that your
work lacks it also. . . . What can we do about it? It is all very well to say
that we admire Mies, and that some discipline is a good thing for young
minds, but what if one is bored . . . ? If you go to Germany you will see
the local versions of Lever House; they are worse. Or go to Denmark and
look at the S.A.S. building—by far the worst of all. It has no scale and is

rather like a piece of blotting paper with a drawing on it. . . . The discouragement, as one wanders around, becomes deeper and deeper, and the only outcome is that one gallops off in all directions."

Yet he remained true to one direction—his historophilia, intimating, ironically again, that history provided the best salve for the contextual sores the 1960s were beginning to blame on the bad medicine of modernism: "I was in Bath yesterday, visiting the new American museum down there. It does seem an oddity. . . . Mr. [Frederick] Gibberd has a very ugly building right in the middle of town. But, after all, I am not so sure that it is ugly. How can you do modern work when you see the old Bath around you? How can you do a housing project after you have seen the Crescent? . . . When you build a new college at Oxford, we are told, you must not copy the Gothic or the Renaissance but strike anew. I am not so sure anymore."

It was a long lecture, and the longer it lasted, the more he warmed to it, gradually giving way to observations that originated, like those of his 1953 Smith College talk, as much in autobiography as in quotidian reality: "I studied philosophy as an undergraduate, instead of architecture. Perhaps that is why I have none now. I do not believe there is a consistent rationale or reason why one does things. . . .

"In Rotterdam in 1925 [he meant to say 1929] I saw my first Neo-Plasticist building, and for the first time I found everything serene, simple and uncluttered. Primary little colors were things one could defend. One could defend the straight line." Now he grew more confidential, even if his audience did not know quite what he meant: "One could, and did, feel passionately about things, as about politics in the thirties. All my friends were members of the Communist Party then, or close to it. [This was a falsehood, although of little consequence to his argument.] They do not mention those things now! It is a great help in life if one can feel passionately about things. I am too far gone in my relativistic approach to the world really to care very much about labels. I have no faith whatever in anything. It neither hurts nor helps my architecture, though it may produce some rather funny results at times."

And then: "I am not interested in politics. It perhaps comes from the fire that one had originally dying out somewhat, but there is no cause for discouragement. One should use the very chaos, the very nihilism, the relativism of our architectural world, to create whimsies."

While his mocking tone was motivated partly by the urge to hit back at an unfriendly British audience, it was also a reflection of the strain he was under in the early 1960s, unsettled in his personal life, uncertain of the direction of architecture, his own and everyone else's.

. . .

Unsurprisingly, tears once so freely shed were shed not at all at the passing of Homer and Louise Johnson, who might have been better off had they died earlier. Their health was too good; it kept them alive past the point of usefulness to themselves or others. In 1950, they had moved from the big old house on Overlook Road to smaller quarters in the Alcazar Hotel on Cleveland's East Side, where they remained until 1957. By that time Homer, ninety-five, accepted the fact that he could no longer make the daily trip to his downtown office, a routine he had followed for sixty years. He and Louise changed their address again, establishing themselves in New London, in the family house on Main Street, and living the genteelly isolated life of the town's most respected elders.

Thus they had ample reason to be as unsentimental about the imminence of death as their son had grown about life and the search for its secrets. Louise, having been saved in her mid-eighties from a bout of pneumonia by the efforts of a local country doctor, made it clear in the hours following the heart attack she suffered one afternoon in the hairdresser's in 1957 that she wanted no extraordinary measures taken to sustain or restore her. Homer was at her side when she expired. She was eighty-eight. There was a brief funeral for family members only, with Jeannette, Philip, and Theodate in attendance. She was interred in the family plot in Lakeview Cemetery in Cleveland.

Homer had not quite three years left, each of them spent in New London, each of them lonely. Few if any of his friends were still around to make an occasional call. Most of his hours were passed with a male nurse, while Jeannette's family life in Cleveland, eighty miles away, restricted her to occasional visits. Philip assumed she was closer than she was. "So I was spared any problem," he told a later interviewer. "And I am a very selfish, egotistical man. I didn't give a damn what my father wanted. They [father and mother] were expendable. He wasn't any use in the world."

Homer succumbed to heart failure in 1960, in his ninety-eighth year. Once again, Philip and Theodate—he, if not she, more out of duty than devotion—made their way from New York for the burial, which took place at Lakeview. In accordance with Homer's instructions, there was no funeral, no eulogy at the grave site, only a prolonged silence that Jeannette described as deeply moving. The only moment of ceremony was the briefest of gestures from Philip to the grave diggers, who lowered the coffin into the ground. Philip remembered being fascinated by the gently rocking motion of the lift mechanism.

THE SIXTIES: LAURELS

AND ASS'S EARS

The older he grew, the more Philip attracted controversy, not least because he recognized it as an ideal way of holding people's attention. The criticism he increasingly drew down upon himself was driven not just by the force with which he enunciated his views but by what seemed at times a shiftiness, a tendency to conceal what we have affirmed as his underlying system of values behind several sometimes-contradictory guises.

In November of 1961, he sat down with a panel of his architectural peers to discuss and diagnose the condition of the modern city, which his colleagues, to a man, viewed with alarm. No doubt to upstage them but also to continue the cynical line he had expressed in his London lecture, he freely admitted that the city was "more mess, more jungle, more chaos. . . . For me [however], a lovely, creative, delicious chaos where I feel at home and content. To switch it quickly to city planning—that other dull subject we are to talk about tonight—the cities dearest to my heart now from a city planning point of view are São Paulo, Brazil, and Tokyo, Japan and if you know what I mean they're in a real mess.

"The city today is of more interest to idealists, do-gooders, real estate speculators, lovers of the automobile than it is to any artist."

To that, Peter Blake replied: "I am delighted to find that Philip Johnson thinks the chaos of cities is delicious. I also note that he lives in splendid isolation in the middle of a forest about 50 miles from New York. . . ."

Blake's sarcasm hardly touched Philip, who came back with some of his own, compacting it in a statement that disparaged not only the most earnest efforts of contemporary city planning but the alternative proposals of social critic Jane Jacobs, who had argued that cities developed most wholesomely if left to the vernacular actions of the common people who lived in them. "Very soon," said Philip, "Brasilia [a city recently and scrupulously laid out deep in Brazil but criticized by many for its studied abstractness and artificiality] will be like Mrs. Jacobs's city with its accretion of lovely little advertising things and garbage pails."

Yet fully contrary to the cynicism of these remarks was the injured righteousness of the piece Philip wrote in 1963 for *Response,* under the heading "Crisis in Architecture." There he declared: "Every color supplement carries pictures of spaghetti tangles of cross-roads, cloverleafs and superhighways, but when was the last great monumental building unveiled? . . . The small number of great buildings merely serves to accent the desert of ugliness which, thanks to our poor, poor patrons, is the American scene."

Evidently enough, this sentiment was at odds with his earlier remarks. Yet the fact is, he vastly preferred beauty to chaos, by such a margin that his purported delight in chaos was little more than a perverse disguise of his belief that beauty in the vulgar modern world was attainable only by the solitary artist and only in small parcels, not on a collective basis. It was enough to remember Lincoln Center.

The conflict between his dream world and the one he was obliged to live in was made never more apparent than in the commencement address he delivered at Mount Holyoke College in 1966: "I must admit that at sixty I am getting a little bitter, so I dream up cities where I should like to live and, meanwhile, try to figure out why, outside my dreams, the city decays. . . .

"My favorite Roman emperor, Augustus, used to boast that he had found Rome a city of brick and left it a city of marble. Now we, on the contrary, actually are proud to say that we find a city of stone and brick and are leaving it a city of precast concrete and corrugated tin."

Old evangelical impulses were hard to resist: "I do not propose that we appropriate tomorrow the 20 to 50 billion it would take in today's money to build the equivalent of the Parthenon. It is not in the cards. But . . . should we not appropriate some of our billions to make our houses, our cities beautiful, if not for posterity and immortality like the Greeks, then for ourselves for the same selfish reasons we dress well, decorate our bedrooms and grow gardens? Call it beautification if you will, can we not be surrounded by beauty?"

Philip then proceeded to a specific, patently unrealistic proposal for a national tax: "A thousand dollars on each car. If we can afford $2000 for a car, we can afford $3000. . . . At 7,000,000 cars a year that will bring us in 7 billion a year which would help. . . . A good tax. Another one might

be a 10% tax on war. Another nuisance tax on one of our best loved occu-
pations. (It must be loved or we would not spend so much on
it.) . . . What dream cities we could build. What heaven on earth."

Philip knew how absurd this new proposal was, knew well enough, in
fact, to make sport of it. Yet the very act of burlesquing a fundamental
plea for beautiful cities signified that he had little faith in such a goal.

To some observers who had more experience with Philip than the
graduates at Mount Holyoke had, his harlequinade was not funny at all,
nor did it gain him sympathy. They found it a kind of double-dealing and
him a double-dealer, and they let him know it, none of them quite so
witheringly as the British critic Robin Middleton, whose open letter to
Philip, published in 1967 in *Architectural Design,* is worth quoting from at
length:

> Dear Philip:
>
> When you came last September to England, I was about to review
> your lushly illustrated monograph *Philip Johnson: Architecture 1949–
> 1965.* Now, having met you, I think the less said about it, the better. It
> is strictly a book for old friends—or clients. You did well to review it
> yourself for *Forum.*
>
> This, of course, is one of the problems of encountering face to face,
> an object of despite. If someone is not exactly a monster you have to
> start making allowances for their fads and opinions. . . . The difficulty
> becomes even more acute when you find that you positively like
> them. . . . All anger is stilled. So perhaps I should try to explain sim-
> ply, why you are so often and so rudely dismissed in those off-the-cuff
> comments that appear in *AD*'s Cosmorama. Neither I myself, nor any
> other contributor, has a vendetta—though, re-reading some of the
> items, I am inclined to agree with you that they are unnecessarily
> nasty, not to say bitchy—it is simply that you appear infinitely more
> intelligent and articulate than most American spokesmen for architec-
> ture, that not only are you impassioned and wise on the subject of
> architecture but, distinguished amateur that you are (and I mean this
> in the best possible sense of the term) you have been able to influence
> not only a wealthy and cultured minority in New Canaan and New
> York, but a far greater range of art conscious hangers-on than you
> realize. In America you are an authority on architecture—whether
> you or other architects like it or not. You are an architectural power.
> You have to be taken seriously. It would be much easier of course, not
> to take you seriously. A busy, eclectic architect, a master of tech-
> niques, a detail-at-a-time genius, a scholarly romantic, a demolisher of

all over-earnest beliefs, a scandalmonger, you raise delicious questions—are you in fact earnest? a charlatan? a mountebank? a juggler?—that are the very stuff of which architectural magazines are made. You are good copy, even in *Fortune*. But this won't do. You are a devil's advocate. Even if you had built nothing, your ideals would have to be denounced as heresy. . . .

Your early buildings are beautiful contrivances, your Glass House, I am sure, is an object still of pilgrimage. But then there are the post-Miesian designs, most of which I imagine, are unvisited by architects from abroad. What went wrong?

Most obviously, your style-mongering has proved upsetting. Your architecture is now an *exercise de style*. If you see something and admire it, at once it has to be assimilated and subordinated to your own idea of formal, classical completeness. . . .

You certainly perceive the essential things in the way of beauty, but you adapt them inaccurately and unnecessarily, turning architectural realities into meaningless fictions and fantasies. . . . You revere the idea of beauty in architecture. You uphold it as an ideal. You conjour [*sic*] up the image of Periclean Athens—though you don't make it clear whether you see yourself in the role of Pericles, or Ictinius [*sic*] or even Phidias. You seem to be genuflecting somewhere, along a processional route, before an ideal image of Art, mysteriously sustained by private means. . . . Each of your buildings is imbued with the dull complacency of wealth. . . .

Art and architecture then are rarefied and remote—and expensive. Your ideals seem altogether inadequate. When architects in Europe talk about "the route," they usually mean "the street," as a teeming and lively part of a town; when you talk about "the route," you think in terms of a stately and unencumbered processional way (with yourself, possibly, in the second or third row of dignitaries). . . . But whether static or moving you judge architecture always in terms of organized space and volumes, a concept so formal and inadequate to twentieth century requirements as to be meaningless. . . .

You seem unaware of, or deliberately to ignore, the real problem of twentieth century architecture—to build an adequate living environment for an ever increasing mass of people. . . . Your work should be shrugged off and dismissed. But it is accepted and defended by other intellectuals in America. This makes me worried and restive. Ridicule and argument are not enough. The dark springs of your activity lie at a deeper level than that of the intellect, and to understand and to stem them critics will have to look beyond reason and policy into the structure and psychology of your whole society. Of all the grim and depressing episodes of modern architecture, your post-Miesian phase is the most curious and perplexing. One only wishes it was unique. But there are a spate of architects attempting to design in exactly the same spirit. The movement you represent has grown horribly in power. And it seems so prissily opposed to all the buoyancy and vigour that is represented to us by the USA itself. In an exuberantly active and expansive country you have the determination and courage, at least, to be effete.

Yours, Robin.

It would be wrong to suppose that this lengthy scolding did not draw blood. But Philip also recognized that Middleton's argument rested at its roots on the old doctrine of social responsibility that he, Philip, had regarded as irrelevant to the art of architecture as early as the days when he first heard Lewis Mumford preach it. He had not altered his view in the meantime, even if by the 1960s his own architecture seemed to change in manner, as Middleton charged, from commission to commission.

Middleton was right about the "style-mongering." Yet in the heat of his animus, he was unwilling to acknowledge that Philip, however eclectic and formalistic his motives, however indifferent to "an adequate living environment for an ever-increasing mass of people," however much the "diabolist" Bertrand Russell once called him, could design good architecture as well as bad. If some of the efforts of his "post-Miesian" period were mediocre (one thinks of such academic buildings as the dormitories of 1960 at Sarah Lawrence College and the Epidemiology and Public Health Building of 1965 at Yale University) and some clumsy in the extreme (e.g., the pseudo-Gothic monastery wing at St. Anselm's Abbey of 1963 in Washington, D.C.), others were distinguished enough to warrant credit in any fairminded history of American building of the 1960s.

Philip himself showed a strong and justified partiality to the jewel-like Museum for Pre-Columbian Art at Dumbarton Oaks in Washington, D.C., completed in 1963. He saw a trace of Mies in the modularity of the plan, which consisted of nine circular pavilions, each twenty-five feet in diameter, arranged in adjacencies of three to form a square, with the central circle accommodating a fountain, open to the sky. More fundamentally, however, he was inspired by the superb Dumbarton Oaks collection of Byzantine art and letters assembled in the 1920s by Mr. and Mrs. Robert Woods Bliss. Later these holdings had been augmented by the pre-Columbian material for which the Blisses asked Philip in 1962 to design a home. Having visited Istanbul—the historic Byzantium—as early as 1939 (see p. 137), he remembered the compartmentalized organization of buildings and gardens traditional to that city and especially notable in the work of the sixteenth-century Ottoman master Sinan. The garden at Dumbarton Oaks reinforced the association.

The museum Philip completed in 1963 remains one of the most exquisite designs in the Johnson catalogue. The dome of each pavilion is supported by eight stout round columns in Illinois marble that interlock with the columns of the adjoining chambers, leaving room at the interstices for plantings. The floors are of teak rimmed in green Vermont marble and the Plexiglas showcases are freely arranged in each room. The scale throughout is small, appropriate to the exhibits, most of them decorative artifacts. Even more arresting than the elegance of materials is the light, which enters each pavilion from the dome above and the curved glass walls all around, finding its way through the filter of the ubiquitous green of the garden interstices and the larger garden that girdles the whole structure.

By the time the Dumbarton Oaks museum was finished, Philip had given up his visiting critic's post at Yale, but he continued his relationship with the school at a no-less-profitable level. He was awarded several architectural commissions, one of which was intended to produce a complex of six units to be known as the Kline Science Center. Three were built: the Geology Laboratory (1964), the Chemistry Building (1965) and the Kline Science Tower (1965). The last of these was the dominant member of the group and exceptional in several respects. It was the first high rise Philip not only designed independently but completed. Moreover, unlike most of his work of the period, it was a piece of pure modernism, almost totally devoid of historical reference. No ornament adorned a frame that was as structurally declarative as anything Sibyl Moholy-Nagy might have wished. The tower was also one of the most imaginatively conceived and carefully detailed tall buildings of its time; it was surely equal to the best of the numerous skyscrapers Philip put up later, in the 1970s and 1980s. Cruciform in plan, it rose seventeen stories on powerful drumlike brick-faced columns that housed exhaust ducts. The stone spandrels were set smartly into window spaces indented behind the protruding girth of the columns, one independent spandrel per space, thus allowing each column to rise in an uninterrupted line from the lobby floor at podium level to the strikingly tall cornice. The resultant pattern of the facade, while straightforward as in any Mies high rise, was an inventively original variation on the master's curtain wall, already grown rather tiresomely standard by the mid-1960s.

MUSEUM FOR PRE-COLUMBIAN ART,
DUMBARTON OAKS,
WASHINGTON, D.C.,
1963: PLAN

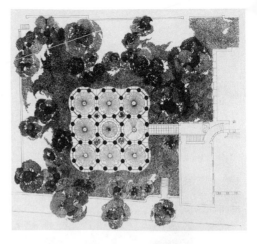

MUSEUM FOR PRE-COLUMBIAN ART, DUMBARTON OAKS: INTERIOR

KLINE SCIENCE TOWER,
YALE UNIVERSITY,
NEW HAVEN, CONNECTICUT, 1965
(RICHARD FOSTER, PARTNER)

Richard Payne

It was in the area around the tower that Philip remembered a bit of history, but his attention was given mostly to that special preoccupation of his, the processional. "What I intend there," he wrote, "is space seen in motion. . . . Walking up the hill at the upper end of Hillhouse [Avenue], you enter through a propylaeum, a covered, columned portico. . . . Before you a paved square section with a colossal statue placed, I hope, inevitably; a point around which movement can circulate. Dominating your view is, however, immediately to your left, the Tower with its 100-foot wide entrance steps. (It is too bad that the great increase in population has made great staircases obsolete. It was contrariwise lucky that the Mayans did not mind steep inclines. . . .)"

The wall that surrounded the space at the base of the Kline Tower was meant to reflect similar usages of the tower in the courtyard that were commonplace at Yale. Dumbarton Oaks was also symbolically enclosed by a wall, even if it was there before Philip added his museum structure. In two other major earlier works, the rampart was his own design; moreover, in each instance the space it enclosed and protected was the site of a single formidable, detached, and distinctly iconic object. Little wonder he referred to each of those spaces as a temenos, with the implication of an ancient sacred enclosure. Appropriately, one of them housed a church, put up in 1960 in a sleepy rural town in southern Indiana. No less appropriately, if ironically, the other was a nuclear reactor, built the same year on, of all places, the bleak coastal plain of Israel.

Typically, Philip gained both commissions on account of confidence placed in him by friends. Late in the 1950s, Dominique de Menil, still in love with the house he had built for her in 1949, introduced him to Jane Blaffer Owen, a woman of means—oil—who was related by marriage to the Owenite movement of the early nineteenth century. Robert Owen, a native Scotsman, had taken over the Christian Rappite settlement of Harmonie, Indiana, in 1825, renaming it New Harmony and turning it into a center unique for its experiments in democratic living and public education. When Philip visited it in the late 1950s, he found a town remarkably preserved in its nineteenth-century architecture and in the palpable sustenance of the Rappite-Owenite spirit. Jane Owen, herself committed to New Harmony and its history, asked him to design a church that would convey something of the community's tradition. Having heard him speak at the University of St. Thomas several years earlier, she was convinced he was the ideal architect for the job.

He saw no reason to disagree, but both he and his client ended up paying a price for an initial accord that did not last long. A bad personal chemistry developed in the course of the construction of Philip's design, and it finally spilled into the courts. Symbolically, the brick wall that surrounded what Philip called the Roofless Church began to disintegrate several years after it was finished in 1960; hence the lawsuit that required his traveling to the courthouse in Evansville, a river town so much less sophisticated than New York, or Berlin, or even Cleveland, that sheer boredom, together with the desire to be free of Jane Owen and all she signified, prompted him finally to settle out of court and pay for the repair of the fallen wall.

Before that episode, and after, the Roofless Church stood as one of the most engaging trophies of its designer's compulsive stylistic prowl. The plan was rectangular, with the long axis of the open 130-by-230-foot court leading from the east entry gate westward past flower beds and a stand of trees that Philip, mindful of the wall, introduced in memory of the medieval enclosed garden, the *hortus conclusus*. (He could just as easily have recalled his own walled garden at The Museum of Modern Art.) At the far end of the court stood the fifty-foot-high parabolic dome of the baldachin, by far the most arresting component of the whole ensemble. Bearing a faint outward resemblance to an Indian stupa, as if crossbred with one of the fantastic "pumpkin" domes of Hadrian's Villa at Tivoli,

ROOFLESS CHURCH, NEW HARMONY, INDIANA, 1960: VIEW TOWARD BALDACHIN

it looked even more like a cloth draped over a convex surface, the "folds" hanging somewhat stiffly and the points of the folds perched—weightlessly, it seemed—on six concrete posts elliptical in plan.

Likenesses did not end there. The words of the prophet Micah, "Unto thee shall come a golden rose," interpreted by the Harmonists as foretelling the second coming, were carved in the cornerstone of the Roofless Church, prompting the community's chronicler Don Blair to add that the "dome is shaped like an inverted rosebud and casts the shadow of a full blown rose." A viewer less conversant with Scripture might have seen in the baldachin, which is not golden at all but tawny brown, something more like a bat with folded wings.

Undoubtedly, the cedar shingles covering the wood-framed structure were lighter in tone when the baldachin was built, but in any case, Philip denied all symbolic intent, insisting as usual that his interests were confined to the form of the thing.

Although he never repeated it in his later work, the baldachin remains a compelling object, open at its base along six sides, so that the viewer approaching it can see from afar the "altarpiece" it shelters: a bronze by

Jacques Lipchitz, usually referred to as *Descent of the Holy Spirit,* but featuring in addition to the sacred dove the figure of a woman and this legend: "Jacob Lipchitz, Jew, faithful to the religion of his ancestors, made this virgin for the better understanding of human beings on the earth so that the spirit may prevail."

Philip's own faith, which was art in matter and power in the abstract, was strong enough to compensate for his indifference to the communitarian religion New Harmony embraced. That is a real irony: His belief in religious monuments was purely esthetic, yet—or thus—he gave the town an authentic religious monument. Moreover, the Roofless Church, whatever its inspiration and however different the modern look of it from that of the humble old buildings that make up the rest of New Harmony, is almost touchingly compatible with them. The brick wall is appropriate in color and in scale, and the colonnade on its north side looks out on the rolling cornfields of southern Indiana, as if the Lord's realm were directly visible to those in the very act of praising Him for it.

Surprisingly little is to be found in the literature on the circumstances leading to Philip's design of the nuclear reactor in Rehovot. As an architectural image the building, completed in 1960, was striking enough to prompt most contemporary critics to restrict their assessments of it to the formalist criteria that dominated their thinking at the time. In fact, it is doubtful that any of them actually saw it. Philip himself never did. They must have judged it from photographs, just as he configured it on drawing paper.

Evidently, the commission came from the then deputy defense minister of Israel, Shimon Peres, who is said to have imposed no budgetary condition on the architect. Asked about this in his late seventies, Philip claimed that Peres "was always a fan of mine. He had been to the Glass House, and one night he asked me, 'How come you've never done anything in Israel?' 'Nothing would please me more,' I said. Rehovot was the result."

The credibility of that recollection was compromised immediately by Philip's follow-up remark: "You know, far from being an anti-Semite, I've always been a violent philo-Semite."

Philip may indeed have been on good terms with Peres, but there is reason to believe that his old friend Edward Warburg, former chairman of the United Jewish Appeal and continuously active at the time in pro-Israel causes, played no less significant a role in arranging the commission. Philip and Eddie were contemporaries not only at Harvard when they were young but close friends later at The Museum of Modern Art, where Warburg was a member of the advisory committee at the same time, the early 1930s, that Philip headed the Department of Architecture.

For all his devotion to Israel, Warburg was a worldly man and a cosmopolitan Jew, who while knowing of Philip's political background considered it more fatuous than flagrant and, by 1960, a chapter of the dead past anyhow. Nevertheless, despite Philip's earlier efforts at expiation, most notably his design for the Kneses Tifereth Israel Synagogue (see pp. 238–40), he was still, in the late 1950s, regarded with suspicion and/or distaste by a small but significant segment of the New York Jewish community.

Historian Nicholas Fox Weber, who knew Warburg well, did not recall whether it was Warburg or Philip—but surely one of them—who proposed that the former use his influence to persuade the authorities in Israel, eager at the time to make and keep American friends, to offer Philip a building commission on Israeli soil. Beyond that lay the ultimate goal: to persuade Philip's American antagonists to recognize that he had at last and formally been washed clean of his sins, by no less an entity than the government of the Jewish state itself.

If Weber was right, it appears that a Jew was required to save Philip from his anti-Jewish past. How complete that conversion was (which seemed truer to the "Saul-Paul" metaphor than Philip's constant use of the image to describe his sudden embrace of architecture at age twenty-two) was no more certain in 1960 than it had been in 1954, the year of the Kneses Tifereth Israel Synagogue. Philip during his whole life never fully succeeded in controlling his hyperconsciousness of Jews, although he tried, after his own complicated fashion. In his professional world, he could not avoid the company of Jewish colleagues, and his own perception forced him to admit that more than a few of them were not only personally competent but admirable, and even attractive. Moreover, he knew he had a dubious past, for which he would occasionally overcompensate by lavish gestures of fellowship and generosity to Jews. Warburg, citing a trip he and Philip made to Israel in 1966 and another in 1970, recalled that on both occasions Philip made fast friends. "He insisted regularly on helping me raise money for Israel," Warburg added. "He became a great buddy of [Teddy] Kollek [mayor of Jerusalem]. Everyone coming from Israel came to him and became his pal. Lots of lunches together. Keep in mind that Philip is not just a salesman but a gracious salesman. He gave jobs in his office to all sorts of people."

On the 1966 trip, Philip came close to capturing another assignment that would, if realized, have added to the ironies that seemed to reflect from all facets of his encounter with Israel. This would have been a new

ABOVE: NUCLEAR REACTOR, REHOVOT, ISRAEL, 1960.
BELOW: VIEW OF COURT. (PHOTOGRAPHS ©ARNOLD NEWMAN)

plaza, to be built in front of a Christian monument, one of the most hallowed in the Holy Land: the sixth-century Church of the Nativity in Bethlehem. Financing was promised by Nelson Rockefeller, that eminent Gentile, with the blessings of Philip's new friend, Mayor Kollek. The project never materialized. Nor did a proposal for the Lod Airport (now the Ben-Gurion Airport). Conceived in 1971, again at the prompting of Peres, Philip's design proved to be far too expensive, not least because of an acreage of exterior glass that would have been altogether out of place in the Israeli climate.

As with the Roofless Church in New Harmony, the Rehovot reactor remains the the most lasting thing Philip left to Israel. Its similarity with the church in form is nearly as evident on first glance as is its dissimilarity in mood. A four-sided battered wall interrupted only by an entrance on one of its short faces surrounds an open court, with a single solid and powerful form looming up at the far end. That dominant latter object, also battered, is central in plan and ridged in its twenty-sided elevation, while the baldachin of the church, also centrally planned, is six-sided and curved. Both are perceptibly sculptural, attesting to a more pronounced influence from Le Corbusier in each of them than was normal for Philip.

Those likenesses are matched by the obvious differences. The unitary single room of the reactor, sealed, windowless, and built of expensively molded concrete, is heavier, lonelier and more psychically isolated, more protective of its interior, and more protected by its outer wall. It brings to mind an ancient Egyptian temple, in which a wall-girded courtyard, open to the sky, led to the sheltered hypostyle hall and the secret sanctuary.

At Rehovot, the wall is thick enough to contain offices that give onto a walkway punctuated by downward-tapering columns. The actual machinery in the core was designed not by Philip but by appropriately trained engineers. The structure was to have been the hub of a research complex that would, or should, have grown around it. Philip's building, however, proved to be too self-contained to allow for any such extension. It remains a solitary monument in today's landscape, austerely beautiful, minimally functional. The commonality of a temenos produced a contrast between a stronghold in Israel and a meeting place in Indiana. If one remembers that Philip was playing with ballet classicism at the same time these two buildings were under way, they are yet another evidence of the variability of his designs at the turn of the 1960s and thereafter. A chronic mental fitfulness had transferred itself from his psyche to his architecture.

NEW CANAAN

When Philip built the Glass House and the Guest House in 1949, he had no idea he would later purchase a piece of land adjacent to his original five acres, and then another and another, eventually putting up enough buildings on the land he bought that some critics would see the resultant compound as a total considered work of architecture. Surely by 1985, when the library-study, the Gehry Ghost House, and the Lincoln Kirstein Tower had been finished following the previous additions of the pond pavilion, the painting gallery and the sculpture gallery, and a pruning of the woods into an ever more perceptibly unified arrangement, it was tempting to see the whole estate as a *Gesamtkunstwerk*. The notion was all the more fetching because Philip's assembled efforts seemed in many ways not only a digest of the phases of his career but a compacted stylistic summary of forty years of American architecture.

The fact is that for most of those three decades, the place followed no master plan but rather was enlarged a component at a time. A swimming pool was installed, close by the Glass House, in 1955. At the time of its completion, Philip was already owner of a broad strip of land to the north of his original parcel. On this new space he had thought of putting up a small studio (1953) and, later, a dining pavilion (1957), rejecting both schemes in favor of a more ambitious work, an art gallery, finished in 1965.

While Philip at the time was already known as an art collector, it was a role he had pursued more casually than rigorously. Mostly he favored Abstract Expressionism, usually buying at the occasional recommendation of Alfred Barr. His new companion, David Whitney, on the other hand, had the appetite and zeal of the dedicated collector, an eye no direc-

JOHNSON RESIDENCE, NEW CANAAN, LATE 1960S: SWIMMING POOL IN FOREGROUND;
SCULPTURE BY JACQUES LIPCHITZ, LEFT; GLASS HOUSE IN BACKGROUND

plined as it was true, and a taste for the generation of artists who were coming of age at the turn of the 1960s, chiefly Jasper Johns, Robert Rauschenberg, Frank Stella, and Andy Warhol. He persuaded Philip, who needed little prodding anyhow, to construct a gallery that would house the collection Whitney had already begun to assemble. The requisite space, however, would be so large that it was sure to compete with the Glass House as the dominant element of the landscape.

So Philip buried it. More exactly, he heaped a huge berm around it. All that showed externally was the flat roof and an entryway, the latter carved out of what seemed no more than a gentle rise in the slope upward from the Glass House to Ponus Ridge Road. Philip could not resist likening the entry to the dromos, or pathway, that leads in similar fashion to the Treasury of Atreus, a celebrated Mycenean underground tomb of the fourteenth century B.C. The resemblance ended there, since Philip's entry gave onto a unique interior whose plan was taken up mostly by a cluster of four tangential circular lobes of varying diameters—hence the slightly bent axis—making for a large asymmetrical unpartitioned space. In the

JOHNSON RESIDENCE, NEW CANAAN, PAINTING GALLERY, 1965: ENTRANCE.
SCULPTURE BY ROBERT BART, TO THE LEFT;
PAINTING BY JASPER JOHNS, VISIBLE THROUGH DOORWAY

PAINTING GALLERY: INTERIOR.
PAINTINGS, LEFT TO RIGHT, BY ANDY WARHOL, ROY LICHTENSTEIN, ROY LICHTENSTEIN,
FRANK STELLA

center of each of the three widest lobes was a drumlike column to which the short sides of large horizontal carpeted panels were attached so that they could be swung around the column by hand, like postcards on a rack.

Thus the panels, seven in the smallest lobe, nine and twelve, respectively, in the two larger ones, could be positioned so that six panels in three flattened pairs, and the paintings hung on them, were visible from the central area at any one time. Since the panels could be moved by the viewer, he could change the "group exhibitions" at will.

As usual, Philip came up with his reason—or rationalization—for the novel interior arrangement he had invented, citing it as a way of minimizing the "museum fatigue" he associated with normal perambulation from one exhibition gallery to the next. Here in his *Kunstbunker*, as he fondly called it, the viewer could sit and the paintings would move—provided someone moved them for him, of course: If he was alone, he would have to do it himself, getting up from one of the little stools Philip had equipped with casters so that guests, while seated, could trundle themselves from spot to spot. That exercise was hardly taxing, but he finally did grow impatient over the frequency with which his sculptures, which were housed in the same building, in the central area, interfered with the sight lines toward the paintings and one another. Making the sculptures movable by affixing wheels to the platforms on which they sat did little to alleviate their intrusiveness. Clearly, a separate gallery for three-dimensional objects was called for, and Philip, forever eager to attack a new idea, obliged himself.

The painting gallery in its bermed state did little to disrupt the topography of the landscape, but it required access, which Philip had already provided earlier in the form of a footbridge over a narrow gulch on the slope leading up to Ponus Ridge Road. "I wanted the thinnest bridge floor that technology could produce," he recalled. "It should be made of the thinnest possible layer of steel, with a high camber and no handrail, so that it would be springy. And precarious, with the uneasy feel of a rope bridge!" Danger was always a delight to him, so long as the odds ensured that it was kept at a safe physical distance. Close to the bridge, at a place free of trees and other visual impediments, he built a wooden platform from which, he liked to point out to visitors, one could sometimes observe the sun set at the same moment the moon rose.

With several acres added in the late 1960s still farther north of the land he had earlier bought, he decided to remove the Lipchitz sculpture, reasoning that the pivotal position it had occupied on the original acreage was unbalanced by all the new land. He also realized how much the row of old maples just west of the painting gallery resembled the border of an allée. Irresistibly, they led to a space at the end of his property where, no less surely, the new sculpture gallery would have to be sited.

Even so, the building, completed in 1970, seems modest and unprepossessing as one approaches it. It is partly obscured by the maples; what shows is a low structure with a slanting roof, its slightly shedlike look only somewhat dressed up by the white-painted brick of the exterior and the all-glass surface of the roof. The impression made within, however, is transfixing. Like the painting gallery, the sculpture gallery is one of Philip's "inside" buildings, indeed the most virtuoso organization of interior space that he ever carried out. He relished describing it, differently, it seemed, each time he talked about it: "two almost-squares that have been partially twisted" or "a square with a triangle stuck on it." In fact, the plan is asymmetrically five-sided, with one side taken up by the entry wall and each of the others by a long room running alongside it. One of these rooms is rectangular; each of the other three features a sharply acute-angled corner. Yet this description, too, is meaningful to the visitor only after he has followed the key component of the building, the staircase, as it leads through the large unitary space down and around the various subspaces to the base floor—"like a dog," in Philip's famous analogy, "turning around several times as he settles into his bed." It is this crisply articulated stair, with its steps paved in dark brown brick and its low sawtoothed balustrade, also of brick but painted white, that most produces the sensation of a complex, shifting space. Because the plan is irregular, the space seems unpredictable, but without the stair there would be little perception of constant movement through three dimensions. In his irrepressible appetite for historical reference, Philip further compared the space to a "classical square with bays off it," adding, however, virtually to contradict himself, that "the square is really a pentagon." Actually, the sculpture gallery is so unclassical in its spatial surprises and ambiguities, yet such an important entry in the Johnson catalogue, that it challenges everything we have said about Philip's classicist predisposition. At the same time, it is clearly modernist in style, moreover a spectacular enactment of his belief in architecture as procession. The visitor yields eagerly to the down-and-around pull of the stairs, fascinated as much by the shifting perspectives, the occasional slots in walls or railings, or the unexpected doorway he encounters at the base as by the sculptures the building was meant to exhibit. Even then, as one studies these pieces, all of them major efforts by the likes of Donald Judd, Robert Morris, Claes Oldenburg, George Segal, Richard Serra, Frank Stella, Mark di Suvero, and Andy Warhol, he is likely to recall how expertly the architect followed the original functional program: Using all these subspaces, Philip

saw to it that each piece occupied its own autonomous place, uninterrupted by the silhouette of any other, while the whole ensemble
remained visible from virtually any position in the building.

If attention is drawn downward at first by the direction of the stair, it
turns quickly enough to the roof and its structure. The rafters attach

JOHNSON RESIDENCE,
NEW CANAAN,
SCULPTURE GALLERY,
1970: INTERIOR.
SCULPTURES BY
CLAES OLDENBURG,
FLOOR LEVEL;
DONALD JUDD,
ON WALL;
MARK DI SUVERO,
UPPER LEVEL

Richard Payne

unevenly to the diagonal steel ridge beam, one row meeting the beam at
its top edge, the other at its lower, in a manner common to the barns that
had charmed Philip on an earlier tour of the Spanish countryside. The
rafters, moreover, separate the long strips of mirror glass that not only
keep the interior cool by deflecting most of the sun's rays but allow
enough light inside to produce yet another display of movement in the
form of the shifting patterns of rafter shadows that play on the multitude
of planes below.

With the completion of the sculpture gallery, twenty-one years after he
moved into the Glass House, Philip had put up five buildings, each with

its own function, on what was now a thirty-three-acre property. For a time, however, the sculpture gallery stood out among these in Philip's mind and intentions. Partly he was moved by pride in what he rightly regarded as a successful piece of work, partly by the realization that the building, for all the specificity of its purpose, might in fact be an alto-gether-satisfying domicile, not just an exhibition space. It was certainly as open an interior as the Glass House, with its relative complexity suggest-ing a differentiation of uses that might actually prove preferable in some respects. Shortly after he finished it, he laid out a plan that assigned por-tions of the building's five levels to living, dining, sleeping, and service areas. That is as far as he went. He used the gallery briefly as a working atelier before deciding that any secondary or alternative employment of it was finally less appropriate than the one he had originally conceived.

"With me it seems to be flibbertigibbet, an amateurish sort of thing, that I'm enjoying hugely. We do live in a very strange, pluralistic world, where the mind jumps around at cybernetic speed, and we all want to do something different every day."

So spoke Philip in his mideighties, leaving truth visible through a curtain of exaggeration that did not close out recollection of several modestly consistent attributes in his work of the 1950s and 1960s. Ballet classicism with its "toed" columns and elliptical arches was the most obvious among these, while influences from a variety of Near and Far Eastern cultures were only slightly less so. His fondness for the temenos was evident in buildings as disparate as Dumbarton Oaks, the Kline Science Tower, the Roofless Church, and the Rehovot nuclear reactor, while three works completed within months of one another in 1965—the painting gallery, the James Geier House near Cincinnati, and the library at Hendrix College in Conway, Arkansas—were surrounded by berms. The berm and, for that matter, the frequent use of the drumlike column may have been reflections of a deeper, albeit on-again, off-again, fascination with sculptural form that Philip claimed took hold of him after he surrendered to the impact of Le Corbusier's great 1955 chapel at Ronchamp.

Granting that much, however, presupposes his self-characterization as a quick-change artist. And if his guises varied as much as they did in his best architecture of the period, they were no less mixed in his lesser efforts. The New York State Pavilion, for one, designed for the 1964 New York World's Fair, was one of his zanier adventures in form, all in all unlike any other work he did at the time.

Its dominant element was a 250-by-320-foot assembly hall, elliptical in plan and open to the air. Sixteen concrete pylons—recognizable as Johnson only insofar as they were drumlike—furnished support for a raffishly multicolored Plexiglas roof-cum-oculus, a velarium of sorts, suspended on cables from curious spikelike projections that were attached to the steel roof rim.

Oddities were sometimes closer to the norm for him than apart from it. If he never returned to the stupa form of the Roofless Church, he also found no further use for the configuration of the New York State Pavil-

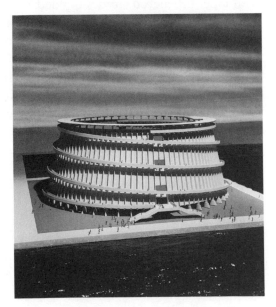

PROJECT, NATIONAL SHRINE,
ELLIS ISLAND, NEW YORK, 1966

ion. Nor is there anything on his books that resembles, except in the most generally sculptural way, the Ellis Island project of 1966.

In that unrealized work, meant as a national shrine honoring the 16 million men, women, and children who filed through the immigration facilities at Ellis Island between 1892 and 1954, Philip proposed as a centerpiece a huge, truncated, hollow, vertically ribbed cone 300 feet in diameter and 130 feet high. On helical ramps descending from the cornice to the ground, within the building and without, would have been placed plaques bearing all the names retrievable from the passenger lists of the ships that carried the immigrants to the United States. While the idea preceded by fifteen years Maya Lin's concept for the Vietnam memorial in Washington, D.C., Philip would have inscribed the names not on a wall, as Lin did, but on the surfaces of a bulky zigguratlike volume—frequently dubbed Johnson's Tower of Babel—that would have been large enough to be visible across the Narrows from Manhattan but deferentially shorter, by twenty feet, than the pedestal on which the Statue of Liberty stands.

Philip's residential designs of the 1960s were marked by the same stylistic restlessness, punctuated by occasionally single-minded streaks. For the most part, he also enjoyed big budgets, especially in the Henry C. Beck, Jr., House in Dallas (1965), the Eric Boissonas House II in Cap Bénat, France (1964), and the David Lloyd Kreeger House in Washington, D.C. (1968). The Beck House was a rambling affair faced on both of its floors with long, unrelieved arcades molded in the ballet classicist manner. The Boissonas House, commissioned by the same client for whom Philip had designed a house in New Canaan in 1956 (see pp. 251–52), was a qualified realization of the idea put forward in the Burden and Chrysler house projects (see pp. 214–16), with a nod to his own Glass House: five perceptibly Miesian pavilions separated physically and in function, with the eastmost trio astride a podium and sheltered partially by an undulating concrete parasol, the kind of "wavy roof" Philip had associated in his 1958 Yale lecture with the architecture of Matthew Nowicki and Eero Saarinen. The five structures, with circulation conducted mostly in the open, convey the impression of a tiny Mediterranean village poised on two levels that have been cut into a hill overlooking the Côte d'Azur. Eastern ideas, on the other hand, dominated the pasha's palace that Philip completed in 1968 for the Kreegers, a couple wealthy enough to afford what he gave them: a lavish collection of modular spaces in two and three tiers, reflective of the plans of medieval Arab structures that Philip had seen on an earlier trip to Cairo. The central section was dominated by a two-story-high grand hall spacious enough to accommodate musicales and most of the copious Kreeger collection of modern French art, while the modular areas on the top floor were crowned with a spectacular array of groin-vaulted domes.

By the mid-1960s, critical reaction to Philip was unanimous only in acknowledging that he was a figure of consequence in the architectural world: a star. Otherwise, the spread between praise and opprobrium was broad. If Robin Middleton deplored his gallimaufry of styles, summing it up as "effete," other writers found it a reflection of creative vitality and versatility from which they, too, could draw generalizations. In an unsigned article of November 16, 1964, titled "Architect of Elegance," *The New York Times* remarked: "Mr. Johnson calls himself a classicist and

MR. AND MRS. ERIC BOISSONAS HOUSE, CAP BÉNAT, FRANCE, 1964

MR. AND MRS. DAVID LLOYD KREEGER HOUSE, WASHINGTON, D.C., 1968
(RICHARD FOSTER, PARTNER)

a traditionalist, but a traditionalist who likes to take tradition and 'improve it, twist it, and mold it; to make something new of it.'

"The result is that he has been called both a rebel and a reactionary— perhaps rebelling and reacting against the same thing: the architectural establishment. But as one observer has said, he now is the establishment."

Certainly at The Museum of Modern Art, he was as solidly entrenched as anyone who bore a name other than Rockefeller. Moreover, he might have found his position there preferable to that of the Rockefellers, since as the unofficial architect-in-residence of the institution he could make his authority manifest in the more material form of a monumental building of his own design.

Thus, in 1964, he completed a combined east wing and garden wing at the museum, working in a manner appropriate to the institution's thirty-fifth anniversary. Six years after he had sounded the "retreat from the International Style" in a lecture at Yale, he chose to build the facade of his addition in unmistakably International Style black steel and gray-amber glass, softening any Miesian rectilinearity only a little by gently curving the intersections of the framing verticals and horizontals. He added space to his own sculpture garden at the rear of the building, preserving its character—as if obedient to an urbanist impulse—rather than altering it. The Vermont marble floor was extended eastward past newly planted trees that matched the old ones. The climax of the processional was a grand staircase that led upward via several levels to a plaza from which the whole garden and all the elevations of the museum building could be securely, proudly, magisterially surveyed. The space beneath the plaza housed the museum's art classes, while the east wing that rose to the same height as the original museum contained new exhibition galleries as well as trustees' meeting rooms and enlarged facilities for the photography, prints, and architecture departments.

While Philip's interior design was most effective in his plan of the gallery areas, which he kept handsomely open and free of pier supports, some of his museum colleagues—chiefly René d'Harnoncourt—were less than happy with his extravagant use of carpeted walls in the twenty-foot-high Founders' Room and the marble walls in the lobby, on which paintings could not be hung. Even so, the annex drew a near-rave review from the bright new critic of *The New York Times,* Ada Louise Huxtable, who had joined the paper in 1963, nearly twenty years after working for Philip in his department at the museum. She wrote:

> [The new addition] is one of New York's most subtly effective structures, its refined simplicity quietly understating the care of its detail-

ing and the sensitivity of its relationships to older buildings and commercial and residential neighbors. . . .

What Johnson is bringing to New York, and to a good many cities
across the country, is a kind of architectural elegance that has not
been seen since the turn-of-the-century days of McKim, Mead and
White and the splendid "Renaissance" palaces built for the business
aristocracy. . . .

It is beauty that he is really after, and history and structure are his
convenient tools. This sometimes turns an artful device into "art for
art's sake," and even makes structure look a little thin. But beauty is
seductive, and so are his buildings. . . .

As a man, Philip Johnson is as soigné as his architecture, with the
kind of knowing discernment that eschews the too silken necktie, the
too obvious gold cuff links, the too smooth, overtly rich effect. . . .

[Philip is quoted.] "My ambition? I'd like to be *l'architecte du roi*."
There is a quick smile, a sidelong glance, to see if the dropped phrase
has been understood, and if it has had the proper shock value. "The
king's architect," he goes on. "We have no phrase for it today, but I
mean the country's official architect for its great public buildings. I'm
not thinking just of myself, but of all our top talent." He offers
another calculated heresy: "I want to take the dirty connotations out
of the words 'official' and 'academic.' "

From the glass house and the glass-walled office in the Seagram
Building, Johnson continues to throw well-selected, beautifully pol-
ished stones; the royal rebel is growing gracefully into the next generation's grand old man.

Philip's remarks to Huxtable were evidence of an intention long held to
reconcile the modernist esthetic with its traditional enemy, "official" and
"academic" culture. Surely some of his professional colleagues who had
been taken aback by his celebration of urban chaos in the early 1960s
wondered whether he was merely seeking publicity when he marched at
the head of the line of pickets protesting the 1963 demolition of New
York's Pennsylvania Station. Of course he was—did he not always revel in
it?—but his later lamentation over the loss of the great McKim, Mead &
White concourse ("That romantic, magnificent room is gone") was as
sincere by his own lights as the disenchantment of his persistent accompanying realization that one could not stop such depredations in today's
capitalist commercial world. All one could do is act individually, as he did
in 1966 when he furnished the seed money that enabled the Chicago
architectural community to save from demolition the John J. Glessner

House, a masterpiece by Henry Hobson Richardson and one of the city's authentic architectural jewels.

Philip's consciousness of urbanism grew, and grew in complexity, as the 1960s wore on. Not only were architects as a whole increasingly preoccupied with the issue of city planning; a related interest in urban reform and the upgrading of the metropolitan fabric was evident at the national and local political levels. President Lyndon B. Johnson's plans for a Great Society, which sustained and enlarged upon the policies of the John F. Kennedy administration, were reflected in New York, especially in the late 1960s, in the liberal Republicanism of Governor Nelson Rockefeller and Mayor John V. Lindsay. In Weimar Germany at the turn of the 1930s, with his future linked to The Museum of Modern Art, Philip could afford to express his disdain for mixing economics and politics with the art of building. Now, as a practicing architect with commissions to seek, he found it harder and harder to maintain that stance professionally, although he continued to see urbanism as much as possible through his cherished esthetic glass. In 1966, having completed a long journey that took him among other places to Egypt (hence the Kreeger House plan) and India, he reported on what he had seen to an Indian friend, the architect Patwant Singh:

"The easiest things for me to grasp are the city plans, but that may be only because my eyes are peeled at the present time for aspects of cities rather than buildings. The top of the list is, of course, Fatehpur Sikri, with Tughlaqabad second."

Then, yielding to another old ambivalence, he added: "Perhaps the sharpest disappointment of my trip was Chandigarh . . . in no way [because of] the architecture. Corbusier remains the great master of interlocking space modulators. . . . But the *city* of Chandigarh as a place for humans to congregate, strikes me as a total disaster. Even if he did want to create monuments out in the open countryside, even granting that this might be a viable approach to a city, there is no possible relation physically among the three buildings that are there, nor any possible relation of the government center to the city they are in. Even L'Enfant's Washington was a better idea. It seems to me that Corbusier must have taken his idea for a government center from Louis XIV's Versailles."

By the time he wrote that, he had decided to test the waters himself, as if—once again—to put behind him the cynicism of his earlier remarks about city planning. In July of 1965, he joined Lindsay, then running for mayor, and a fellow architect, Robert L. Zion, for a helicopter tour of all five boroughs of New York City as well as a pair of neighboring islands. The survey was done as part of the preparation of Lindsay's campaign platform, which promised a major redevelopment of the city's infrastructure. "I'm very depressed at what we saw," Lindsay said, "but excited by the potential." Commenting on the proposed Lower Manhattan Expressway, a project he opposed, he continued, "If it can't be stopped legally, change the law."

That was the sort of sentiment, implicitly autocratic, that Philip could find supportable. He echoed Lindsay: "The only green we saw in Brooklyn was for the dead—in the cemeteries," and "Expressways ruin everyone's life along the way and destroy historic sites." A year later, tracking an urbanistic path on his own, he made a brief foray into electoral politics, his first in nearly three decades, when he ran for a seat in the General Assembly of Connecticut on a platform that stressed the need for environmental planning. After losing by a two-to-one margin, he admitted he had mostly wanted to learn whether such issues were of interest to the voters. "Obviously they aren't," he concluded. "Voters are more interested in things like the PTA." Clearly, Connecticut was far too rural, much too domestic, probably too damned smug to care about such things. Philip turned his attentions back to New York.

Nothing in the record suggests that he expected to become the city's new Baron Haussmann or that he coveted any specific city commission. On the other hand, in view of his personal history, there is as much irony in his first major city assignment, announced in August of 1967, as there was frustration in the loss of it. It was the design of a $220 million sewage disposal plant on a Hudson River site in West Harlem, between 137th and 145th streets.

Philip knew the difference between hydraulic engineering and architecture; still, his proposal underscored his imprinted estheticism. In his remarks to the press he stressed that he intended to cover the plant's twenty-two-acre roof with ornamental pools and a group of fountains capable of shooting water two hundred feet into the air. "There will be great water displays rising high above the level of the Henry Hudson Parkway," he said cheerfully, "with the fountains set among the sculptural shapes of ventilators and doorways on the roof of the plant."

Slightly more than a year later, the city dropped his plan, as the *Times* reported, "in favor of something more 'meaningful' to the community" and, in the words of Environmental Protection Administrator Merril Eisenbud, "something 'more useful than fountains, and I agree.'" More irony, if not insult, was added when Lindsay appointed a steering committee of local residents to prepare the plans for whatever was to go up on and around the plant.

While the whole experience clearly did little to stimulate his urbanist ambitions—such as they were—Philip pressed on. So did fate. Together with Wallace Harrison and William Conklin, he was named in April of 1968, by Rockefeller in concert with Lindsay, to draft a master plan for a vast residential and commercial complex on 104 acres of the West Side of Lower Manhattan. Philip accepted his place in the commission despite the unpleasant memory of his earlier involvement with Harrison at Lincoln Center. Eventually, it didn't matter much. Like the great washout farther up the Hudson, Battery Park City, as the project was usually called, never materialized as Philip might have envisioned it. (It was finally built, in the 1980s, by a different team of architects, with Cesar Pelli getting most of the credit.)

To the extent that Philip enjoyed success as a planner, it occurred more in the private than in the public sector, and even then not without travail. No venture illustrated the trade-off more than the nearly decade-long project that was conceived originally as a large-scale reconstitution of the New York University campus at Washington Square.

In the course of the free and easy social life that kept him constantly in the company of financially as well as intellectually influential people,

GOVERNOR
NELSON ROCKEFELLER,
MAYOR JOHN V. LINDSAY,
AND PHILIP JOHNSON,
C. 1965

Philip struck up a friendship with Mr. and Mrs. Charles Wrightsman that flourished during the 1960s. It was Mrs. Wrightsman who, in the culture whirl of Manhattan, discovered Philip, succumbed to his charms, and commended him to her husband.

Charles Wrightsman stood for *big oil,* the stuff that had already greased the wheels of Philip's carriage of ambition more than once—witness his earlier relations with the Rockefellers, the de Menils, and Jane Blaffer Owen. Oil also nourished Wrightsman's aspirations, earning him a trusteeship at the Metropolitan Museum of Art and the directorship of the 1964 New York World's Fair, positions that by themselves brought him close to Johnson. Relations grew closer still on several summer voyages on the couple's yacht around the islands of the Aegean Sea.

Wrightsman was also a figure of consequence in the councils of New York University, the largest single institution of higher learning in the country in the early 1960s. That was a very good time for American academe as a whole, a period of optimism and apparently boundless growth, and NYU, owner already of much of the land around Washington Square, felt called upon to expand itself on those holdings. By then not only friendly with Philip but convinced that he was the architect to carry out such a development, Wrightsman persuaded university president James Hester to hire him. In December of 1964, Philip, together with Richard Foster, whom he had coaxed into rejoining him for this and several other commissions, disclosed plans for a huge rebuilding program that would not only have added to but substantially altered the neighborhood mostly to the east and south of Washington Square Park.

The square had a long history cherished by the people who lived on or around it. Its west and north edges, notable for a number of handsome small-scaled early-nineteenth-century row houses, had been declared a historic district by the city, while the south edge was marked in its own right by several distinguished works, chief among them McKim, Mead & White's Judson Memorial Baptist Church of 1893. Yet it was along this south apron and the area to the east that Philip proposed putting up a group of large new buildings. His keystone structure would be a library designed to rise to a height of 150 feet, more than twice that of the limits of the cornice lines along the south edge. While an even more dramatic component of his plan—the transformation of Washington Place eastward off the square into a three-block-long mall covered by a glass-covered galleria—was dismissed at an early stage of the planning, the rest of the big-boned Johnson-Foster project was promoted aggressively by the university.

It was no less vigorously opposed, mostly by the residents of the Greenwich Village community, whose clamorous resistance was addressed partly to the intrusiveness of the building Philip wanted to carry out, partly to the ambition of the university, which they feared would institutionalize the neighborhood, effectively taking it over. Both grievances were tartly summed up by Philip's old bane Jane Jacobs, who, mindful that the library would cast a long shadow on the square, declared, "All the glamour of Philip Johnson won't save that corner of the park from gloom." She then added, "The two elements most destructive of urban parks are highways and educational institutions."

In the interminable wrangling among battalions of debaters from both sides, Philip gave as good as he got, arguing that the square could accommodate itself to height since its erstwhile modest scale had long since been modified by several tall buildings on the east edge that his opponents had learned to live with. In the end, he and NYU won some but, especially in view of the loss of the galleria, a good deal less than all of what they had campaigned for. The library, named the Elmer Holmes Bobst Library in honor of the NYU trustee who donated $6 million to it, was completed in 1973, a great boxy red sandstone monolith in the generic modernist mode, with an interior dominated by a capacious four-sided atrium that was promptly dubbed "the square Guggenheim." It belongs neither to his more nor to his less persuasive achievements, and its acceptance by the neighborhood has remained all in all loveless. Two other buildings, Tisch Hall (1972) and the Hagop Kevorkian Center for Near Eastern Studies (1973), plus the facade of the André and Bella Meyer Hall of Physics (1972), were realized, completing the sum of the Johnson-Foster team's nine long years of urbanistic exertion.

OUTPACED AND RESTORED

BY THE YOUNG

In the late 1960s, Philip felt his age for the first time in a variety of ways. In July of 1966, he passed his sixtieth birthday and slightly more than a month later was subjected to a ruder and more abrupt lesson in his own mortality. On their return to New York from work on the Kreeger House in Washington, he and Richard Foster missed their scheduled flight and agreed to join three other men who had chartered a single-engine airplane that would carry them all to Danbury, Connecticut. Several miles short of the airfield, the motor died and the pilot's efforts to restart it failed. Philip remembered the situation clearly, especially the "curious serenity" that overcame him as he found himself detachedly studying the configuration of the treetops visible through the window and rising rapidly to meet him. The plane drifted in eerie silence for a few minutes, setting itself down at last in a field and slowing its forward speed enough that when it hit a rut and flipped over, the shock was not enough to cause anyone more than minor injury. Philip escaped with a bruised arm. Apprised of the accident, David Whitney hurried over from nearby New Canaan to fetch his friend, whose unearthly calm quickly gave way to an overwhelming desire for a stiff drink, which he satisfied back at the Glass House, more than once or twice, until he gave himself up to his bed and, next day, to a massive hangover.

Death summoned his attention with less force but no less gravity three years later, in 1969, when he realized that during the previous single decade the giants had passed, all the great men whose work had been the model and measure of the modern architectural world he knew: Wright in 1959, Le Corbusier in 1965, Gropius and Mies in 1969. Closer to home, The Museum of Modern Art, his refuge and personal pulpit for what had seemed a lifetime, accepted the resignations of Alfred Barr in 1967 and of René d'Harnoncourt a year later.

Other changes were subtler. Toward the end of the 1960s, it gradually dawned on him not only that a new generation was at hand but that it was the first to steal from him the position at the forefront of the van that he had so long and so easily maintained. He was suddenly uncomfortably close to being old hat.

To some extent he had himself to blame. He let his cutting edge go dull, as two pieces of his own writing from the late 1960s bore out. Still wrestling with the issue of city planning, he chose the popular magazine *Look* as the forum for an article published in 1968 under the title "Architecture: A Twentieth Century Flop." In the opening passages, he argued, typically, for the cause of great monuments: "After all, everyone in Athens worked on the Acropolis, even Socrates. What great communal project do you and I work on? No, civic pride is not an 'in' sentiment right now . . .

"Cities of the last century have not vied with each other for beauty, but for belching smoke, freight-car loadings and population growth. It was incidental that even single monuments were ever built."

This much of his prose seemed an echo of his lifelong hostility toward mobocracy, commercialism, parliamentary government, all the rot of the modern world. Then, however, he went on to acknowledge that "our problems have changed. . . . Our dimensions, like our wars, have escalated, with millions to house, millions to transport, millions to feed, nothing that mere billions of dollars can help. . . .

"With no help from spiritual fathers, the younger architects have to start dreaming anew. . . . The alternative is too frightening—bigger and bigger slums stretching into megacities like the one we already have on the Eastern Seaboard from Washington to Maine. . . .

"Quite simply," he concluded, "the megacity requires megastructures. The problems are out of scale; the new architecture will appear to some out of scale. The megastructure does not yet exist; the new environment does not exist, but it must, and it will. It will if management is ready. It will if the public is ready. Above all, it will when our civilization is ready to create architecture."

True to his taste for grandeur, Philip was once again proposing a great concept, no mere cut-and-paste affair but an Olympian exercise in city planning so large in scale that he himself could not define it except by the generality of the *mega* prefix.

One must presume he knew that the very abstractness of the solution he offered to the mammoth societal problem he posed was proof that the

problem was beyond his solution—hence his reliance on the dodge of his
own rhetoric, his own salesmanship, which in this instance had very little
to offer a public that did not understand "megastructures" and a body
politic unprepared to give high priority to the control of them.

The new generation, with whom Philip had little close contact but
who were now stirring urgently and audibly, struck a different stance, in
fact several alternative stances vis-à-vis architecture as a whole and urbanism in particular. Great concepts, Gordian knot–cutting solutions and
revolutionary programs, for that matter wistful yearnings after past golden
ages, were precisely what did not interest them—especially one of them,
Robert Venturi of Philadelphia, who produced a book in 1966, *Complexity and Contradiction in Architecture,* that more than any other publication of
the period sounded the death knell of the modern movement. The introduction was written by Philip's old friend from Yale, Vincent Scully, who
judged Venturi's text "probably the most important writing on architecture since Le Corbusier's *Vers une Architecture* of 1923." Venturi's opening
sentence, "I like complexity and contradiction in architecture," was followed by his complaint that "Orthodox Modern architects have tended
to recognize complexity insufficiently or inconsistently. In their attempt
to break with tradition and start all over again, they idealized the primitive and elementary at the expense of the diverse and the sophisticated."

It was a widely encompassing indictment, aimed chiefly at the International Stylists and their heirs, Philip included. Venturi displayed a knowledge of history that rivaled even Philip's but that led him to his own
conclusions. ". . . Peter Blake," Venturi wrote, referring to another old
friend of Philip's, "has compared the chaos of Main Street with the order-
liness of the University of Virginia. Besides the irrelevancy of the comparison, is not Main Street almost all right? Indeed, is not the commercial
strip of a Route 66 almost all right? . . . The seemingly chaotic juxtapo-
sitions of honky-tonk elements express an intriguing kind of vitality and
validity, and they produce an unexpected approach to unity as well."

While Venturi discussing Main Street sounded like Philip in one of his
occasional cynical salutes to urban chaos, the real difference was that Venturi was not being cynical at all and Philip deep in his heart and contrary
to previous protestations had no taste whatever for chaos. And honky-
tonk stood for chaos. Worse still, it stood against monumentality, the
architectural condition that Philip had striven for through all his shifts of
manner.

There were other differences, as well. In 1966, the same year as Venturi's book, Philip wrote a review of a book, *The Puzzle of Architecture,* by
the Australian critic Robin Boyd, that he found a "description of the sit-

uation today in the world of architectural design [that] is completely convincing." Unlike Venturi, Boyd was less critical of the modern movement than absorbed with dividing it as of the mid-1960s into three phases, the first, in Philip's paraphrasing, roughly equivalent to the International Style ("Today Mies is the lone giant . . . of the First Phase"); the second, preoccupied with "arbitrary shapes" and "preconceived geometric volumes" (Philip identified himself and to a degree Paul Rudolph, Edward Durell Stone, and Kenzo Tange with this phase); the third, with "functional elements . . . picked out and exaggerated to make breaks and strength of intent," as in passages in Kahn, James Stirling, and John Johansen.

Johnson's own friends came to find Venturi's analysis more penetrating than that of either Philip or Boyd. Robert A. M. Stern, one of the younger architects with whom Philip was close in the mid-1960s, and later one of his more-than-occasional champions, remarked in 1979 on the two differing positions:

"Johnson was fascinated by [Boyd's] book, which for a long time he felt offered a Rosetta stone to the new directions in architecture and which now, rather contrary to Boyd's intentions, seems little more than an account of modernism in disarray. All three of the 'phases' that Boyd discusses and Johnson makes so much of merely document parallel tendencies in the Modern Movement as it was playing out its hand in the mid-1960s and do not touch on the really new directions, which were then already quite clearly articulated in the work of Venturi, [Charles] Moore and [Romaldo] Giurgola—work that Johnson was aware of but felt unsure about."

Philip was indeed just that—aware and unsure. He knew who Venturi was, and Stern, too, having already treated both, the latter especially, with his characteristic professional generosity. In 1965, asked by the Architectural League to run a program of exhibitions, he recommended instead that the assignment go to Stern, one of the brightest Yalies of the Johnson years, often described by Philip as "the best student I ever had." The most widely discussed of Stern's efforts—which were monitored by Johnson—was "40 Under 40," a review of younger American architects, among them Venturi and Charles Moore. As for Venturi's book, Philip supported its publication by The Museum of Modern Art and recognized its importance. Even if he did not rejoice in the message it conveyed, he credited its author with the attribute, intelligence, that he prized more highly than all other human conditions.

Yet he kept his distance from the Stern-Venturi-Moore contingent and from the architect they seemed determined to elevate to the stature of a modern master of first magnitude, Louis Kahn. Philip had, after all, successes of his own that seemed to him grounds for ample self-satisfaction. The high place that Ada Louise Huxtable accorded him was a measure of his good standing in the social and cultural Establishment, even if it left him proportionately further from a younger architectural set he would surely have known intimately ten years earlier.

Moreover, the latter group was hardly homogeneous. By the mid-1960s, another identifiable faction, just as intent as the Venturi circle on using verbal argument to stake out a radical position, was making noises in the New York architectural world. They were purists to the ultimate, equally indifferent to Venturi's contextual concerns and the social and economic priorities long promoted by Lewis Mumford. They went Philip one better in their belief in architecture as an art, professing a passion for abstract form and heavy theory that he, self-confessed "functional eclectic," after all, had customarily been too pragmatic to espouse. "Architecture beyond accommodation" was the way one of them, Charles Gwathmey, expressed their most earnest commitment. "We all try to make buildings that are also ideas." Most closely identified with Gwathmey, in attitude if not in individual architectural style, were four others, all in their thirties: Peter Eisenman, Michael Graves, John Hejduk, and Richard Meier. Together they became known as "the Five," a name attached to them more or less formally in an exhibition staged at The Museum of Modern Art in 1972.

The most aggressively intellectualizing of the group was Eisenman, who in his special passion for verbal exchange was largely instrumental in founding the Institute for Architecture and Urban Studies in 1967. A combined school and discussion forum that prided itself on its nontraditional approach to whatever it touched, the institute invited artists, architects, and thinkers at large from all over the world, the more problematical the better, with the prime purpose of talking, talking, and talking some more about architecture and writing as much of it down as privately collected funds permitted.

Philip knew what Venturi, Stern, Eisenman, and the rest were doing. But he did not much like the buildings any of them designed and he had more pressing things to do than spend time seeking any of them out—or so he thought.

On the other hand, the time had come at last for traditional modernism, long criticized, long agonized over, but widely practiced anyhow in one form or another, to be confronted with several effectively combative alternatives. The late 1960s were nothing if not driven by the winds of revolution in all corners of the United States. It was common to associate the frustrations that attended the Vietnam war and the civil rights movement with the shredding of national community and the blurring of urbanistic purpose, not to mention the reactive growth of a counterculture that looked with distaste on high art, high culture, and bourgeois morality. There is little wonder then that Venturi, reasoning from a culturally disenthralled point of view, found new satisfaction in *Learning from Las Vegas* (the title of his second book, published in 1972) and in promoting the "decorated shed" as a more valid architectural model than the heroic postulations of the modernists.

In turn, the same perceptions led Eisenman and his theory-prone, abstraction-minded colleagues to move in a direction that was similar in its very oppositeness: to recognize the ineffectiveness of a dying cause but to quit the humdrum and herd, to reject the vernacular rather than ally themselves with it, to aspire instead to a realm of pure ideation and form qua form.

None of this was lost on Philip, who nevertheless found himself for the first time in his adult life positioned off the pace. Younger architects, Stern later remembered, were increasingly critical of him, identifying him with conservative rather than forward-looking values. Even his office schedule was suffering. He had been without a working associate since Richard Foster walked away in 1962 to seek his own fortunes as an independent architect. Foster returned several years later to help on the NYU project, but that was temporary and both he and Philip knew it. Philip also recalled how much better he fared when he had someone at his side who could not only assist in designing but, more important, could deal with administrative matters for which he had historically shown little aptitude.

With these various goblins, ideological as well as practical, making a racket in his brain, he called upon one of his fundamental characterological assets, resilience, a faculty that had helped him rebound more than once from adversity, to begin a slow process of restoring confidence in himself and luster to his career. The sensible first step was to reorganize his practice. In 1967, he welcomed thirty-four-year-old John Burgee of Chicago into his office.

Their meeting occurred in the normal course of business. Philip had agreed to seek the commission for a major new airport in Philadelphia in tandem with his old Harvard chum Carter Manny, now a principal in the huge and highly successful Chicago firm of C. F. Murphy Associates.

With Burgee as his assistant, Manny had headed Murphy's mammoth O'Hare airport project several years earlier, and Burgee was among the team Manny took to the job interview in Philadelphia. Philip, much taken by Burgee when he met him, passed his compliments on to Manny, who relayed them to his young colleague. Burgee was as quick to seize an opportunity as to sense it. He was shortly in touch with Philip.

Burgee had grown up in Chicago, in a quintessentially architectural environment. His father had been a partner at Holabird, Root & Burgee, one of the city's oldest offices, where John worked briefly after taking his architecture degree from the University of Notre Dame in 1956. Fully at ease in the atmosphere of a utilitarian city that regarded utilitarian architecture as more nearly a way of life than an art, he moved on to Murphy, where he quickly became one of the firm's ablest younger players. C. F. Murphy Associates was among the offices most affected by and deferential to Mies van der Rohe's immense authority in Chicago; among its principal designers were Jacques Brownson and Gene Summers, both former students of Mies at Illinois Institute of Technology—as was Manny. Burgee learned not only an architectural frame of reference at Murphy but the mastery of practical methods and working techniques, assets for which Chicago firms as a whole were widely renowned.

On paper, then, as well as in person, he looked promising to Philip. Tall, poised, and articulate, Burgee cut a fine figure in meetings, where he left no doubt about what he wanted and how it should be realized. Philip made it clear he wanted him, withholding a formal offer only long enough to avoid the appearance of plundering Murphy's ranks.

Ironically, when the Johnson-Murphy team came close to winning the airport commission, Philip found his relations with Burgee even more conflicted: "My God," he said, "we might get that job commission. Then we could never get together!"

They didn't and they did. The selection committee recommended the Johnson-Murphy team, but the local political kingpins overruled them, awarding the commission to Philadelphia architect Vincent Kling. Philip then disclosed his intentions to Manny, who tried to retain Burgee by sweetening the pot at Murphy. It was no use. Within several months, Burgee had begun a new and ultimately fateful phase in his own career and Philip's.

If Burgee was the most important person to enter Philip's professional life in the 1960s, his equivalent at the personal level was Philip's last and most enduring lover, David Grainger Whitney.

Had Whitney been so inclined, he could have cut nearly as colorful a swath through the New York world of the arts as Philip did; he had all the wit, talent, and intelligence that color required. But he was as uninterested in publicity as Philip was drawn to it, a difference that made the two of them more compatible, if anything, not less. Even so, they visited a good deal of connubial discord upon each other, certainly in their early years together, if not in far serener later ones. It was just as well that the public image Philip enjoyed was more than enough for both of them.

Born in Worcester, Massachusetts, in 1941 to a banker's family that he recalled with more resentment and bitterness than Philip retained of his own upbringing, Whitney spent several prep school years as a classic misfit at Loomis Institute in Windsor, Connecticut, moving on for a final year and a protohippie life—that is, a happier one—at Woodstock Country School in South Woodstock, Vermont. He then "wandered around" the Rhode Island School of Design for nearly five years, finally picking up a bachelor of architecture degree in 1963. He was still an undergraduate when he heard Philip lecture at Brown University in 1960. Following the talk, the two exchanged a few words that prompted Whitney to ask Philip whether he could see the Glass House sometime.

His interest piqued, Philip said by all means yes, and Whitney on a visit paid shortly thereafter was made welcome enough to spend the night with his host. At the time, Philip's love life was contrapuntally entangled. He had recently broken up with John Hohnsbeen but was still involved with Peter Vranic in a relationship he later described as "very violent, very sexual, very physical, and very short." Thus, with Whitney on the scene before Vranic made his exit, Philip had his hands full. Once Vranic departed and Hohnsbeen moved to Italy, David was available to comfort Philip, even at the distance that separated New York from Providence, where David lived until his graduation from RISD. Thereupon, in 1963, he took a small place of his own in Manhattan, a decision that seemed, at least to him, a happy turn of events until Hohnsbeen came back from Venice for a visit. Philip couldn't resist the prodigal: "You've always been wife number one," he told Hohnsbeen at about the same time he suggested to Whitney that he find something else to do with himself.

Whitney found more solace in the bottle than he could handle. Alcohol became a serious, long-lasting problem, even before Hohnsbeen returned to Venice and Philip invited Whitney back, now to share the Fifty-fifth Street apartment. In brief, then, the Johnson-Whitney relationship in its early stages showed little promise of a stable future. By his own confession, Philip continued for a time to treat his young friend shabbily, leading Whitney to take up counseling with a psychotherapist who advised him to remove himself from a love affair that was the immediate cause of most of his emotional torment. That, Whitney told him, is the one thing I cannot do, therewith fixing in place one of the foundational supports that kept him and Philip together for life. The other leg of the relationship, to be sure, was provided by Philip. It was his age. When he met Whitney, he was in his mid-fifties, hardly old enough, in view of his rather steady concupiscence, to worry about who would care for him in his final years. Still, for all the bad times with Whitney, there were more good ones that sustained the relationship until Philip began think-

DAVID WHITNEY,
C. 1975

ing more seriously about a time that might call for other, less sensate attractions in a companion. Thus Philip's strongly felt need for a partner in the 1960s was filled as surely by Whitney as by John Burgee.

Smoothly handsome but saturnine in disposition, David was probably the smartest of Philip's lovers, surely the most committed to the arts and the most independently accomplished in them. Philip could talk shop with him without feeling he was involved in a monologue. When Whitney moved into the Fifty-fifth Street digs, he gave up any architectural ambitions. "It would have been ludicrous to do that kind of work while I was living with Philip," he recalled, certifying the more passive or feminine role in the relationship that he, like the others before him, played. Instead, he set his critical sights on the art of painting, serving as a designer in the Department of Painting and Sculpture at The Museum of Modern Art until the museum closed for the renovations that led to the 1964 unveiling of the East and Garden wings. Thereafter, he had a series of connections with major Manhattan commercial galleries, fulfilling his duties there with more devotion than John Hohnsbeen had shown toward his own ten years earlier. After stints at Kornblee, Green, and Leo Castelli, Whitney became the assistant to one of the rising stars of the Castelli group, Jasper Johns, and even had a gallery of his own from 1968 to 1971.

For all the political and social unrest of the sixties, they were the decade in which the whole world, not just the American arts and their hangers-on, almost unanimously recognized the ascendancy of the United States to global leadership in painting and sculpture. As Abstract Expressionism and its roster of masters, Jackson Pollock, Willem de Kooning, Mark Rothko, Franz Kline, et al., had dominated the fifties, the sixties belonged to Pop and hard-edge abstraction and such leading representatives of both as Jasper Johns, Roy Lichtenstein, Robert Rauschenberg, Andy Warhol, Morris Louis, Kenneth Noland, and Barnett Newman. Moreover, in the passing of the decades and their respective generations, there seemed if anything a gain rather than a loss in corporate national creative vitality.

Thus it was Whitney's decade, too, and his close relations not only with Philip but with several of the new Manhattan art stars enabled him gradually to supplant Alfred Barr as Philip's chief counselor in buying works for the Johnson collection. His professional activities extended well beyond the household he shared with Philip. From the 1970s onward, the art world came to regard him as a first-rate freelance curator and editor. The solo exhibitions of Jasper Johns, Cy Twombly, David Salle, and Eric Fischl that he organized for the Whitney Museum of American Art (no family relation) remain among the major documents of the work of those artists, while the books he edited and produced on the paintings of Salle, Fischl, and Brice Marden, and on Philip's own Glass House, attained a wide and responsive public.

These labors provided him with the pleasure, to some extent the consolation, of a social life spent largely independent of Philip's. While American life as a whole was freer of sexual taboos in those years than it had been in the 1950s, reformist views had not advanced so far that homosexual relationships were openly tolerated by society at large. And since Philip had long consorted with mainstream types, he continued in the company of Lee Radziwill, John Gielgud, and comparable public icons while making solo appearances at the Wrightsmans, or at Brooke Astor's, or at comparably gilt-edged social functions. This left the openings, vernissages, and studio parties for the most part to David. "High society," Whitney once said, "knows exactly who is living with whom, but they don't want to see you together." Thus David's everyday life in the 1960s was occupied almost as much by Andy Warhol as by Philip. David and Andy would spend an hour each morning sharing gossip about friends and enemies alike.

Whitney was remembered nonetheless as a jealous lover, and not only by Philip. Theodate saw him that way, too, although her longtime closeness with her brother, more than a little possessive in its own right, did not ensure her objective judgment.

At the beginning of the 1960s, she had little immediate cause to see David as a rival. Not only was he a recent fact of Philip's life, but she, taken up with duties as the new publisher of the magazine *Musical America,* had lately been involved in a romance of her own with Scott Severns, a Manhattan dentist, which led to a marriage—her third—in 1961. Philip was best man at the wedding. On the way out of the office of the justice of the peace, he remarked offhandedly, "Oh! I almost forgot your wedding gift," then handed Theodate and Scott the deed to a choice flat in the distinguished old Dakota apartment building on Central Park West. Not content with that, he granted them the use on weekends of a big old brown farmhouse that stood at the eastern edge of his property in New Canaan. Such largesse was as much a part of Philip's makeup as a willingness to withdraw it as summarily as he offered it. Theodate never forgot or quite recovered from an encounter with him in the mid-1960s when he stopped her on the New Canaan grounds and announced—abruptly, as she recalled it—that if she had any furniture of her own in the brown house, she'd better get it out of there quickly: "David and I need that house for ourselves." From that day forward, her place in Philip's life was never the same and she never stopped blaming David for it. Philip, on the other hand, according to Burgee, claimed that his reasons for removing his sister stemmed from her possessive affection for him, something David—especially David—was not likely to endure gladly.

For all of that, Philip never gave up control of his own society, including his time spent with women. Sexual encounters were rare, sexual entanglements rarer still; yet his ease in commanding not only the respect but the affection of women led to several of the most civilized relationships of his life. His friendships with Iris Barry, Blanchette Rockefeller, and Sibyl Moholy-Nagy have been reported here. Later, he would form similar bonds with others, including, notably, the art critic Rosamond

Bernier, the Museum of Modern Art trustee Barbara Jakobson, and the president of the museum, Agnes Gund. Yet none of these women ever surpassed the steadfast tenderness offered him for most of half a century by Eliza Bliss Parkinson Cobb.

The niece of Lillie Bliss, one of the founders of the museum, Eliza met Philip early in the 1930s when she and he were involved in committee activities at the then-still-young institution. She was not only moneyed and well placed but, in Russell Lynes's words, "as earnest as she was pretty," and Philip had no trouble liking her immensely. It was less her marriage in 1932 to John Parkinson, which lasted only briefly, than Philip's departure from the museum in 1934 that kept her apart from

PHILIP JOHNSON AND
ELIZA BLISS PARKINSON,
C. 1970

Philip until he returned to New York in the mid-1940s. Thereafter, and especially during the 1950s and 1960s, they were frequently and fondly in each other's company. She was a regular at the Sunday-afternoon gatherings in New Canaan, and she became one of his favored partners on vacation trips. They spent winter holidays occasionally at Cuernavaca and summer idylls even more often at Eliza's ranch, Silvertip, in Montana.

For him, these were special periods of respite and she was ideally suited to share them with him. Since he took them for relaxation, a condition he welcomed precisely because it did not come naturally to him, he delighted in what he described as her unclinging devotion and her intelligence, which, if not schooled, was equal to all their exchanges. And they could be silent together. Best of all, she knew how to put up with him and his caprices and to like him all the more for it, a gift that seems to have been common to the best of Philip's women. "Today I'm feeling depressed," she confessed to him one day when they met. "Thank God," she remembered his responding. "I am, too. And I've been saying to myself, If she's in an up mood today, I won't be able to stand it."

Eliza had her own very affirmative image of Philip. She was struck by something about him that would have surprised his city friends: He was quite at home in the forests and hills around Silvertip, where they made a point of going almost annually for twenty years. He knew the local flora cold, as if the botany his mother had drilled him in on the front lawn at Townsend Farm had been fully and permanently assimilated. He was, Eliza further claimed, an excellent horseman.

More and more, talk around New York in the late 1960s had it that Eliza and Philip were lovers. She had been unmarried for more than thirty years, but she was still attractive. It seemed clear enough that she cared for Philip as much as he appeared to care for her. His liaison with David, while familiar to intimates, was not known or else not taken seriously by many of the tattlers around town who savored speculation about the private lives of public people. Might he marry Eliza? Perhaps when he retires? Or when he turns seventy, or seventy-five?

The truth, of course, was that neither he nor she harbored any such intentions. David belonged to Philip and Philip and Eliza knew it. What Philip, the accomplished old networker, did not know was that Eliza had a real lover, whom she had been seeing for most of the time she was close to Philip, although Philip didn't learn of this until after the lover died.

Eliza did at last take a second husband, Henry Ives Cobb, whom she married in 1982. She and Philip remained the best of friends.

PART FIVE

SUPERSTARDOM

1967-

John Burgee was equal parts ambition and circumspection when he moved into Philip's office in the Seagram Building in 1967. While he was obviously the junior man, he was not content to be an employee; he wanted, and got, a percentage of the profits in an arrangement that he presumed—rightly, as matters turned out—would lead someday to a formal partnership. At the same time, he was unclear about the reasons for the departure of Philip's most recent assistant, Richard Foster, and uneasy as well, especially when Foster declined to discuss the matter with him. On arrival at his desk, he learned, moreover, that there was less work on hand than he had led himself to expect. Philip was living in customary grand style, but he had more jobs in his head, as Burgee remembered it, than in his hand. An addition to the old McKim, Mead & White Boston Public Library was in the works, but it had already gone through several costly stages and appeared on the verge of cancellation. Philip had secured a contract to design an American headquarters building for Mercedes-Benz, but the scheme he proposed was never built. Neither were a shopping center, Broadway Junction, and a high-rise apartment development, Chelsea Walk, meant respectively for sites in Brooklyn and Manhattan. Burgee heard talk of a possible move from the Seagram Building quarters to a less expensive place.

More positively, Philip did succeed in bringing the design of two buildings to completion several years later, the Neuberger Museum for the State University of New York at Purchase and the Niagara Falls Convention Center. Meanwhile, however, Burgee spent most of his time in the early months of his tenure shuttling back and forth to Boston and finish-

ing the library project, while he began to entertain doubts that there
would be enough work in the office to keep two people busy on a sustained schedule.

Luck struck abruptly and unexpectedly from out of the west, and with
comparable suddenness the Johnson-Burgee relationship achieved a complementarity each man had longed for. At first, no signs of it were apparent in their meeting with the people from Minnesota who approached
them with a potential commission. Two major corporations, the
Investors' Diversified Services and the Dayton Company, had joined in a
plan to put up a fifty-one-story building in the city both were quartered
in, Minneapolis. A local architect, Edward F. Baker, had already produced
a scheme for them when Ken Dayton, who was a serious collector of
modern art, proposed they check it out with a famous architect. He suggested they show it to Philip Johnson.

When the Minneapolis delegation showed up at the Seagram Building,
they encountered a cool, unresponsive Burgee. "What is it you want us
to do?" he asked. "You've already got a plan. We are not interested in
putting a skin on Mr. Baker's building. It's not what we do."

This was Burgee talking the Chicago tongue he had learned at C. F.
Murphy, where big buildings were standard fare and negotiations over the
control of them were usually conducted in short declarative sentences.
Philip, who had done most of his work at smaller scale and as often as not
for personal or institutional friends, listened in quiet fascination as his
young colleague let the Minneapolitans know that if they wanted John-
son/Burgee at all, they would get all Johnson/Burgee and nothing and
nobody else. With that much understood, Philip was in a perfect position
to take over, to do what he could do far better than anyone, Burgee
included—namely, persuade his listeners that they had hired a major creative artist, who happened to have an enforcer working for him.

On one of their examinations of the Minneapolis site, which took up
one half of a block on the Nicollet Mall, Johnson and Burgee observed
that it provided room for their tall tower and nothing more—nothing,
that is, like a plaza or similar open space, which, following the classic
example of the Seagram Building, had become a popular appurtenance to
high-rise buildings in the late 1960s. If their IDS building was to be all it
could be and justify its far greater height than any of its neighbors in
downtown Minneapolis, it would have to have the whole block to itself.
The clients proceeded at considerable pains to provide them with that.

Effectively, Johnson and Burgee clipped the four corners off a rectangular plan, thus slimming the building volume perceptibly. Each clipped
edge was articulated in a rank of serrated notches that provided corner

IDS (INVESTORS' DIVERSIFIED SERVICES) CENTER, MINNEAPOLIS, 1973
(JOHN BURGEE, PARTNER)

Richard Payne

views for fully thirty-two offices per floor. Whatever similarity an observer may have noted between their octagonal plan and that of a recently completed building in New York that both of them despised— the Pan Am Building (designed in large part by Philip's old bugbear Wal-

IDS CENTER:
VIEW OF
CRYSTAL
COURT

Richard Payne

ter Gropius)—was diminished not only by the serrations but by cladding the entire six-hundred-foot shaft in a newly developed chrome-coated reflective glass that produced an abundance of shifting light and shadow effects on the building's surface. The result was a structure clearly modernist in style but exceptional in profile, an inventive deviation from the Miesian rectangular prism that had become one of the clichés of the American urban skyline.

What Johnson and Burgee did at ground level was more exceptional still. Since the negotiations that secured the entire block had transformed the project into a program of mixed use, the designers, abetted further by an awareness of the cold Minneapolis climate, decided to erect a building at each of the four corners of the site—the fifty-one-story tower, a nineteen-story annex with a three-story bank at its base, a sixteen-story hotel, and a two-story retail unit—and to roof over the space in between them. Thus the plaza was transformed into a huge atrium—the Crystal Court— made more visually engaging by an open three-dimensional network of plastic- and glass-defined cubes overhead and more socially attractive by the amenities installed within a climate-controlled interior. Philip's description of the atrium as "the Seagram Building turned inside out" seemed reasonable enough, although the asymmetry of the plan and elevation at IDS, together with a repetition of the exterior motif of serrations, created a spatial syncopation very unlike the stately rhythms of the Seagram Building.

The IDS Center was not only the first striking critical success of the Johnson/Burgee office but one of the most significant redefinitions of the form of the tall building to appear in the post–World War II years. While the Museum of South Texas in Corpus Christi, a bandbox of concrete that resembled a finely crafted soap sculpture, was finished a year earlier and well received at the time, it was the Minneapolis complex that carried two noteworthy reminders to the profession, especially to the young radicals: that Philip remained a figure of consequence and that the modernist manner itself might still be employed more inventively than many of its detractors, himself included, had been saying for a decade or more.

Moreover, no other style name is more readily applicable than modernism to the Fort Worth Water Garden, begun in 1970 and completed in 1975 and one of the most lightsome and mesmerizing works in his catalogue. It was commissioned by the Amon Carter Foundation, which had bought a patch of ground in a dilapidated section of Fort Worth and instructed Johnson and Burgee to put a public park on it. The result was a grouping of paved and planted spaces that rose capriciously to the height of hillocks or descended the same way to pools and fountains, all via pathways and terraces that in plan resembled a geometrically abstracted contour map. The layout of IDS was brought to mind by the placement of major features centrifugally away from a central open area. The most thoroughly engrossing element was a waterfall that rushed downward over various levels of slotted stone until increased pressure funneled it into a small basin at the bottom that was forever abroil with foam. To follow the water over the rock surfaces was an experience at once bracing and daunting, exactly what Philip had in mind when he spoke warmly of danger as a motive in the art of design.

Richard Payne

FORT WORTH WATER GARDEN, FORT WORTH, 1975
(JOHN BURGEE, PARTNER)

By the end of 1972, the signs of unease John Burgee had perceived in the Johnson office five years earlier had almost completely dissolved. Philip had agreed to make him a formal partner. Equally important, the firm's fortunes were on the rise, propelled by a force that more and more originated in Texas, where prosperity had been a fact of life for well over a decade, seemingly with no end in sight.

In the same year, 1970, that Philip began work on the Water Garden, he and Burgee received a call from a Houston developer who identified himself as Gerald Hines. No leader in his field—in fact, a wary, even timid man, as they both remembered him from their first encounter—he had never heard of them nor they of him. He found their names in the phone book, acting on the request of his client, I. S. Brochstein, a tough-minded Russian immigrant who had grown rich in Texas as a builder and who now wanted to construct something on land he owned at the western edge of the city. If Hines didn't know the two New York architects he had rung up, Brochstein did. His own experience in the construction field had convinced him that Johnson was the man he wanted for the job.

Thus, the relationship between Johnson/Burgee and Hines began neutrally, even unimpressively, with no hint of the immense success that they would enjoy together in years to come. Meanwhile, Philip got on famously with Brochstein as soon as he met him. The commission granted, he proceeded with the design of Post Oak Central I, II, and III, a trio of speculative buildings that recalled, of all things, the Art Moderne manner that Philip had so detested during its salad days of the 1930s but that he was willing to imitate now for reasons of economy. "We thought of the cheapest things you could do," Burgee explained, "and they were ribbon windows, setbacks, and curved corners."

Richard Payne

POST OAK CENTRAL I, II,
AND III, HOUSTON, 1976–
1981 (JOHN BURGEE,
PARTNER)

Before the first phase of Post Oak was finished in 1976, Gerald Hines was busy with another Houston client, a corporate executive with his own reputation for hardheadedness who might be willing to sit still for Johnson and Burgee. J. Hugh Liedtke of Pennzoil was an old wildcatter from the oil fields of Pennsylvania who both sounded and smoked like one. Pennzoil wanted a new building big enough to make an impact on the landscape but not so big that it would only tempt a competitor to erect something bigger nearby next week. "This is Texas," Liedtke explained, adding his overriding desire that people would think PENNZOIL when they looked at his building. *Identity* was what mattered, he declared, not size. Reasonably, he didn't want "another upturned cigar box," yet the very rectilinearity he deplored Hines thought most saleable, and Hines's opinion counted, since he wanted space in the project for his own speculative purposes.

After considerable reflection and Hines's acquisition of a second major tenant, the Zapata Corporation, Johnson and Burgee proposed a scheme that was close to the one finally built. If Hines didn't care for it, Liedtke did, and the major decisions rested finally with him. It consisted of two buildings trapezoidal in plan, with the obtuse angle of each very nearly touching that of the other, across two triangular-shaped lobbies that narrowed as they approached the point of "the kiss," as the buildings' close adjacency has been called. An implicit path carried diagonally from one corner of the block to the other, and it was the diagonal as a formal element that prompted Burgee to propose a design for the tops of their two structures. Each thirty-six-story volume would be lopped off at a forty-five-degree angle, with both towers sloping downward, in opposite directions from the point where they faced each other. Hines didn't like that idea, either. Liedtke did. It stayed. Liedtke had also made it clear he hated aluminum and "that shiny-shit glass"; don't use them, he instructed the architects, who used them anyhow, anodizing the aluminum bronze and coming up with a softly bronze-tinted glass coated with a substance that reflected the sun's rays while preserving the transparency of the glass.

Liedtke was placated. He especially found the roof line a splendid device by which a uniquely Pennzoil image could be conveyed. Identity, that precious desideratum, was further readable at the base of the building, where reliance on the diagonal led Johnson/Burgee to roof over each triangular lobby with a frame of glass that made the buildings as recognizable from the street as from the air. Or from the local expressways: Houston was and is an automobile town, and Pennzoil's exceptional silhouette traced against the vast Texas sky is one of the visual phenomena most readily seized and remembered in the few seconds available to viewers who ride more often than they walk.

The January–February 1973 issue of *Architectural Forum* was devoted entirely to the recent work of Philip Johnson, whose portrait by Andy Warhol appeared on the cover. It was the most public signal that he had recovered much of his stature within the profession, although the magazine's prose was so unstinting in its affirmation that no inference could be drawn about the ambiguous position he occupied in the mid- to late 1960s. In the lead essay Paul Goldberger even seemed unpersuaded that there had been any dip in his fortunes: ". . . his work since [the early 1960s] is notable for a freshness of form that confirms his movement away from Mies and his position as one of the most original as well as eminent architects in America today."

PENNZOIL PLACE, HOUSTON, 1976
(JOHN BURGEE, PARTNER)

At a distance of two decades, that assessment may read as immoderate; it is less easy in the 1990s to think of Philip as an "original" architect than as one who followed, ratified, and refined (on rare occasions even caricatured) forms invented by someone else. Yet in 1973, the IDS Center had just been completed and Pennzoil was under construction, two buildings that appeared to have substantially revitalized the skyscraper as an architectural genre. While neither was executed in strict International Style, both reflected a cleanly abstracted geometry that could be tracked to the Miesian example. In retrospect, one may be tempted to wonder how much Philip, had he sustained the momentum implicit in both works, might have done to revivify the modernist esthetic in architecture.

No sooner born, the temptation dies, or surely gives way to major qualifications. Everything in Philip's history suggests that he has not been good at sustaining an expressive position. Anyhow, no clear majority of the architectural world agreed with the *Forum's* extravagant praise. Philip was still in the process of adjusting to the onset of the younger architects who had worked so strenuously to take over the leadership of the van, and there were so many of them in such variety, and so ironclad in their convictions, that the period would have required a circumstance of tremendous cultural gravitational force—or a singular genius—to pull them into one or even several clearly traceable orbits. The centrifugal movement of the 1960s did not stop, but only accelerated.

Indeed, pluralism became a standard term, not to say bromide, of critical parlance in the 1970s, a device meant to encompass expressive views various enough to discourage encompassment. In addition to the groups already mentioned here who jockeyed for a central position in the avant-garde, the more conservative forces—one thinks of the Miesian loyalists in Chicago or the Corbusian brutalists everywhere—were still plentiful, still active. Added to these were new rationalists, representationalists, semioticists, organicists, ad hoc urbanists, and hybrids of all of these and more; proponents of "high-tech" materials and prefabricated systems; unclassifiable eccentrics of the widest assortment; and designers of demonstrable talent emerging in major and minor countries in Europe and Asia, where little seemed to have happened in the first two postwar decades. Upholding the values of the counterculture and the New Left were the ranks of the loudly disaffected, who declared that architects did not deserve the luxury of regarding themselves as artists: It was building—or tearing down—that was called for in a corrupt America, not "architecture." Meanwhile, running alongside, or beneath, or above, or through these various developments was the crippling recession of the early 1970s, which diminished the possibilities of actual construction everywhere in the country.

Architecture, ironically, had grown into a sphere of activity that fulfilled
or even exceeded the goals of an ancient yearning of Philip's: It had
become not only an arena of argument but a near Babel, where new journals and new critics strove to outdo one another in the abstruseness of their
prose and where intellectual contention threatened to replace design as the
currency of the profession. Accordingly, some of the debaters maintained
that that was a false distinction: Theory *was* architecture and vice versa;
certainly the two could not be separated. Philip had never been comfortable in the confinements of theory. But that kind of talk, and the kind of
people who most indulged in it, captured his attention, partly because he
adored talking, hardly less because he realized he had lost touch with the
young while he was riding in the woods with Eliza Parkinson and sunning
himself on the Aegean with the Wrightsmans. At the turn of the 1970s, he
began to involve himself in the activities of the Institute for Architecture
and Urban Studies, where the fiercest polemics were daily fare.

The IAUS was founded in the fall of 1967, mostly by people who had
spent much of the 1960s in enterprises connected with city planning.
Among them was Arthur Drexler, who, earlier the same year, had made
his Department of Architecture and Design at The Museum of Modern
Art the stage for an exhibition—"The New City and Urban Renewal"—
that was made up of work by members of the faculties of four major
university architecture schools: Columbia, Massachusetts Institute of
Technology, Princeton, and Yale. One of the Princeton team was Peter
Eisenman, whose involvement in the show led to a close friendship with
Drexler and the mutual decision to create an organization that would foster more and better intellectual exchange among practitioners, students,
and lay friends of contemporary architecture. The IAUS was the result, "a
halfway house," as Eisenman characterized it, "between academe and the
profession."

Philip was not party to these germinal activities. His principal institutional relationship was with the museum, and Drexler, according to
Eisenman, preferred to keep him, together with his generosity, focused
on the Architecture and Design Department. On the other hand, on
behalf of the fledgling institute, Drexler gained the blessings of MoMA
director René d'Harnoncourt and the agreement of MoMA trustees Lily
Auchincloss and Armand Bartos to join the new board of the IAUS.

Eisenman was named to the directorship. While he barely knew Johnson at the time, he was aware that Philip knew just enough about him to
hold his work in rather low esteem. He had lately concentrated on the
design of aggressively unfunctional houses, white, abstract, severe, and

outwardly somewhat reflective of the cuboid forms used by Le Corbusier in the 1920s. Philip found them ungainly and ill-proportioned. Nevertheless, Eisenman was as compulsive and ambitious a promoter of his new institute as Philip was a likely candidate for interest in and support of it. Each responded to the other and to the pleasure both took in self-salesmanship. It was only a matter of time before they were linked by highly personal ends in a growing symbiosis.

Privately funded, the IAUS functioned as a research center, development agency, nonaccredited school, and forum for exhibitions, programs, and publications. Its faculty of designers, critics, and historians included such aspiring figures as Kenneth Frampton, Anthony Vidler, Rem Koolhaas, and Emilio Ambasz, while visitors from the United States and abroad—Aldo Rossi, Bernard Tschumi, Arata Isozaki, Leon Krier, and others of similar stature—made sure to find their way into and around the institute's quarters. Throughout the 1970s, the IAUS was unsurpassed as a crucible of innovative architectural thought in the United States.

Some of the heat seeped into the administrative offices, where an argument between Drexler and Eisenman over the leadership of the institute led the former to distance himself from it and the latter to take it over almost completely. By 1972, the IAUS had become intimately identified with Peter Eisenman.

Meanwhile, he and Philip grew ever closer together in the inner councils. Philip anted up all the money Eisenman hoped he would, using his own powers of persuasion to talk Gerald Hines, the ultimate businessman, into contributing, too. Gradually, Eisenman recalled, Philip assumed the persona of the institute's éminence grise. Accomplished master and celebrant of the word that he was, he lectured formally and conversed informally, lending corollary support to the organization's publications and occasionally writing for them. The most important of these was the journal *Oppositions,* edited by Eisenman, who kept its contents geared to a level of rarefied discourse virtually without precedent in the annals of American architectural periodicals. The clamor of views and pronouncements in the early 1970s prompted Philip to remember all over again how much propaganda meant in elevating and fixing cultural reputations, his own included. (In 1977, *Oppositions* devoted a whole issue to him.) In the absence of the dead heroes of the past, whose authority had served as a model of judgment and conduct among other architects, it was more vital than ever to establish and promote *images,* and no better medium to that end existed than published criticism. Where the cultural press is, there reputations are shaped, and nowhere else; there is power. In the 1970s, that was New York. The fact was not lost on Eisenman, nor on Philip; that shared knowledge did much to cement their friendship and sustain it over the years.

Philip's allegiance to the IAUS was constant but qualified. He was never comfortable with the leftists of the group, chiefly Kenneth Frampton and his close cohorts, for whom he felt no more sympathy than he had for the "sociologues" of Weimar Germany. Eisenman reported doing what he could, and most of that successfully, to keep Philip close to the activities of the institute. But he had less effect upon Philip's taste, little at all on the kind of architecture that emerged from the Johnson/Burgee office. In that regard, the influences Philip felt during the mid-1970s were collected as surely from outside as inside the institute.

To be sure, he made a point of paying attention to what Eisenman and his colleagues were doing, recognizing that they were attracting more and more ink in the New York architectural press. In the postscript he added to the book *Five Architects,* produced in conjunction with The Museum of Modern Art's 1973 exhibition of Eisenman, Graves, Gwathmey, Hejduk, and Meier—the ideationally puristic "Whites," as they were also called—he wrote: "In common, all they have is talent: they are interested, as artists millennia before them have been, in the art of architecture. I feel especially close to them in this world of functionalist calculation and sociometric fact research. . . .

"If they be too young for me really to understand them, at least I can express a certain empathy and sympathy.

"Alphabetically, Peter Eisenman, weighted down by erudition and intellection, nevertheless is most original in his search. I look at House II, for example, and rejoice in its interpenetrating richness. Rigid complexity is all anyone can hope for. What would he do in a large building?"

It was fluent Philipese, flattering one moment, slyly critical the next, but sufficiently self-abasing to soften the criticism, and never genuinely dissembling. In any case, Eisenman was, or appeared to be, rising in his estimation.

Meanwhile, he was listening to other voices. Arrayed more or less at a polar position opposite the Whites were the "Grays," so called because they were less purist in their objectives, less "rationalist" in their means, more alert to the architecture of contextual accommodation that Robert Venturi had promoted. While Philip never bought into strict Venturianism, he was fascinated by a viewpoint increasingly identified in the 1970s as postmodernism and by its relationship to some of Venturi's thoughts. Most important, he sensed that it was drawing ahead of the multifarious pack of movements around it.

Then as now, there was no consensus definition of postmodernism, a phenomenon too complex and contradictory—to paraphrase Venturi's terminology—to permit simple summation, but among its effects on the architecture of the period was a growing respect for a sentiment that was well formulated by the Italian critic Umberto Eco: "The post-modern reply to the modern consists of recognizing that the past, since it cannot really be destroyed, because its destruction leads to silence, must be revealed: but with irony, not innocently."

In a sense, Philip hardly needed to be told by Eco that history cannot be profitably avoided in contemporary expression. He had been promoting that argument ("You cannot *not* know history") after his own fashion, ever since his days at the Harvard Graduate School of Design. But in his own work, references to the past had been conceptual rather than mimetic, made more in emulation of the spirit of a model than in the copying of it—in short, were more abstract than representational. Postmodernist architecture, on the other hand, as it developed in the 1970s and 1980s, treated the history of building as one immense source book. What modernism might have considered a pier, postmodernism would as easily call a column—and crown it with a Doric, Ionic, or Corinthian capital; or it might feel free to span an opening with a molded arch, not just a naked beam, and the arch might be pointed as readily as round. Thus regarded, postmodernism appeared to offer up the most workable stylistic alternative to modernism of any movement of the post–World War II period.

No one provided Philip with more instruction in the new way than his former student Robert Stern. Stern was now practicing architecture in New York, but Philip remembered that he had been as promising an architectural historian at Yale as he was a designer. Stern was, in fact, currently at work on a biography of George Howe, Philip's old friend, Stern's erstwhile mentor, and an architect who himself had unblushingly relied on historical styles in many of his house designs. And Stern was in sympathy with Venturi and the Grays, especially with their willingness to use architectural conventions to communicate more literally with society and tradition. By contrast, he wrote, "I disagree with Eisenman's stance most vehemently in regard to his belief that one can and presumably should divorce architectural experience from culture."

Thus Philip, true to form, kept company with Stern and Eisenman at the same time, the early 1970s, while continuing, just as characteristically, to carry out his own work in a variety of modernist idioms that had little to do with White, Gray, or any other more recent stylistic coloration. Gradually, however, as the decade unfolded and especially as it turned into the

ROBERT A. M. STERN
AND PHILIP JOHNSON, 1983

1980s, it became evident that he had taken far more from Stern's historicist outlook than from the hermetic abstractions of Eisenman and the Whites.

His frankest reprise of history to date was begun in 1971, when a charitable religious foundation in Dallas commissioned Johnson/Burgee to design a chapel that would celebrate the nonsectarian institution of Thanksgiving. Philip worked on the project during the early and mid-1970s, completing it as late as 1977.

Is Thanksgiving Square, as it is formally called, the first postmodernist work in the Johnson catalogue? Certainly in the 1950s and 1960s, he had used history subtly rather than overtly, applying it to structure and plan and only rarely to ornament or even building shape. On the other hand, the dominant feature of Thanksgiving Square, the chapel itself, is so strikingly similar in overall form to the great ninth-century mosque at Samarra that it seems "contemporary" only in the smooth abstraction of the spiral wall that rises to the sky, candidly mimicking the conventional look and remembering the conventional function—the call to worship—of the minaret that crowned the Samarra mosque. Otherwise, admittedly, the design of the remainder of Thanksgiving Square can be traced to Philip's own recent work. It occupies a slender triangular block in the heart of the Dallas business district. The visitor enters it at the narrowest point of the triangle, continuing through a gateway of four planar columns, surmounted by a carillon, into a garden laid out in what Nory Miller calls "an agitated geometry with angular wedges fitted tight against one another." A rushing stream runs immediately parallel to the path that leads toward the chapel through plantings and spaces both sunken and raised that recall the Water Garden at Fort Worth. In all of his work, Philip's emphasis on the role of procession in architecture is nowhere made more convincingly clear than in a perambulation through Thanksgiving Square.

Early in 1975 Philip noticed suddenly that he could not walk a block without growing short of breath. Spells of fatigue overcame him, usually in the afternoons, prompting him to nap on the floor of his office. Since

THANKSGIVING SQUARE, DALLAS, 1977 (JOHN BURGEE, PARTNER)

Richard Payne

he had long ago put the hypochondria of his youth behind him, he found these new symptoms cause for genuine worry. "Philip," John Burgee said, as if to soothe him, "you're sixty-eight. You do have a right to be tired once in a while. We've been keeping quite a pace."

Philip was not soothed. Neither was his physician, who diagnosed a heart condition but added that for the moment there was no reason to take drastic action. Philip decided that since he was scheduled shortly to give a lecture in Houston, he would use the occasion to look up Michael De Bakey, the physician widely renowned for his pioneering efforts in heart surgery. Burgee reports:

"Philip phoned me from Houston. 'Well, this is it,' he said. 'De Bakey says it's worse than we imagined. But he has an opening in his schedule tomorrow morning. Double bypass. They're prepping me at the hospital now.'

"I couldn't believe there was such an urgency. 'Philip,' I said, "have you checked this out with your doctor?' 'No. Openings in De Bakey's schedule are too rare not to take advantage of this one.'

"So I called a heart specialist I knew, who reinforced the caution I felt. He said before he did such an operation he was required to get the opinion of another surgeon, a doctor, and the hospital board. I phoned Philip back and told him not to have the operation but to stay in the hospital, that I'd pick him up. I caught a night plane to Houston and found him next morning sitting in a chair in his hospital room, all dressed up and ready to leave. I asked to see De Bakey, who refused because we'd gone against his orders. So Philip returned to New York and saw several more doctors. Two said do the operation; two said don't do it. He did it—at St. Luke's."

Less than two weeks later Philip was up and around, nearly frisky as ever, and back at the office on a daily basis.

He loved his operation, judging from the many times he was later quoted by the press in variations of the statements "Everybody should have one" and "Life begins at seventy."

Life by his standards was indeed very good to him as, in 1976, he completed the transition from his seventh decade to his eighth. He had a right to claim credit for the euphoria. His practice with Burgee was going well and he had worked hard to make it so. With the recession easing and commissions arriving in a fairly steady flow—better still, being realized often enough—he and John achieved a position among the major larger American architectural firms of the time. Yet the factor that more and more defined his personal and growing prominence in the field was his unique ability not only to remain conversant with but to support, materially and morally, the various raucous, problematical movements around him. He kept his own table at the Four Seasons in the Seagram Building, where he presided, most accomplished of hosts, over lunch with anyone who mattered. Not everyone around town liked him, and vice versa, but everyone could be sure he would be as interesting tomorrow as he was today.

Having recovered from his crisis of the late 1960s, Philip learned a lesson about staying alive. None of his generational age-mates learned it as well. Some of them continued to prosper professionally, like Pei and Barnes, some of them faded somewhat from view, like Rudolph and Johansen, while the one most critics judged the greatest, Louis Kahn, died in 1974. Thus, while a majority of his peers permitted themselves to become locked in historical place, Johnson by consensus emerged in the course of the 1970s as the swinging dean of American architecture, having earned that place not by age alone but by ongoing productivity, tireless networking, and the added, perfectly expectable dividend of the fixed and fascinated attention of the media.

He could, moreover, be as generous with the press as he was with all the instruments of culture. It was his idea to turn his compound at New Canaan into a stage for the wedding of Rosamond Bernier, founder and former editor of the magazine *L'Oeil* and one of New York's most popular lecturers on art, to John Russell, chief art critic of *The New York Times*. Philip was best man. Cohosts were appropriately eclectic: the de Menil family and Andy Warhol—tradition arm in arm with Pop. Warhol brought along his band, the Velvet Underground, and arranged them north of the Glass House on the moon-viewing platform, where they filled the suburban night with rock 'n' roll until the local police instructed them to pack it in.

Later in the same year, 1975, which was various enough to begin with, Philip shifted his attentions from the earthly domain of Connecticut to a realm with spiritual aspirations a full continent away. Sometime during the autumn, John Burgee was informed by his secretary that a man from California had phoned to ask for an appointment with him and Philip. The caller had "worked" with the distinguished architect Richard Neutra, the message went on, leading Burgee to presume he was "some kid looking for a job." With Philip out of town at the time, Burgee had little interest in seeing the man until his secretary told him several days later that he had turned up in the office: "He says his name is Dr. Schuller. He looks a little funny. Has on a green suit, with a big medal hanging around his neck. But he's very earnest and he's come all the way from the West Coast."

Dear God, thought Burgee, a California hippie. He consented to give a few minutes to Dr. Robert Schuller, who, displaying his Good Shepherd emblem and identifying himself as a man of the cloth, greeted him effusively. Burgee recalled their conversation, more or less verbatim:

"God brought you to me," said Schuller, adding that he normally spent a lot of time in airplanes—close to Him—where he had recently seen in a magazine a photo of the Fort Worth Water Garden and, shortly thereafter, another reference in the press to Philip. The coincidence convinced him: Philip must be the man for the job.

The job, he hastened to explain, was a new church he wanted built for something he called "The Hour of Power." The structure must be big enough to contain four thousand seats.

In a sense the meeting was a reprise of the first encounter between Gerald Hines and Johnson/Burgee. Until Schuller's consecutive readings of Philip's achievements, neither he nor the architects he was now visiting had ever heard of one another. Burgee was interested (four thousand seats?) but guarded. "What sort of budget have you for a church with four thousand seats?" he asked.

"Don't worry about that. God will provide."

The answer did little to diminish Burgee's skepticism. On the other hand, Schuller seemed both intelligent and informed, and Burgee thought it best to run him past Philip before deciding what to do with him. "Tell me something about Mr. Johnson," said Schuller. "Will I have a spiritual experience with him?"

"I'll guarantee that," replied Burgee. "You'll have a spiritual experience of some kind. Be sure of it."

Burgee's research verified both Schuller's story about himself and "The Hour of Power," which was, in fact, a televised worship service that originated in a church in Garden Grove, California. Richard Neutra had built it between 1959 and 1961, in dimensions indeed too small for the kind of sanctuary Schuller had in mind as the pastor of one of the Christian ministries that proliferated rapidly throughout the United States in the 1970s and 1980s, offering a message based more on ego motivation and the guilt-free pursuit of worldly success than on traditional Christian theology. Schuller had gotten his start as a young man preaching from the roof of a kiosk at a drive-in movie theater. He had learned to attract an ever larger audience by exploiting two of the technological tools of the late twentieth century that are most useful and familiar to ordinary people: television and the automobile. But he still wanted a piece of architecture handsome enough to provide a setting that would bring the faithful to the parking lot or the video screen.

He and Philip were meant for each other, both of them masterful communicators, showmen first, salesmen second, missionaries only a little later. Philip watched "The Hour of Power" as it dawned on him that he was only one of a nationwide audience of 2 or 3 million. Then he phoned Schuller in California to tell him he was a fan. The minister's commission followed forthwith.

Only rarely was a client a full step ahead of Philip at the start of a project. That this was such an instance became apparent almost as soon as Johnson and Burgee showed Schuller their first proposal, a scheme in the form of a Greek cross, with masonry walls. The preacher's lack of enthusiasm was as obvious as it was uncharacteristic. "I was hoping for a great idea," he said, "You've given me a traditional church. I'm not traditional.

This is California. People here don't come to church to be closed up in a box. They want to be close to green, to water and sun."

This guy wants to preach in a greenhouse, Burgee thought to himself, adding later in conversation with Philip that Schuller was, after all, a tent preacher: "He'd like a big glass tent." Philip had already arrived at the same conclusion, while realizing that any such unconventional house of worship might be in its own way as monumental as anything he himself was in the habit of dreaming about. All systems were rearranged and work began on Schuller's "great idea," a tabernacle of glass, a Crystal Cathedral, the ecclesiastical counterpart of Philip's own Glass House.

The finished structure, which Schuller opened to his flock in 1980, is a perfect example of an "inside" building, in Philip's terminology. On approach, its exterior is even something of a disappointment, a vitreous polyhedron with no immediately perceptible logic to its shape and a site that hardly distinguishes it from the motley of the town around it, Garden Grove, a yard-goods suburb of Los Angeles. In fact, the plan is a four-sided star, although that configuration doesn't imprint itself on the mind of the viewer until he has recovered from his eye-popping first sensation of the interior space. It is an immensity, a vault of shimmering transparency whose scale—207 by 415 feet along its two axes and 128 feet tall at its high point, with a column-free span of 200 feet—seems an appropriate materialization of Schuller's "great idea." The normally cloudless California sky and radiant California light are abundantly visible through glass walls effectively in 360 degrees, their support provided by a vast three-dimensional trusswork of welded steel tubing painted white and so continuous in its modularity that it seems to the eye fully as decorative as it is structural.

The short axis is given to the nave, so that the congregation is brought closer to the chancel, where a space for an orchestra and tiers for the choir are backed by two balconied banks in oak that accommodate the organ. Schuller's pulpit is located on the right apron of the altar area, where it may be seen from the huge parking lot through a door twenty feet wide and ninety feet high, the single component that deviates from a symmetry of plan. This is the business end of the Crystal Cathedral, encapsulated in one of the two short arms of the star plan, the remaining three assigned to balconies and seating for the congregation. The main aisle is divided by a long trough filled with fountains, an echo of the Fort Worth Water Garden.

The Crystal Cathedral has no heating or cooling plant. The local climate is naturally benign enough that air conditioning is not the requirement it would be in Houston or even Minneapolis. In any case, louvers

CRYSTAL CATHEDRAL, GARDEN GROVE, CALIFORNIA, 1980; BELL TOWER ADDED, 1990
(JOHN BURGEE, PARTNER)

CRYSTAL CATHEDRAL, GARDEN GROVE, 1980: INTERIOR (JOHN BURGEE, PARTNER)

in the glass wall all along the periphery provide ample cross-ventilation, while the reflective glass of the windows resists most of the heat generated by the sun's rays. While the great space frame is designed to withstand an earthquake of 8.0 magnitude on the Richter scale, many of the ten thousand windows would be lost in any major tremor, along with the names etched on their glass surfaces, each representing donors whose individual contributions of one thousand dollars were a vital part in paying the building's $18 million cost. More modest contributors were awarded their own mylar stars, suspended from the ceiling and twinkling in the constant air currents. Schuller, in short, made good on the Lord's promissory note.

Whatever functional miscalculations and inconveniences in the Johnson/Burgee design, including poor sight lines from several places, capricious acoustics throughout, and, sorriest of all, the unavoidable reduction of seats to fewer than three thousand, the building remains a showpiece worthy of the talents of the two virtuosos, Philip and the preacher, most responsible for it. Schuller's sanitized Christianity was expertly conveyed to a TV audience that was encouraged to identify the good reverend's perfect teeth and sculpted hairdo with the secular success he kept telling them could be theirs, too. He magnified the call with witnesses as luminously self-confident as himself and with singers and instrumentalists who, close as they were to Hollywood, offered music to the faithful with finely honed Hollywood skill and unashamed Hollywood taste.

Philip's architectural tasks were carried out with more genuine elegance than Schuller's white-bread evangelism, and a majority of critics have taken the Crystal Cathedral seriously enough to place it among its designer's most impressive efforts. Moreover, for sheer pulpit cheek, Schuller could never outdo Philip, who, in 1990, having built a new bell tower for the church, agreed to be part of "The Hour of Power" when the structure was dedicated. There he stood, before a national television audience, side by side with Schuller, who asked him solemnly, "Tell us, Philip, what went through your mind when you designed this beautiful building?"

As profoundly atheistic as ever, and just as disdainful of Christian ceremony even when acted out with a humility foreign to Schuller's nature, Philip responded by drawing close to the preacher and speaking in a subdued, nearly inaudible voice. "I thought I knew history. I thought I knew what the Gothic spires of old stood for. The Romantic period and the thirteenth-century period were the highest periods, perhaps, in spiritual Christianity. I thought I knew how to combine these things to create a great tower. I was wrong. I could not have done this—I have to say it humbly, and I don't ever feel humbly, but I do this morning—I got help, my friends. I think you all [voice breaks] know where that help came from." Schuller beamed in transcendent acknowledgment. "Philip Johnson, we love you!" he cried.

Later, when asked by an interviewer who knew him well enough, "Philip, how *could* you?", Philip briefly buried his head in his hands in mock shame, then grinned and replied, "Wasn't that *awful!*"

In stylistic terms, the Crystal Cathedral must be called modernist, a classification appropriate to most of the other works produced by Johnson/Burgee in the 1970s, including the General American Life Insurance Company Building in St. Louis (1974–1977), the National Center for the Performing Arts in Bombay, India (1974–1980), the reconstruction of Avery Fisher Hall in New York (1975–1976), Century Center in South Bend, Indiana (1975–1977), 80 Field Point Road in Greenwich, Con-

FACADE, 1001 FIFTH AVENUE, NEW YORK CITY, 1979 (JOHN BURGEE, PARTNER)

necticut (1976–1978), the Terrace Theater in the Kennedy Center for the Performing Arts in Washington, D.C. (1977–1979), and the Peoria Civic Center (1977–1982). Nevertheless, given Philip's near-total embrace of postmodernism in the 1980s, signs of an increasing affection for it were apparent before the previous decade ended. They were not promising.

In 1977, he accepted a commission to add a facade to an apartment building at 1001 Fifth Avenue in New York, most of which had already been constructed to the designs of the architect Philip Birnbaum. Having agreed to effect some measure of contextual unity between his scheme and the building's sobersided neighbors, a 1903 French town house and a 1911 McKim, Mead & White Italian palazzo, Philip made use of what the champions of the postmodernist esthetic referred to as "double coding," the commingling of historical and modernist elements in a single design. Thus he crossed the four vertical ribbon windows that were the dominant and clearly modernist features of his facade with a series of stringcourses lifted from classical vocabulary. The combination was just uninteresting enough to be innocuous, but Philip did himself no further favors b, mounting the cornice of the building with a bizarre trapezoidal panel th. resembled a mansard roof when viewed from the front but that was in fact nothing more than a sheet of stone propped up from behind by struts, giving it, at three-quarter view, the look of a slightly makeshift movie set. It was a joke, right? Well, no, not on muttonchops Fifth Avenue, hardly the place to turn limestone into cardboard or a neoclassical edifice into a decorated shed. If there was intentional irony in his effort, there was an unintentional measure of it in his decision to apply it at all to a context that hadn't the capacity to appreciate it in the first place.

The third phase of Philip Johnson's architectural career, following his Miesian devotions of the 1950s and his formalist venture in the 1960s and early 1970s, began on March 30, 1978, when the American Telephone and Telegraph Company announced plans for a new 660-foot-high head-quarters building to be erected on New York's Madison Avenue between Fifty-fifth and Fifty-sixth streets.

In no significant respect was the structure technically unique or stylisti-cally innovative. Yet it had the effect, even before ground was broken, of elevating Philip from star to superstar status in the architectural world. Moreover, during the years required for its completion in 1984, and in all the time following, there has been no agreement among the critics as to its intrinsic merit, despite a public consensus that it made the man who designed it the most famous architect alive. Before it was anything else, then, the AT&T Building was a triumph of the image-making process that had increasingly taken command of the arts in the 1970s. *Time* mag-azine, unsurpassed in its prominence as an international medium of com-munication, featured Philip on the cover of its January 7, 1979, issue. He was photographed looking slightly down at the viewer, while holding an effigy of the facade of the building. The metaphor was clear: Moses and the tablets of the Law.

No one could have appreciated the unwitting irony more than Philip himself, who had known ever since he shifted his esthetic allegiance from Plato to Nietzsche that in the arts fact could not be established but opinion could be made weighty enough to serve as a convincing substitute for it. Thus there were no laws, Mosaic or otherwise, only the force of persuasion.

The lead article in that issue of *Time* only bore all this out. Written by Robert Hughes, with the style and authority he customarily brought to his critical prose, it took the revolution of postmodernism as its subject and treated Philip as its central figure. Nowhere was it claimed he had started it, but given the size of his new building and the reputation of AT&T as the largest business in the world, given as well his fame and nearly steady proximity to the front of every architectural vanguard of the previous half century, it seemed indubitable that he more than anyone had legitimized the postmodernist movement. That identity was further fixed by the roles Hughes assigned other architects in his piece. Several of them, like Charles Moore and Robert Stern, had been working in the postmodernist manner longer and with more commitment than Philip had, while at least two others, Robert Venturi and the Californian Frank Gehry, had made more demonstrably original contributions. Yet here they were given positions secondary to Philip, who emerged not just dean of the school but king of the hill.

The commission can be traced to the fall of 1975, roughly the same time that Philip was recovering from his bypass operation and beginning work on the design of the Crystal Cathedral. AT&T sent out forms to twenty-five of the nation's leading architectural offices, Johnson/Burgee included, expressing its intentions to put up a big building and asking the standard questions about the various firms' approaches to pertinent architectural problems. According to Burgee, he and Philip were the only ones who didn't answer. It was an exceptionally busy time for them, he said, adding, however, that they had confused the form with a request for an update of an old file from an AT&T branch office in Chicago. Once they learned who the client was and how large the project might be, they lost no time in offering their services. Even so, finding themselves at last on the short list of three candidates, they made their presentation to AT&T board chairman John D. deButts and his committee with a disarming minimum of props—just two photographs: one of the Seagram Building, the other of Pennzoil. Otherwise, they relied on conversation, on Philip's inimitable mixture of wit and willing but hardly eager urbanity together with Burgee's complementary cool expertise. "We did a good sister act," John recalled, "and it worked. We got the job."

DeButts left no doubt that a high budget could be counted on but that the product must be appropriately unique. The song of the client: Philip recognized it when he heard it. But the earnestness of deButts's rendition took on special meaning as soon as he went on to say that he regarded the

Seagram Building as a work of such stature that AT&T must match it—
but by doing something other than copying its metal-and-glass slab form.

That meant a top, thought Philip, recalling Hugh Liedtke's injunctions
at Pennzoil, but it might also suggest stone, a material that deButts would
surely prefer to glass. Stone was making a comeback lately in any case, as
the oil shortage of the 1970s drew attention to the high cost of heating
and ventilation in most glass-walled buildings. Both prospects, a pronounced attic story and a granite shaft, carried Philip backward in his
thoughts to the past, to the 1910s and 1920s when skyscrapers like the Tribune Tower, the Woolworth, Chrysler, and Empire State buildings glo-
ried in the embellished singularity of their crowns and the palpable
sturdiness of the materials they were made of. But history, as Stern and
Moore were arguing, was now as much an inspiration to the present as it
was a receptacle of the past. Philip's goal virtually defined itself: a building that he could endow with a premodern—amend that—a postmodern
look, a structure, moreover, that would be far more monumental than the
smaller-scaled things his younger colleagues had had to be content with.
This, in short, would be the first postmodernist skyscraper, a marriage
between an ambitious new movement and an established artist that would
not only validate the one but give new life to the other. And the media
would preside at the union.

The momentum of Philip's thinking was interrupted by the necessity—
the nuisance, as he saw it—of listening to twenty-odd of the top AT&T
executives offer up their views of what the company stood for and how the
building might symbolize it. "If we had our portrait painted," one of them
wrote in a memo, "it should be by Norman Rockwell. If we were ancient
builders, we would have built the Roman aqueducts instead of the Cathedral of Notre Dame. . . . If we were a state, we would be midwestern,
probably Iowa. Twenty years ago, we would have been Nebraska."

Philip reacted to most of this with controlled tolerance. He knew that
some of the AT&T managers wanted a hard-calloused, practical, less
expensive building, not the splendid object deButts had in mind. But he
took heart from his perception of the chairman as a strong-willed executive who ran a "democracy of one"—precisely the kind of unassailable
authority figure he associated with ideal architectural patronage.

Philip and Burgee were not long in deciding that the building's form
should be a rectangular tower, with a symmetrical facade on the long
Madison Avenue side. Zoning laws requiring not only a plaza but
ground-level shops that would have been arrayed close enough to the
entrance to deprive it of the grandeur Philip wanted for it led him and
John to the inventive idea of raising the whole structure sixty feet off the

ground and supporting it on massive columns. The lobby would be smaller but kept at grade, and the shops would be moved to a glazed galleria at the rear of the tower. The open area, whose great piers reminded Philip of an Egyptian hypostyle hall, would be given over to benches and café seating, thus providing the public amenities expected of a plaza. The very raising of the building left the facade with a surface area large enough to guarantee a spectacular entrance.

It was at the ground level and at the top of the building that Philip, remembering a similar double treatment of IDS and Pennzoil, imposed the design elements that granted the building a unique image, moreover in the historical forms the postmodernists claimed communicated more directly with an urban audience than did the abstracted lineaments of the International Style. The entrance was conceived as a mammoth 116-foot-high round arch flanked on each side by three shorter 60-foot rectangular openings that create the effect of an arcade. Well before any of this was built, the critics couldn't resist drawing associations from history: Was the facade a variation of the famous Palladian motif? The Pazzi Chapel by Brunelleschi in Florence? Alberti's Church of Sant' Andrea in Mantua? Moreover, guessing games aside, would it work? Was it too vast for the narrowness of Madison Avenue? Or was its very super scale the appropriate use of postmodernist irony?

These issues paled by comparison with the reaction to the crown of the building. There, Johnson and Burgee had decided that the best alternative to a flat roof would be a gable form of some sort. "We felt," Philip was quoted as saying, "that a pediment, by raising the middle higher, was the only way to unify the verticality and the symmetry of the facade. Perhaps one could put a tower there, but we were classicizing, and this was clearly the most classical solution." Weeks of fussing over the exact profile of the pediment followed, with the final product taking the form that has since become as famous as any building top of the twentieth century. A cylindrical trough was cut into and along the crest of the gable and a cornice line was added to the top of the facade surface, flaring horizontally at the outer ends.

The pediment excited even more historical free association than the arched entryway. Its most obvious antecedent was the broken pediment, a form traceable to the ancient Romans but more popularly identified with the Baroque period. Some observers, mindful of Philip's suggestion that steam from vents within the trough might be made to rise from the building like huge puffs of smoke—and floodlit at night—were reminded of the fantastic projects of the eighteenth-century visionary French architect Étienne-Louis Boullée. And since the pediment sat atop a tall four-

AT&T (AMERICAN TELEPHONE AND TELEGRAPH) CORPORATE HEADQUARTERS,
NEW YORK CITY, 1984 (JOHN BURGEE, PARTNER)

sided shaft, the overall resemblance to a grandfather clock or an eighteenth-century highboy was sufficiently apparent that the building has
become known, whether Philip Johnson liked it or not, more as the
"Chippendale skyscraper" than as the AT&T Building.

Did he like the simile? Surely he wasn't thinking about furniture when
he designed the pediment, but he did not object to the publicity given it

AT&T BUILDING: ENTRY
(JOHN BURGEE, PARTNER)

Richard Payne

by a press that found a representational architecture more engaging to discuss than the abstract stuff turned out by the previous several generations.

A further reason for the attention concentrated so intensely on the
crown of the building was the effect it had on the skyline. The Miesian
slab was so generic and so commonplace by the late 1970s that from a distance the collective profiles of American cities looked nearly indistinguishable one from another. Thus in the midst of a jungle of squarish
boxes, the AT&T pediment, hardly a complicated form in itself, was
enough to reawaken New Yorkers to the uniqueness of the Manhattan
architectural silhouette.

Indeed, both the top and bottom of the building were studies in simplicity by contrast with the treatment of the interior. There, Philip pursued most cheerfully the postmodernist notion of "multivalence"
promoted so eagerly by critic Charles Jencks. The granite walls of the
lobby were set upon classical arcades and crowned by a groin vault. The
columns conveyed no historical pedigree except for their capitals, whose

Byzantine origins were double-coded with a bit of modern by the abstracted smoothness of their surfaces. Two huge oculi faced each other across the lobby. The floor was paved in black-and-white marble in a pattern derived from the conservative early twentieth-century English architect Edwin Lutyens.

In the center of this space stood the most arresting single component of the entire interior ensemble. Overriding a proposal to install a large sculpture there by Isamu Noguchi, Philip persuaded deButts instead to let him salvage a statue that had been placed in 1916 on top of the old AT&T building downtown. It was the *Genius of Electricity* by Evelyn Beatrice Longman, a larger-than-life winged nude male figure painted gold, mounted on a pedestal, poised on a globe of the world and carrying a rolled length of cable and several lightning bolts. It was as close to a stroke

EVELYN BEATRICE LONGMAN: *THE GENIUS OF ELECTRICITY,* 1916;
MOVED TO FOYER OF AT&T BUILDING, 1984

of genius as Philip gave the whole project: an unmistakable symbol of a solidly conservative corporation, at the same time a piece of beefcake and high camp, a weightless gay fantasy levitating in the middle of all that straight hard rock. *This* was PoMo irony, undiluted.

AT&T's insistence on a tight security system necessitated a second foyer, the so-called Sky Lobby, one floor above street level. Since access was restricted to AT&T personnel, it seemed to Philip a fitting place for one more expression of corporate magnificence. Enormous circular openings in the walls counterposed against equally powerful posts and lintels, all parts executed in Breccia Strazzema marble, created an effect of opulence that provided a definitive model for the material pomp that became a near requisite of skyscraper lobbies during the Reagan 1980s.

Critical reaction to the AT&T Building was as mixed as judgments of Johnson himself had been ever since he was old enough to be ejected from the classroom of one prep school teacher while winning the affection and deep respect of another.

Vincent Scully wasted no words: ". . . Philip Johnson's A.T. & T. giant on Madison Avenue takes charge of the street. It both acknowledges its flow and rounds it out into an event. It shapes an urban place of enormous authority, instantly making the International Style skyscrapers on either side of it look captious, insubstantial and obsolete—in fact, not like buildings at all. The lift of Johnson's pediment has the effect of making us wonder why we ever allowed people to build skyscrapers with flat tops."

Another critic, on the other hand, with a record of loyalty to Johnson that had lasted longer than Scully's, now violently reversed herself. Ada Louise Huxtable was not impressed: not by postmodernism as a movement and most emphatically not by Philip Johnson as its latest protagonist. She wrote: "Architects may be rediscovering the past, but their knowledge of it is still so spotty, their enthusiasms so arbitrary and episodic, that a lot of what we are getting is do-it-yourself history, with a long way to go for [an] assured and able synthesis. . . ."

And then, more to the point of Philip and AT&T: "What Mr. Johnson has produced, from that Pop pediment on down, is a pastiche of historical references and evocative spatial experiences drawn from his admiration of bits and pieces of earlier monuments, blown up gigantically in unconventional and unsettling relationships. . . . But this building is a monumental demonstration of quixotic aesthetic intelligence rather than art."

. . .

The final years of the 1970s had this much in common with the critics' assessment of AT&T: They were filled with honors and reproach, uncommonly good fortune and uncommonly bad, all of it made bearable by the increased attention—call it fame—that praise and blame in great quantity conferred together.

Major commissions for big, high-paying commercial projects seemed to flow unsolicited into the Johnson/Burgee office from all over the country. Such unremitting activity viewed against the backdrop of Philip's long and colorful professional life set off an eruption of prizes and awards. In 1978 alone, in the course of work on the Crystal Cathedral and AT&T, he received the R. S. Reynolds Memorial Award for an outstanding building in aluminum (Pennzoil), the City of New York's Bronze Medallion, and the University of Virginia's Thomas Jefferson Medal—and one more, most prestigious of all, the American Institute of Architects Gold Medal, of which he was the fortieth recipient, following such historic luminaries as Louis Sullivan, Frank Lloyd Wright, Le Corbusier, and Mies van der Rohe. One year later, in 1979, he was named the first winner of the new and highly publicized Pritzker Prize, which carried a check for $100,000 to accompany the parchment bearing his name. Granted by a jury of his peers, the prize signified the recipient's special accomplishments in the profession.

By that time, however, he had also been involved in a small professional dispute that effectively ended in a draw and a very large one that he lost, sustaining a blow to his ego from which he was years in recovering. The first instance was minor only relative to the second and only to him personally, not to the governing commission of Miami, which was disappointed by his design of a cultural center the city had hoped would symbolize its ambitions to become, in its own terms, a "New World Center." The commissioners had approached him in 1977, understanding him to be a first-rate modern architect who would give them a first-rate piece of modern architecture. By that time, however, he was already bitten by the postmodernist bug. "The modern way of being modern," he was quoted, "is to hook into regionalism." Hence his design, a recapitulation of the Spanish Mediterranean manners and materials associated with Addison Mizner and Burrell Hoffman, the locally famous Florida architects of the 1910s and 1920s: round arched arcades, terra-cotta-tiled barrel roofs, cream-colored stucco walls, and a battered podium of shell limestone. Grudgingly, Miami let him build it. "It would be," said County Manager Roy Goode, "the ultimate community insult, in terms of our national image, if we selected a nationally famous architect and rejected his work."

Philip ran into far less pliable opposition in suffering his most painful professional defeat of the 1970s.

He had sought and lost commissions before; the experience is familiar to all architects, the immortals included. In this case, however, the client who walked away from him was none other than The Museum of Modern Art, and the work in question was by far the most ambitious architectural effort that institution had ever undertaken. Early in the 1970s, confronted by rising costs and expanding physical needs, the museum elected not only to add more gallery and office space to its existing structure but, extraordinarily, to build a luxury apartment building close by. The galleries and offices would be appropriate to the celebration of the museum's fiftieth anniversary, forthcoming in 1979. The revenue-producing apartment tower was meant strictly to ensure the museum's fiscal survival. It was a daring and debatable move with a $40 million price tag on it, but once voted on by the trustees, it led soon enough to the question of the right architect.

Over a quarter century, the major additions to the museum—two wings and a garden—had been designed by Philip and Philip alone. Whether he admitted it publicly or not, he regarded himself as the house architect and, given the success of his recent partnership with Burgee, all the more obviously the ideal candidate for the job.

Thus it was that he was jolted to learn in 1976 that the Building and Development Committee of the board of trustees had recommended against him. Queried late in life, he offered his own interpretation of the event. He reported that he first learned of his rejection through a museum leak. Only later was he invited to lunch by Blanchette Rockefeller, who, as president of the museum, had been assigned by the trustees to impart the bad news. He went on to claim that she was "in love with Eddie boy and she wanted him to do the building." That, he contended, not without a generous measure of petulance, was the reason he lost the commission.

Eddie boy was Edward Larrabee Barnes, a fellow architect whom Philip had disliked ever since their days together at the Harvard Graduate School of Design. Like Philip, he was a trustee of the museum, although he had not served on the Building and Development Committee of the board that had ruled against Philip. Neither had Philip, of course, or the two other architect trustees, Gordon Bunshaft and Wallace Harrison. Philip didn't care for them, either, and the feelings were mutual.

Barnes recalled that there had been talk early on of the possible selection of one of those four architects, but he made it clear at the time that
whoever might be chosen should forthwith resign his trusteeship. It is
certain that Philip, given his personal history at the museum, would have
found that proposal repellent. Barnes added that yes, Blanchette did seem
to have something of a special fondness for him, but that there was nothing serious about it and it figured not at all in the final selection process.
In fact, the board shortly decided to disqualify all four architects and to
ask them instead to recommend an architect from outside the museum.
This they did, narrowing the list of candidates finally to I. M. Pei, Romaldo Giurgola, and Cesar Pelli. Late in January of 1977, the museum
announced that Pelli had been awarded the commission.

Despite, or rather because of, the museum's studious efforts to keep its
deliberations to itself, suppositions and speculations abounded, one of
them Philip's own rankling suspicion about the motives of a woman,
Blanchette Rockefeller, who he was sure was once smitten with him. In
fact, he had identified the right family, but hardly the only member and
hardly that member's principal motives. At a luncheon in the early 1980s
attended by several of the museum staff, Marga Barr declared that David
Rockefeller in communication with board chairman William S. Paley
had promised a hefty contribution of $5 million to the building expan-
sion, conditional on Philip's not being named the architect. By nature a
sober soul of unhurried makeup, David Rockefeller had never favored
Philip quite the way his more expansive brother Nelson had, but in any
case, he was not the only trustee with reservations about Philip. There
were enough of the others to bring him down—including Blanchette
Rockefeller, who, according to everyone but Philip, appeared to be
moved by considerations more fiscal than amorous.

The case against him rested on the twofold argument that he had been
insufficiently mindful of budgetary constraints and overly proprietary in
his previous building efforts for the museum and that he would thus have
found it difficult to mediate among the varied commercial, institutional,
and political factors that comprised a highly complicated project. Since
the expansion program was driven by the hardest financial facts, there
could be no place in it for anyone, least of all the architect, who might be
indifferent to economies or other practicalities. The decision to withhold
the commission from any of the trustee architects, so as to avoid any possible conflict of interest, was a defensible reason for eliminating Philip, but
a secondary one.

He, in turn, had enough sense, or should have had, to know that The
Museum of Modern Art by the late 1970s was a much vaster, more

impersonal and more convoluted organism than it had been when he and Barr and Hitchcock sat around in the early 1930s and reorganized the universe. Alfred himself was in his late seventies now and suffering symptoms of Alzheimer's disease, long since bereft of the position and potency he had had in the good old days. Philip, spiritually most case-hardened of men, who built his career on a belief in power in human intercourse, had collided with a corporate business entity tougher and stronger than he and anchored by an ancient immovable object still in place: the Rockefellers.

It was the very fact of his personal involvement that kept him from sizing up the situation as rationally as he might have. If over the years he had profited immensely from the museum, and from the Rockefeller clan, he had given greatly of himself to both, and it is in the nature of things that giving increases vulnerability. Ever since the emotional buffeting of his youth, he had made it a goal of his life to avoid vulnerability, yet he had let his defenses against such a condition down, and he was crushed, humiliated, and embarrassed. The loss of the commission caused him what may have been the most serious inward suffering he had ever known.

Hence his reaction, which was to reverse the intentions he had earlier had for the disposal of his estate and *not* to leave the museum his collection of painting and sculpture or even his country property in New Canaan. He relented a little in the early 1980s when he invited William Rubin, the museum's curator of Painting and Sculpture, to select a limited number of his holdings and take them into the permanent collection. Later still, he added a few more donations; he couldn't help himself. But the property and by far the major portion of his collection were formally bequeathed in 1987 to the National Trust for Historic Preservation.

The museum, then, may have paid its own price for its unsentimentality and fiscal single-mindedness. The program overseen by Cesar Pelli, with Jaquelin Robertson, architect for the developer, Arlen Properties, and Richard Weinstein, architect and planner, was not completed until 1986 and it encountered its own not-inconsiderable cost overruns. Moreover, it was and remains a work of only modest architectural distinction. Pelli was obliged to encroach on the terrace of the Johnson garden in order to gain more space for the main lobby and its bank of escalators. He also had to sacrifice the upper level of the east wing to make room for a restaurant. The forty-eight-story tower, a rather garrulously patterned exercise in the late modernist manner, is a respectable accomplishment and substantially nothing more. One cannot help yielding to hindsight and the suspicion that Philip would have produced a better piece of work.

CESAR PELLI: GARDEN COURT
AND MUSEUM TOWER,
THE MUSEUM OF MODERN ART,
NEW YORK CITY, 1984

He would probably have put his very heart into it, knowing that he was old enough—his early seventies—that this would almost certainly have been the last important architectural contribution he could have made to an institution that had been his very life.

That, of course, is speculation, finally as bootless as any dream that may have troubled his sleep in the melancholy days after the commission evaporated.

THE POMO REVEL

Philip did not forget the MoMA debacle, but he did not waste time brooding over it. Indeed by 1980, having turned his attentions fully back to his practice with John Burgee, he stood on the brink of a decade that by its completion had won him probably more attention than it granted any of his peers. There would be the usual endless quarreling over the architectural quality of the buildings he made in the 1980s but also unanimous acknowledgment of his unmatched gift for being somehow everywhere at once. The master of culture politics had returned from the marginal place he occupied briefly in the late 1960s to a position of centrality from which he consciously and skillfully built lines of connection and influence that reached to all corners of the architectural world. Philip was unique in understanding the priorities of both the intellectual and the commercial realms of the period and, more remarkably, in recognizing how those two communities, normally perceived as antithetical, if not hostile, toward one another, could be persuaded to share the same goals. In a time of hot materialistic pursuit—the eighties—the theoretician learned to like public attention as much as the real estate developer did. And Philip showed them both how they could have what they wanted and get along with each other at the same time.

This was evident as early as the turning of 1980 into 1981, when Ada Louise Huxtable, summarizing events of the year for the *Times,* reflected on the confrontation between the big old Establishment firms like Skidmore, Owings & Merrill and "the high priests of post-modernism, represented by Robert Stern, Michael Graves, Jorge Silvetti and Steven Peterson, who build a little and write and talk a lot about why firms like SOM are passé."

"The 1980 prize," she proceeded to say, "for having it both ways goes to the firm of Philip Johnson and John Burgee, now dressing the big, basic, corporate tower in post-modernist, historically allusionist clothing. . . ." Just a year later, in February of 1981, Arthur Drexler staged a symposium at The Museum of Modern Art under the title "New York: Building Again." Six major architects, Philip among them, sat down together to discuss the commercial building boom that was already under way in Manhattan and elsewhere, destined to become one of the salient architectural facts of a decade acquisitively obsessed. Reporting on the event, also in the *Times,* Paul Goldberger cited one of the panelists, Der Scutt of Swanke, Hayden & Connell, as providing the "most revealing insights into where skyscraper design is going. Mr. Scutt proudly proclaimed his interest in lively shapes, and peppered his presentation with words such as 'excitement' and 'image' and 'people-pleasing.' . . . The highest praise a building can get, in some circles at least, is that it has an interesting shape."

The "high priests" mentioned by Huxtable could hardly take issue with the pleasing of people through exciting images, since postmodernism tended to regard communication as an important architectural goal, most readily attained by reference to forms—images, after all—familiar from the past. And certainly Stern and Graves negotiated the transition from the high road of theory to the canyons of commerce, and of fame, during the 1980s, both profiting not only from the example of Philip Johnson but from his personal encouragement and professional intercession on their behalf. Philip was the dominant voice advising the jury that in 1980 selected Michael Graves's design for the Portland Public Services Building, a work completed in 1982 that quickly became an architectural icon of the decade and "the second most important postmodernist building," as John Brodie wrote, "after Johnson's AT&T Building."

Meanwhile, Philip was hardly idle at his own drawing board. His successes at IDS and Pennzoil, not to mention his continuing association with Gerald Hines, left him convinced that the period craze for designer apparel to which the names of "creative" couturiers were attached—St. Laurent, Cardin, de la Renta, Lauren, et al.—had its logical parallel in signature buildings erected to emphasize the unique identity not only of the client but of the architect. To this kind of architecture, the postmodernist, with his freedom to roam at will through history, was as well suited as the classical modernist, in his narrowed search for structural and spatial universals, was not. And no one matched Philip either in his knowledge of history or in the caprice of his mind, which darted from one idea to the next like a bee in clover, all the while aware that there was a specific client to please or— it was much the same thing—to overwhelm with apparently superior knowledge and understanding of the problem.

Mies was gone for good, *deo gratias,* or so it seemed. And Philip, in a ferocious burst of energy over a five-year period, designed and finished a sequence of buildings that had no equal in twentieth-century architecture for multiple personality of authorship. Most of them recalled identifiable historical styles or even perceptibly individual buildings of the past, while some were further variations on modernist ideas of no specific provenance, as distinct from postmodernist forms. It was as if Philip, well aware of Mies's famous remark, "We don't invent a new architecture every Monday morning," decided to do just that. He made other audibly oedipal sounds in the eighties. Remembering another Miesianism ("I don't want to be interesting; I want to be good"), he fixed his tongue firmly in his cheek before sticking it out: "I wouldn't know how to be good."

A double inference followed: On the one hand, he was content instead to be interesting; on the other, his remark was another instance of a familiar habit of self-deprecation that masked an aggressiveness and bravado especially evident in his work of the early 1980s. One moment he was a French classicist, then, without skipping a beat, a medieval castellator, and—next Monday morning, so to speak—a borrower from the Northern Renaissance. Moreover, his extraordinary quick-change act was carried out on the big center stage, where everyone could see him. Several of his works took the form of high rises, large enough to make Philip known to an ever-widening public, sufficiently provocative to earn him and them ample space and heated critical debate in the professional journals.

He became a circuit rider to the national corporate frontier, carrying his message to big businesses all over the United States. His first major accomplishment following AT&T was the PPG (originally Pittsburgh Plate Glass) Corporate Headquarters Building (1979–1984), a complex of six structures that was meant to enliven a run-down section in Pittsburgh adjacent to Market Square while addressing the downtown business district to the west. Appropriate to the client's product, the exterior of each parcel is composed almost totally of glass. The articulation of the elevations in alternating square and triangular sectional protrusions crowned with turrets creates a quick-step rhythm of light against dark, with the result that the dominant element of the group, a 630-foot-high tower, bears an unmistakable resemblance to the Houses of Parliament in London. PPG, then, is a study in postmodernist Gothic. The glass does triple expressive duty, partly suggesting Gothic fenestration; partly, in its mirror opacity, the solidity of medieval stone shafts; partly, in its sheer plenitude, the mass-produced character of twentieth-century machine technology. Philip further exercised the freedom typical of PoMo thinking by arranging his six buildings around a formal classicist piazza, with a distinctly unmedieval granite obelisk in the middle. And the Gothic is still further qualified—formally by the abstraction of the hundreds of turrets; functionally by the addition of a winter garden to the west.

Philip's conscious use of heterogeneous devices is underscored by the jarringly dissimilar impressions PPG makes up close and at a distance. At the level of the piazza, it conveys, like so many late Johnson works, the look and curious insubstantiality of a stage set, while from the bluff overlooking the Monongahela River, it makes up one of the most dramatic and authoritative—and unmistakably solid—passages of the Pittsburgh skyline.

Completed just a year after PPG, although otherwise contemporaneous with it, is another skyscraper, in Houston, developed and promoted by Gerald Hines. The Transco Tower (1979–1985) is as much a celebration of mirror glass as PPG but it projects a palpably different stylistic image. Built at a height of nine hundred feet (the tallest building in the Johnson catalogue) at a considerable distance from the downtown area, it stands in stunning solitude, physically and in a sense psychically aloof from its squat city's-edge environment. Predictably, Philip relied on a historical source, or two, or three, but for the most part relatively recent ones. His tower rises from a base to a symmetrical series of setbacks that bring to mind the New York skyscrapers of the 1920s, most of all Raymond Hood's American Radiator Building, although Philip himself saw a kinship between the profile of Transco, with its low pyramidal cap, and Bertram Goodhue's state capitol in Lincoln, Nebraska (where, not incidentally, Johnson erected his 1963 Sheldon Memorial Art Gallery). A notching of the elevations of Transco by v-shaped bays is an inversion of the same device in PPG, but it creates a comparable verticality, the more pronounced in the former building by its lonely station on the flat Texas prairie. Typically unwilling to let things remain stylistically consistent, Philip turned the entryway into an enormous masonry panel that framed a sixty-foot-high portal done up in classical moldings. Even then, with eclecticizing energy to spare, he laid out a formal park to the south of the tower, where a lawn led to a gabled screen wall penetrated by three Renaissance arches. Beyond and visible through it at a greater height stood a monumental semicylindrical structure with an inner wall covered totally by a waterfall. To all appearances, such untamed *richesse* sat very well with the Transco management. Jack Bowen, the company's chief executive officer, was

Richard Payne

PPG (PITTSBURGH PLATE GLASS) COMPANY CORPORATE HEADQUARTERS,
PITTSBURGH, PENNSYLVANIA, 1984
(JOHN BURGEE, PARTNER)

PHILIP JOHNSON AND JOHN BURGEE AT TOPPING OUT CEREMONY FOR PPG BUILDING,
PITTSBURGH, 1984

quoted in a local newspaper: "The 64-foot-high water wall corresponds
to the 64-story height of the tower and . . . to the all-time high on the
stock market for Transco stock."

While Philip during the 1980s built in places as various as San Francisco, Denver, Chicago, Cleveland, New York, and Boston, it was Texas
where most of his work was done, moreover frequently to his own spirited satisfaction. He was drawn to the state's affection for materiality at
large scale, which dovetailed with the sense of architectural adventure that
postmodernism awakened in him. This congeniality of outlook was
expressed nowhere more strikingly than in another skyscraper commissioned by Gerald Hines and completed in Houston in 1985.

Sited as it was directly across from the modernist/minimalist towers of
Pennzoil, the RepublicBank Building brought into focus as few other
structures of its time the changes that had overtaken architecture with the
ascendancy of postmodernism. Its great height—772 feet—made the two

Richard Payne

TRANSCO TOWER, HOUSTON, 1985 (JOHN BURGEE, PARTNER)

PHILIP JOHNSON AND
GERALD HINES,
C. 1985

uncommon setbacks that punctuated its shaft seem more uncommon still. They are quite clearly based on the step gables that tourists easily remember from the guildhalls and town halls of late medieval northern Europe, especially Holland and Germany. That such forms were altogether foreign to the tradition of the skyscraper as a genre seemed to have made them only more enticing to Philip at a time when his history source books were growing dog-eared. He mounted turrets on the gables of the facades, subjecting them to more than a little double-coded "modernist" streamlining, meanwhile leapfrogging historical periods elsewhere in the design. At the base of the shaft is a smaller building that accommodates the banking hall and serves as a hall of entry to the larger building behind it. It, too, is gabled and, on the north elevation, turreted. Yet on the east, where the steps of the gables are most obvious, a giant round arch over the main entry strikes a defiant, consciously dissonant classical chord. A similar mixture of period effects is apparent in the banking hall itself. There, the walls and the vaults that trace the rise of the gables are articulated by very unmedieval segmented round arches. Nor could Philip resist adding nineteenth-century street decor to the interior in the form of elaborate five-globed lampposts and a comparably ornate floor clock. Meant strictly as ornamental detail, these last objects were the most unabashedly unoriginal components of the design, the parts that most looked as if Philip had purchased them at an antiques shop.

The furious pace set by Johnson/Burgee elicited equally quick reactions from the critics, prodded not only by the fact of Philip's fame—which

NCNB CENTER (FORMERLY REPUBLICBANK), HOUSTON, TEXAS, 1984
(JOHN BURGEE, PARTNER)

NCNB CENTER, HOUSTON:
VIEW OF FOYER
(JOHN BURGEE, PARTNER)

Richard Payne

only grew the more they wrote about him—but by the buffet of architectural forms he set before them. As always, the opinions were as various as the menu. *Architectural Record* quoted architectural historian K. B. S. Toker on PPG: "one of the most ambitious, sensitive and public-spirited urban developments since Rockefeller Center." Paul Goldberger in *The New York Times* was no less enthusiastic about the trail Philip had left in Houston, calling Transco and RepublicBank together "among the most emotionally powerful tall buildings that have been constructed anywhere in recent years."

The case for the negative was no less felt. Ada Louise Huxtable, who had soured greatly on the whole current scene, summing it up in a 1980 lecture to the American Academy of Arts and Sciences titled "The Troubled State of Modern Architecture," was more unforgiving of Philip than of all the other postmodernists. Dismissing PPG along with AT&T as a "stand-up joke," she said, "I take that back. I take them very seriously, because they are such shallow, cerebral design and such bad pieces of architecture. . . . It takes a creative act, not clever cannibalism, to turn a building into art."

Even more virulent in his scorn was Michael Sorkin, critic of *The Village Voice,* who carried the attack ad hominem:

> [Philip Johnson] is the architectural analogue of Ronald Reagan, another seamless producer of a seemingly endless series of contradictory statements. Both men resolve the manifest conflict by forcing attention away from their acts and onto themselves. . . . The two are true epi-

gones of the age of television, apostles of a consciousness that transcends traditional structures of logic, ethics, and—for that matter—time and space. Television invents via juxtaposition and re-juxtaposition. On TV, no sequence is precluded, anything can follow—or go with—anything else. Indeed we're perfectly habituated to the segue from starving babies in Ethiopia to Morris the Finicky Cat, from Mr. T. to Mother Theresa [*sic*]. . . . This is the world which Ronald Reagan inhabits (our side freedom fighters, their side terrorists) and which Philip Johnson designs. Mies today, Mizner tomorrow—what's the difference, it's only images.

Sorkin, as his previously quoted (see pp. 143–44) indictment of Philip's politics of the 1930s bears out, was a critic to whom intemperateness came easily. But Philip, especially in the 1980s, was no less immoderate in the games he played, architectural and otherwise. He continued to design as he had, in any manner or combination of manners that took his fancy. In a sense, he was not really unlike the Johnson of the sixties in the short-ness of his attention span; it is only that postmodernism gave him the license to make the bold, not to say extreme, gestures that a Vincent Scully or a Paul Goldberger found powerful, or that simply infuriated Huxtable and Sorkin. For freedom of attitude extended to critics, too, leaving so wide a gap and so many different gaps among them that an out-side observer might search in vain for either a cultural consensus or the conditions amenable to one.

Nevertheless, despite the pleasures of rule bending that the pluralism of the seventies and the eighties allowed, postmodernism could be a danger-ous game for an architect who, beneath Philip's outer layers, was more a classicist than a romantic, more persuasive when governed by discipline than when tempted by extravagance. None or at most few of his more ardent champions would have suggested that any of his postmodernist buildings of the 1980s was as fine or as effective a piece of work as the Glass House or the Sculpture Garden at The Museum of Modern Art or the first Boissonas House or Dumbarton Oaks or Pennzoil. Even AT&T, PPG, Transco, and RepublicBank—assuming these to be the best or close to the best of his postmodernist output—are so manifold in their emphases and directions that Johnson could not keep any of them free of assorted imperfections. If AT&T and PPG were as urbanistically com-manding as Scully and Toker claimed, it was nonetheless easier to admire the latter from across the river than from the piazza, and all too easy to feel cold and unwanted in the cavernous AT&T ground-floor arcade that Philip originally meant to make a sociable place. Transco hardly gains from the granite portal that seems uneasily fixed to its glass base, like a tombstone propped against a shop window, and Goldberger qualified his own praise of RepublicBank by complaining that the interior had been filled "with all kinds of things that seem intended to make it intimate and friendly, but end up only making it seem cute."

As a matter of fact, Philip exhibited no stranger or more surprising habit during the 1980s than the involuntary but all-too-frequent tendency to undercut the judgment of his friend Scully, who had said of him that "Johnson at his best . . . [possesses] the most ruthlessly aristocratic, highly studied taste of anyone practicing in America today." Now and then and often enough, his designs in the PoMo mode reveal a descent to the level of kitsch that appears less camp in its motivation than simply and unmitigatedly cheap in its effect.

In view of his rearing, his education, and his faithful membership as an adult in the world of high culture, one hesitates to call anything Philip voluntarily created meretricious, but there is no apter word for several of the works he imposed on the 1980s. None comes more readily to mind than the Crescent (1982–1985) in Dallas, a complex of office towers, shopping mall, hotel, and garage. The failure of this work lies less in its olio of manners and devices, although the recitation of them is breathtaking enough: Second Empire in the elevations qualified by modernist fenestration, Victorian grillwork with Mogul tracery in the balconies, mannerist classicism in the rusticated base. Rather it is the tawdriness of parts and sum: the papery masonry, the machine-stamped look of the metalwork, an overall tolerance of ersatz that falls just short enough of burlesque that one must assume Philip was serious when he did it. A similar vulgarity (Philip Johnson *vulgar*?) infects such efforts as the frail-walled Two Federal Reserve Plaza (1982–1985) in New York and the one build-

THE CRESCENT,
DALLAS, TEXAS,
1985
(JOHN BURGEE,
PARTNER)

Richard Payne

Richard Payne

COLLEGE OF ARCHITECTURE, UNIVERSITY OF HOUSTON, 1986
(JOHN BURGEE, PARTNER)

ing Philip designed for Chicago, 190 S. LaSalle. John Burgee's claim for
the latter, "We wanted our building—as a gesture to [John Wellborn]
Root and the Rookery [by Root and Daniel Burnham]—to be of the
same solidity and calmness," identifies the two Rootian qualities—solidity and calmness—that are most glaringly absent from it.

Philip's most audacious exercise in stylistic disentombment was the
School of Architecture (1983–1986) of the University of Houston, a work
so close in outer appearance to a specific building of the past—as opposed
to a type—that it was arguably less an act of derivation than of freeboot-
ing. Once again, the great Nicolas Ledoux had spoken to him and he
echoed back, following so closely the elevation of that master's neoclassical project for a House of Education (1773–1779) in the ideal city of
Chaux that most viewers would find it necessary to examine both designs
side by side in order to see the difference between them. An argument
ensued over whether, as Charles Jencks put it, "a good copy of a good
prototype [might be] an acceptable if modest goal." Jencks attributed a
remark to Philip himself—"It's better to be good than original"—that
sounded in sympathy with the very principle, Mies's "I'd rather be good

than interesting," rejected by Philip in another context (see p. 359). The issue never spread much beyond the ateliers in Houston; most of the critics agreed with Jencks's judgment that Johnson and Burgee had "managed only to thin out the original, in appearance at least, by subtracting its base and adding extraneous windows that lessened its *gravitas.*"

PETER

While there has never been a clear consensus about the merit of Philip's architecture overall in the 1980s, it seems fair to affirm that he arrived at the end of the decade better known than ever but no closer to the stature of a major master than he had been at the beginning. Too few of the buildings he made garnered the praise sufficient to overcome or compensate for the many that aroused genuine critical hostility. The way had not yet been found by which he might elevate himself above the reach of the perennial judgment "controversial," which at the same time he remained both vivacious and combative enough to make the most of, since it was clearly better than being ignored or even tepidly admired. Immortality, if it was ever to be conferred upon his architecture, would have to wait.

Meanwhile, he had more to do than design buildings. His approach to the universe of architecture called for action and confrontation at both the public and professional levels, and in those contexts he had lost none of the luster attributed to him in 1979 by Martin Filler, a critic who could hardly have been called a staunch admirer:

> . . . Philip Johnson has established for himself a unique place in the cultural world of New York (and, consequently, the nation). He is not only trustee, board member, and man-about-town: he is the Godfather, the Power Broker, the Gray Eminence, the Fount of all Honors for the architectural profession (and, consequently, the nation). Through his support of several institutions and many young architects, his frequent job referrals (Johnson has accepted only a fraction of the architectural commissions offered him, and habitually passes on the

rest), and his easy movement between the shapers of ideas and the holders of power, Johnson has consolidated a position unequaled by anyone else in the architecture world today.

Filler's words were part of a review for *Art in America* of *Writings*, an anthology of Philip's own critical prose, written between 1931 and 1979. It was published in 1979 at the urging and with the help of the two younger architect-colleagues, Peter Eisenman and Robert Stern, who were and would long remain among Philip's most committed supporters. Eisenman wrote an extended, lucid, and insightful introduction. Stern contributed short commentaries, similarly intelligent, on the pieces by Philip that followed. Vincent Scully added a foreword.

This was a formidable group of gun bearers, a sign of the high station ascribed to Philip by Filler, whose dislike of Johnson the designer ("the perverse inflictor of architectural jokes on an unsuspecting public") did not prevent him from finding these "articles and lectures . . . consistently high in quality. . . .

"After Johnson's flirtation with Fascism in the late 1930s . . . [he] re-emerged at a time when intellectual discourse on architecture in the U.S. was more or less a vast wasteland, bracketed on one side by the earnest, anti-formalist criticism of Lewis Mumford and on the other by the senile maunderings of Frank Lloyd Wright's crusade against the International Style."

Indeed these writings, for their intellectual substance, straightforward-ness of expression, and unfailing transparency of style, are the very antithesis of the agglutination of motifs that occurs in the worst of Philip's postmodernist buildings. He reminded the reader, who had cause to know it from the past, that he was by habit, if not by nature, a more crit-ical than creative mind and intellectually secure enough that he never felt the need to hide behind verbal obfuscation. The same reader should also have remembered, however, that there was no way so faceted and fidgety a mentality could have been content to choose between a career as a writer and one as an architect—not to mention the other routes he fol-lowed in the expenditure of his prodigious energies.

Happy with the publication of *Writings*, Philip entered with Eisenman into another literary project that aborted in short order, under circum-stances best described as bizarre. It was Philip's autobiography, to be related, as Eisenman later remembered it, in a book-length series of interviews. That much agreed, the two men sat down together in New Canaan in the summer of 1982 with a notepad and a tape recorder.

Eisenman was as much a talker as Philip, and rather more aggressive about it; his questions frequently ran as long as the answers. Moreover, he seemed to be having so good a time with his assignment—he and Philip loved mixing it up with each other anyhow—that what is left of the transcripts suggests a rambling conversation more than a prepared interview. A competent editor would have had little trouble putting it in order, but the two men never got far enough into their project for that.

What interfered appears traceable in part to another conversation, between Eisenman and John Burgee, which the latter reported took place at a party in Manhattan. "Peter got a little drunk," Burgee recalled. "I said, 'How's the book coming?' He said, 'Come into the other room.' We were sitting there when he said, 'I'm going to get him. I've got the goods on him. I've got photographs of him riding in a Nazi car. Lovers in Cambridge during school. I'm going to pull him down for good this time.' Those were Peter's words.

"I waited a few days and then went to Philip. I was uneasy about putting myself between those two. But I had a stake in this. It was my partnership, too. I said to Philip, 'Do you know Peter's intentions?' And I told him what I had heard. Philip said, 'Oh come now; everyone knows all about that stuff! I'm a colorful character.' He was reveling in it!

"I said, 'Philip, he's going to use the book to pull you down. You've got to get out of it.'

"Philip finally changed his mind and bought off Peter for ten thousand dollars. His [Philip's] lawyer drew up the contract.

"And then he and Peter got cozy all over again. There was really no bad blood. Peter needed the money—since the book was out of the question now—and Philip gave it to him. It was a good deal for both of them and they resumed their friendship, with no further conflict!"

Apprised of this account, Eisenman insisted he had no memory of any such encounter with Burgee and, in any case, no intention of blackening Philip's name. Philip did later confirm that a growing uneasiness over Peter's intentions had led him to pay the ten thousand dollars in the form, in publishers' parlance, of a kill fee, moreover, and that only a short time passed before he and Peter were chums again. Peter admitted to only one breach of faith: While working on the interviews, he had discussed them with a board member of the IAUS, thus violating his agreement with Philip that the book project would remain confidential until the time of publication.

. . .

"That's Peter" was Philip's usual and, so far as it mattered to him, sufficient way of explaining Peter's conduct, whatever it was. Sometimes he would add, as much to excuse as to characterize him, "He lies a little."

Even so, in crucial respects they were a perfect match. Each was driven by a personal ambition he knew was far more easily achieved if the other was kept a friend rather than made an enemy. Besides, they were charmed by each other's company. Quick off the mental mark and as passionate about architecture as about architectural gossip, they gossiped with each other as happily and indefatigably as David Whitney with Andy Warhol.

And Peter did know a lot, having earned a Ph.D. from Cambridge University, even if one of the things he knew was that he was not as well educated as Philip. Thus he drove himself all the harder to delve into the esoterica of the avant-garde and to talk about it so that he would ensure his recognition as the leading intellectual of the architectural brotherhood. Philip was enough of a Nietzschean to realize that Peter was good at getting and using power, the very things he had always wanted, and still did, for himself.

And so they sustained their friendship, turning it to pleasure and advantage in the two cultural milieus, upscale society and academe, that they regarded as vital to their respective professional advancements. In both instances, Eisenman was the driving force, Johnson the provider of cachet: prime minister, as it were, and sovereign.

Nothing illustrated that aspect of their relationship more graphically than the series of dinners, beginning in the late 1970s and continuing into the 1990s, at the Century Club, one of New York's premier private social organizations. Catering to people of note in philanthropy, government, and the arts and letters, the club was a perfect place for Eisenman, Johnson, and a small company of their peers to meet, eat, and confabulate. It was ideally ancient, founded in 1847 and housed in a well-pedigreed building completed in 1891 by McKim, Mead & White. The glow radiating from the list of its members—Jacqueline Onassis, Tom Wolfe, Tina Brown, Arthur Schlesinger, Jr., Paul Goldberger, to name a few— guaranteed prestige to any function carried out on its premises.

It was Eisenman who saw to it that in such a setting form and ritual were observed, even, or rather especially, among architects known for the radicalism of their work. Dinner jackets were obligatory. No women were invited. Meetings took place in the small private dining room containing the library of the architect Henry Pratt, with a normal complement of eight to twelve guests on any occasion. There might be an honored invitee, who was normally expected to discuss his work.

Philip Johnson would occupy the head of the table, flanked by the likes of Michael Graves, Robert Stern, Richard Meier, Jaquelin Robertson, Frank Gehry, Charles Gwathmey, Eisenman, and an assortment of carefully chosen others. Philip's high place was taken for granted, testimony to his unchallenged deanship of the group and his equally unmatched ability at the end of each meeting to sum up the substantive discussion that had taken place. Everyone in attendance retained a deadly respect for his intellectual authority, and while their regard for his architectural accomplishments varied from individual to individual, there was enough of it collectively, buoyed by his general renown, that the Century Club dinners became identified with him more than with anyone else.

They were also the talk of New York and of architects everywhere. Those who regarded them as formalizations of professional snobbism and self-promotion were invariably those who were never invited. Surely the meetings were more than intellectually profitable to their participants, who by their contact with one another were kept within reach of some of the most desirable clientele in the world. Philip himself recommended Graves as well as Gwathmey and Meier to the trustees of the Whitney Museum of American Art when they were looking for someone to add a wing to the building Marcel Breuer had built for them in 1966 on the East Side of Manhattan. Philip claimed a similar influence growing out of his exchanges with Michael Eisner, the chairman of the Walt Disney enterprises, who in the mid-1980s was seeking designers to carry out huge programs in Florida, California, and France. "I gave him the names," Philip is quoted as saying, "of young architects—Gehry, Eisenman and Graves."

Thus the decision to transfer the choreography of the Century Club dinners to an academic setting made only the most eminently good sense. In November of 1982, at the University of Virginia in Charlottesville, twenty-five men convened, all of them invited by Eisenman, all internationally known but no less notable for their own largely self-conferred status as the avatars of the East Coast Establishment. Given that, their meeting had an exclusivist air about it, made more rarefied by their agreement not to talk about the event in any formal way before it was undertaken. Its contents would, of course, be taped and later published.

The whole affair had, as Jaquelin Robertson wrote in his introduction to *The Charlottesville Tapes*, "a familiar Peter Eisenman trademark, the architectural 'twofer,' or how to use the Architectural Event to generate both publicity (in this case, the anti-publicity to be derived from 'open secrecy') and a provocative publishing opportunity."

The conference was to have been staged in New York by the Institute for Architecture and Urban Studies, but that body had become so financially strapped by 1982 that Eisenman quit the directorship. Hence the shift of venue to the University of Virginia, whose School of Architecture was chaired by Robertson, Peter's friend of long standing and another of the boys.

At each session, one of the architects would present a previously unpublished work for scrutiny and criticism by his colleagues. Philip, who showed a project for a pair of high-rise towers in Boston called International Place, flavored his presentation with a statement destined to resound down the corridors of architecture in the 1980s. It was made in response to a fusillade of criticism of his work by several of his peers, including the Luxembourger Rob Krier, who went so far as to declare, "We do not need high-rise buildings anywhere in the world. Not in America or anywhere else."

Philip, cool but defensive and annoyed, answered Krier: "I have read your book [*City Space in Theory and Practice*] and I agree with it completely, but I am a whore and I am paid very well for building highrise buildings. I think that going into an elevator is one of the most unpleasant experiences a man can have, and I do not see why we need them. We have all the room in the world. If you fly over this country you wonder where all the people are."

Of all the statements made at the conference, many equally provocative, "I am a whore" was the one seized upon most resolutely by the press, the very "outsiders" (Robertson's word) the conference sought to exclude from its colloquies. The critics, of course, read the published book and, with it, this figuratively engraved invitation, tendered by Philip, to box Philip's ears.

Why? What prompted such a remark, not so much self-deprecating as self-destructive? Philip might argue it wasn't self-anything; it was his way of chiding Krier for being a pharisee as well as a dreamer. Maybe he was right, but it was also part of a pattern of behavior to which he became habituated in his adult life, not least because it customarily worked so well for him. Normally, and especially if faced with an audience he perceived as hostile, he might say something so critical of himself that an antagonist was likely to feel robbed of an effective rejoinder. "He is disarming," wrote architect Denise Scott Brown in *The Saturday Review* of March 17, 1979. "To the student's question: 'Some of us may feel that some of your buildings are facile?' he counters, 'That is because I am a bad architect.' "

On the other hand, his response to Rob Krier in 1982—based on somewhat the same strategy—did not silence criticism so much as it inspired it. By the second half of the 1980s, those observers of the scene who did not appreciate Philip Johnson had arrived at a near consensus about him, most of it brought into focus by his Charlottesville self-evaluation. Diane Ketcham in an article written for *The New Criterion* of December 1986 said: ". . . Johnson's cynical verbiage does tell us something profound about his recent architecture. For his utterances are the spiritual equivalent of the soullessness characteristic of his buildings. In his commentary on the Charlottesville proceedings, Jaquelin Robertson . . . charges him with responsibility for 'the peculiar rich emptiness' typical of the latest American architecture." Three years later, Robert Campbell echoed Ketcham in *Lear's* of September 1989: "Playful, cynical impostorship—that, I propose, is the essential persona of Philip Johnson." Even the political columnist of *The New York Times,* Anthony Lewis, commenting on the building Philip had presented at Charlottesville, wrote: "I think Mr. Johnson is expressing his disdain for people, and for the society, by showing that he can produce absolutely any design, however insultingly inappropriate, and get it built." Charles Jencks, the American-born, mostly London-based writer who had been one of the most determined tormentors of Johnson since the early 1970s, seemed less harsh and more resigned, but hardly enthusiastic: ". . . only large commissions beget other large commissions and if one isn't large one isn't on the corporate lists. When this isn't a vicious circle it's extremely entertaining and Johnson has decided to enjoy it: it confirms his Nietzschean view of the world as founded on power relations and the will to art and immortality."

Any observer was misguided who thought that the barrage of criticism leveled at Philip in the eighties was enough to jolt him out of the orbit

PHILIP JOHNSON
IN HIS OFFICE AT
885 THIRD AVENUE,
NEW YORK CITY,
C. 1985

into which he had launched himself. Nothing really new had been adduced; he had already heard worse from Frank Lloyd Wright and Robin Middleton, to name just two of his earlier disparagers already quoted here. Besides, there were far more than a few figures of consequence in the 1980s who admired him for his talents and his achievements or recognized the weight he carried and the power he wielded in American culture, artistic and architectural, corporate and institutional. Even Robert Campbell, in the aforementioned article for *Lear's,* felt compelled to acknowledge that Philip was "widely considered to be one of [Thomas] Jefferson's successors as the greatest patron and practitioner of his time."

PHILIP AND DAVID AT HOME

The compound in New Canaan is not the only one of Philip's residences that he designed himself. In 1972, he and David Whitney moved from their apartment on East Fifty-fifth Street to a house Philip had leased on East Fifty-second Street—the same one he built in 1950 as a guest house for Blanchette Rockefeller. They remained there until 1979, when Philip was taken with the notion of a Fifth Avenue address. He chose a flat in the building at 1001 Fifth Avenue that he had completed the same year after another architect's plans (see p. 343). In 1983, he and David moved again, to an apartment in, of all places, the Museum Tower at 15 West Fifty-third Street, the building Philip had so ached to design before The Museum of Modern Art gave the commission to Cesar Pelli. Mostly recovered from the loss, he further consoled himself by buying a space on the eleventh floor that disclosed a splendid view of the AT&T Building to the east. He redecorated the flat, of course, spending most of his energy on the living room, which he crowned with a low, curving ribbed vault in emulation of an old favorite of his, John Soane. A table and chairs by Robert Venturi were added. The mood was postmodernist.

This was a small apartment, something of a pied-à-terre, with room for himself and David and no one else. Since David, an excellent cook, did not favor making meals there, he and Philip, who was only a little better than useless in the kitchen, took dinner on each of their Manhattan evenings—Monday through Wednesday or Thursday—at nearby restaurants. David was more attentive in the apartment to another art he had mastered, the cultivation of the flowers he grew in his greenhouse in New Canaan and brought into town.

The domestic strife that had marked the early phases of the Johnson-Whitney relationship, when John Hohnsbeen and Peter Vranic were symptomatic of Philip's cavalier expression of his freedom of movement, had largely abated. Philip was hardly the prowler in his seventies that he had been in his young years. He was also brought up short one evening, as he recalled it, by the television personality Barbara Walters, who shared a table with him and Jacqueline Onassis at a party hosted by the singer-actress–arts administrator Kitty Carlisle Hart. Walters wanted to know why Philip never invited his companion to such functions, since, quite evidently, the stigma attached to homosexual partners socializing together, even at society events, was fading in the 1970s. Judging from his behavior, if not from his motivation, Philip hadn't taken active notice of the change. He had no answer for Walters, who proceeded to scold him until—Philip remembering again—he left the party, feeling maladroit and just guilty enough to want to be left alone.

Thereafter, he and David were seen more regularly as a couple around town, although David's own emotional problems, which would probably have plagued him with or without Philip, continued to the point that the effects of his drinking threatened their relationship and earned him a sour reputation for rude comportment, especially among the upper crust. No less than Andy Warhol, who, one might suppose, was above being taken aback by this sort of thing, was more than once taken aback by David. While Warhol's busybody diary is hardly a piece of scholarship, it does refer repeatedly and consistently to several of David's habits and proclivities. In an entry to his diary dated December 4, 1983, Andy wrote: "Steve Rubell called and said he was picking me up at 6:30 with Bianca [Jagger] and Ian Schrager to go to the Helmsley Palace for the Philip Johnson retrospective exhibition with Jackie O[nassis] at the Municipal Art Society benefit in the Villard House. Got into black tie. . . .

"Philip was sort of cute. He said that it wasn't his exhibition, it was his execution. David Whitney was having martinis and he said that as soon as Philip popped off he and I could get together. . . . And Philip gave a speech and David laughed and clapped. He's smart, David."

The August 7, 1984, entry includes the following: "I was meeting David Whitney and Philip Johnson for dinner at the Four Seasons. Invited Keith [Haring] and Juan [Hamilton] and Jean Michel [sic] [Basquiat]. Philip goes to bed at 9:00, so he wanted to have dinner at 6:30 but I made it 7:30. . . .

"Then David got drunk and started what he always starts when he's had a few drinks, that when Philip kicks the bucket he'll move in with me. It's scary."

Elsewhere in the diaries, Warhol noted David's drinking habits and the shift in them, observing on November 24, 1985, that "David was having his first of about seven martinis and a beer. And he was talking again about 'when Pops pops off.' But David will probably pop off before Pops," then adding, however, on January 12, 1987, that "he [David] . . . and [Robert] Rauschenberg have given up drinking so I guess they'll live forever."

David did stop, not just the drinking but, judging from the Warhol diaries, all further badinage with Andy about future plans. The two developments would have been enough to strengthen his relationship with Philip, which grew stronger anyhow, and remarkably, in the wake of Philip's coronary relapse in 1986.

Suddenly overcome with a weakness that reminded him of the conditions leading to his bypass operation eleven years earlier, Philip made

DAVID WHITNEY AND ANDY WARHOL
AT OPENING OF ART MUSEUM OF SOUTH
TEXAS, CORPUS CHRISTI, 1972

straight for his physician, who lost no time himself in bundling his patient into New York Hospital for an angioplasty. It was June 7, 1986, the eve of the New Canaan gala Philip and a retinue of friends, family, and staff had planned in celebration of his eightieth birthday. Upward of two hundred people were invited; the guest list read like the condensation of a New York society columnist's black book. As reported on the first page of this narrative, Philip's enforced absence compounded by the remorseless rain that fell on June 8 could have defeated the whole affair. But the very opportunity to see the compound as a whole and the Glass House in particular, an offering not previously extended to all the invitees, pulled a multitude of them out there, many further attracted by the irresistible prospect of rubbing up against one another.

David acted the host and Theodate the hostess, a partnership formed more out of necessity than amity. But they performed their duties handsomely, and the party in retrospect seemed all the more successful because of the very obstacles fate had put in its way.

Even people who knew the Johnson compound from past experience liked to visit it as often as it was made available to them, if for no other reason than that it was in a more or less constantly changing state. Since the completion of the sculpture gallery in 1970, a two-column entry gate to the grounds had been added, plus three independent structures, the most conspicuously architectural of which was the library, finished in 1979. Until it materialized, Philip had been without a satisfactory working space on the property. As reported, he never carried through the studio project he had meant for a site close to Ponus Ridge Road, and he later abandoned the notion of using the sculpture gallery as combined atelier and living area.

The new library, on the other hand, fulfilled its special requirements in several respects. Its very diminutiveness was functionally ideal: There was space in its compact one-room interior for Philip and, at most, a single guest. Moreover, a conical skylight admitted light that fell virtually shadow-free on his working table below, from which, if he glanced up, he saw books and more books lining the walls of the room, interrupted only by the window directly across from him. That, in turn, revealed a view of the woods and especially the curious, useless—well, evocative—little concoction made wholly of chain-link fencing, the Gehry Ghost House, named partly in honor of Philip's friend Frank Gehry, partly because it rose from the ruined foundation of an ancient farm building.

Sited at a distance of several hundred yards from the Glass House, the library was itself a strange and striking object. Intended as a retreat, it looked the part in its chalky whiteness and utter isolation, a cylinder locked into, or embraced by, a cube, with the latter hollowed out slightly to accommodate an entry. A fireplace chimney rose from one corner of the cube, diagonally across from the conical skylight that crowned the cylinder, creating an overall effect of lean sculptural geometry. Silhouetted against a stand of trees, silent and aloof, the library brought to mind the paintings of one of Philip's favorite artists, Giorgio de Chirico. So Philip loved it. It was spare and disconnected from everything, with no telephone, no running water, no plantings around it or pathway leading

JOHNSON RESIDENCE,
NEW CANAAN:
LIBRARY/STUDY, 1980

Richard Payne

JOHNSON RESIDENCE, NEW CANAAN:
GEHRY GHOST HOUSE, 1985

JOHNSON RESIDENCE, NEW CANAAN:
LINCOLN KIRSTEIN TOWER, 1985

to it—so much for Philip's normally cherished processional—to unite it even with the ground it stood on.

The birthday party guests were among the first to see the Gehry Ghost House and another new addition to the compound, both of them finished a few months before the celebration. On the rise of a hill west of the pond stood the Lincoln Kirstein Tower, an arresting sight whether viewed up close or from the Glass House. It was more a piece of sculpture than of architecture, but it was clearly built, an assemblage of informally composed concrete blocks that rose to a height of thirty-six feet. No sooner seen, it inspired the average visitor to climb it; no sooner mounted, it daunted him. The blocks were wide enough for a foothold but not sufficiently articulated for a sure handhold. Thus the adventurer more likely than not faltered about halfway up and never read the inscription Philip had embossed on a plate embedded in the topmost block. A tribute to Kirstein, its exact sentiment was kept secret to any and all who did not complete the ascent. (Philip himself made it with the agility of a mountain goat until he was in his early eighties.)

Apart from David, for whom Philip in the 1960s designed two unbuilt houses on the south property, later purchasing and remodeling an old Shingle Style house for him nearby, Kirstein was the second person honored by name in a structure on the Johnson grounds. Frank Gehry, of course, was the brilliantly idiosyncratic California architect whom Philip admired probably more than any other active member of the profession during the 1980s. Kirstein, on the other hand, was a personal friend of long standing for whom Philip felt not only affection but undying gratitude. He had been chiefly instrumental in securing Philip's commission at Lincoln Center (not named after him, though he may have assumed, David would dryly note, that it was) and, no less vitally, had written a letter in 1944 (see p. 164) that sought to absolve Philip of the political sins he was burdened by at the time. Widely regarded as a formidable intellectual, Kirstein was also given to abrupt and violent shifts of temper. While he was without peer as an impresario of modern ballet, he held much of modern painting, especially the abstract variety, in contempt and had even alienated Alfred Barr with an article in *Harper's* in 1948 that attacked the alleged abstraction-biased policies of The Museum of Modern Art.

But he revered Philip. In Kirstein's eyes, Philip could do no wrong architecturally. And the regular Sunday get-togethers the two men enjoyed in their later years only solidified Philip's reciprocal desire to dedicate a monument to him. Besides, Barr, an even dearer friend, was dead now, having surrendered what was left of his once exquisitely structured mind to Alzheimer's in 1981. Philip nonetheless designed a monument

GEORGE BALANCHINE, PHILIP JOHNSON,
AND LINCOLN KIRSTEIN,
C. 1984

PHILIP JOHNSON AND
EDWARD M. M. WARBURG,
C. 1985

MEMORIAL TABLETS DESIGNED
BY PHILIP JOHNSON FOR GRAVES OF
ALFRED AND MARGARET SCOLARI BARR,
GREENSBORO, VERMONT, C. 1983

for him, too, his tombstone in Greensboro, Vermont, in a form that imitated the profile of the AT&T Building, and he had the wisdom to end his eulogy of Barr at a memorial service in The Museum of Modern Art with a recollection of Christopher Wren's epitaph: "in Latin because it makes you remember it better: *Si monumentum requiris, circumspice.*"

Philip did not confirm any significance in the dedication of two buildings at New Canaan to very close friends. Nevertheless, one may speculate that the gesture was a reflection of his years, of the more or less natural impulse to bequeath something to somebody near to him or somebody deserving. By the mid-1980s, he was still financially secure but not wealthy enough, in fact, to provide the National Trust out of pocket with the money necessary to endow the New Canaan compound. Thus it was agreed that whatever was needed to make up that amount could be assured by the sale of some of the paintings he owned. Following his death, the National Trust would, of course, open the place to the public, keeping just enough of the paintings to comprise sufficiently presentable displays in the painting gallery. David would get most of the rest of Philip's assets, including the New York apartment and the Shingle Style house he already occupied on the Ponus Ridge Road edge of the New Canaan property. (Another old house on the property would continue to serve as a caretaker's cottage.) Modest sums would also go to Philip's sisters, Jeannette and Theodate.

At eighty, Philip was, after all, an old man by most standards, which certainly seemed applicable to him in the wake of his second coronary illness. He went on reciting his favorite adage, "Life begins at seventy," but more and more he would add with a touch of bitterness, "and it ends at eighty." The fact is, he did not rebound from the angioplasty with anything like the magical recovery he made following the 1975 bypass. For well over a year, he was in an often-enervated state, unable to function without daily naps and even then occasionally coming to the close of a day looking forward, surely for the first time in his life, and very introspectively indeed, to the end.

As he described it, what he saw was a blackness, a nothingness, thinkable only as surcease from the misery of the present moment. If presently he was to feel a little better, he would recoil from the blackness, hating and fearing it. Normally keen to accept any interesting invitation to lecture or to travel, he gave up both. He made his way to work every day, for as long as he could manage, but there the prospect filled him with only more gloom. For relations with Burgee were not what they once had been. The mood around the office had grown tense.

While the corporate entity Johnson/Burgee thrived in the 1980s, John Burgee began early in the decade to enjoy his success less and less and to change, gradually, from a confident to a frustrated man. His chief objective in joining Philip in the first place, in 1967, had been to take command of the office upon Philip's retirement, which he presumed would occur while he was still young enough to establish his own independent reputation.

But Philip did not retire, either at sixty-five or at seventy or at seventy-five. Nor did he modify his long-standing insistence that his name be removed from the firm upon his death. Moreover, he could not help drawing public attention to himself, at the expense, at least in John's eyes, of John. In 1983, when Philip was seventy-seven, the two men sat down together in an effort to ameliorate the situation worsening between them. Philip said he would do what he could to share the spotlight with John— a virtually unenforceable agreement—and the name of the firm was changed from Johnson/Burgee Architects to John Burgee Architects with Philip Johnson.

It was a nominal move, effectively little more. Regardless of his attempts to minimize himself, at which he was constitutionally ill-suited anyhow, Philip continued as the office's central design figure, absorbing so much of the media light that none was left for the luckless Burgee.

In 1985, less than a year before Philip's eightieth birthday, the office was moved from the Seagram Building to a new high rise at Fifty-third Street and Third Avenue in Manhattan, a work completed after a Johnson/ Burgee design and developed by the ever-ready Gerald Hines.

Even those who disliked it had to admit it was a spectacular object, and more than a few critics called it one of the best buildings Philip and John had ever presented to the public. It quickly got a nickname, the Lipstick Building, on account of its elliptical plan and the two setbacks in its elevation, which endowed its shaft with the look of a giant retractable lipstick tube. Since its facade was a great looping curve, it deviated from the generally straightfaced look of Third Avenue, but there was something rather refreshing about that, especially since New York architecture is not a study in formal consistency to begin with. Moreover, it was mercifully free of most of the postmodernist historical ornament that Philip had lately employed, more than once, with dubious taste.

In any case, it was Philip who got nearly all the glory, or the heat, for the Lipstick Building. In the year of its completion, a book promoted by the firm, illustrating its output since 1979 and published under the title *Philip Johnson/John Burgee: Architecture, 1979–85*, only certified what the public never stopped believing, right or wrong, that even John Burgee Architects with Philip Johnson only meant Philip Johnson.

PHILIP JOHNSON IN THE HOME
OF FRANK LLOYD WRIGHT,
OAK PARK, ILLINOIS,
C. 1984

Once again, John confronted Philip, who offered in 1986 to withdraw entirely from the firm. In substance, this proposal was accepted, Burgee amending it only to allow for a period of transition in which Philip would operate not as a partner but as a consultant, while receiving a $250,000 annual salary, an office of his own, and a secretary.

Neither Philip's angioplasty, which occurred in the same year, nor anything else that ensued seemed to work to the benefit of John's effort to establish his personal image. Finally, at wit's end, in April of 1988, he sent a memorandum to Philip that had the effect of an ultimatum. Excerpts follow:

> First it has become clear in a variety of ways that the perception of the firm is such that it would or could not continue without your total and central involvement. This obviously is not acceptable to me as I must prepare for the time when this is not possible. . . . The most drastic action which I feel I must take if nothing else will work is to become totally independent now with your immediate retirement and take my chances. . . .
>
> What I propose is that you really become "design consultant": consulting with the firm on design issues just as other consultants consult on lighting design, landscaping, graphics, etc. It is a different role than

FIFTY–THIRD STREET AND THIRD AVENUE (ALSO KNOWN AS 885 THIRD AVENUE
AND/OR THE LIPSTICK BUILDING), NEW YORK CITY, 1985
(JOHN BURGEE, PARTNER)

you have had in the past and will require modification of working
process. . . .

    . . . there is unanimous agreement that no one in the profession can
match your public image and as long as you want to, it will overshadow any image the firm might try to project. As long as you are
working with the firm . . . the public perception will not accept qualifications. . . . Therefore there must be no more interviews or public
appearances as long as you continue as design consultant to the
firm. . . . I know this will be hard for you because you do enjoy it.
Requests, no doubt, will continue—you are a "celebrity" with "star
quality" and the press eats it up and age only enhances it. I see no
other way than just eliminating it all. This also includes interviews,
unveilings, ground breakings, openings, and other special events
unless we agree beforehand that it would help the firm. . . .

    As your role is reduced you may find you don't need to be in the
office as much and can spend more time in the country or at other
activities. . . .

It must be kept in mind that Burgee issued his draconian memorandum
at a time when Philip lacked the physical capacity, if not the will, to
mount a workable counterattack. If he had contested John's demands and
won, he would be left with a terminally unhappy partner or, worse, control of an office of sixty employees whom he had neither the aptitude, the
will, nor the strength to keep in line all by himself. Alternatives were
available to him, but it seemed to him best and simplest to try to live with
the conditions of the memo.

Thus Burgee did manage to put a lid on Philip, but it was not airtight.
He could not police him day and night, nor were the media easily discouraged from their habitual pursuit of a man who loved being pursued.
Just one month after Burgee wrote his memo, and five years after Philip
had been dropped to second billing in the firm's name, Paul Goldberger
in an article in the *Times* twice credited the newly completed IBM Building in Atlanta to "Philip Johnson and John Burgee."

Moreover, the clients, that collective sine qua non of the architectural
profession, were themselves naturally drawn to Philip's name. One of the
most ambitious efforts ever undertaken by the Johnson/Burgee firm was
the reconstitution of Times Square (see pp. 403–04), which began in 1983
and did not die until the recession of the early 1990s rendered it unbuild-
able. Since several schemes for it were proposed early and late, each of
them principally by Philip, the project's principal developer, George

Klein, insisted until the very end that Philip be kept involved, not merely as a "consultant" but as a major player in the overall planning.

The old cat had not run out of lives. By late 1988, strength was returning to Philip's eighty-two-year-old body—his mind having never deserted him—and it occurred to him once or twice, never sentimentally, of course, that a measure of gratitude might at last be due his long-lived parents for the genetic makeup they had passed on to him.

At the beginning of his ninth decade, then, and following an example he had set for himself several times earlier, he summoned the resources to make the most of his situation. It is likely that he was motivated to some degree by a fear of the bottomless pit into which he had gazed following his angioplasty: For as long as he could function professionally, he could keep his distance from it. Yet he had more affirmative cause to look ahead, to stay clear of the slough that retirement from Burgee might have suggested.

A perceptible and enduring calm had settled over his own household. David and he were in the process of turning their life together into a happy marriage, a condition to which he had never given much thought, or effort, in any of his earlier close relationships. An increasing need of David appears to have led him to behave with sustained decency toward his younger companion, to leaven their partnership with a humor and forbearance for which, again, he had not been famous in his more hell-bent years.

David, in turn, had given up his own previous violent indulgences. The drinking was over, and the smoking, both replaced by, of all things, a regime of physical exercise. Otherwise, he continued his own life, practicing his uncommon talents in the New Canaan greenhouse while occasionally curating an art exhibition and editing and supervising the publication of an art book. A Philip Johnson archive, meticulously assembled, took shape in his upstairs quarters at the Shingle Style house. Insuring the preservation of Philip's memory, David magnified him. Around the house and even in the presence of guests, he was free as a wife of comfortably long standing to be as sharp and withering as he pleased with Philip, who found his barbs funny—which they invariably were—rather than demeaning. The two of them attended any and all social functions together, traveled together, talked together, intelligently and with a common purpose, spent time alone together, all in a comradeship matched in its growing harmony by few couples of whatever age or gender.

If much of this good feeling grew from Philip's age and fragility, none of it was a sign of his dotage. In fact, with the recovery of his old energy came the restoration of his resilience. He pursued new commissions, working on them in his library at New Canaan and the office Burgee had given him and paying Burgee staff members—his old loyalists mostly, like designer John Manley—to negotiate the technicalities. He resumed his old travel schedule, traversing the country and carrying on as far as Europe and Japan.

But as he kept busy with his practice, he grew busier still with the conscious renewal and extension of his lordship of the realm by other means, launching, in 1987, a project that at the beginning drew heavily on his fame—and notoriety—and at the end added more weight to both.

DECON

No critic anywhere had as uncharitable a view of Philip as Michael Sorkin did, and no architect preyed on Michael Sorkin's mind as did Philip. It was reasonable, then, that Sorkin took the opportunity to record the scenario that led to the "Deconstructivist Architecture" exhibition of 1988, which Philip curated—for the first time since the early 1950s—at The Museum of Modern Art. In an article of December 1987 titled "Canon Fodder," Sorkin reported that a pair of young Chicago architects, Paul Florian and Stephen Wierzbowski, had conceived an idea as early as 1984 for an exhibition of recent architecture marked, in Sorkin's words, "by a prevalent tendency, shared with the culture in general." It was "an architecture obsessed with fragmentation and instability, 'torn between history and technology.' "

Having assembled a list of forty to fifty suggested examples, Florian and Wierzbowski applied to the National Endowment for the Arts for grant assistance. They were turned down twice. They then reduced the size of their show and added a title: "Violated Perfection: the Meaning of the Architectural Fragment." Another application was prepared and rejected.

Enter Aaron Betsky, employed at the time as an architect in Frank Gehry's Los Angeles office: Lunching one day with Wierzbowski, Betsky was much taken with what he heard about the show and said he would try to find a place for it on the West Coast. Sometime later, he changed his mind, deciding the whole idea was better presented in the form of a book, which he proceeded to peddle to a New York publisher. Florian and Wierzbowski would collaborate.

Sorkin continued: "However, the same day that Betsky cut his deal at Rizzoli, he had lunch with Philip Johnson."

Now Sorkin thickened the plot, noting that all this was happening against the backdrop of a search for someone to fill a greatly coveted position at The Museum of Modern Art, the directorship of the Department of Architecture and Design, open since the recent death of Arthur Drexler and tended on acting basis by the Curator of Design, Stuart Wrede. Johnson had taken it upon himself to conduct a search for Drexler's successor, subjecting a number of bright young men to scrutiny over lunch at the Four Seasons. One of these was Betsky, another Joseph Giovannini, a writer for the *Times*, who was himself at work on a book dealing with a subject roughly like that pursued by Betsky. Both Betsky and Giovannini informed Johnson of their respective studies, and Johnson, conversing with Betsky, said he thought "Violated Perfection" would make a splendid exhibition at MoMA.

Meanwhile, Wrede, who had hopes of securing the Architecture and Design job for himself but who was "widely considered," in Sorkin's words, "to be without Johnson's support," entertained a phone call from Philip, which included a spirited proposal that the exhibition be put on at the museum. Sorkin wrote:

> Poor Wrede. If ever a man were trapped between a rock and a hard place, it was he. Here's the guy who holds the key to his future, "all enthusiastic" to do a show as soon as possible, demanding a favor. . . . Finally, though, this is the portrait of a man with only one choice, and he made it: the show's being hustled into a slot in June, absolute record time as these things go. . . .

Part of the reason for such alacrity was that Wrede, on his own and more independently than Sorkin implied, was strongly in favor of the show and wanted to press forward with it. Even so, this had little effect on Philip's personal momentum. Sorkin went on:

> Now, of course, Philip was obliged to perform power-brokering's primary act: deciding who's in and who's out. . . . The initial cut had been done by Florian, Wierzbowski, Giovannini, Betsky, et al., but things needed to be finalized, and so the scene was set for a ritual of consensus and complicity, a transfer of rights from the originators to the appropriator. And, as with so many of the ceremonies of the Johnson cult, this one was enacted at a boys-only dinner at—where else?—the Century Club.

On October 28, the following gathered in a private room: Philip, John Burgee, Peter Eisenman, Frank Gehry, Aaron Betsky, Joe Giovannini, and Peter Zweig and Mark Wigley, two young academics recently elevated to the Johnson retinue. . . . Not present were Florian and Wierzbowski, completely cut out, never having received, as Wierzbowski recently wrote me, a single "letter or phone call regarding 'Violated Perfection,' our opinions about it, or a request for permission to use the title."

Philip's reply to the charges against him was, as Martin Filler reported, "that the idea was as much 'in the air' as the architecture itself." In his catalogue preface, he did acknowledge Florian and Wierzbowski for inventing the name "Violated Perfection," even though the museum, which found it unpalatably suggestive, disallowed it in favor of "Deconstructivist Architecture."

Nonetheless, by the time the show was ready for mounting, Philip's maneuvering had already done damage to his own position and was about to do more; seldom, in fact, has an exhibition been so scalded before it went on view as was this one. After charging him with "an abuse of power [and] intellectual shoddiness," Herbert Muschamp, writing two months before the opening, added, ". . . I hope it is a great show. But I'm not so sure—it seems to me a strong possibility that Philip Johnson resembles the persona Walter Pater fashioned for the Mona Lisa, a figure 'older than the rocks among which she sits; like the vampire, she has been dead many times, and learned the secrets of the grave.' "

That was a rhetorical back-of-the-hand, of course, but the whole exhibition was overgrown with rhetoric, the densest of it appearing in the literature written to rationalize the work of the architects represented. There were eight exhibitors, all with internationally respected credentials: Frank Gehry (based in Los Angeles), Bernard Tschumi and Peter Eisenman (New York), Zaha Hadid (London), Rem Koolhaas (Rotterdam), Daniel Libeskind (Milan), and Wolfgang Prix and Helmut Swiczinsky of the firm Coop Himmelblau (Vienna). While each of them was distinguishable from the others, their work as a whole tended toward several discernible expressive characteristics: the use of warped and disengaged planes, deviations from parallels and right angles, and, in Philip's own words in the catalogue preface, "the diagonal overlapping of rectangular or trapezoidal bars." The emphasis in most of the projects was aggressively formalist, as if little concern had been felt by the designers, let alone shown, for the goals of convention as communication that much of postmodernist architecture had set for itself.

If the exhibition could have been presented more nearly independently of all the talk about Philip's motives and all the sweaty theoretical strug-

gles over the concept of Deconstructivism, it might have made a more
affirmative impression on the critics. But motives and theory were so
much at the heart of it that public attention to the work itself was greatly
diverted to the margins of consciousness. The irony was that Philip, who
had always depended on his eye rather than on theory in judging architecture, had now invited Mark Wigley to write the main catalogue essay,
which turned out to be a litany of theoretical maunderings that generated
more critical heat than the work it was meant to be about.

Wigley began with several massive generalizations as debatable as they
were encompassing and undocumented:

"Architecture has always been a central cultural institution valued above
all for its provision of stability and order. These qualities are seen to arise
from the geometric purity of its formal composition.

"The architect has always dreamed of pure form, of producing objects
from which all instability and disorder have been excluded."

He then sought to establish a link between Deconstructivism and the
efforts of the early Russian Constructivists, whose " 'impure,' skewed,
geometric compositions" stood for "a critical turning point where the
architectural tradition was bent so radically that a fissure opened up
through which certain disturbing architectural possibilities first became
visible. Traditional thinking about the nature of the architectural object
was placed in doubt. But the radical possibility was not then taken up.
The wound in the tradition soon closed, leaving but a faint scar. These
[Deconstructivist] projects reopen the wound. . . .

"If [they] in a sense complete the enterprise, in so doing they also
transform it: they twist Constructivism. This twist is the 'de' of 'deconstructivist.' . . . The forms themselves are infiltrated with the characteristic skewed geometry, and distorted. In this way, the traditional
condition of the architectural object is radically disturbed. . . . The internal disturbance has actually been incorporated into the internal structure,
the construction. It is as if some kind of parasite has infected the form and
distorted it from the inside.

"The rooftop remodeling project in this exhibition, for example [by
Coop Himmelblau], is clearly a form that has been distorted by some
alien organism, a writhing, disruptive animal breaking through the corner. Some twisted counter-relief infects the orthogonal box. It is a skele-
tal monster which breaks up the elements of the form as it struggles out."

Wigley went on to say that "the more carefully we look, the more
unclear it becomes where the perfect form ends and its imperfection
begins: they are found to be inseparably entangled. . . . It is as if perfection had always harbored imperfection, that it always had certain undiag-

nosed congenital flaws which are only now becoming visible. Perfection is secretly monstrous. Tortured from within, the seemingly perfect form confesses its crime, its imperfection."

Wigley's explicit denial that the work on view was an application of the literary theory of deconstruction hardly cleared things up, especially in view of the claim lodged about the same time by Giovannini: "And just as a literary text, according to advocates of deconstruction such as Jacques Derrida and the late Paul de Man, doesn't have a unifying wholeness or fixed meaning, but several asymmetrical and irreconcilable ones, a building can consist of disparate 'texts' and parts that remain distinct and unaligned, without achieving a sense of unity."

Indeed, Wigley's constant references to parasites and other alien organisms and invasive monsters bore a suspiciously strong resemblance to the usages of Derrida, but no less to the favorite phraseologies of Peter Eisenman, whom Wigley knew through common connections at Princeton University. Eisenman, who was promoting Derrida heavily at the time, while seeing a lot of Philip, loved to apply words like *contamination* and *transgression* to architecture, sprinkling them throughout the conversations he had with Philip as early as their failed series of biographical interviews in 1982.

The press was collectively unsympathetic toward the exhibition, scoring it over and over, as Brendan Gill wrote, with "reviews so harsh that even the Broadway euphemism 'mixed reviews' . . . would amount to an overly benign summary of them." Douglas Davis attacked as "preposterous" Wigley's assertion that the Decon architects were "shocking," adding that "it overlooks the virulent, mocking, anti-art tradition that has coursed through the entire century." Herbert Muschamp was heard from again, in no happier a mood following the show than prior to it: "Nor do the ideas with which Wigley promotes the doctrine of impure form arise from the center of architectural practice (or, for that matter, from Russia during the teens). They have drifted into his impressionable mind from post-structural philosophy as it developed in Paris following the student uprisings of 1968: buzzwords like strategy, agent, intervention, subversion, undermine, disrupt, extremity, enigma; prêt-à-penser modes like the ecstasy over instability and the collapse of meaning. . . ."

Thus Wigley caught more of the critics' displeasure than did the architects, whose work on the whole was greeted with polite praise ("I don't see much theoretical intensity in Zaha Hadid's work, but her visual intelligence is acute," said Muschamp) or something close to a shrug ("There is nothing abrasive or startling in these buildings," wrote Jane Holtz Kay). Philip himself was seen, by consensus, as the string-pulling mastermind of the event. Some observers, unwilling to accept his claim that Decon was not a style or a movement or a creed but just a "confluence of a few important architects' work of the years since 1980," insisted he was trying to do again what he had done in the MoMA "Modern Architecture" show of 1932; namely, illuminate the most promising pathway that a vital new architecture might follow—specifically, in this case, away from an aging postmodernism to something called Deconstructivism. Probably these critics were right, nor would they have resented him for such a motive, taken by itself. What most aggrieved them was their impression that he had achieved his ends through an imposition of naked power: "the use of MoMA as a platform for old boy promotion," as Douglas Davis declared just before enunciating his central complaint: "that the exhibition had little to do with the art of architecture and everything to do with polemics."

Once again, Philip was trapped in an irony. His practiced eye—no one contended it was less than that—was evident in the overall merit of the eight architects he chose, but it was compromised by his willingness to avert it, to allow the theoreticians to take command of the temple.

Therewith, another parallel with his experience in the 1932 exhibition comes to mind. He always freely admitted he had profited in that venture from all he learned from two brilliant colleagues, Alfred Barr and Henry-Russell Hitchcock. Equally a matter of record is his own observation that he was customarily less comfortable in his professional pursuits when he conducted them all by himself than when he had some such partner at his side. In the case of the Deconstructivist show, the voice whispering in his ear, more exactly declaiming, belonged to Peter Eisenman.

There can be no extensive account of Philip's later years without some considerable space allocated to Peter, who was the first to acknowledge his uncommon ability to make space for himself anywhere, anytime. Quick-witted, talented, intellectually ambitious, vain, articulate, immensely sociable, and capable of the boldest manipulations in the service of professional power, he had manifestly so much in common with Philip, and was in the nature of things so close to him, that the two men seemed virtually destined to an ambivalent relationship that neither could relinquish or fully resolve. Although Peter admitted sharing confidential passages of the 1982 biographical tapes with an outsider, thus arousing Philip's suspicions, he also claimed that Philip's affection for him derived from his efforts to defend Philip against those who charged him with fascist sympathies. And he was full of praise for Philip's generosity in helping him recoup business losses by making him a loan of ten thousand dollars—a sum Philip insisted was no loan at all but the kill fee already reported here (see p. 373).

Nevertheless, once they reconciled, they stayed that way. In 1990, Philip was best man at Peter's second marriage, to Cynthia Davidson, at Chicago's posh Racquet Club. Peter, in turn, delivered an eloquent encomium to Philip at a celebration of the latter's eighty-fifth birthday at Seton Hill College in Greensburg, Pennsylvania, in 1991.

If there was one thing they did not share, it was an opinion about psychoanalysis. Philip had done without therapy long enough to dismiss analysis as mostly nonsense. Peter saw it as the route to ultimate truth. Muschamp once spoke of Eisenman's "quirky desire to insinuate his private psychoanalytic history into his public persona." Peter certainly considered himself an expert on the subject even though his perceptibly Jungian opinions were at odds with the more advanced social standards of 1992. On the subject of Philip's politics in the 1930s, Peter reflected thus:

"He was run by his unconscious, what I would call his anima, which is very active in the homosexual personality. If you've been in psychoanalysis, you realize that part of homosexuality is the female side, the unconscious female side out of control. When Philip runs afoul of everybody, the anima is still the thing that strikes out, and bites, and is nasty. It's this anima that is basically sated through his physical, homosexual, his very satisfactory relationship with David. The anima is fine there. But sometimes it still bites, strikes. If you've been analyzed as long as I have . . . I've changed. I've come to understand Philip and to be able to deal with the anima, and so it doesn't threaten me. But I think that Philip went out of control in the thirties. . . ."

Needless to say, that statement was not made in the presence of Philip, even though he was not only accustomed to what he regarded as Peter's addiction to high-flown flummery but most of the time tolerant of it. Frequently, if not typically, he would be offended by something Peter said, then get over it and forgive him. As late as 1988, six years after the payment of the kill fee, Peter, referring to the notorious articles Philip had written in 1939 for Father Coughlin's *Social Justice,* remarked, "He [Philip] sees nothing wrong with them."

That was hardly fair of him, Philip rejoined privately, remembering that he had never said anything to Peter on the tapes that warranted such a simplistic summation, moreover out of context. But the friendship held fast. Eisenman recalled the Fifth International Exhibition of Architecture

LEFT TO RIGHT:
PETER EISENMAN,
PHILIP JOHNSON,
FRANK GEHRY,
1991

of the Venice Biennale in 1991, to which Philip, having been appointed commissioner of the American entry by the exhibition director Francesco Dal Co, chose to show Peter and Frank Gehry.

"I can tell you," Peter said, "how he chose us. You see, all of these things are so goddamned complicated. . . . We got him to be the commissioner so that we could be appointed. . . . Frank and I are not naïve or blameless. Dal Co came to see me and he said, 'I want you and Frank to come to the United States [slip of the tongue; Peter meant Venice]. How do I work that?' . . . I said, 'I can't guarantee you that a committee from the Guggenheim is going to appoint Frank and me. . . . The only way I can see it to work it is to get Philip as the [American] commissioner. . . . He's got enough credibility to do it.' . . . And then Philip said to me, 'Well, what should I do? I can either do the young people or do Frank and you.' I said, 'Frankly, Philip, you should have me and Frank.' He said, 'Okay!' That's as truthful as I can be about it."

BURGEE: DISCARDED

BY THE DISCARDED

Peter's willingness to admit wielding influence over Philip's judgment at Venice without ensuring that he was talking off the record was a form of daring, a reflection of his conviction that an image of brazenness profited him in the long run. People were certain to talk about him; he would stand out in a crowd. If such an outlook was not a consequence of his own calculation, it had to be something he learned from Philip, who had made great capital of it over the years, frequently and merrily comparing himself with Peck's bad boy. Most important, both men believed that the offense critics took at their behavior was only rarely of lasting consequence in the world of cultural power.

Yet it is vital to observe that each of them could back up his bravado. Philip's achievements as architect, critic, curator, and patron were demonstrably unique in the arts of the twentieth century, while Peter himself had grown by the late 1980s into an architect of substance, as his convoluted but inventive—and highly publicized—design for the Wexner Center at Ohio State University (1990) testified. Moreover, his intelligence, wit, and persuasiveness were real. He had as much a right to that place in the Venice Biennale as any of his rivals, and Philip, notwithstanding his wire pulling and dial turning, agreed. Eisenman and Gehry seemed to him at the very top of the middle generation of American architects.

If Peter had much to gain from Philip, he had also much to give. Philip was convinced that Alfred Barr had been a better-trained, all in all more distinguished intellect, not to mention a more reliable friend and nobler character. But Barr was dead now, like Mies and all those others already mentioned here. Hitchcock, too, in 1987, lost a bout to cancer that had robbed him of his mental vigor some years earlier. Thus Eisenman, as well as Stern, Gehry, and the rest of "the kids," as it pleased Dean Johnson to call them, were the most engaging people closest to him, each grateful for his interest and more capable than anyone he knew of keeping him where he forever wanted to be, close to the forward edge of the van.

PHILIP JOHNSON AND
HENRY-RUSSELL HITCHCOCK,
C. 1985

Peter also introduced Philip to a group of young men he had gathered around himself. Wigley was one. Another was Jeffrey Kipnis, whose familiarity not only with deconstructionist theory but with Nietzsche and Heraclitus, more Johnson favorites, so engrossed Philip that Kipnis became his mentor/protégé in the late 1980s and early 1990s. Thus the close connection with Kipnis and Eisenman seemed the best sign that Philip, and they, had been neither defeated nor derailed by the critics' hammering of the Decon show. In 1990, Philip went so far as to publish at his own expense a limited edition of aphorisms by Kipnis, *In the Manor of Nietzsche,* and to contribute the introduction, which began with a confession:

"I have heretofore taken a stand against Theory in architecture. . . . All the exegeses of various theories seemed to me murky, tiresome, boring and, what is more important, not applicable to the problem in front of us: how to build a building.

"Now I am converted. The theoretical framework suggested by Kipnis' aphorisms seems to fit my mental work habits. . . . I need some useful paradigm of an architectural 'truth.' I have to believe. Theory is an actual necessity for design."

In fact, what Kipnis was about was not architectural theory in the standard sense but a kind of deconstructionist-based play with ideas—for example, "a) The meaning of any work is undecidable. b) In as much as they aspire to the meaningful, conventional ways of working, whether radical or conservative, always seek to repress undecidability."

Theory or whatever, such a statement was music to Philip's anti-Platonic ears; nor could he resist this one: "All the letters of architecture, all of its theories, its histories and its criticisms desire to design. Distrust those that protest to the contrary; they protest too strongly." Obviously, that was not theory at all, but something of a rationalization of Philip's own career as an architect. However much Philip protested, he never really gave up believing in Mephistopheles's counsel to the student in *Faust, Part I:* "All theory, dear friend, is gray." Thus he satisfied himself with listening, dutifully enthralled, to Kipnis and Eisenman and Wigley and the rest, and even sitting down with Kipnis in front of eager audiences in the United States and Japan. Kipnis knew his Derrida, which made up for the fact that Philip had read just enough of the Frenchman to be put off by what he found a steady impenetrability—just as he had balked at Whitehead's metaphysics during his undergraduate years. So he and Jeffrey talked at length, brightly and learnedly.

Few fields suffered more than architecture in the recession of the late 1980s. The national economy slowed for nearly everyone, but with the dissolution of the confidence that had led to a headlong overbuilding of towns and cities across the country, architectural firms were hit especially hard. The new decade dawned inhospitably, with too few commissions on the books, too many architects in the offices, and a herd of them forced one by one to find some other line of work. To the extent that Philip Johnson and John Burgee maintained their connection, tenuous though it was, they, too, watched as profit curves plummeted.

The similarities in their respective careers, however, were altogether overshadowed by the differences. Philip—typically—survived; John did not.

The relationship they had agreed upon in 1988 remained in effect for several years, but with no measurable decrease in uneasiness between them. Philip's so-called design consultant status was never fully stabilized, largely on account of his virtually unavoidable involvement in projects not yet completed. Meanwhile, the economic slowdown grew only worse. Several commissions that he had earlier secured for the firm, including major developments in Washington and London, were canceled. The Times Square project, a scheme that would have walled the junction of Forty-second Street and Broadway behind four gargantuan high-rise buildings containing 4 million square feet, was in imminent

danger of being aborted altogether. Few tears were shed outside the
Burgee office; by consensus, the Times Square design represented the
worst of the architecture of the 1980s in general and of the Johnson/
Burgee partnership in particular. The first stage, proposed in 1983, was
little better than a caricature of postmodernist historicism, with mansard

PROJECT FOR TIMES SQUARE CENTER,
NEW YORK CITY, 1989
(JOHN BURGEE, PARTNER)

roofs mounted atop shafts whose paste-on panels looked as if they could
be peeled away like plastic wrap. Later versions were tricked up with a bit
of Deconstructivism and a soupçon of high tech, none of it effecting any
substantial esthetic improvement. In 1991, when progress ground to a halt
on the massive affair, Burgee released Philip, severing all his legal ties with
the office.

Philip was then free to compete with John for new works, a condition
whose benefit was undercut by the sluggishness of the market. He made
several attempts to strike up a working relationship, formal or informal,
with Kohn, Pedersen & Fox and Skidmore, Owings & Merrill, two of the
largest firms in New York. These efforts were of no avail; he was left with
no choice but to find new quarters for himself and start all over again.

However sobering that prospect may have been, John Burgee had it
worse. Late in 1988, he became embroiled in another dispute with one of
his firm's partners, Raj Ahuja, who he said made the unacceptable
demand of exclusive control over certain of the office's projects. Ahuja
denied the allegation, but Burgee, persuaded that Ahuja also wanted to
see Philip's name restored to the firm's letterhead, dismissed him anyhow,
with an offer of a $1.8 million partnership draw for the year. Ahuja,

whose contract permitted him to carry the matter to arbitration, countered with a claim for compensation from future profits on works not completed. The arbitration panel ruled in his favor. Ahuja was awarded $13 million, plus $3.7 million interest, a staggering sum by all professional standards. If not financially destroyed, Burgee was so crippled that he filed for Chapter 7 and Chapter 11 bankruptcy protection, applicable to himself and his firm, respectively.

And Philip the luck child, stripped of his partnership and fully removed from the firm, was free of any and all of its debts.

Fate, however, had not finished punishing John. The news of the Ahuja verdict, especially viewed against the backdrop of the collapse of the once-powerful office of Johnson and Burgee, was hot copy, too fetching for the media not to seek out and follow up. Burgee nursed the hope that if the story could stay out of the major newspapers, he might be able to begin the laborious process of a comeback. Suzanne Stephens had already reported it in *Oculus* and John Brodie in *The New York Observer,* but both periodicals appealed to specialized readerships. The trick was to keep the national popular press at bay, the *Times* and *The Wall Street Journal* most notably. Publicity, which Burgee had earlier wanted so earnestly to cultivate, he now desired even more devoutly to stifle. It was no use. *The Wall Street Journal* ran the whole story on column one of the front page of its September 22, 1992, issue. By the end of the year, Burgee, his office in the Lipstick Building closed, was an architect on paper only. His eventual return to professional activity, if at all foreseeable, would be painful and grueling.

Philip attributed John's defeat to the latter's inflated belief that he was a better designer than he actually was. John ascribed it no less certainly to Philip's overweening love of center stage. Each of them, that is, defined the bad seed that blighted their relationship as hubris—the other guy's, not his own. Insofar as they agreed on anything, it was on the obvious: They had had a spectacular flight together as long as it lasted; and John suffered by far the greater fall.

Economically, Philip, in his new independence, held his own. He retained his Lipstick Building address, 885 Third Avenue, moving into a more modest space there, with his assistant Donald Porter leading a smaller staff that meant most likely smaller commissions. He followed his new Deconstructivist muse in projects for Seton Hill College, the University of Houston and the University of St. Thomas and, most spectacularly, in the three small pavilionlike attachments he added to a large,

zany, and very expensive house designed by Frank Gehry for the insurance magnate Peter Lewis in Lyndhurst, Ohio.

While Gehry had been one of the exhibitors in the Deconstructivist
exhibition of 1988, his Lyndhurst house, like more than a few of his
other works, deserved some other stylistic label or none at all. He was sui
generis, one of the most authentically original architects of the last quar-

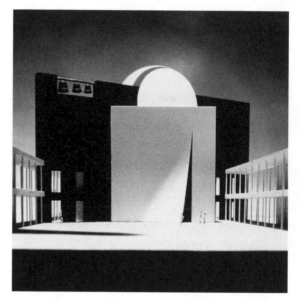

PROJECT FOR CHAPEL,
UNIVERSITY OF ST. THOMAS,
HOUSTON, 1992

ter of the century. Philip knew it, too, proffering him the sincerest com-
pliment by making him and the ground-creeping, knockabout,
antigeometric forms of the Lewis House the chief source of several of his
own most serious design projects of the early 1990s. Evidence of this
special homage, somewhat apparent in the pear-shaped profile of the
inner dome he inserted in a preliminary scheme for one of his three
attachments to the Lewis House, is patent in the scattered volumes he
proposed in a project for the Pelican Marsh Center for Learning in
Naples, Florida. Meanwhile, well into his eighties, he remained true to
another habit as old as his willingness to follow the readiest influence—
namely, to deviate from it just as forthrightly. His design for the town
hall of the Disney-built community of Celebration, Florida, was as far
from Decon and Gehry as the American vernacular tradition, to which
it bowed low, can get.

Philip had once again discarded an old wardrobe and gone shopping for
a new one. Postmodernism had passed from his favor; the return to historical motifs by the designers of the 1980s had failed more often than
not, he decided, because that generation was not only ill-educated in the

craftsmanship such detailing called for but too remote from the spirit of those periods (Philip did not or could not bring himself to say *Zeitgeist*) that found classical ornament a natural expressive language. That he did not excuse his own work from the indictment hardly erased all memory of the devotion with which he had only a few years earlier embraced a diametrically opposite point of view. Even so, if his about-face was altogether in character, so was the nimbleness with which he now negotiated it. Dropping just one word from his famous aphorism, he announced to an audience in Fort Worth in 1993, "You cannot know history!"

THE SUMMING UP: BERLIN, 1993

Many of Philip's designs of the early 1990s were either not built or put on indefinite hold by their clients. The recession was partly responsible for this, but in his new, smaller quarters he could not easily attract large commissions anyhow. He had once again to scramble, to dip into the reserves of his other talents and the records of his other accomplishments, therewith to keep at bay that bleakest of prospects, total retirement.

In both his mind and his movements, Philip quite belied his age. Otherwise, in 1993, he looked every one of his eighty-seven years. All of his hair was gone except for the snow white fringe around the edges that he kept close-cropped in the manner of a crew cut. The scored lines in his face and a slightly bent, perceptibly frail frame were the most obvious signs of how much he had lost of his former handsomeness and dash. But he was still capable of the swift, darting gesture and an equivalent quickness in his eyes, the latter visible as they had been for years through the owlish black-rimmed spectacles he had loosely copied from the still-more-famous prototype of Le Corbusier. That he dressed, if anything, more elegantly than ever, in his Armani suits, only led anyone in conversation with him promptly to forget his age and to take him for the youthful—more precisely, the timeless—intelligence he actually was.

He not only kept alive his connections at The Museum of Modern Art; he drew upon the dividends they yielded. The appointment of a new director of the Department of Architecture and Design did not rest with him, especially since Stuart Wrede had been finally and formally elevated to the post. But the fact was, he did not take to Wrede, even after Wrede had cleared the decks for the Deconstructivist show. More important, officially assigned or not, Philip felt sure that his voice in the matter carried further than anyone's within range of the board of trustees, an opinion shared by the men he scrutinized over lunch at the Four Seasons, including Aaron Betsky, Joseph Giovannini, Colin Amery, Heinrich Klotz, and Michael Sorkin. Michael Sorkin? "Of course. He is very bright," said Philip, isolating the supreme virtue, even if there were lesser ones to consider in this case, like the ability of whoever took the job to get along well with those who needed to be gotten along with. So when Wrede had the courteous good sense to tender his resignation, the directorship went to Terence Riley, a young New York architect who in 1992 emerged seemingly from nowhere to stage an impressive documentation at Columbia University of the sixtieth anniversary of the now-fabled Johnson-Hitchcock-Barr exhibition "Modern Architecture."

Philip took further advantage of his fame and the power it conferred by acquiescing to nearly all the journalists, critics, historians, and scholars, real and counterfeit, who asked him to submit to their various forms of inquiry. In his later years, an article appeared almost annually in one or another of the slick-paper magazines, each purporting to be some sort of definitive summation of the man. The authors invariably had an easy time of it; Philip was far more likely to answer a question than fend it off, even if he damaged himself in the process. In a piece for *Vanity Fair,* Kurt Andersen accurately quoted Philip's assessments of Denise Scott Brown ("a sour apple"), Gerald Hines ("the world's dullest man"), and Brendan Gill (". . . he doesn't know anything about architecture. And he never will"), and Philip found himself obliged to make exculpatory phone calls to the offended. Surely some of the offended were aware, as Philip himself must have been, that the private apology carried less weight than the public offense.

He had an equally volatile relationship with television. Since he was so much at ease and so effortlessly articulate in any setting akin to a podium, he was a natural on the small screen, where he enjoyed himself as much as did the producers who watched him. Several years earlier, he had been especially good with Rosamond Bernier, an expert interviewer who brought out the best in him in a documentary program of 1986 that was part of the PBS series *American Masters.* But TV could do mischievously more than watch and record. A good video editor could cut and paste far more acrobatically than his counterpart on the printed page, with a result that might be as effectively distorted as it was technically accurate. Seasoned performer that he was, Philip should have been familiar with the perils that lurked in the medium, but he was usually too eager to hear himself talk, and no more cautious in front of a camera than before a tape recorder. Thus the 1993 British Broadcasting Corporation production

Philip Johnson: Godfather of American Architecture succeeded all too well in showing its subject less as the creator of a significant body of architectural work or a figure of lasting cultural consequence and more as the calculating, manipulative power broker so many of his antagonists were convinced he was before all else. He appeared in one sequence sipping and savoring a glass of red wine while the voice-over likened him to a vampire with "plenty of fresh, talented young virgins around from whom he can suck the creative juices. . . ." He did further harm to himself, voluntarily and involuntarily. A passage in which he confessed involvement with fascist causes in the 1930s was followed by the dubious voice-over claim that he had been an admirer of the work of Hitler's trusted architect Albert Speer. Still later, shots of the Pennzoil and RepublicBank buildings were shown with a boisterous orchestral excerpt from Wagner's *Götterdämmerung* in the background. It was television at its most totalitarian; did it remind him, while he was watching it, of how little means of appeal any tyranny—including those he had once admired—permits those it tyrannizes? The worst of it all, nonetheless, was his own fault. No one forced him into offering his services on camera to the swaggering Donald Trump in so deferential a manner that the viewer was torn between disgust at both of them and sadness over the spectacle of such an eminent personality playing up to such an unappetizing one.

If Philip made up for that embarrassment, and he did, it was in his triumphant return to Berlin in 1993, an occasion in which—passionate historian that he was at heart—he took the most resourceful advantage of his own past endeavors.

He had been given a commission there by Ronald Lauder of the Estée Lauder cosmetics firm. With Germany's economy robust and America's lagging at the time Lauder hired him, he was hardly the first architect to recognize the obvious: Several U.S. firms had already opened offices in Berlin. In fact, his own assignment consisted of no more than a modestly scaled building on the Friedrichstrasse, close by the former Checkpoint Charlie, a single component in a development that Lauder initially called the American Business Center, later dropping the word American from the name, out of courtesy to the Germans. Moreover, Philip was obliged to abide by Berlin zoning laws that he found uncomfortably strict in their stipulation of height measurements, subdivisions of site, and materials. The piece of commonplace modernism that he finally submitted was hardly a noble work, still less one in accord with the Decon-Gehryesque manners that had lately taken command of his fancies.

Thus his alternative: to offer Berlin and the Berliners not merely a building, only a little distinguishable from most other seven-story structures in the Friedrichstadt district, but a far more arresting work of art: himself, the mature public Philip Johnson, updated and reissued, more than an architect, indeed all he otherwise was, as well: critic, scholar, salesman, irresistible human force.

DAS BUSINESS CENTER,
BERLIN, 1992;
COMPLETION EXPECTED 1995
(DRAWING BY LOUIS BLANC)

In his last years, Philip had lost a taste for writing. It was no longer a necessity in his life, and he did it reluctantly when he did it at all, in bits and pieces, seldom with the crispness and flair of his earlier efforts. His lectures, furthermore, were usually given off the cuff. He much preferred working the podium in tandem with an interviewer, such as Jeff Kipnis.

But in June of 1993, having accepted the invitation to present a formal lecture to the public in the Renaissance Theater in Berlin, he turned this all around. He labored for months on the finished work, writing and rewriting, directing its translation into German, practicing his diction and inflection, the total oratory.

Nothing he said would have surprised anyone familiar with his previous public utterances. All his well-known biases were intact, undergirded by his mastery of history as a whole, of architecture and architects in particular, and the normal complement of lies charming and less so.

The presentation was nonetheless extraordinary. In an hour's time, he returned himself to the bosom of Berlin, the same man, older and wiser, full of memories of all that had once made the city great and all that gave him license to identify himself with it and to give it sage counsel for the future. More than that, less than a month shy of his eighty-seventh birthday, he summed up his vision of himself.

"I am interested only in the art of architecture," he began. "Even the art of painting leaves me less than ecstatic, perhaps with few exceptions—Caspar David Friedrich, Paul Klee, Piero della Francesca. Politics interests me only insofar as it fosters or impedes the production of architectural beauty."

For his own good, he would have been wise to omit the next sentence: "For example, I loathe Hitler but love Friedrich Wilhelm IV: bad client, good client." But his listeners let him get away with it, either out of courtesy or ignorance of his political past or the wish to hear the rest of his message. He got closer to the heart of it:

"Then, of course, comes the supreme expression of architectural art: city planning. I love Siena, Priene, the Rome of Sixtus, the squares of London, the gardens of Le Nôtre's Vaux-le-Vicomte or the romantic gardens of Wörlitz.

"Then I have my hates: all the city plans of Le Corbusier and [Ludwig] Hilberseimer. In fact, I know of no plans of the International Style, even [Bruno] Taut's Hufeisen or Gropius's Siemensstadt, that I can bear. How very sad that, in the end, the modernists were brilliant builders but abysmal planners. Doubly sad for me because much of my lifetime was spent promoting modern architecture, preaching the beauties of buildings by such geniuses as Le Corbusier and Mies.

"Which brings me to the city of Berlin."

Philip proceeded to recall his salad days during the Weimar period and the unfolding of the modernist outlook: ". . . the air we breathed, the people we came to know, the restaurants, the Kurfürstendamm, the sex life were all new, all thrilling to a young American. The world was being created here. . . ."

And then another bit of unnecessary dissimulation: "In my intoxication with Berlin's modern life, I completely missed the underlying political difficulties that were developing. . . ."

Rescuing himself in time, he returned to the point: "Of the city planning of Berlin, however, I knew little."

The remainder of the lecture, fully three-quarters of it, presented Philip at his truest, always eager for some kind of forward movement—and forever the unreconstructed elitist—but compelling in the presentation of his case to an audience arrested by his easy erudition and the fluency of his German. And all of it so *vornehm*.

Having titled his talk "Berlin's Last Chance—Schinkel, [Alfred] Messel, Mies van der Rohe—and What Now?", he lost little time in establishing his objective, the proposal of a workable approach to city planning in Berlin. He had a lofty and definitive exemplar on which to build his argument, the great Schinkel, a hero he could be sure he had in common with his audience:

"His [Schinkel's] concept of city planning is shown best in the engraving of a view from the balcony of the Altes Museum looking toward the Schloss and the Friedrich-Werderschekirche across the Lustgarten. Each building is very different from the other, as the Friedrich-Werderschekirche, the Bauakademie, the project for the State Library and the Kaufhaus show. They are autonomous, self-contained images, remotely related, just the opposite of the unified aspect, for example, of the two eighteenth-century Baroque squares at Nancy . . . each building is in a different 'style' of architecture, if you will, and placed at an ad hoc angle with respect to the other, though both face the park of Sans Souci."

Architecture in the late twentieth century, he continued, devoted as it is to making the realistic best of an ineluctably pluralistic environment—rather than seeking, like the early modernists, to recreate the whole thing—could learn from Schinkel in Berlin. "The twenties," Philip continued, "were the days of utopias . . . when many were convinced of the end of style, convinced that functionalism would triumph over monumentality, symbolic, emotional or spiritual architecture. . . .

"There were, however, some who resisted that conventional wisdom, of which I was one. I felt that history itself taught us the ephemerality of styles, the inevitable changes that occur in our vision, our sense of space, our understanding of what is great, what is beautiful and what is desirable."

Schinkel's concept, then, was "a city plan to rival any capital in the world: a large square, a small intimate square, a Baroque allée, all very loosely connected. . . . [His] great invention was Intervention, a word [now] much used by city planners faced with existing fabrics into which to insert more designs. My young friends today speak of a 'new cohesiveness' in planning. . . . It seems to me that Schinkel achieved precisely that effect in his Lustgarten scheme."

Thus Philip demonstrated anew his way of reconciling a love of history and a commitment to the advanced concepts of the moment. He criticized—gently—the plan lately decided upon for the Friedrichstadt district, a scheme to which his Lauder building was forced to conform.

Cunningly, then, he offered his audience a second proposal for that building, the sketch of a fantastic iceberglike massing of interlocking blocks, "primordially organic," as one Berlin newspaper later called it. It was directly indebted to Frank Gehry and to an artist who had even more recently caught Philip's roving eye: the painter-sculptor Frank Stella, busy himself now with architectural form. Hints of Decon were likewise present, although less obviously.

"The old man was amazing," reported Lorenz Tomerius in the *Berliner Morgenpost*, "not only in his physical freshness, but even more in the

PROJECT,
"BERLIN FANTASY,"
1993

witty and lightning-sharp style of his formulation and delivery of thoughts that were not always comforting but that the public was jolted into agreeing with."

If Philip achieved nothing else, he had, in the course of a single lecture, added Germany to the United States among the cultures that could not deny having seen a manifestly rare and untamable being in their midst. And whether he knew it consciously or not, he had rendered a comforting judgment of himself, rationalizing his habitually polymorphous approach to architecture by finding it at the heart of the work of the unimpeachable Karl Friedrich Schinkel.

WORK IN PROGRESS

With the coming of the warm weather in 1994 Philip thought more and more about the various ways in which he might observe his ninetieth birthday two years hence. A couple of summers earlier, in 1992, his older sister Jeannette Dempsey had negotiated her own ninetieth, not only enduring but gaining strength from several hours of standing on the lawn of her son Bourne Dempsey's spacious lakefront estate in Cleveland, where she received well-wishers in the hundreds, nearly all of them perceptibly moved by her easy grace and wit, and, above all, by her unfailing stamina.

Why not me?, Philip had begun to ask himself, conjuring a prospect that had been quite beyond his imagining at the time of his eightieth birthday, which he spent in a hospital bed, exhausted by the effects of the passage of a balloon through the vessels of his heart. Now, eight years later, he and the heart were getting on very well together, thanks partly to the benefits of medical technology, but mostly to a greater gift, the ultimate legacy, of Homer and Louise Johnson's genes.

His musings about a halcyon future were more than fantasies. If as a young man he had dreamed of the romance of marching troops and the dangerous life, as an old man he was content to dwell on the things he could make happen in the everyday world, and he had proven himself altogether competent at that. In fact, The Museum of Modern Art had already settled on plans for its own tribute to him in 1996 that would consist of a special honorific publication and an accompanying exhibition of the paintings, sculptures, and design objects he had given the institution over six decades. Therewith another dividend of Philip's well-developed tempering of ambition with realism: Despite his resentment over the loss of the commission for the museum tower in 1979, he and MoMA were friends again, restored in their ancient symbiosis.

PHILIP JOHNSON,
C. 1988

In his office, too, the mood was high. He claimed to be almost as busy in 1994 as he had been during the peak years of his partnership with John Burgee. Not all his activity was given to design, and not all the design was realized. He lost a pair of competitions, one for the expansion of a large commercial complex in Riyadh sponsored by the King Faisal Foundation, the other for a Federal courthouse in Omaha. But the Times Square project, inglorious or not, had been resurrected, with Philip by himself the principal architect; and Donald Trump, now an apparently steady suitor, had put him in charge of two works: the immense Riverside South development on New York's West Side, an enterprise long on Trump's mind, and the conversion to expensive apartments of the lofty old Gulf-Western tower near Columbus Circle. Philip meanwhile continued his collaboration with Frank Gehry on the Peter Lewis House in Lyndhurst, Ohio, which grew increasingly fantastic as the months passed. By the spring of 1994 Gehry's ever-changing design, pumped up by Lewis's apparent willingness to spend money at a rate that lifted the budget well into eight digits, consisted of more than a dozen structures strewn casually about the landscape, most of them sheltered by a vast tent. Three of the buildings were still the guest houses done by Philip, now Expressionist-inspired, the liveliest shaped like an octopus.

Even as he was thus occupied, Philip completed the remodeling or redevelopment of several of his own older efforts, including Thanksgiving Square in Dallas and the Amon Carter Museum in Fort Worth. He took special personal pains to design and build a visitors' center for the New Canaan compound, that would become functional as soon as the National Trust took over the property following his demise.

If the Trust had been in any hurry, the pace of Philip's schedule would have discouraged the anticipation of an imminent tenancy. He was designing, building, and carrying on his practice as if undiminished either by age or the recent economic slump, which in any case was beginning to ease. By midsummer he had set up a partnership with two former members of the Johnson-Burgee office, Alan Ritchie and David Fiore. The name of the new firm, Philip Johnson, Ritchie & Fiore, reflected Philip's position as chairman and chief designer. Nor did this in-house activity prevent him from making himself available to the little army of writers who wanted to publish something about him, now that he was hugely famous and still alive to talk to. The authors of no fewer than five books besought him for his time in the early 1990s, and he gave it as freely, as eagerly, as they requested it.

It was an old story with Philip, this habit of close involvement with several societies at once, hardly least among them now the company of closest professional intimates: Kipnis, Eisenman, Gehry, and Stern. Indeed, only because Zaha Hadid, Rem Koolhaas, and Wolfgang Prix were an ocean away did he have slightly less contact with them, although on his increasingly frequent travels he visited with them as surely if not as often as he phoned them from home. In a single month, December of 1993, he was in Saudi Arabia, Nebraska, and California on separate trips from New York that only punctuated his regular flights to Berlin, a city rapidly becoming a routine part of his life, another symbiosis. In May 1994 he was the guest of honor at the International Architecture Forum in Dessau, his name appearing on the program just below that of the principal patron of the event, Chancellor Helmut Kohl. And only a month earlier he had been in Vienna, offering the formal opening remarks at an exhibition in the Austrian Museum of Applied Arts. The subject was Stalinist architecture, and Philip used the occasion not only to demonstrate again that his basic view of the world was as consistent as the styles of his architecture were not, but to affirm an opinion he had seldom had the opportunity to express: his admiration for a boulevard in the former East Berlin that had been the object of almost unanimous scorn among Western critics. It was the notorious neoclassical Stalinallee, later renamed the Karl-Marx-Allee, still later, after the fall of the Berlin Wall, the Frankfurter Allee. Philip had long found a grandeur in it that others had dismissed as totalitarian pomposity. Now he called it "the new Champs-Élysées," a product of "romantic daring" and "the dream of the East for monumentality. . . . We might prefer Mies van der Rohe's Friedrichstrasse Bahnhof project to [Boris Mikhailovich] Iofan's Palace of the Soviet, but who can find the functionalist metro stations in the West more attractive than Stalin's monumental ones?

"All these thoughts confuse me. They convince me all the more that joy, tears, excitement have more to do with architecture than dour morality or political causes or considerations. . . ."

Clearly Philip was capable as ever of taking the outrageous position. Yet the audacity required to praise Stalinist architecture in spite of all that Stalinism stood for, while typical of his habitually formalist views, was no less intellectually de rigueur, fully in step with the spirit of revisionist criticism that has grown out of the various disenchantments the twentieth century has felt about modern historiographic orthodoxies. At eighty-eight, he was where he was always most comfortable, at the head of the parade of contemporary taste. The reports seemed eminently credible that a *Festschrift* in honor of his ninetieth birthday was being prepared by Peter Eisenman, Jeffrey Kipnis, and Phyllis Lambert.

Did life begin, after all, at eighty-eight? By 1994 he was hinting as much from time to time, obviously fully recovered from the malaise that beset him in his early eighties. He had even decided he did not need Prozac, the much-publicized wonder drug, the way he thought he needed it just a little earlier. If pressed, he would have acknowledged that life in fact begins more than once and ends more than once and repeats the process, on and on. His own life might have been his own model, a succession of rises and falls that figuratively mirrored the manic-depressive cycle of his youth. Yet he found no more consolation or assurance in his most recent new beginning than he had learned any chastening or corrective moral lesson from previous ill fortune. In his old age, active, healthy, materially secure, and festooned with honors, he held firm to his view of life as a process that did nothing to sustain or even engender faith in the normal sense of the word. Of cycles he had learned what he needed to know from Heraclitus, whose fragments he liked to recite verbatim: "Everything flows and nothing abides; everything gives way and nothing stays fixed." Even more emphatically, he would call to mind "War is the father and king of all; some he has shone forth as gods and others as men, some he has made slaves and others free."

Philip found grim truth in both aphorisms, or more precisely, a realistic sense of things, since each reinforced his conviction that an ultimate and immutable "truth" was beyond man's capacity to determine, thus effectively did not exist. He had cultivated these thoughts for years, well before it was fashionable to use "deconstructionist" theory to build a case against verifiability. He had derived them mostly from his reading of Nietzsche, whom he never stopped calling his philosopher of choice and who confirmed for him the only "faith"—art—that sustained him. Further nourishment had come from the "black thinkers," whom he had learned to admire chiefly with the help of his friend the historian Isaiah Berlin: writers who had in common one or another form of anti-Platonic or anti-Enlightenment or antiliberal sentiment, for example, Giambattista Vico, Johann Gottfried von Herder, Vilfredo Pareto, Joseph de Maistre.

Philip's philosophical reflections were further animated by the several years late in his life when he conversed at length with a graduate student from the University of Chicago, Ujjval Vyas. As fascinated by Johnson the thinker as by Johnson the architect, Vyas developed his findings into a doctoral dissertation.

Early in their numerous discussions, Philip acknowledged to Vyas that he had long admired the Sophist school of Greek philosophy, siding with its members in their famous arguments with Socrates. Contrasted with Socrates, Vyas recalls, "the Sophists . . . believed that questions of value were much more fluid, the result not of cosmic certainties but of human existence." Thus they were "forced to engage in a discourse which understood truth in a relative and contingent manner while remaining effective in the realm of human action."

So arguing, the Sophists affirmed the necessary pluralism of philosophical positions, with the acceptability of any one of them dependent on the ability of its proponent to persuade his audience, since "proof" in any dialectical sense was not possible. For the Sophists, the discipline of rhetoric was at the heart of human things.

Vyas thus helped to cast light on the ways Philip not only thought but acted: on Philip the architect of many manners, the harlequin of exchangeable masques; Philip the promoter and propagandist, Philip the ruthlessly objective observer; Philip the wielder of power, conferrer of fame, and subverter of reputations; Philip pragmatic, Philip idealist, Philip eternally generous; Philip possessed and Philip distracted; charmer, seducer, dissembler, yet no less authentically dedicated to the making of art and the patronage of culture; the most critically disposed of architects, the most architecturally involved of critics; at once admired and detested, as easily loved as loathed.

All this, moreover, he knew about himself; he needed no instruction. Asked by what image he would be most remembered in history, he said, "as an *Anreger*, an inciter, a preacher of the art of architecture as distinct from its lesser aspect, the function of it. As to the place of my own architecture, I have absolutely no idea. It would be almost impossible to build in as many directions as I have and not hit it once in a while. But I don't feel like a prophet the way all my good architect friends do. Mies was convinced, as Wright was, that he was the end of architecture: 'Why would anyone want to do architecture after I've done mine?'

"Perhaps more than any of my contemporaries I have bridged the gap between making buildings and thinking about them. I'm not, however, as good a scholar as Hitchcock or as good an eye as Alfred Barr. And I'm not as good as Mies. But I have changed and I think I do change the climate of architecture in this country."

These remarks, made in an informal conversation in the spring of 1994, were as much a rationalization of his ongoing mission as a summation of himself. There was no way he could stop working; it would likely kill him more readily than any somatic ailment might. The prospect of death, meanwhile, neither stayed his hand nor quickened it. "Because I don't believe in the good, the true or the absolute, or in justice or mercy, I don't worry about the end, which is just that—the end, the end of everything. Every animal faces it." He was reminded that his attitude was more relaxed than it had been in 1987 when he was feeling desperately poorly and talking about the blackness of the beyond.

"My plans," he replied, just a little more earnestly than tongue-in-cheek, "are to retire on my one-hundredth birthday. Then I will move to Rome."

NOTES

PART ONE: ORIGINS
AND DIRECTIONS, 1652–1934

p. 5 The Museum of Modern Art: Theodate Johnson Severns, interview, 10
July 1987.

9 biblical name: Information pertinent to Philip Johnson's genealogical background has been drawn from his family records, most of them in the possession of his sister Jeannette Johnson Dempsey, and from personal interviews
with her, Johnson himself, and their sister Theodate Johnson Severns.

14 identified him in an editorial: "Homer H. Johnson," no byline, *Cleveland
Plain Dealer,* 28 March 1960, 36.

15 on the East Side: General information about the Homer Johnson-Louise
Johnson relationship, marriage, and family life has been taken from conversations with Philip Johnson, Jeannette Dempsey, and Theodate Severns,
1986–1994.

17 "how the flowers melted": Jeannette Johnson Dempsey, interview, 14 July
1989.

18 hovering over him: Philip Johnson, interview, 8 July 1986, and Severns,
interview, 20 June 1988.
ghost to resent: Severns, interview, 17 February 1990.

19 like a girl's: ibid.
showing, or of withholding, them: This was underscored repeatedly in
interviews with Johnson—e.g., 6 January 1990—and Severns—e.g., 17
February 1990.
Alcohol was never served: Johnson, interview, 6 January 1990.
"her intelligence makes up for it": ibid.

21 who was more than a friend: Johnson, interview, 8 July 1986, and Severns,
interview, 10 July 1987.
limited to "serial monogamy": a term frequently used in interviews by
Johnson, who said it was a favorite self-characterization of his friend the
architect George Howe.

23 neatly attired and quite alone: Johnson, interview, 8 July 1986.
Philip stuttered: Severns, interview, 9 July 1986.
cold water into his face: Severns, interview, 8 July 1986.

27 he made no reply: Johnson, interview, 11 July 1987.
of her as a "cold fish": Johnson, interview, 6 January 1990.
she replied: Severns, interview, 20 June 1988.

28 to unleash upon one another: Dempsey, interview, 14 August 1986.
29 plan of Paris: Johnson, interview, 3 July 1987.
30 once ejected from class: Johnson, interview, 8 July 1986.
31 altogether competent: Carleton Sprague Smith, interview, 14 July 1987.
    among the class of 1923: *The Hackley,* published by Hackley School, Tarry-
    town, New York, 1923.
    could not act upon it: Johnson, interview, 8 July 1986.
    "talking to the masters": *The Hackley.*
    after Philip left Hackley: Johnson, interview, 8 July 1986.
32 "Noble thoughts. Clichés": Johnson, interview, 6 January 1990.
33 signified upscale status: Johnson, interview, 24 April 1993.
    advantageous start in life: Dempsey, interview, 14 August 1986, and Johnson,
    interview, 10 October 1987.
35 between desire and shame: Johnson, interview, 8 July 1986.
    "That's all?" asked Philip: The conversation was recalled in these terms by
    Johnson, interview, 8 July 1986.
    "You'll be all right": Johnson, interviews, 8 July 1986 and 3 July 1987.
    several more weeks, it did: Johnson, interview, 8 July 1986.
36 he succumbed to her: ibid.
    "that is the whole story": Johnson, letter to Jeannette Johnson, 13 Octo-
    ber 1925.
    life as a concert pianist: Johnson, interview, 10 October 1987.
37 "I have not done a thing": Johnson, letter to Louise Johnson, November 1925.
    "much less than I do": Johnson, letter to Louise Johnson, 19 January 1926.
    "a poetic idea of his to abolish it": Johnson, letter to Louise Johnson, 10 Jan-
    uary 1926.
    young men among the Buchmanites: Johnson, interview, 8 July 1986, and
    Dempsey, interview, 6 November 1986. The Buchmanites were followers
    of Frank Nathan Daniel Buchman (1878–1961), an American evangelist
    best known for the international movement he organized in the 1920s as
    the Oxford Group—at Oxford University, where he preached "world
    changing through life changing"—and later, in the 1930s, as Moral Re-
    Armament.
    "greatest philosopher we have today": Johnson, letter to Louise Johnson, 16
    January 1926.
38 " 'something else, I suppose' ": Johnson, letter to Louise Johnson, 19 Jan-
    uary 1926.
    "in the quiz this morning": Johnson, letter to Louise Johnson, 27 Febru-
    ary 1926.
    contemptuous of her: Jeannette Dempsey, interview, 14 August 1986.
    quirkiness on the other: On the origins of the children's names: Philip
    claimed his mother thought his name was "euphonious—it tripped off the
    tongue." Jeannette maintained, similarly, that her parents simply regarded her
    name as "pleasant." Theodate, meaning "gift of God," was named for her
    great-grandmother Theodate Stackpole, who was seen as one of the great
    matriarchal figures of the family. Theodate Pope Riddle, christened Effie,
    assumed the name she went by, likewise with Stackpole as her inspiration.
    "in short beneath contempt": Henry James, letter to Riddle, 12 January
    1912, published in *Henry James: Selected Letters,* ed. Leon Edel. Cambridge,
    Mass.: Harvard University Press, Belknap Press, 1987, 394–95.
    "cracked when we got out": Johnson, letter to Jeannette Johnson, 13 Octo-
    ber 1925.

39 "clambered all over the place": Johnson, letter to Louise Johnson, 13 July 1926.
"at their house overnight": Johnson, letter to Louise Johnson, 4 July 1926.
"verger's time by asking": Johnson, letter to Louise Johnson, 13 July 1926.
40 most of his travels were: Severns, interview, 10 July 1987.
"I ought to be able": Johnson, letter to Homer Johnson, undated, 1927.
41 "over the mountains, within sight": Johnson, interview, 10 July 1993.
sexual experience: Johnson, interview, 8 July 1986.
42 sit out the autumn semester at Harvard: Johnson, interview, 1 October 1989.
44 "He knew it": Johnson, interview, 10 October 1987.
"always remain far from me": Friedrich Nietzsche, *Thus Spoke Zarathustra,* trans. with a preface by Walter Kaufmann (New York: Viking-Penguin, 1966, 1987), 87.
"the Sated and the Permanent": ibid., 86.
45 force of the embrace: These recollections are numerous and familiar to most students and many friends of Johnson. They were repeatedly called up in interviews in the late 1980s and early 1990s.
46 innovative exhibition fare: For an extended discussion of the Harvard Society for Contemporary Art, see Nicholas Fox Weber, *Patron Saints* (New York: Alfred A. Knopf, 1992).
47 declined to seek him out: Johnson, interview, 8 July 1986.
ring of truth: Johnson, interview, 8 January 1988.
planned to Europe: Johnson, in an interview of 8 January 1988, recalled that Barr discussed the eventual possibility of a place for Johnson on the staff of the not-yet-realized museum.
48 "in a hurry though": Johnson, letter to Louise Johnson, 8 November 1929.
transatlantic trip: Johnson, interview, 8 January 1988.
50 "red and white stone": Johnson, letter addressed "Dear Family," 13 August 1929.
"German heart would never understand": ibid.
51 "often none at all": Johnson, letter to Louise Johnson, 18 August 1929.
"but I really am not": Johnson, letter to Louise Johnson, 22 September 1929.
"to write my letters to": Johnson, interview, 6 January 1990.
"more or less vague": Johnson, letter addressed "Dear Family," 6 August 1929.
"The Romanesque is the best part": Johnson, letter addressed "Dear Family," 13 August 1929.
52 "articles on architecture": ibid.
"famous modern architects": Johnson, letter to Louise Johnson, 18 August 1929.
for the most part white: For an extended discussion of the Weissenhofsiedlung, see Karin Kirsch, *The Weissenhof: Experimental Housing Built for the Deutscher Werkbund, Stuttgart, 1927* (New York: Rizzoli, 1989), or Richard Pommer and Christian Otto, *Weissenhof 1927 and the Modern Movement in Architecture.* Chicago: University of Chicago Press, 1991.
"for me to begin on": Johnson, letter to Louise Johnson, 18 August 1929.
"three greatest living architects": ibid.
"perhaps the finest masters": Alfred H. Barr, Jr., "Notes on Russian Architecture," *The Arts,* February 1929, 103.
"greatest of them all": Johnson, letter to Louise Johnson, 18 August 1929.
53 "there is no better style": Johnson, letter to Louise Johnson, 20 August 1929.
"as this for a rest": Johnson, letter to Louise Johnson, 1 September 1929.
"going day after tomorrow": ibid.

53 "is as usual staggering": Johnson, letter to Louise Johnson, undated, 1929.
neither of them acted out: Johnson, interview, 3 July 1987, and Severns,
interview, 9 July 1986. Severns claimed that her brother was more smitten
with Coward than his own recollection acknowledged.
"J. J. P. Oud": Johnson, letter to Louise Johnson, 22 September 1929.
"each of the big men": ibid.

54 "I would not admit it": Johnson, letter addressed "Dear Family," 18 November 1929.
"*gastfreundlich*": Johnson, interview, 10 October 1987.

55 "majesty and simplicity which are unequaled": Johnson, undated letter to
Louise Johnson, probably October 1929. In a postcard to her postmarked 18
October 1929, he added, "This is one of the most beautiful buildings in the
world. You must see it some day. We are reveling in having reached our
Mecca at last."
"greatest man there": Johnson, letter to Louise Johnson, undated, fall of 1929.
judged him anew as "great": Johnson, letter to Louise Johnson, 18 November 1929.
"sometimes pathetic, sometimes amusing": Johnson, letter to Alfred Barr,
undated, fall of 1929.
"at his age of 26": ibid.
"colors would only be bits": Johnson, letter to Louise Johnson, 3 October
1929.

56 "as much as possible": Johnson, letter to Louise Johnson, 26 October 1929.
one Wagnerian movement he resisted: Johnson, interview, 8 July 1989.

57 "Bohunks, I calls 'em": Johnson, letter to Louise Johnson, 26 October 1929.
formally in New York City: Louise Johnson's interest and involvement in
Johnson's affairs are suggested by excerpts of a letter she wrote to Alfred Barr
on 31 October 1929:

> My dear Mr. Barr,
> Only recently I learned that you had been appointed Director of the
> new Museum of Modern Art and I wish to express to you the pleasure
> and the congratulations of the Johnson family because this honor has
> come to you. I was keenly interested when I read of the probable
> establishment of such a museum and now we shall all have a double
> interest in its progress.
> Philip writes most enthusiastically of his architectural pilgrimage
> through Holland and Germany. Just now I believe he is in Dessau and
> will return to Berlin soon for some intensive work at the University in
> the German language. . . . He feels he has much to thank you for in
> giving him an opportunity for some delightful contacts.
> I hope you will let us know where to find you in New York for I feel
> sure Philip will wish to see you immediately on his return in January
> to tell you of his satisfactory experiences. . . .
> Truly yours,
> Mrs. Homer H. Johnson

59 "rearing to race": Margaret Barr, notes written to provide information to
Calvin Tomkins for his article "Forms Under Light," *The New Yorker,* 23
May 1977, 43–80.
"begging him to finish": ibid.

"called his analyst": In an interview of 24 April 1993, Johnson identified the "analyst" as the aforementioned (see p. 35) Dr. Sandy MacPherson.

"sick to my stomach": Johnson, letter to Margaret Barr, 30 April 1930.

60 "turning over a new leaf": Johnson, undated letter to Margaret Barr, probably May 1930.

Modern Architecture: Romanticism and Reintegration: Henry-Russell Hitchcock, Jr., *Modern Architecture: Romanticism and Reintegration* (New York: Payson & Clarke, 1929).

less affecting basis: Johnson, interview, 1 October 1989.

61 "Russell's big book": Johnson, letter to Louise Johnson, 20 June 1930.

The International Style: Architecture Since 1922: Henry-Russell Hitchcock, Jr., and Philip Johnson, *The International Style: Architecture Since 1922* (New York: W. W. Norton, 1932).

"of an apprentice": Johnson, letter to Louise Johnson, 7 July 1930.

"horizontal method": offered by Johnson in numerous interviews in the late 1980s and early 1990s.

"many warm friends": Johnson, letter to Louise Johnson, 20 June 1930.

62 "Russell is a genius": ibid.

"But oh gosh!": Alfred H. Barr, Jr., letter to Margaret Barr, undated, 1930.

63 "definitely become less close": Johnson, letter to Louise Johnson, 7 July 1930.

"my very good friends": Johnson, letter to Louise Johnson, 20 June 1930.

"certainly exciting to see": ibid.

64 "nevertheless very elegant": Johnson, letter to Louise Johnson, 4 July 1930.

"the people stupid": ibid.

66 *Vers une architecture*: Le Corbusier, *Vers une architecture* (Paris: Editions G. Crès, 1923); trans. as *Towards a New Architecture* (London: John Rodker, 1927).

67 "aesthetic stock of their work": Johnson, letter to Louise Johnson, 6 August 1930.

"propagandistic building": ibid.

predictable results: In a letter to J. J. P. Oud, 17 September 1930, Johnson describes his meeting and early conversations with Mies:

> After seeing some of the rooms that he had decorated here in Berlin, I got the idea of getting him to do my room in New York for me. I went to call on him with my best friend, a German, Jan Ruhtenberg, who is beginning to study architecture. Mies was most polite but distant, but we were lucky to be going to Dessau the same day that he was going, so we took him with us in the car, and then he opened up and talked all the way, always impersonally, but very openly. . . . It was so refreshing for me to meet a German architect who has no illusions about Sachlichkeit or Technic [*sic*] or Material. . . . He tells amusing stories about Gropius' Acht vor der Technic [respect for technology]. He worships it because he knows so little about it. [This seems to be the first clear evidence of Johnson's waning regard for Gropius.] Especially Mies hates this Zweckmässigkeit [functionalism] carried to extremes. . . . He says Zweckmässigkeit is more subjective than rein [pure] Aesthetik.

68 and his wife, Grete: As reported, Johnson never saw the German Pavilion. At the time he met Mies, the latter's only realized buildings in the modernist

manner—aside from the Tugendhat House (itself not completed until November 1930)—were the Wolf House in Guben (1925–1927) and the Lange and Esters houses in Krefeld (1927–1930).

68   "is a frightful sum": Johnson, letter to Louise Johnson, undated, probably late August 1930.

"He knew only the plan": Johnson, letter to Henry-Russell Hitchcock, Jr., 20 August 1930.

"best looking house in the world": Johnson, letter to Hitchcock, 2 September 1930.

69   "to the board of trustees": Johnson, letter to Louise Johnson, 6 August 1930.

"to be met by his family": Johnson, letter to Louise Johnson, 1 September 1930.

70   "apartments that we now have": ibid.

71   three principal divisions: Johnson, memorandum to A. Conger Goodyear, undated, probably December 1930.

published by the museum: Johnson, "Built to Live In," (New York: The Museum of Modern Art, March 1931), 1–14.

72   several years earlier: Alfred H. Barr, Jr., "The Necco Factory," *The Arts,* May 1928, 292–95.

"unnecessary and merely imitative": Johnson, "The Skyscraper School of Architecture," *Arts,* May 1931; reprinted in Johnson, *Writings* (New York: Oxford University Press, 1979), 38–42.

"younger and omitted men": Johnson, speech to Architectural League, New York, 1965; quoted in part in *Writings,* 44.

following her son's recommendation: Johnson, "Rejected Architects," *Creative Art 8,* no. 6 (June 1931): 433–35; reprinted in *Writings,* 44–47.

"in the International Style": Johnson, "Two Houses in the International Style," *House Beautiful,* October 1931, 307–309, 356.

73   "last days of Louis XVI": Julien Levy, *Memoir of an Art Gallery.* New York: G. P. Putnam's Sons, 1977, 67.

for the American press: See Johnson, "In Berlin: Comment on Building Exposition," *The New York Times,* 9 August 1931, VIII, X5, and "The Berlin Building Exposition of 1931," *T-Square,* January 1932, 36–37.

"handled as art": Johnson, "In Berlin: Comment on Building Exposition."

"God forbid": Johnson, letter to Hitchcock, 12 June 1930.

74   "his worship of it": Johnson, letter to Hitchcock, undated, probably 1931.

"American invasion": Johnson, interview, 11 July 1987.

75   reach of the new architecture: For an extended discussion of the "Modern Architecture" exhibition, see Terence Riley, *The International Style: Exhibition 15 and The Museum of Modern Art* (New York: Rizzoli/Columbia Books of Architecture, 1992).

76   appeared in the catalogue: The catalogue was published in two forms, with identical texts: Henry-Russell Hitchcock, Jr., Philip Johnson, and Lewis Mumford, *Modern Architecture: International Exhibition* (New York: The Museum of Modern Art, 1932) and Alfred H. Barr, Jr., Henry-Russell Hitchcock, Jr., Philip Johnson, and Lewis Mumford, *Modern Architects* (New York: W. W. Norton, The Museum of Modern Art, 1932).

77   "benefit of human living": Hitchcock, Johnson, Mumford, *Modern Architecture,* 179.

"to Frank Lloyd Wright": ibid., 12.

"a new aesthetic": ibid., 19–20.

78   "ornament or artificial pattern": ibid., 12–17.

79 *Internationale Architektur:* Walter Gropius, *Internationale Architektur.* Munich: Bauhausbücher, 1925.
    According to Marga Barr: Margaret Barr, notes to Johnson, November 1986.
    an article of February 1929: Alfred H. Barr, Jr., "Notes on Russian Architecture."
    "The New International Style, 1922–32": Otto Haesler, letter to Johnson, October 1930.
    "problems of urban building": See Riley, *The International Style,* 31.
80 "and it must be good": Johnson, letter to Hitchcock, undated ("Tuesday"), probably 1931.
    "with a fresh severity": Ralph Flint, "Present Trends in Architecture in Fine Exhibit," *The Art News,* 13 February 1932, 5.
81 "slavery to the machine idea": H. I. Brock, "Architecture Styled International," *The New York Times Magazine,* 7 February 1932, 11, 22.
    "of modern imagination": Douglas Haskell, "Architecture: What the Man About Town Will Build," *The Nation,* 13 April 1932, 441–43.
    "the Exhibition displeases them": Johnson, letter to J. J. P. Oud, 17 March 1932.
82 and "all formalism": Mies van der Rohe, "Bürohaus," *G* (Berlin), June 1923, 3.
    with the "internationalists": "Symposium 'International Style,' Exhibition of Modern Architecture, Museum of Modern Art," *Shelter,* April 1932, 6.
    "propagandists of atheism": ibid.
    as they conceived it: Johnson, in a letter to Oud, 16 April 1932: "Frank Lloyd Wright was included only from courtesy and in recognition of his past contributions." In another letter to Oud, 14 July 1932, Johnson wrote: "I am also sending you the Wright book. I cannot read it. His style infuriates me."
    In a letter to Johnson, 19 January 1932, written before the exhibition opened, Wright—continually vacillating between participating in the show and withdrawing from it—offered his own view of things in one of his most affecting, not to mention prophetic, statements:

> I find myself a man without a country, architecturally speaking, at the present time. If I keep on working another five years, I shall be at home again, I feel sure. [By then—1937, at age seventy—Wright had completed the great Kaufmann House, Fallingwater, a work that more than any other restored his international reputation.]
> . . . I see too much at stake for me to countenance a handpicked group of men in various stages of eclecticism by riding around the country with them as though I approved of them and their work as modern, when I distinctly do not only disapprove but positively condemn them.

83 "best younger contemporaries": Alfred H. Barr, Jr., in foreword to *Modern Architecture,* 15.
    "a high-powered salesman": Frank Lloyd Wright, telegram to Johnson, 18 January 1932.
    "the guise of invention": Wright, "Of Thee I Sing," *Shelter,* April 1932, 10–12.
    "open in the circumstances": Wright, letter to Johnson, 19 April 1932.
84 "Henry-Russell Hitchcock, Jr.": Hitchcock, letter to Wright, 22 April 1932.
    "Yours [etc.]": Johnson, letter to Wright, 25 April 1932.
85 "personal toward no one": Wright, letter to Johnson, 24 May 1932.
86 "*modern* architects": Peter Blake, "Modern Architecture Revisited," *Interior Design,* May 1992, 238–39.

88   classicist Karl Friedrich Schinkel: Johnson, interview, 6 January 1990.

89   Philip put Persius aside: ibid.

"get us an invitation": Johnson, quoting Read, interview, 11 July 1987.

"harangue the crowd": ibid.

90   passage back to the States: Virgil Thomson, *Virgil Thomson: An Autobiography* (New York: Alfred A. Knopf, 1967), 212.

he later remembered: Johnson, interview, 16 March 1988.

92   "given cocktails later by the host": Thomson, *Autobiography,* 215.

93   has characterized it: Thomas Bender, *New York Intellect,* New York, Alfred A. Knopf, 1987, 322. See also Warren Susman, *Culture as History.* New York: Pantheon, 1984, chapter 9.

94   "as host and entertainer": Thomson, *Autobiography,* 217.

than he expected to be: Johnson, interview, 10 October 1987.

95   "hate to move their lips": Thomson, *Autobiography,* 217.

"the navel of the world": Johnson, lecture at Hartford Atheneum, Hartford, Connecticut, 25 February 1984.

96   Thomson's word for it: Thomson, interview, 4 March 1989.

97   "had left smiling": Thomson, *Autobiography,* 217.

angry end to their affair: Johnson, interview, 10 October 1987.

98   "the Beaux Arts 'modernistic' ": Johnson, foreword to "Work of Young Architects of the Middlewest." New York: The Museum of Modern Art, 1933, unpaginated.

"by [Ernest] Grunsfeld": Johnson, letter to Alfred H. Barr, Jr., undated.

99   "Brancusi and Fernand Léger": "Talk of the Town" (no byline), *The New Yorker,* 17 March 1934, 18.

"achieved in this country": Helen Appleton Read, "Machine Art," *Brooklyn Daily Eagle,* 11 March 1934, 14BC.

100   "but always and absolutely": Alfred H. Barr, Jr., foreword to catalogue, *Machine Art.* New York: The Museum of Modern Art, 1934, unpaginated.

"Mathematics is Mathematics": quoted by Royal Cortissoz in "Machine Art and the Art of Some Artists," *New York Herald Tribune,* 11 March 1934, VII, 10.

"direction of the crafts": Bulliet quoted in "Veering to Crafts" (no byline), *The Art Digest,* 1 October 1934, 20.

said the *New York Sun* of Philip: Henry McBride, "Museum Shows Machine Art in a Most Unusual Display," *New York Sun,* 10 March 1934, 11.

added *The New York Times:* Edwin Alden Jewell, "The Realm of Art: the Machine and Abstract Beauty," *The New York Times,* 11 March 1934, X, 12.

PART TWO: THE INGLORIOUS
DETOUR, 1934–1946

105   response as he had wished: Johnson, interview, 10 October 1987.

106   "the other great moderns": Johnson, letter to J. J. P. Oud, 23 November 1933.

"a Le Corbusier or a Wright": Johnson, interview, 10 October 1987.

According to Marga: Margaret Barr, interview, 3 July 1987.

107   domains of politics and economics: Johnson, interview, 10 October 1987.

Nazi attitudes toward the arts: Johnson, "Architecture in the Third Reich," *The Hound and Horn* 7 (October–December 1933): 137–39.

108   "when I go to Bruenn": Johnson, letter to Alfred H. Barr, Jr., dated only July but written in 1931.

neoclassicism in 1934: Recent scholarship has shown persuasively that some buildings put up by the National Socialists, including a number done for Hermann Goering's Luftwaffe, were executed in a manner much closer to *Sachlichkeit* modernism than were the formal or ceremonial structures often exclusively identified with Nazi esthetic doctrine.

not lost on Philip: Within a month after Hitler's accession in January 1933, homosexual rights organizations were officially banned in Germany. See David F. Greenberg, *The Construction of Homosexuality*. Chicago: University of Chicago Press, 1988, 438n.

109 his book *Is Capitalism Doomed?*: Lawrence Dennis, *Is Capitalism Doomed?* (New York: Harper & Brothers, 1932).
"living religions": ibid., 85.
"out of the world of profits": ibid., 86.

111 text for *The International Style:* Alan Blackburn, interview, 10 December 1987.

112 between 1932 and 1934: ibid.
Philip's new preoccupations: Severns, interview, 17 February 1990.
Theodate scornfully recalled them: ibid.

113 denounce the profit motive: "Two Quit Modern Art Museum for Sur-Realist Political Venture," *New York Herald Tribune*. 18 December 1934, 1, 17.

114 "shape human destiny": *Is Capitalism Doomed?, 317.*

115 discreet public silence: Johnson, interview, 18 September 1988.
stunned and embarrassed: Helen Franc, interview, 8 January 1987.
"Minister of Fine Arts": quoted in Russell Lynes, *Good Old Modern* (New York, 1973), 93.

117 "how to shoot straight": "2-man Third Party Heads South to Size Up Long." *New York Herald Tribune*, 23 December 1934.
back to Ohio and "organize it": Johnson, interviews, 10 October 1987 and 17 March 1990.
returning to New York: Johnson, interview, 17 March 1990.

119 rather as he preferred it: ibid.
arrived a day too late: Johnson, interview, 10 October 1987.

121 "protest against low milk prices": Geoffrey Blodgett, "Philip Johnson's Great Depression," *Timeline* 4, no. 3 (June–July 1987): 7.

122 "A lot of people liked them": Lee Ignat, interview, 3 January 1990.

123 "a 100 percent strike": Blodgett, in *Timeline,* 8.

124 "I've got lots of company": ibid., 8.

125 "murderers of unborn people": ibid., 9.
declared himself a Democrat: ibid.

126 more of him during the campaign: Johnson, interview, 10 October 1987.
state representative in Ohio: ibid.
"solitary figure of the priest": *Chicago Tribune,* 7 September 1936, 1, 4.
to make himself heard: Johnson, interview, 8 July 1989.
nation's economic vitality: Ironically, Roosevelt's principal opponent, Gov. Alfred M. Landon of Kansas, had been nominated at the Republican National Convention in Philip's home city of Cleveland.

128 closeness and Philip's wealth: Johnson, interview, 10 October 1987.
restless young locals: Johnson and Blackburn drew back from Coughlin following the 1936 election. In an interview, 10 October 1987, Johnson claimed that Coughlin was depressed and a little unhinged by his defeat, which prompted Johnson to suggest that he give up the priesthood. "What?" he remembers Coughlin's responding. "Would you have me do a Luther!"

128   "distressed Philip no end": Richard Bowers, interview, 3 January 1990.
130   Mies liked it: Johnson, interview, 11 July 1987.
       Weltanschauung, Science and Economy: Werner Sombart, "Weltanschauung,
       Wissenschaft und Wirtschaft," included in *Probleme des deutschen Wirtschafs-*
       leben. Berlin and Leipzig: Walter de Gruyter & Co., 1937.
       two years later, in 1939: Johnson's translation was published by Veritas Press,
       New York.
       lottery he had set up: Blodgett, in *Timeline,* 13.
       poker with local friends: Johnson, interview, 10 October 1987.
       to his native Australia: That Johnson had had earlier dealings with Secretary
       Perkins when he was still with The Museum of Modern Art is attested by a
       letter of 14 September 1933, addressed to him by Assistant Secretary of the
       Treasury L. W. Robert, Jr., who referred to a letter Johnson wrote to
       Perkins in August 1931 promoting the idea of modern architecture for fed-
       eral buildings. Johnson did not recall whether his former museum connec-
       tion had prompted him to seek Perkins out in 1937.
131   "but back to New York": Johnson, interview, 6 March 1988.
132   in the spring of 1938: Johnson, interview, 17 March 1990.
       subsequent winter in New York: It is hard to believe that in his visits with
       Barr during this period Johnson would not have heard of an American proj-
       ect by Mies, but Johnson repeatedly insisted in interviews—e.g., 8 January
       1988 and 25 August 1990—that he had no such knowledge until much later.
       whose title, *The Coming American Fascism:* Lawrence Dennis, *The Coming*
       American Fascism (New York: Harper & Brothers, 1936).
133   uppermost in Philip's mind: Johnson, interview, 6 January 1990.
       house of a local family: ibid.
134   "even more staggering": ibid.
       "carried away by it all," Philip recalled: ibid.
135   married to Maj. Gen. Karl Bodenschatz: ibid.
136   "out of my depth": Johnson, interview, 17 September 1988.
       "covered with black": ibid.
137   a Jew and a homosexual: Johnson, interview, 18 September 1988.
       "how long I can talk to you": Johnson, ibid.
       powerless to do anything: Johnson, interview, 10 July 1993.
138   Coughlin agreed: Johnson, interview, 10 October 1987.
139   reread it himself late in life: Johnson, letter to the author, 30 July 1990. He
       writes: "The William James article in this magazine [see following note]
       shows him in a new light. His ecstasy at the burning of San Francisco
       reminds me of my exultation during the first days of the war.
           "How can terrible things be so thrilling?"
       "personal battlefield experience": R. W. B. Lewis, "William James in 1906:
       Earthquake Perils and Mental Daring," *National Humanities Center News Let-*
       ter 11, no. 2 (Winter 1989–90): 1–13.
142   what to do with himself next: Johnson, interview, 10 October 1987.
       in the fall of 1939: Federal Bureau of Investigation file no. 100–32734, entry
       of 23 December 1942.
       "great struggle in Europe": FBI file no. 100–32734, undated entry.
       "a German agent of some sort": Johnson, interview, 17 March 1990.
143   "allowed to make one large mistake": Lynes, *Good Old Modern,* 93.
144   by his earlier foolishness: Two examples were the British Broadcasting Cor-
       poration television documentary *Philip Johnson: Godfather of American Archi-*

tecture, produced by Sharon Maguire, 1993, and an article, "Philip the Great," by Kurt Andersen, *Vanity Fair,* June 1993, 130–38, 151–57.

146   (What is good?): The question "What is noble?" is discussed at length by Nietzsche in both *Beyond Good and Evil* (New York: Vintage Books, 1966), trans. with commentary by Walter Kaufmann, and *The Will to Power* (New York: Vintage Books, 1968), trans. Kaufmann and R. J. Hollingdale, ed. Kaufmann.

148   not Philip's cup of tea: Johnson, interview, 16 March 1988.

149   "I don't see any problem": Johnson, interview, 10 October 1987.
"practicality or cost": Carter H. Manny, Jr., letter to his family, 12 October 1940.
"true meaning of modern architecture": Manny, letter to his family, 27 October 1940.
"like a drunken sailor": Manny, letter to his family, 17 November 1940.
in a jury critique: Manny, letter to his family, 24 November 1940.

150   as he later called him: or, in a variation, "pious, pompous, Prussian, and Protestant," Johnson, interview, 11 July 1987.
relationship with him gone sour: Johnson, interview with Robert A. M. Stern, Oral History Program, Temple Hoyne Buell Center for the Study of American Architecture, Columbia University, 2 May 1985: "Hudnut and I got together a great deal . . . we used to get together in hate-Gropius fests."

151   "None of the profs can touch him": Manny, letter to his family, 21 May 1941.
in one of Manny's letters: Manny, letter to his family, 22 July 1941.
"No discipline whatsoever": Manny, letter to his family, 1 June 1941.
"is progressing nicely": Manny, letter to his family, 27 September 1941.

152   "a few bored grunts": William L. Shirer, *Berlin Diary: The Journal of a Foreign Correspondent, 1934–41* (New York: Alfred A. Knopf, 1941), 212–13.
an antifascist patriot: Johnson, interview, 25 August 1990.
"is none too kind to him": Manny, letter to his family, 27 September 1941.

153   altogether likable adversary: Arthur Schlesinger, Jr., interview, 4 May 1989.
"we must go the whole way": Manny, letter to his family, 30 October 1941.

155   " 'with a cad you agree with' ": Freda Utley, *Odyssey of a Liberal: Memoirs* (Washington, D.C.: Washington National Press, 1970), 265.

156   knew his own mind: Karl Schlubach and John Wisner, interview, 7 December 1991.

157   "along the garden expanse": Manny, letter to his family, 9 May 1942.
now pursuing a master's: Johnson, interview, 8 July 1989.

158   four decades later, in 1979: Johnson, *Writings,* 56–60.

161   gotten out of the army alive: Johnson, interview, 17 March 1990.
"only they call it 'soopel' ": Johnson, letter to Louise Johnson, 2 May 1943.
"military bearing and strict discipline": Johnson, letter, probably to his family, incomplete and undated, probably July 1943.
"German accent that is so annoying": Johnson, letter to his family, undated, probably summer of 1943. His attachment to his mother, which he later disavowed, seems still strong at this time, witness this passage: "Dear mother, it was so wonderful having you here that if I stay another season, I think you will have to take a home near here. It was the best thing I have had since I joined the army."
in New York early in 1943: FBI file no. 100-32734, entry of 13 February 1943, which reports that the interview took place on 23 January 1943.

162   *The Dynamics of War and Revolution:* Lawrence Dennis, *The Dynamics of War and Revolution* (New York: The Weekly Foreign Letter, 1940).

162   "whatever that may mean": Johnson, letter addressed to "mother and father," 14 November 1943.
       "gone through in years": Johnson, letter to Louise Johnson, 18 October 1943.
       tell the court about him: Johnson, interview, 5 May 1990.

164   "Pvt. Lincoln Kirstein [etc.]": Fifty years later, in a letter to the author dated 15 April 1994, Kirstein confirmed a recollection he had offered in an interview of 13 August 1986:

> I think . . . that either Philip or his father gave my father [Louis Kirstein, prominent in Jewish circles in Boston in the 1940s] a considerable sum of money, then around $300,, for the relief of European Jews, subsequent to my letter [of 5 January 1944].
> I am not certain about the date or the sum, but Philip may recall.

Johnson did not recall, but added that his father might have made such a contribution without advising him.

165   embassy building in Bogotá: Johnson, interview, 25 August 1990.
       soul of the institution: In November 1944, Barr's title changed again, to chairman of Modern Painting and Sculpture. In February 1947, he was named director of the Museum Collections. Following his retirement in June 1967, he was designated councillor to the board of trustees.

166   "It had lots of glass": Johnson, interview, 25 August 1990.

168   "one-half Wright, one-half Persius": ibid.

PART THREE: REBIRTH
AND RENEWAL, 1946–1953

171   issue of that magazine: Richard Pratt, "As Simple as That," *Ladies' Home Journal,* July 1945, 118. A second house by Johnson was published in the same periodical in another article by Pratt, "A House for a Millionaire with No Servants," April 1946, 227.

173   parapet cornice of the building: Johnson has claimed that the Goodwin-Stone design incorporated one of his own suggestions, the extension of the ribbon windows nearly to the west edge of the building. Since he was no longer connected with the museum at the time he would have made this proposal, one is led to presume it was conveyed to the architects through Alfred Barr.
       tend to grow accustomed: See Russell Lynes, *Good Old Modern,* 221.

174   She evidently never had a chance: Johnson, interview, 23 February 1991.

175   "commission better artists and architects": Johnson, "War Memorials: What Aesthetic Price Glory?" *Art News,* September 1945, 8–10, 24–25.

176   "Symbols are out": Frank Lloyd Wright, letter to Johnson, 3 October 1945.
       German Democratic Republic: Following negotiations with the authorities of the German Democratic Republic, Mies's papers were retrieved in 1964. They were given to The Museum of Modern Art, which installed them in 1968 in the newly established Mies van der Rohe Archive.

177   "tell us no doubt very soon": Johnson, letter to J. J. P. Oud, 27 April 1946.

178   "Mies van der Rohe is least known": Philip C. Johnson, *Mies van der Rohe* (New York: The Museum of Modern Art, 1947).
       the exhibition as a whole: Edwin Alden Jewell, "A Van Der Rohe Survey," *The New York Times,* 28 September 1947, II, X7.

180 voluntary contact with Wright: See Franz Schulze, *Mies van der Rohe: A Critical Biography* (Chicago: University of Chicago Press, 1985), 237–38.
opened at the museum: Mary Barnes, interview, 23 February 1991.
"No conversation": anonymous interview, 27 July 1992.

181 most of his curatorial endeavors: Peter Blake, interview, spring 1992.
former place by Alfred Barr: Rockefeller's absence from 1941 to 1946 was occasioned by his service in governmental posts during World War II.

184 encounter with Jon Stroup: Jon Stroup, interview, 26 October 1989, and Johnson, interview, 1 May 1988.

186 drawings he might do for them: Johnson, interview, 25 August 1990.
as an architectural stillbirth: Landis Gores, *Memoirs,* unpublished manuscript, 1986, unpaginated.
"a raised podium": Gores, ibid.
"commissioned by . . . Stanley Resor": ibid.

187 collapse of a leasehold transaction: ibid.
he had bought the place: Stroup, interview, 26 October 1989.

191 distinguishable approaches among them: Gores, *Memoirs.*
walls all of glass: ibid.

192 ensured intimacy and privacy: Kenneth Frampton, "The Glass House Revisited," *Catalogue* 9, Institute for Architecture and Urban Studies, 12 September to 31 October 1978, 39–59.
"in neo-classic mold": Gores, *Memoirs.*

193 the Glass House scenographically: Frampton, "The Glass House Revisited," 40.

194 fifty yards east of the Glass House: Gores, *Memoirs.*
Die Entwicklung der Autonomen-Architektur: ibid.

195 "newly promulgated esthetic": ibid.

197 like a Rorschach blot: Johnson, interview, 26 August 1990: "My burnt-out house association is made up. I do well on Rorschach tests."
Mies would never tolerate: See *The Mies van der Rohe Archive,* ed. Franz Schulze. New York: Garland, 1993. Vol. 13.105 (Museum Acquisition Number 1002.65); 150 (Mies van der Rohe Archive Number 4505.16).
and asymmetrical planning: Stroup, interview, 26 October 1989.

198 the outskirts of East Hampton: ibid.
" 'How absolute can you get?' ": Gores, *Memoirs.*

200 "under way in the U.S.?": Peter Blake, letter to Johnson, 3 May 1951.

202 "Johnson was a timid designer": Henry-Russell Hitchcock, introduction to *Philip Johnson: Architecture 1949–1965* (New York: Holt, Rinehart and Winston, 1966), 9.
"the worst house I ever built": Johnson, interview, 25 August 1990.

203 "late nineteenth century French painting": Gores, *Memoirs.*
developing a crush on him: Johnson, interview, 8 July 1989.
"coming through firm and clear": Gores, *Memoirs.*

204 "one-story house in New York": Johnson, interview, 8 July 1989.
"looking for Philip Johnson": Rita Reif, "Manhattan Town House Being Sold," *The New York Times,* 27 March 1989, C14. Reif reported that the building was the first house ever auctioned by the Sotheby auction firm.

206 "its neighbor on either side": Gores, *Memoirs.*

209 "would probably have designed it symmetrically": Johnson, quoted in *MOMA: A Publication for Members of the Museum of Modern Art,* Summer 1975, unpaginated.

210 "a piazza in New York": "Outdoor Room" (no byline), "Talk of the Town," *The New Yorker,* 25 April 1953, 24–25.

210 "Or possibly Dali": Johnson quoted in *MOMA: A Publication.*
with names appended: Gores, *Memoirs.*

211 not to bother speculating: Johnson, interview, 1 May 1988.
"accommodating environment of New Canaan": Gores, *Memoirs.*

214 "design the pavilion above": Johnson quoted in Hitchcock, "Philip Johnson," *Architectural Review,* April 1955, 236–47.

216 as the third Mrs. Johnson: John Hohnsbeen, interview, 15 April 1991. (Stroup claimed in his interview of 26 October 1989 that it was he who introduced Johnson and Hohnsbeen.)

218 "more than he loved her": ibid.

219 "The perfect psychosomatic illness": ibid.
"It was our happiest time together": ibid.
"brings out the best in me": Johnson, interview, 7 December 1991.

221 "tradition of western classicism": Robert A. M. Stern, "Yale 1950–1965," *Oppositions* 4 (October 1974): 35–62.
"Architecture exists only in *time*": Johnson, "Whence and Whither: The Processional Element in Architecture," *Perspecta* 9/10 (1965): 167–78; reprinted in Johnson, *Writings,* 150–55.

222 his "Seven Crutches" lecture: Johnson, "The Seven Crutches of Architecture," informal talk to students, School of Architectural Design, Harvard University, 7 December 1954; published in *Perspecta* 3 (1955): 40–44; reprinted in Johnson, *Writings,* 136–40. The title is a tongue-in-cheek reference to John Ruskin's famous book of 1849, *The Seven Lamps of Architecture.*

223 one such visit: Wright, letter to Johnson, 6 August 1948.
"to love each other do we": Wright, letter to Johnson, 6 September 1948.
" 'The prince visits the king!' ": Gores, *Memoirs.*
"a decade or two behind": Why Johnson never organized a major retrospective of Frank Lloyd Wright has never been made clear. Johnson claimed he had no such thing in mind at any time, but Gores in his memoirs writes, "There had never been a moment's hesitation on Philip's part about . . . the propriety of a major solo exhibition to balance his Mies show. . . ."
"And is it architecture?": Wright quoted by Selden Rodman, "Frank Lloyd Wright (I), *Conversations with Artists* (New York, 1957), 50.

224 " 'Wonderful, wonderful' ": Johnson quoted in Rodman, "Philip Johnson (I)," *Conversations,* 56.
"a house of glass": Wright quoted in Rodman, "Philip Johnson (I)," *Conversations,* 70.
Philip's "foreign legion": Wright, letter to Johnson, 7 March 1949.
"ashamed of yourself? F. LL. W.": Wright, note to Johnson, undated, probably 1950.
"leaving them out in the rain?": This anecdote has been repeated endlessly, its phraseology changing almost as often, probably because the event happened suddenly enough that no one recorded it exactly. See Rodman, *Conversations,* 53, and Meryle Secrest, *Frank Lloyd Wright: A Biography* (New York, 1992), 394.

225 "practice architecture seriously": Johnson quoted in Rodman, "Philip Johnson (I)," *Conversations,* 52.

226 natural gift for writing: Arthur Drexler, in "Architecture Opaque and Transparent," *Interiors,* October 1949, 90–101, wrote one of the first important reviews of Johnson's Glass House.

227 "has come of age": *Built in U.S.A.: Post-War Architecture,* edited by Henry-Russell Hitchcock and Arthur Drexler. New York: The Museum of Modern Art, 1952, 8–9.

PART FOUR: BREAK WITH
MODERNISM, 1953–1967

230 at Smith College in 1953: Johnson participated in a "Symposium on Art and Morals" at Smith College, 24 April 1953. His lecture has never been published.

232 " 'we may not perish through truth' ": Nietzsche, in an essay of 1873 titled "On Truth and Lying in an Extra-moral Sense," puts it this way:
"What is truth? a mobile army of metaphors, metonyms, anthropomorphisms, in short, a sum of human relations which were poetically and rhetorically heightened, transferred, and adorned, and after long use seem solid, canonical, and binding to a nation. Truths are illusions about which it has been forgotten that they *are* illusions, worn-out metaphors without sensory impact, coins which have lost their image and now can be used only as metal, and no longer as coins." See *Friedrich Nietzsche on Rhetoric and Language*, eds. and trans. Sander L. Gilman, Carole Blair, and David J. Parent (New York: Oxford University Press, 1989), 250.

233 "The Seven Crutches of Modern Architecture": This talk was delivered to students, School of Architectural Design, Harvard University, 7 December 1954.

234 English critic Geoffrey Scott: Geoffrey Scott, *The Architecture of Humanism: A Study in the History of Taste* (New York: Charles Scribner's Sons, 1924).

239 "in this country in recent years": Johnson quoted in "Model Is Shown of Memorial to 6,000,000 Jews," *New York Herald Tribune*, 18 January 1950, 25.

240 Philip's oval to the Baroque: Henry-Russell Hitchcock, Jr., introduction, *Philip Johnson: Architecture 1949–1965*, 11.

242 all the time she asked for and then some: Phyllis Lambert, interview, 11 November 1991.

243 "Wright, Le Corbusier, and Mies": ibid.
"all the more beauty to it": Lambert, "How a Building Gets Built," *Vassar Alumnae Magazine*, February 1959, 14.
to back him up, someone local?: Lambert, interview, 11 November 1991.

245 "what you see in him or in it": Johnson, interview, 23 September 1993.
when he was twenty-six: This was the house for Mrs. Helene Kröller-Müller, meant for Wassenaar, near The Hague. Neither Berlage's scheme nor Mies's (see p. 192), nor another by Peter Behrens, was ever built. The house finally materialized in Otterlo, in 1938, after the design of Henry van de Velde.
a routine that was already fixed: The one major dislocation stemmed from the actions of Wiley, in whose house Mies had spent the night following the famous Berlage fight. Presenting himself to both Mies and Johnson as a financial expert, Wiley had not only offered advice to Mies in the course of the Seagram project but secured Johnson's power of attorney. In fact, Johnson entrusted him with several hundred thousand dollars before suspecting him of fraud. Investigation confirmed that Wiley was not a member of the Wall Street brokerage he earlier claimed to be. Shortly after Philip confronted him with his findings, Wiley committed suicide. (Johnson, interview, 7 December 1991.)

246 the new two-headed arrangement: Richard Foster, interview, 15 March 1989.
"it is taken": Gene Summers, conversation, April 1992.
"to asking me not to leave": Foster, interview, 15 March 1989.

248 added consistency to the overall effect: In 1958, following the recommendation of Alfred Barr, Johnson asked the eminent American painter Mark

Rothko to produce a series of monumental canvases for the larger of the two Four Seasons restaurants. The project came to naught. Rothko did the paintings, fully three sets of them. He elected, however, to sell the first group as individual objects, then abandoned the second, and finally, after finishing the third, withheld it from Johnson. As finicky as he was indecisive about the settings in which his work was shown, Rothko decided to resent the idea of hanging his painting in "a place," as his biographer James E. B. Breslin quoted him, "where the richest bastards in New York will come to feed and show off." James E. B. Breslin: *Mark Rothko.* Chicago: University of Chicago Press, 1993, 376.

Johnson's indignation over Rothko's change of mind was followed by another frustrating encounter with him. Commissioned by Dominique de Menil to design a chapel in Houston where Rothko's paintings would be the featured decoration, Philip wrangled constantly with the artist about the makeup of the place. His—Johnson's—wish to surmount the structure with a very high conical dome was rejected by the de Menil family and he withdrew from the project, which was completed in 1970 by Howard Barnstone and Eugene Aubry. While those architects retained Johnson's octagonal floor plan, he refused to claim the otherwise-altered building as his own.

249 to the building's entrance: Johnson, interview, 7 December 1991.
aqueous plaza scheme in favor of his own: Lambert, interview, 11 November 1991. She claimed the placement of pools in the plaza was originally Johnson's idea, not Mies's. Johnson in his 7 December 1991 interview confirmed this.

252 the University of Virginia in mind: Johnson, interview, 9 August 1992.
253 British critics who invented it: ibid.
255 "that little stretch of water": Johnson, interview, 28 March 1986.
"a boy's for a tree house": ibid.
"the Gothic church of St. Séverin": Johnson, interview, 9 August 1992.
258 rendered in the modernist idiom: See Victoria Newhouse, *Wallace K. Harrison, Architect* (New York: Rizzoli, 1989).
259 the physical planning of the project: ibid.
260 as Philip remembered it: Johnson, interview, 5 December 1992.
"How much blood would be shed?": Harold C. Schonberg, "Six Architects in Search of a Center," *The New York Times Magazine,* 8 February 1959, 22.
together in a single structure: Johnson, interview, 5 December 1992.
263 rose from its concentric center: ibid.
265 "threatened several times to kill him": John Hohnsbeen, interview, 15 April 1991.
266 "I refused": ibid.
"knew I knew from the Seagram project": Johnson, interview, 7 December 1991.
267 conscious homage to Le Corbusier: ibid.
early days of the Hitler regime: For the best discussion of Mies's politics, see Richard Pommer, "Mies van der Rohe and the Political Ideology of the Modern Movement in Architecture," *Mies van der Rohe: Critical Essays,* ed. Franz Schulze (New York: The Museum of Modern Art, 1989), 96–145.
"feeding architecture to the multitude": Sibyl Moholy-Nagy, letter to Johnson, 30 September 1962.
268 "humanizing experience of the last 10 years": "Earthly Bliss" is Sibyl Moholy-Nagy's variation of "Heavenly Bliss," a name she meant for Eliza Parkinson, née Bliss, then a close friend of Johnson and likely a target of Moholy-Nagy's jealousy.

"whether you might have a free evening": Sibyl Moholy-Nagy, letter to Johnson, 13 December 1958.

"in the post-cubist abstract period": Johnson, letter to Sibyl Moholy-Nagy, 1 May 1956.

"[his National Farmers' Bank in Owatonna, Minnesota]": Johnson, letter to Sibyl Moholy-Nagy, 19 December 1956.

269 "Long live Change!": Johnson, letter to Jürgen Joedicke, 6 December 1961, published in John M. Jacobus, Jr., *Philip Johnson* (New York: Braziller, 1962), 120–22; reprinted in Johnson, *Writings,* 125–26.

"forms of unlimited variety": Sibyl Moholy-Nagy, letter to Johnson, 21 December 1961.

"don't always use structure expressively": Johnson, letter to Sibyl Moholy-Nagy, 12 May 1959.

"Retreat from the International Style of the Present Scene": Johnson, lecture, Yale University, 9 May 1958, published in Johnson, *Writings,* 84–97.

270 at the Architectural Association: Johnson, lecture, Architectural Association, School of Architecture, London, 28 November 1960, published in Johnson, *Writings,* 104–16.

restricted her to occasional visits: Jeannette Johnson Dempsey, interview, 21 November 1992.

272 "He wasn't any use in the world": Johnson, interview with Robert A. M. Stern, Oral History Program, Temple Hoyne Buell Center for the Study of American Architecture, Columbia University, 18 March 1985.

Jeannette described as deeply moving: Dempsey, interview, 21 November 1992.

the gently rocking motion of the lift mechanism: Johnson, interview, 19 December 1992.

273 "than it is to any artist": Johnson quoted in "Modern Architecture and the Rebuilding of Cities," abridged transcript of a panel discussion at the Graham Foundation for the Advanced Studies in the Fine Arts, Chicago, *Arts and Architecture,* February 1962, 16–17, 30–32.

"about 50 miles from New York": Blake, quoted in ibid.

274 "advertising things and garbage pails": Johnson quoted in ibid.

"is the American scene": Johnson, "Crisis in Architecture," *Response* (journal published by Princeton University), April 1963, 5–6.

"a city of precast concrete and corrugated tin": Johnson, "Our Ugly Cities," commencement address, Mt. Holyoke College, 5 June 1966, published in *Mt. Holyoke Quarterly* 1 (Summer 1966): 86–88.

275 published in 1967 in *Architectural Design:* open letter, Robin Middleton to Johnson, published in "Cosmorama," *Architectural Design,* March 1967, 107.

278 reinforced the association: Johnson, interview, 14 November 1992.

280 "the Mayans did not mind steep inclines": Johnson, "Whence and Whither: The Processional Element in Architecture," *Perspecta* 9/10, 1965, 167–78; reprinted in *Writings,* 150–55.

281 the repair of the fallen wall: Johnson, interview, 7 February 1993.

282 "the shadow of a full blown rose": Don Blair, *The New Harmony Story* (New Harmony, Ind.: New Harmony Publications Committee, undated), 63.

283 "Rehovot was the result": Tom Buckley, "Philip Johnson: The Man in the Glass House," *Esquire,* December 1983, 270–82.

284 a building commission on Israeli soil: Nicholas Fox Weber, interview, June 1993.

"jobs in his office to all sorts of people": Edward M. M. Warburg, interview, 9 July 1987.

290   one exhibition gallery to the next: Johnson, interview, 7 January 1989.
"the uneasy feel of a rope bridge!": Johnson, interviews, 19 December 1992 ("I love danger when it isn't dangerous") and 7 February 1993.

291   "that have been partially twisted": Reif, "An Estate Has Evolved from a Single Glass Box," *The New York Times,* 12 December 1970, 44.
"a square with a triangle stuck on it": Johnson, interview, 7 February 1993.
"several times as he settles into his bed": Johnson, interview, 17 March 1991.
"the square is really a pentagon": Johnson, interview, 7 February 1993.

292   virtually any position in the building: Johnson may have been influenced in this notion by Alfred H. Barr, Jr., who had expressed the same motive in the plan of the first sculpture garden at The Museum of Modern Art (see p. 207).

293   the one he had originally conceived: Johnson, interview, 7 February 1993.

294   "do something different every day": Johnson, quoted in "Master Builder" (no byline), *Cleveland Plain Dealer,* 13 October 1991, 1H, 6H.

299   "the next generation's grand old man": Ada Louise Huxtable, "He Adds Elegance to Modern Architecture," *The New York Times Magazine,* 24 May 1964, 18–19, 100–01.
("That romantic, magnificent room is gone"): Johnson, "Our Ugly Cities," *Mt. Holyoke Quarterly* 1 (Summer 1966): 86–88.

300   one of the city's authentic architectural jewels: Johnson, interview, 19 December 1992.
"Fatehpur Sikri, with Tughlaqabad second": Johnson, letter to Patwant Singh, 18 January 1966.
(Johnson on several occasions has named his "ten greatest architectural works of all time." Actually, the list includes fourteen—just on the occasions I have heard him recite them: They are: Imhotep's funerary district of King Zoser in Sakkara, Egypt; the Parthenon in Athens; the Pantheon in Rome; the Cathedral of Chartres; Fatehpur Sikri in India; Ryoanji in Japan; Brunelleschi's Church of Santo Spirito in Florence; Borromini's Church of San Carlo alla Quattro Fontane in Rome; Le Nôtre's gardens at Vaux-le-Vicomte in France; Schinkel's Gardener's Cottage and Roman Baths in Potsdam; Gaudí's Parque Güell in Barcelona; Mies van der Rohe's German Pavilion in Barcelona; Frank Lloyd Wright's Johnson Wax Building in Racine, Wisconsin; Le Corbusier's chapel at Ronchamp in France.)
"from Louis XIV's Versailles": ibid.

301   "If it can't be stopped legally, change the law": Lindsay quoted in Huxtable, "Lindsay Surveys City from Copter," *The New York Times,* 24 July 1965, 8.
"and destroy historic sites": ibid.
"interested in things like the PTA": Johnson quoted in "Johnson in Political Foray," no byline, *Progressive Architecture,* December 1966, 54.
"doorways on the roof of the plant": Johnson quoted in "Architect Hired for Sewage Plant" (no byline), *The New York Times,* 17 August 1967, 39, 42.
" 'more useful than fountains, and I agree' ": Merril Eisenbud quoted in David Bird, "Beauty Loses Out to Efficiency in Design for Sewage Plant," *The New York Times,* 11 November 1968, 43.

303   east and south of Washington Square Park: For an extended discussion of the New York University project, see "An Urban Problem: the People Object," signed "E.P." (Ellen Perry), *Progressive Architecture,* June 1966, 181–93.

304   "highways and educational institutions": ibid.

306   "single monuments were ever built": See Johnson, "Architecture: A Twentieth Century Flop," *Look,* 9 January 1968, 30.

307   *Complexity and Contradiction in Architecture:* Robert Venturi, *Complexity and Contradiction in Architecture* (New York: The Museum of Modern Art, 1966).

308 "[that] is completely convincing": Johnson, review of Robin Boyd, *The Puzzle of Architecture* (New York: Cambridge University Press, 1965), *Architectural Forum,* June 1966; reprinted in Johnson, *Writings,* 129–33.

"aware of but felt unsure about": Robert A. M. Stern, introduction to Johnson review of Boyd, Johnson, *Writings,* 128.

"the best student I ever had": Johnson, interview, 3 February 1991.

310 second book, published in 1972: Venturi, Denise Scott Brown, and Steven Izenour, *Learning from Las Vegas* (Cambridge, Mass.: MIT Press, 1972).

rather than forward-looking values: Robert A. M. Stern, interview, 15 July 1987.

311 "Then we could never get together!": Johnson quoted in Barbara Lee Diamonstein, interview with John Burgee, *American Architecture Now II* (New York: Rizzoli, 1985), 29.

Philadelphia architect Vincent Kling: Carter H. Manny, Jr., letter to author, 13 September 1993.

312 bachelor of architecture degree in 1963: David Whitney, interview, 13 November 1992.

"very physical, and very short": Johnson, interview, 14 November 1992.

find something else to do with himself: ibid.

313 him and Philip together for life: Johnson, interview, 7 February 1993.

"while I was living with Philip": Whitney, interview, 13 November 1992.

315 "they don't want to see you together": ibid.

about friends and enemies alike: ibid.

the magazine *Musical America*: Theodate was the publisher of *Musical America* from 1960 through 1964.

Dakota apartment building on Central Park West: Theodate Severns, interview, 15 March 1989.

"need that house for ourselves": ibid.

was not likely to endure gladly: John Burgee, interview, 9 May 1993.

316 "as earnest as she was pretty": Russell Lynes, *Good Old Modern,* 76.

317 "I won't be able to stand it": Eliza Parkinson Cobb, interview, 6 January 1987.

until after the lover died: Johnson, interview, 7 December 1991, confirmed by Cobb, interview, 6 January 1987.

PART FIVE: SUPERSTARDOM,

1967–

320 to discuss the matter with him: John Burgee, interview, 22 April 1993.

321 "It's not what we do": ibid.

324 "the Seagram Building turned inside out": Johnson, interview, 16 May 1992.

325 nor they of him: Burgee, interview, 22 April 1993.

326 "setbacks, and curved corners": ibid.

"This is Texas," Liedtke explained: ibid.

327 the transparency of the glass: ibid.

"eminent architects in America today": Paul Goldberger, "Form and Procession," *Architectural Forum,* January–February 1993, 32–53.

330 "between academe and the profession": Peter Eisenman, interview, 13 November 1992.

331 the institute's éminence grise: ibid.

332 the "sociologues" of Weimar Germany: Johnson, interview, 24 April 1993.

332   "What would he do in a large building?": Johnson, postscript to *Five Architects: Eisenman, Graves, Gwathmey, Hejduk, Meier,* preface by Arthur Drexler, introduction by Colin Rowe, "Frontality vs. Rotation," by Kenneth Frampton (New York: Oxford University Press, 1975), 136.

333   "but with irony, not innocently": Umberto Eco, Postscript to *The Name of the Rose* (New York: Harcourt Brace Jovanovich, 1984), 67.
        "architectural experience from culture": Robert A. M. Stern, "Stompin' at the Savoye," *Architectural Forum,* May 1973, 46–48.

334   "tight against one another": *Johnson/Burgee Architecture,* text by Nory Miller (New York: Random House, 1979), 95.

335   "keeping quite a pace": Burgee, interview, 9 May 1993.

336   "at St. Luke's": ibid.

337   an appointment with him and Philip: Burgee, interview, 22 April 1993.
        Burgee recalled their conversation: ibid.

339   "to green, to water and sun": ibid.

341   "when you designed this beautiful building": included in the documentary film *Philip Johnson, Godfather of American Architecture,* produced by Sharon Maguire, the British Broadcasting Corporation, 1993.

342   "Wasn't that *awful!*": Johnson, interview, 28 October 1990.

345   the only ones who didn't answer: Burgee, interview, 9 May 1993.
        "We got the job": ibid.

346   "we would have been Nebraska": an AT&T executive quoted in Craig Unger, "Tower of Power: the Extraordinary Saga of the A.T & T. Building," *New York,* 15 November 1982, 51.
        "democracy of one": a favorite Johnson expression, applied to powerful corporate figures.

347   "the most classical solution": Unger, "Tower of Power," 52.

350   a large sculpture there by Isamu Noguchi: Burgee, interview, 9 May 1993.

351   during the Reagan 1980s: After 1983, when AT&T's historical control of the telephone industry was broken by the federal courts, the company shrank in size. In 1992 it moved its corporate headquarters farther downtown in New York City, leaving the Johnson/Burgee tower on Madison Avenue to the Sony Corporation, which converted the arcade space into a closed area given over to commercial shops. Later in 1992 AT&T also removed the Golden Boy figure to the company's rural campus in Basking Ridge, New Jersey.
        "build skyscrapers with flat tops": Vincent Scully, "Buildings Without Souls," *The New York Times Magazine,* 8 September 1985, 66.
        "assured and able synthesis": Ada Louise Huxtable, "The Troubled State of Modern Architecture," *The New York Review of Books,* 1 May 1980, 22–29; reprinted in *Architectural Record,* January 1981, 72–79.
        "aesthetic intelligence rather than art": Huxtable, "Johnson's Latest—Clever Tricks or True Art?", *The New York Times,* 16 April 1978, II, 26.

352   "is to hook into regionalism": Paul Goldberger, "The New Age of Philip Johnson," *The New York Times Magazine,* 14 May 1978, 27.

353   "and rejected his work": ibid.
        a luxury apartment building close by: William Lieberman, at the time a major member of the curatorial staff, has reported that the new building project was under discussion as early as the late 1960s, during the brief (1968–1969) tenure of Bates Lowry, who succeeded René d'Harnoncourt as director of the museum.
        the reason he lost the commission: Johnson, interview, 7 January 1989.

354   should forthwith resign his trusteeship: Edward Larrabee Barnes, interview, June 1993.

not being named the architect: In conversation with the author, September 1993, Museum of Modern Art archivist Rona Roob recalled Margaret Barr's remarks at the luncheon. In turn, Barr, in notes written to provide information to Calvin Tomkins for his article "Forms Under Light" (*The New Yorker,* 23 May 1977, 43–80), declared: "I don't think Philip knows that David Rockefeller, who had pledged 5 million dollars to this project, made it a condition that Philip should not be the architect." In an interview, 14 July 1987, William S. Paley, chairman of the board of the museum from 1972 to 1985, acknowledged that "it was the Rockefellers . . . we didn't want to buck them."

comprised a highly complicated project: In an interview, 14 March 1989, Richard Oldenburg, appointed director of the museum in 1972, said that Johnson was denied the commission because trustees worried about possible cost overruns, given his previous working habits. Oldenburg added that David Rockefeller was one of the worriers.

358 "historically allusionist clothing": Huxtable, "The Boom in Bigness Goes On," *The New York Times,* 12 December 1980, 25–26.

"it has an interesting shape": Goldberger, "Six Architects Ponder Design Rationale Behind New Manhattan Skyscrapers," *The New York Times,* 21 February 1981, 14.

"after Johnson's AT & T Building": John Brodie, "Master Philip and the Boys," *Spy,* May 1991, 50–58.

359 "I wouldn't know how to be good": Johnson quoted in Susan Doubilet, "I'd Rather Be Interesting," *Progressive Architecture,* February 1984, 69.

362 "the stock market for Transco stock": Jack Bowen quoted in Ann Holmes, "Structures Stand Out," *Houston Chronicle,* 17 April 1985, Houston Section, 8.

366 "urban developments since Rockefeller Center": K. B. S. Toker quoted in Darl Rastorfer, "Reflections in a Curtain Wall," *Architectural Record,* October 1984, 193–99.

"constructed anywhere in recent years": Goldberger, "Architecture: Two Skyscrapers in Houston," *The New York Times,* 13 February 1984, C13.

"to turn a building into art": Huxtable, "The Troubled State of Modern Architecture," *The New York Review of Books,* 1 May 1980, 22–29.

367 "what's the difference, it's only images": Michael Sorkin, "The Real Thing," *Architectural Record,* September 1986, 78–85; reprinted in Sorkin, *Exquisite Corpse* (New York: Verso, 1991), 171–77.

368 "only making it seem cute": Goldberger, "Two Skyscrapers in Houston," *The New York Times,* 13 February 1984, C13.

"ruthlessly aristocratic taste": Scully quoted in Tom Buckley, "Philip Johnson: The Man in the Glass House," 282.

369 "the same solidity and calmness": Burgee quoted in Henry Hanson, "Philip of Green Gables," *Chicago,* January 1985, 96–97.

"an acceptable if modest goal": Charles Jencks, *Post-Modernism: The New Classicism in Art and Architecture* (New York: Rizzoli, 1987), 234.

372 "anyone else in the architecture world today": Martin Filler, "The Architect as Theorist," *Art in America,* December 1979, 16–19.

"against the International Style": ibid.

373 "with no further conflict!": Burgee, interview, 4 February 1993.

no intention of blackening Philip's name: Eisenman, interview, August 1993.

375 "Gehry, Eisenman and Graves": Brodie, "Master Philip and the Boys." *Spy,* May 1991, 50–58.

"a provocative publishing opportunity": *The Charlottesville Tapes* (New York, 1985), 6.

376   "you wonder where all the people are": ibid., 19.

377   "and get it built": Anthony Lewis, "The Golden Goose," *The New York Times,* 17 July 1986, A23.
"the will to art and immortality": Jencks, *Post-Modernism: The New Classicism,* 229.

378   "greatest patron and practitioner of his time": Robert Campbell, "The Joker: Philip Johnson, the Corporate Architect as Clown," *Lear's,* September 1989, 108–13, 178.

380   to want to be left alone: Johnson, interview, 25 August 1990.

381   badinage with Andy about future plans: *The Andy Warhol Diaries,* ed. Pat Hackett (New York: Warner Books, 1989), 791. Asked about the Warhol diaries in an interview, 13 November 1992, Whitney confined his answer to the claim that he was never cozier with Warhol than with Philip: "It's just that we were two lonely widows." Warhol, he added (interview, 13 November 1992), was involved at the time with a lover of his own.

384   policies of The Museum of Modern Art: See Lincoln Kirstein, "The State of Modern Painting," *Harper's,* October 1948, 47–53.

386   memorial service in The Museum of Modern Art: See *"A Memorial Tribute,"* Museum of Modern Art, 21 October 1981.
misery of the present moment: Johnson made this clear in several interviews, notably 3 July 1987 and 10 October 1987.

388   *Philip Johnson/John Burgee: Architecture, 1979–85: Philip Johnson/John Burgee: Architecture, 1979–85* (New York: Rizzoli, 1985).
withdraw entirely from the firm: Mitchell Pacelle, "Noted Architects' Firm Falls Apart in Fight Over Control, Clients," *The Wall Street Journal,* 2 September 1992, A1, A9.

390   "or at other activities": Burgee, memorandum to Johnson, 15 April 1988.
"Philip Johnson and John Burgee": Goldberger, "American Gothic Rides High in Atlanta's IBM Building," *The New York Times,* 8 May 1988, 30, 32.

391   "in the overall planning": Johnson, interview, 8 July 1989.

393   " 'torn between history and technology' ": Sorkin, "Canon Fodder," *The Village Voice,* 1 December 1987; reprinted in Sorkin, *Exquisite Corpse* (New York, 1991), 254–59.

395   "as the architecture itself": Martin Filler, "Philip Johnson: Deconstruction Worker," *Interview,* May 1988, 102–04, 107–09.
" 'learned the secrets of the grave' ": Herbert Muschamp, "Ground Up," *Artforum,* April 1988, 12.

396   "purity of its formal composition": Mark Wigley, "Deconstructivist Architecture," Johnson and Wigley, *Deconstructivist Architecture* (New York: The Museum of Modern Art, 1988), 10–20.

397   "without achieving a sense of unity": Joseph Giovannini, "Breaking All the Rules," *The New York Times Magazine,* 12 June 1988, 40–43, 126–30.
"overly benign summary of them": Brendan Gill, "The Skyline: Deconstructivism," *The New Yorker,* 5 September 1988, 90–96.
"coursed through the entire century": Douglas Davis, "Slaying the Neo-Modern Dragon," *Art in America,* January 1989, 43–49.
"instability and the collapse of meaning": Herbert Muschamp, "The Leaning Tower of Theory," *The New Republic,* 29 August 1988, 36–40.
"her visual intelligence is acute," said Muschamp): ibid.

398   "in these buildings," wrote Jane Holtz Kay: Jane Holtz Kay, "Architecture," *The Nation,* 17 October 1988, 358–60.
"everything to do with polemics": Douglas Davis, "Slaying the Neo-Modern Dragon," *Art in America,* January 1989, 43–49.

charged him with fascist sympathies: see John Taylor, "Mr. In-Between: Deconstructing with Peter Eisenman," *New York*, 17 October 1988, 46–52.

399 the kill fee already reported here: Johnson, interview, 10 July 1993.
"into his public persona": Herbert Muschamp, "The Leaning Tower of Theory," *The New Republic*, 29 August 1988, 36–40.
"out of control in the thirties": Eisenman, interview, 13 November 1992.
"sees nothing wrong with them": Peter Eisenman, quoted in John Taylor, "Mr. In-Between: Deconstructing with Peter Eisenman," *New York*, 17 October 1988, 46–52.
Philip rejoined privately: Johnson, interview, 10 July 1993.
"as truthful as I can be about it": Eisenman, interview, 13 November 1992.

403 during his undergraduate years: Johnson, interview, 1 May 1988.

404 legal ties with the office: Pacelle, "Noted Architects' Firm Falls Apart in Fight Over Control, Clients," *The Wall Street Journal*, 2 September 1992, A1, A9.
start all over again: Johnson, interviews, 26 October 1990 and 16 May 1992.
certain of the office's projects: Burgee, interview, 4 February 1993.

405 laborious process of a comeback: ibid.
reported it in *Oculus:* Suzanne Stephens, "Architect Abuse/When Partnerships are Dissolved: Raj Ahuja vs. John Burgee," *Oculus*, June 1992, 8–9.
in *The New York Observer:* John Brodie, "Split Between Johnson and Burgee; A $13 Million Suit and Chapter 11," *The New York Observer*, 15 June 1992, 1, 21.
better designer than he actually was: Johnson, interview, 15 December 1992.

407 "You cannot know history!": Johnson, conversation with author at the Amon Carter Museum, Fort Worth, 18 September 1993.

409 "He is very bright," said Philip: Johnson, interview, 4 June 1993.
exhibition "Modern Architecture": Terence Riley, *The International Style*.
In a piece for *Vanity Fair:* Kurt Andersen, "Philip the Great," *Vanity Fair*, June 1993, 130–38, 151–57.

410 "suck the creative juices": British Broadcasting Corporation television documentary: *Philip Johnson: Godfather of American Architecture*, produced by Sharon Maguire, 1993.

412 "the production of architectural beauty": Johnson, unpublished address, Renaissance Theater, Berlin, 13 June 1993.

414 "into agreeing with": Lorenz Tomerius, "Philip Johnson klagt Mut zum visionären Bauen ein" (Philip Johnson calls for courage in visionary building), *Berliner Morgenpost*, 14 June 1993.

418 "political causes or considerations": Johnson, speech opening the exhibition "The Tyranny of Beauty," Museum of Applied Art, Vienna, 5 April 1994.

419 "nothing stays fixed": see Guy Davenport, *Herakleitos and Diogenes* (San Francisco: Grey Fox Press, 1976).
"and others free": ibid.
"the realm of human action": Ujjval Vyas, *Philip Johnson: An Intellectual History*, Ph.D. dissertation, Committee on the History of Culture, University of Chicago, completion expected 1994.

420 "climate of architecture in this country": Johnson, interview, 27 March 1994.
"Every animal faces it": ibid.
"Then I will move to Rome": ibid.

SELECTED BIBLIOGRAPHY

WRITINGS BY PHILIP JOHNSON
Books and Exhibition Catalogues

With Alfred H. Barr, Jr., Henry-Russell Hitchcock, Jr., and Lewis Mumford. *Modern Architecture: International Exhibition.* New York: The Museum of Modern Art, 1932. This text is identical with that of *Modern Architects.* New York: W. W. Norton, The Museum of Modern Art, 1932.

With Henry-Russell Hitchcock, Jr.: *The International Style: Architecture Since 1922.* Preface by Alfred H. Barr, Jr. New York: W. W. Norton, 1932. Paperback edition with new foreword and appendix, "The International Style Twenty Years After," by Henry-Russell Hitchcock, Jr. New York: W. W. Norton, 1966.

Machine Art. Foreword by Alfred H. Barr, Jr. New York: The Museum of Modern Art, 1934.

Mies van der Rohe. New York: The Museum of Modern Art, 1947; 2d revised edition with added chapter, 1953.

Philip Johnson: Architecture 1949–1965. Introduction by Henry-Russell Hitchcock, Jr. New York: Holt, Rinehart and Winston, 1966.

Selected Writings by Philip Johnson. Edited by David Whitney. Translated into Japanese by Tadashi Yokoyama. Tokyo: ADA Edita, 1975.

Writings. Foreword by Vincent Scully; introduction by Peter Eisenman; commentary by Robert A. M. Stern. New York: Oxford University Press, 1979.

With Mark Wigley: *Deconstructivist Architecture.* New York: The Museum of Modern Art, 1988.

Articles and Published Statements

"The Architecture of the New School." *Arts,* March 1931, 393–98. Reprinted in *Writings.*

"The Skyscraper School of Architecture." *Arts,* May 1931, 569–75. Reprinted in *Writings.*

"In Berlin: Comment on the Building Exposition." *The New York Times,* 9 August 1931, Section 8, X5. Reprinted in *Writings.*

"Architecture in the Third Reich." *Hound and Horn,* October–December 1933, 137–39. Reprinted in *Writings.*

"Are We a Dying People?" *The Examiner,* Summer 1938, 305–20.

"*Mein Kampf* and the Business Man." *The Examiner,* Summer 1939, 291–96.

"London and Paris—Midsummer 1939." *Today's Challenge,* August–September 1936, 19-26.

"Architecture in 1941." *Writings,* 56–60.

"Architecture of Harvard Revival and Modern: The New Houghton Library." *Harvard Advocate,* April 1942, 12–17. Reprinted in *Writings.*

"War Memorials: What Aesthetic Price Glory?" *Art News,* September 1945, 8–10.

With Edgar Kaufmann, Jr.: "American Architecture: Four New Buildings." *Horizon,* October 1947, 62–66.

"The Frontiersman" (on Frank Lloyd Wright). *Architectural Review,* August 1949, 105–10. Reprinted in *Writings.*

"House at New Canaan, Connecticut." *Architectural Review,* September 1950, 152–59. Reprinted in *Writings.*

Preface to *Postwar Architecture.* Edited by Henry-Russell Hitchcock and Arthur Drexler. New York: The Museum of Modern Art, 1952, 8–9. Comments, 72–75.

"Correct and Magnificent Play." *Art News,* September 1953, 16–17, 52–53. Review of Le Corbusier, *Complete Works, vol. V., 1946–1952,* edited by W. Boesiger (Zurich: Girsberger, 1953). Reprinted in *Writings.*

"Where Are We At?" *Architectural Review,* September 1960, 173–75. Review of Reyner Banham, *Theory and Design in the First Machine Age.* London: The Architectural Press, 1960. Reprinted in *Writings.*

Letter to Dr. Jürgen Joedicke, 6 December 1961, published in John M. Jacobus, Jr., *Philip Johnson.* New York, Braziller, 1962, 120–22. Reprinted in *Writings.*

With others: "Modern Architecture and the Rebuilding of Cities." *Arts and Architecture,* February 1962, 16–17, 30–32. Abridged transcript of panel discussion sponsored by the Graham Foundation for Advanced Studies in the Fine Arts, Chicago. Illinois Institute of Technology, Chicago, November 1961.

"Crisis in Architecture." *Response,* April 1963, 5–6.

"Whence and Whither: The Processional Element in Architecture." *Perspecta* 9/10 (1965): 167–78. Reprinted in *Writings.*

Review of Robin Boyd, *The Puzzle of Architecture* (New York: Cambridge University Press, 1965). *Architectural Forum,* June 1966, 72–73, 93. Reprinted in *Writings.*

Review of *Philip Johnson: Architecture 1949–1965. Architectural Forum,* October 1966, 52–53.

"An Open Letter to Mayor Kollek." *The New York Times,* 26 February 1971, 33.

"Beyond Monuments." *Architectural Forum,* January–February 1973, 54–68, 70, 72, 74. Adapted from "Monuments for the Masses," Graham Foundation lecture, Chicago chapter, American Institute of Architects, 15 December 1972.

Vorwort: Helge und Margret Bofinger, *Junge Architekten in Europa.* Stuttgart: W. Kohlhammer, 1983.

"A Personal Note" [on the Wexner Center for the Visual Arts, Columbus, Ohio]. *Architectural Design,* no. 11/12 (1989): profile 9–10.

Introduction to *Peter Eisenman and Frank Gehry,* catalogue of American exhibition, Fifth International Exhibition of Architecture, Venice Biennale, 1991. New York: Rizzoli, 1991.

Lectures and Speeches

Speech: symposium on "Art and Morals." Smith College, Northampton, Massachusetts, 24 April 1953.

Lecture: "The Seven Crutches of Modern Architecture." Harvard University, Cambridge, Massachusetts, 7 December 1954. Published in *Perspecta* 3 (1955): 40–44. Reprinted in *Writings.*

Lecture: "Retreat from the International Style to the Present Scene." Yale University, New Haven, Connecticut, 9 May 1958. Published in *Writings,* 84–97.
Speech: "Whither Away—Non-Miesian Directions." Yale University, 5 February 1959. Published in *Writings,* 226–40.
Informal talk: Architectural Association, School of Architecture, London, 28 November 1960. Published in *Writings,* 104–16.
Lecture: "Karl Friedrich Schinkel im zwanzigsten Jahrhundert." Berlin, 13 March 1961. Published in English, "Schinkel and Mies." *Program,* School of Architecture, Columbia University, New York, Spring 1962, 14–34. Reprinted in *Writings.*
Commencement address: "Our Ugly Cities." Mount Holyoke College, South Hadley, Massachusetts, 5 June 1966. Published in *Mount Holyoke Alumnae Quarterly* 1 (Summer 1966): 86–88.
Lecture: "What Makes Me Tick." Columbia University, 24 September 1975. Published in *Writings,* 258–65.
Speech: "Berlin's Last Chance: Schinkel, Messel, Mies van der Rohe. Now What?" Renaissance Theater, Berlin, 13 June 1993.

Interviews

Interview: "Philip Johnson (I)" and "Philip Johnson (II)," in Selden Rodman, *Conversations with Artists.* New York: Devin-Adair, 52–56, 60–70.
Television interview with Susan Sontag, British Broadcasting Corporation, 1965.
Interview with Francine du Plessix, "Philip Johnson Goes Underground." *Art in America,* July–August 1966, 88–93.
Interview with Paul Heyer in Heyer, *Architects on Architecture: New Directions in America.* New York: Walker, 1966, 279–92.
Interview with John W. Cook and Heinrich Klotz in Cook and Klotz, *Conversations with Architects.* New York: Praeger, 1973, 11–51.
Interview with Lee Radziwill, "Fancy Speaking." *Esquire,* December 1974, 159–61, 220–24.
Interview with Robert A. M. Stern. *Ianus,* May–June 1980, 12–25.
Interview with Barbara Lee Diamonstein in Diamonstein, *American Architecture Now II.* New York: Rizzoli, 1985, 152–60.
"Philip Johnson and John Burgee's Exclusive Interview." *Stone World,* January 1988, 32–42.
Interview with Martin Filler, "Philip Johnson: Deconstruction Worker." *Interview,* May 1988, 102–04, 107–09.
Interview with George T. Kunihiro. *Japan Architecture,* no. 1 (1991): 4–5.
Interview with Peter Eisenman. *Skyline,* February 1982, 14–17.
Philip Johnson: Godfather of American Architecture. Television documentary, produced by Sharon Maguire, British Broadcasting Corporation, 1993.

WRITINGS ON OR RELEVANT TO PHILIP JOHNSON
Books

Jacobus, John. M., Jr. *Philip Johnson.* New York: Braziller, 1962.
Alexander, Ricardo Jesse, and Eduardo Juan Cervera. *Philip Johnson.* Buenos Aires: Instituto de Arte Americano: Investigaciones Esteticas, 1967.
Noble, Charles. *Philip Johnson.* New York: Simon & Schuster, 1972.
Johnson/Burgee: Architecture. Text by Nory Miller. New York: Random House, 1979.

Philip Johnson/John Burgee: Architecture, 1979–85. Introduction by Carleton Knight III. Edited and compiled by Ivan Zaknic. New York: Rizzoli, 1985.
Philip Johnson: The Glass House. Edited by David Whitney and Jeffrey Kipnis. New York: Pantheon, 1993.

Entire Issues of Periodicals

Philip Johnson. Global Architecture. Edited and with photographs by Yukio Futagawa. Text by Bryan Robertson. Tokyo: ADA Edita, 1972.
Philip Johnson. A + U (Architecture and Urbanism), special issue, 1979.
Philip Johnson. Architectural Forum, January–February 1973.
Philip Johnson and John Burgee. Progressive Architecture, February 1984.
Philip Johnson, Kunstfigur/Philip Johnson, Artist. Werk, Bauen + Wohnen, September 1991.
Philip Johnson: Processes; The Glass House, 1949 and the A.T. & T. Corporate Headquarters, 1978. Catalogue 9, Institute for Architecture and Urban Studies, September–October 1978.

Articles

Andersen, Kurt. "Philip the Great." *Vanity Fair,* June 1993, 130–38, 151–57.
Banham, Reyner. "The Post Post-Deco Skyscraper: A.T. & T. New York." *Architectural Review,* August 1984, 22–29.
———. "Actual Monuments." *Art in America,* October 1988, 172–77, 213–15.
Blake, Peter. "Philip Johnson Knows Too Much." *New York,* 15 May 1978, 58–67.
Blodgett, Geoffrey. "Philip Johnson's Great Depression." *Timeline,* June–July 1987, 2–17.
Brodie, John. "Master Philip and the Boys." *Spy,* May 1991, 50–58.
Brown, Nona B. "A Timeless Place" (on Johnson's Museum of Pre-Columbian Art, Dumbarton Oaks, Washington, D.C.). *The New York Times,* 24 May 1964, Section X, 1, 9.
Buckley, Tom. "Philip Johnson: The Man in the Glass House." *Esquire,* December 1983, 270–82.
Campbell, Robert. "A Mover and a Shaper." *Boston Globe Magazine,* 14 August 1983, 10, 50, 52, 54–55, 58.
———. "The Joker." *Lear's,* September 1989, 108–14, 178.
Chira, Susan. "New Designs for Times Square Try to Reflect Neon Atmosphere." *The New York Times,* 31 August 1989, B1, B4.
Ciucci, Giorgio. "The Work of Philip Johnson" (translated by Diane Ghirardo). *Catalogue 9* (September–October 1978): 13–39.
Dal Co, Francesco. "The House of Dreams and Memories." *Lotus* 35 (1982): 122–28.
Drexler, Arthur. "Architecture Opaque and Transparent." *Interiors,* October 1949, 90–101.
"Ellis Island Shrine." *Progressive Architecture,* April 1966, 214–16.
Filler, Martin. "High Ruse." Part one, *Art in America,* September 1984, 152–65; part two, *Art in America,* October 1984, 168–77.
Frampton, Kenneth. "The Glass House Revisited." *Catalogue 9* (September–October 1978); 38–59.
Giovannini, Joseph. "Breaking All the Rules." *The New York Times Magazine,* 12 June 1988, 40–43, 126–30.
Goldberger, Paul. "Philip Johnson's Eminent, Elegant, Practical World." *The Smithsonian,* February 1975, 48–55.
———. "The New Age of Philip Johnson: A Controversial New Vision for Architecture." *The New York Times Magazine,* 14 May 1978, 26–27, 65–73.

Haskell, Douglas. "Architecture: What the Man About Town Will Build." *The Nation*, 13 April 1932, 441–43.

Hitchcock, Henry-Russell, Jr. "Philip Johnson." *Architectural Review*, April 1955, 236–47.

———. "Current Work of Philip Johnson." *Zodiac* 7 (1961): 64–81.

"Houses" (on Johnson House, Cambridge, Massachusetts). *Architectural Forum*, December 1943, 89–93.

Hughes, Robert. "The Duke of Xanadu at Home." *Time*, 26 October 1970, 82–85.

———. "Doing Their Own Thing." *Time*, 8 January 1979, 52–59.

Huxtable, Ada Louise. "He Adds Elegance to Modern Architecture." *The New York Times Magazine*, 24 May 1962, 18–19, 100–101.

———. "Johnson's Latest—Clever Tricks or True Art?" *The New York Times*, 16 April 1978, II, 26.

———. "The Troubled State of Architecture." *The New York Review of Books*, 1 May 1980, 22–29.

Jewell, Edwin Alden. "The Realm of Art: The Machine and Abstract Beauty." *The New York Times*, 11 March 1934, Section X, 12.

Jordy, William. "Seagram Assessed." *Architectural Review*, December 1958, 374–82.

———. "The Mies-less Johnson." *Architectural Forum*, September 1959, 114–23.

Ketcham, Diane. " 'I Am a Whore': Philip Johnson at Eighty." *The New Criterion*, December 1986, 57–64.

Kipnis, Jeffrey. "Philip Johnson" (six recent projects, with interview). *A + U*, April 1992, 10–39.

Kramer, Dale. "The American Fascists." *Harper's*, October 1940, 380–93.

MacPherson, Myra. "The Great Hall: A Mansion Is Attached" (on the Kreeger House, Washington, D.C.). *The New York Times*, 8 September 1968, Section 10, 88.

Middleton, Robin. Open letter, "Dear Philip." "Cosmorama," *Architectural Design*, March 1967, 107.

Moholy-Nagy, Sibyl. "The Syncretism of Philip Johnson." *Perspecta* 7 (1961): 68–71.

Muschamp, Herbert. "The Leaning Tower of Theory." *The New Republic*, 29 August 1988, 36–40.

———. "For Times Square, a Reprieve and Hope of a Livelier Day." *The New York Times*, 6 August 1992, C15, C18.

Owens, Craig. "Philip Johnson: History, Genealogy, Historicism." *Catalogue* 9 (September–October 1978): 2–11.

Pacelle, Mitchell. "Noted Architects' Firm Falls Apart in Fight Over Control, Clients." *The Wall Street Journal*, 2 September 1992, A1, A9.

Page, Homer. "The Man Who Builds Monuments." *Think*, May–June 1965, 19–23.

Pastier, John. "Evangelist of Unusual Architectural Aspiration: Twenty Years in a Neutra Church, Dr. Robert Schuller Is Building a Johnson Cathedral." *AIA Journal*, May 1979, 48–55.

———. "Evaluation: Pennzoil as Sculpture and Symbol." *AIA Journal*, June 1982, 38–43.

———. "Tale of Two Houston Towers: SOM's Allied and Johnson/Burgee's Republic." *Architecture*, April 1984, 38–47.

P(erry), E(llen). "An Urban Problem: The People Object" (on Johnson's project for New York University). *Progressive Architecture*, June 1966, 181–93.

Philip Johnson's lecture with Jeffrey Kipnis. "Transformation of Space." *Japan Architecture*, Summer 1992, 4–17.

Platt, Adam. "A Towering Figure in Architecture." *Insight*, 23 February 1987, 8–16.

Plunz, Richard, and Kenneth L. Kaplan. "On 'Style.' " *Precis*, Columbia University Graduate School of Architecture and Planning. Fall 1984, 33–43.

Pommer, Richard. "Philip Johnson and History." *Artforum*, September 1986, 78–85.

Portoghesi, Paolo. "Una chiesa al settimo cielo." *L'Europa*, 2 March 1981, 75.

"Recent Work of Philip Johnson." *Architectural Record*, July 1962, 113–28.

Russell, James S. "Gridlock" (on redevelopment of New York's Times Square). *Architectural Record*, November 1989, 55.

Schonberg, Harold C. "The Lincoln Center Vision Takes Form." *The New York Times Magazine*, 11 December 1960, 7–10, 101–10.

Scott Brown, Denise. "High Boy: The Making of an Eclectic." *The Saturday Review*, 17 March 1979, 54–58.

Scully, Vincent. "Buildings Without Souls," *The New York Times Magazine*, 8 September 1985, 42, 65–68, 109–11, 116.

———. "Frank Lloyd Wright and Philip Johnson at Yale." *Architectural Digest*, March 1986, 90–94.

———. "Philip Johnson: The Glass House Revisited." *Architectural Digest*, November 1986, 116–25.

Sorkin, Michael. "Philip Johnson: The Master Builder as a Self-Made Man." *The Village Voice*, 30 October 1978, 61–62. reprinted in Sorkin, *Exquisite Corpse*. New York: Verso, 1991.

———. "The Real Thing." *Architectural Record*, September 1986, 78–84; reprinted in *Exquisite Corpse*.

———. "Canon Fodder." *The Village Voice*, 13 October 1987, 123, 150; reprinted in *Exquisite Corpse*.

———. "Decon Job." *The Village Voice*, 5 July 1988, 81–83; reprinted in *Exquisite Corpse*.

———. "Where Was Philip?" *Spy*, October 1988, 138–40; reprinted in *Exquisite Corpse*.

Stern, Robert A. M. "Yale 1950–1965." *Oppositions* 4 (October 1974): 35–62.

———. "The Evolution of Philip Johnson's Glass House." *Oppositions* 9 (Fall 1977): 57–67.

Tafuri, Manfredo. "La cattedrale sommersa: l'ultime opera de Johnson and Burgee" ("Subaqueous Cathedral"); in Italian and English. *Domus*, July–August 1980, 8–15.

Tomkins, Calvin. "Forms Under Light." *The New Yorker*, 23 May 1977, 43–80.

Unger, Craig. "Tower of Power." Part one, *New York*, 15 November 1982, 40–47; part two, *New York*, 22 November 1982, 46–54.

Welch, Frank. "Philip Johnson's Texas Connection." *Texas Architect*, January–February (1993), 48–57, and July–August, 44–54.

Wilson, Forrest. "Philip Johnson's Modern Art at the Enlarged Museum of Modern Art and His Neo-Classic at Lincoln Center's New York State Theater." *Interiors*, July 1964, 85–95.

SELECTED BACKGROUND MATERIAL

Berlin, Isaiah. *The Crooked Timber of Humanity.* New York: Alfred A. Knopf, 1991.

Betsky, Aaron. *Violated Perfection: Architecture and the Fragmentation of the Modern.* New York: Rizzoli, 1990.

Blake, Peter. *No Place Like Utopia: Modern Architecture and the Company We Kept.* New York: Alfred A. Knopf, 1993.

The Charlottesville Tapes. Transcript of the Conference at the University of Virginia School of Architecture, Charlottesville, Virginia, 12 and 13 November 1982. New York: Rizzoli, 1985.

Dennis, Lawrence. *The Coming American Fascism.* New York: Harper, 1936.

Herdeg, Klaus. *The Decorated Diagram: Harvard Architecture and the Failure of the Bauhaus Legacy.* Cambridge, Mass.: MIT Press, 1988.

Hitchcock, Henry-Russell, Jr. *Modern Architecture: Romanticism and Reintegration.* New York: Payson & Clarke, 1929.

Jencks, Charles. *Post-Modernism: The New Classicism in Art and Architecture.* New York: Rizzoli, 1987.

Larson, Magali Sarfatti. *Behind the Post-Modern Facade: Architectural Change in Late 20th Century America.* Berkeley: University of California, 1993.

Le Corbusier. *Vers une architecture.* Paris: G. Crès, 1924. Translated into English as *Towards a New Architecture.* London: John Rodker, 1927.

Lynes, Russell. *Good Old Modern.* New York: Atheneum, 1973.

Riley, Terence. *The International Style: Exhibition 15 and The Museum of Modern Art.* New York: Rizzoli/Columbia Books of Architecture, 1992.

Scott, Geoffrey. *The Architecture of Humanism: A Study in the History of Taste.* New York: Charles Scribner's Sons, 1924.

Shirer, William. *Berlin Diary: The Journal of an American Correspondent, 1934–41.* New York: Alfred A. Knopf, 1941.

Sorkin, Michael. *Exquisite Corpse.* New York: Verso, 1991.

Venturi, Robert. *Complexity and Contradiction in Architecture.* New York: The Museum of Modern Art, 1966.

Vyas, Ujjval K. *Philip Johnson: An Intellectual History.* Ph.D. dissertation, Committee on the History of Culture, University of Chicago, completion expected 1994.

Weber, Nicholas Fox. *Patron Saints.* New York: Alfred A. Knopf, 1992.

Aalto, Alvar, 227, 259
Abbott Academy, 35
Abbott, Jere, 58, 92
Abramovitz, Max, 227; Philharmonic Hall, New York, 260, 263
Abstract Expressionism, 268, 287, 314
Acropolis, Athens, 175, 196–7, 233, 306
Adrian, Gilbert, 113
Aeschylus, 233
African-Americans, 94
Ahuja, Raj, 404–5
Ain, Gregory, 182
Albers, Anni, 182
Albers, Josef, 105, 109, 220
Alberti, Leone Battista, 347; Church of Sant' Andrea, Mantua, 347
Allen, Fred, 123
Alsop, Joseph, 113
Aluminum Corporation of America, 34
Ambasz, Emilio, 331
American Academy of Arts and Sciences, 366
American Fellowship Forum, 141–2, 154
American Institute of Architects, 160
American Society of Architectural Historians, 157
Amery, Colin, 409
Amherst College, 9
Amon Carter Foundation, 324
Amsterdam School, 86

Andersen, Kurt, 409
Anti-Defamation League of B'nai Brith, 238
anti-Semitism, see Jews, Judaism
Architectural Association, London, 270
Architectural League of New York, 72, 308
Armour Institute of Technology, 148
Aronovici, Carol, 101
Art Deco, 70, 72, 85, 98, 119, 173, 326
Art Nouveau, 16, 98
Askew, Kirk and Constance, 92–3, 105, 109, 118, 172
Asplund, Erik Gunnar, 64; Paradise Restaurant, Stockholm, 64
Astor, Brooke, 315
Aubry, Eugene, 436n
Auchincloss, Lily, 330
Augustus Caesar, 274
Auhagen, Friedrich Ernst, 142
Austin, A. Everett "Chick," 92–3, 95
Austrian Museum of Applied Arts, 418
Avon Old Farms, Farmington, Conn., 38

Bach, Johann Sebastian, 56
Baker, Edward F., 321
Baker, Newton D., 28
Balanchine, George, 92, 187, 261
Barnes, Edward Larrabee, 155–6, 227, 270, 336, 353–4

Barnes, Mary, 180
Barnes, Joseph, 141–42
Barnstone, Howard, 436n
Barr, Alfred H., Jr., 5–6, 46–9, 52, 55,
    57–8, 60, 62–3, 67, 70–4, 76–83,
    86–8, 90, 92–3, 95, 98–100, 105–8,
    111, 115, 119, 131–2, 158–9, 163–5,
    172–4, 181–2, 200, 207–8, 217, 225,
    233, 235, 240, 242, 268, 287, 306,
    314, 355, 384–6, 398, 401, 409, 420,
    423n, 424n, 430n, 432n, 435n, 438n
Barr, Margaret Scolari-Fitzmaurice
    (Marga), 58–60, 62–3, 67, 70, 73, 75,
    79, 92, 106, 131, 217, 354, 440n
Barry, Iris, 92, 315
Bartos, Armand, 330
Basquiat, Jean-Michel, 380
Batista, Fulgencio, 267
Bauhaus, 46, 48, 54–6, 59, 65, 76, 97–9,
    105, 107, 149–50, 172, 220, 267, 424n
Bayer, Herbert, 172
Beaux-Arts (tradition and style), 98,
    147–50, 220
Beethoven, Ludwig van, "Hammer-
    klavier" sonata, 260
Beggs, Gertrude, 13
Behrens, Peter, 77, 435n
Bel Geddes, Norman, 71, 75
Belluschi, Pietro, 220, 259–60; Juilliard
    School of Music, 260
Bender, Thomas, 93, 259
Ben-Gurion Airport, Tel Aviv, 286
Benny, Jack, 123
Berlage, Hendrik Petrus, 77, 176, 245;
    Stock Exchange, Amsterdam, 245;
    Kroller-Muller House project, 245,
    435n
Berlin, Isaiah, 165, 419
Berman, Eugene, 92
Bernier, Rosamond, 315–16, 337, 409
Betsky, Aaron, 393–94, 409
Bible, The, 116
Biddle, Francis, 165
Birnbaum, Philip, 343
Birth Control League of America, 124
Black Legion, 128
Blackburn, Alan, 111–31, 141, 152
Blair, Don, 282
Blake, Peter, 86, 180–2, 200–1, 225,
    273, 307
Blakeman, Mrs. Ray Slater, 105

Blancpain, Paul, 184
Bliss, Cornelius, 111
Bliss, Lillie P., 111, 316
Bliss, Mr. and Mrs. Robert Woods,
    277–8
Blisses (family), 181
Blodgett, Geoffrey, 121
Blondel, Jacques Francois, 176
Blunt, Anthony, 235
Bodenschatz, Maj. Gen. Karl, 135
Bodenschatz, Viola, 135–6, 138–40
Boehmer, Dr., 152
Bogner, Walter, 149, 186
Bogues, Frank Ellis ("Daddy"), 31,
    38–39, 47
Booth, Richard and Olga, 186
Boulder Dam, (later Hoover Dam), 113
Boullee, Etienne-Louis, 347
Bowen, Jack, 360–2
Bowers, Richard, 128, 132, 141
Bowes, Major Edward, 123
Bowman Brothers, 71, 76
Boyd, Robin, 307–8; *The Puzzle of
    Architecture*, 307
Boysen, Ed, 156, 165, 202
Brancusi, Constantin, 99
Breslin, James E. B., 436n
Breuer, Marcel, 55, 74, 147–51, 155,
    158, 166, 182, 186–7, 192, 206, 214,
    216, 227, 243, 259, 270, 375
Bridges, Harry, 131
British Broadcasting Corporation,
    408–9
Brochstein, I. S., 325–6
Brock, H. I., 81
Brodie, John, 358, 405
Bronfman, Samuel, 240, 242–3, 266
Browder, Earl, 153
Brown, Tina, 374
Brown University, 312
Browns (family), 91
Brownson, Jacques, 311
Brunelleschi, Filippo, 347; Pazzi
    Chapel, Florence, 347
Buchholz Gallery, 216, 218
Buchman, Frank Nathan Daniel, 422n
Buchmanite movement, 37, 109, 422n
Bulliet, C. J., 100
Bunshaft, Gordon, 260, 270, 353;
    Library and Museum of the Perform-
    ing Arts, Lincoln Center, 260

Burdens (family), 181
Burgee, John, 310–11, 313, 315, 320–7, 332, 335–40, 342, 345–7, 352–3, 357–8, 364, 369–70, 373, 387–92, 394, 403–5, 416–17, 441n
Burnham, Daniel, 87, 369; The Rookery, Chicago (with John Wellborn Root), 369
Buttes Chaumont Park, Paris, 28–29
de Butts, John D., 345–6, 350

Cage, John, 92, 97, 112
Cairo Museum, 41
Calder, Alexander, 175
Callery, Mary, 179, 198, 202, 235
Cambridge University, 374
Camp Atterbury, 167
Camp Devens, 160
Camp Ritchie, 161–2, 165
Campbell, Robert, 377–8
Canterbury Cathedral, 39, 51
Cantor, Eddie, 123
Capone gang, 114
Capron, Charlie, 128
Carey, John, 145
Castelli, Leo, Gallery, 314
Castello Plan of Nieuw Amsterdam, 11
Castro, Fidel, 267
Century Club, 374–5, 394–5
Chamberlain, Houston Stewart, 141
Chapman, Mae, 24, 29
Chartres Cathedral, 45, 177, 188, 194
de Chirico, Giorgio, 382
Christenberry, Earle, 117
Church of the Nativity, Bethlehem, 286
Clark, Stephen C., 165, 173
Clausewitz, Carl von, 140
Clauss and Daub, 72, 76; Johnson House, Pinehurst, N.C., 72–73
Cleveland Museum of Art, 29
Cleveland Orchestra, 29
Cleveland Playhouse, 95, 131
Cobb, Eliza Bliss Parkinson, 316–17, 330, 436n
Cobb, Henry Ives, 317
Columbia Broadcasting System, 123, 151
Columbia University, 330, 409
Committee on Slum Clearance, 258
Committee to Defend America by Aiding the Allies, 152

Conklin, William, 302
Constructivism, Russian, 46, 48, 66, 75, 396–7
Coop Himmelblau, 395–6
Cooper Union, 226
Copland, Aaron, 92
Cornell University, 12, 219
Cortelyou, Jacques, 11
Cortelyou, Lydia, 11
Cortissoz, Royal, 100
Coughlin, Charles E., 123–8, 138, 143, 152, 430n; *Social Justice*, 126–8, 138–140, 142–3, 152, 399
Coward, Noel, 53, 424n
Crandall, Lou, 243
Crane, Mrs. W. Murray, 91
Crescent, The, Dallas, 56, 368
Crescent, Royal, Bath (by John Wood and John Wood II), 271
Cubism, 46
Curtiss, Mina, 186

Dada (Berlin), 65
Dal Co, Francesco, 400
Dali, Salvador, 210
Danforth, George, 178
Daniels, Jimmy, 93–5
Davidson, Cynthia, 399
Davis, Douglas, 397–8
Dayton Company, 321
Dayton, Ken, 321
De Bakey, Michael, 335–6
Deconstructionism, 402–3, 419
Deconstructivism, 393–8, 404–6, 410, 413
Delaunay, Robert, 255
Demos, Raphael, 37–8, 40, 47–8, 156
Dempsey, Bourne, 415
Dempsey, Jeannette Johnson, 16–21, 24, 27–9, 33–6, 41–2, 115, 272, 386, 415, 421n
Dempsey, John, 41
Dennis, Lawrence, 108–10, 112–15, 119–20, 132–3, 140–41, 154, 161–3, 232; *Is Capitalism Doomed?*, 109–10; *The Coming American Fascism*, 132; *The Dynamics of War and Revolution*, 162
Depression, The, 61, 65, 67, 74, 80, 82, 85, 88–89, 91, 106–8, 112–13, 122, 124, 127, 130, 133, 200

Derrida, Jacques, 397, 403
De Stijl, 55, 66, 196, 252
Dillinger gang, 114
Disney, Walt, enterprises, 375, 406
Dix, Otto, 65
Dostoevskian (point of view), 230
Drexler, Arthur, 218, 225–7, 330–1, 358, 394
Ducal Palace, Mantua, 255
Durlacher Brothers, 92
Dyer, J. Milton, 15–16

Eames, Charles, 227
Eco, Umberto, 333
Ecole des Beaux–Arts, 16
Edgell, George H., 147
Eisenbud, Merril, 301
Eisenman, Peter, 309–10, 330–43, 372–6, 394–5, 397–403, 417–18; House II, Hardwick, Conn., 332; Wexner Center, Columbus, Ohio, 401
Eisler, Otto, 136–7
Eisner, Michael, 375
Eliot, T. S., 144
Ellwood, Craig, 270
Emerson, Janette, 131
L'Enfant, Pierre Charles, 300
Exhibitions: "Architecture of the City Plan," 182; Berlin Building Exposition, 73; "Built in U.S.A., 1932–44," 165, 173–4, 226; "Built in U.S.A: Post–War Architecture," 226; Century of Progress Exposition, Chicago, 98; "Deconstructivist Architecture," 393–8, 402, 406, 408; "Early Modern Architecture, Chicago, 1870–1910," 87, 97–8; "Early Museum Architecture," curated by Henry-Russell Hitchcock, Jr., 100, "Eight Automobiles," 226; *Entartete Kunst*, 134; Fifth Exhibition of Architecture of the Venice Biennale, 399–401; "Five Architects," 332; Frank Lloyd Wright: Design of Theater near Hartford, 182; "From Le Corbusier to Niemeyer," 182; "Housing Exhibition of the City of New York," 101; International Exposition, Barcelona, 57; Johnson House project by William Priestley, 100;

"Machine Art," 98–100, 109; Milan Triennale of 1933, 105, 109; "Modern Architecture: International Exhibition" (also known as International Style show), 69–72, 74–85, 90, 97–8, 105, 108–09, 137, 172, 178, 221, 233–4, 398, 409, 60th anniversary exhibition, 409; "The New City and Urban Renewal," 330; "New Posters from 16 Countries," 182; "Objects: 1900 and Today," 98; Philadelphia Savings Fund Society Building by Howe and Lescaze, 100; Recent Work by Skidmore, Owings and Merrill, 182; "Rejected Architects," 72; "Ten Automobiles," 226; Textiles by Anni Albers, 182; "Typographic Competition," 98; "Violated Perfection," 393–5; "The Work of Young Architects of the Midwest" (Robert W. McLaughlin and Howard T. Fisher), 98
Expressionism, 65–66, 77, 86, 417

Fanning, James, 208–09
Fantl, Ernestine, 71, 172
Farnsworth, Dr. Edith, 191
Farr, Warren, 37
Fatehpur Sikri, 300
Federal Bureau of Investigation: investigation of Johnson, 135–6, 139, 142–4, 153–4, 161–3
Federal Office of Facts and Figures, 153–4
Federal Public Buildings Administration, 164
Federal Reserve System, 124
Filler, Martin, 371–2, 395
Fiore, David, 417
Fischl, Eric, 314
Fitzgerald, F. Scott and Zelda, 58
Flint, Ralph, 80
Florian, Paul, 393–5
Flying Wedge, 113, 128
Fort Belvoir, 160–1, 163–5
Foster, Richard, 246, 261, 303–5, 310, 320
Frampton, Kenneth, 192–3, 331–2
Frankfurter Allee, Berlin, 418
Franzen, Ulrich, 270
Freiburg Cathedral, 51

Fried, Ferdinand, 134; *Autarkie*, 134
Friedlaender, Walter, 235
Friedrich, Caspar David, 412
Friedrich Wilhelm IV, 412
Friends of Democracy, 162–3, 165
Frost, Henry Atherton, 150
Fuller Company, 243
Fuller, R. Buckminster, 46, 220, 233; the Dymaxion House, 46

Gabriel, Ange-Jacques, 176
Garbo, Greta, 204
Gebrauchsmusik, 66
Gehry, Frank, 345, 375, 382, 384, 393–5, 400–02, 406, 410, 413, 417; Lewis House, Lyndhurst, Ohio, 406, 417
Geneva: Les Hirondelles, Pensionat Thudicum, 29
Genius of Electricity ("Golden Boy"), *see* Longman, Evelyn Beatrice
German–American Bund, 128
German Embassy, Washington, D.C., 143
German Propaganda Ministry, 152
German-Soviet nonaggression treaty of 1939, 137
Gershwin, George, 92
Giacometti, Alberto, 218, 235
Gibberd, Frederick, 271
Giedion, Sigfried, 210
Gielgud, John, 314
Gienanth, Ulrich von, 133
Gill, Brendan, 397, 409
Ginsburg, Moisei, 79
Giovannini, Joseph, 394–5, 397, 409
Giurgola, Romaldo, 308, 354
Gobineau, Joseph Arthur, 140
Goering, Hermann, 429n
Goethe, Johann Wolfgang von (quotation from Mephistopheles, *Faust, Part I*), 403
Goff, Bruce, 270
"Gold Dust Twins," 128
Goldberger, Paul, 327, 358, 366–8, 374, 390
Goode, Roy, 352–53
Goodhue, Bertram, 360; State Capitol, Lincoln, Nebr., 360
Goodman, Percival, 239
Goodwin, Philip, 172–3, 205, 207–8

Goodyear, A. Conger, 71, 181
Gores, Landis, 155–6, 171–2, 185–6, 191–8, 202–5, 211, 223, 246, 434n
Graham, Bruce, 270
Graham Foundation for Advanced Studies in the Fine Arts, 149
Graves, Michael, 309, 332, 357–8, 375; Portland Public Services Building, 358
"Grays, The," 332–33
Great Sedition Trial of 1944, 154, 161–2
Green Gallery, 314
Greene, Francesca, 35, 37
Gropius, Ise, 172
Gropius, Walter, 48, 52, 55–6, 65–6, 71, 73–4, 76, 79, 85, 147–51, 155, 158, 172, 180, 182, 200, 220, 227, 267, 305, 323, 425n, 431n; Bauhaus, Dessau, *see* Bauhaus; *Internationale Architektur*, 79; Pan Am Building, New York, 323; Siemensstadt, Berlin, 412
Grosser, Maurice, 92, 95
Grosz, George, 65
Groton Academy, 33
Grunsfeld, Ernest, 98
Guggenheim, Peggy, 266
Gund, Agnes, 316
Gwathmey, Charles, 309, 332, 375

Hackley School, 29–34, 36–7, 111
Hadid, Zaha, 395, 397, 417
Hadrian's Villa, Tivoli, 281
Haesler, Otto, 75, 79
Hall, Charles Martin, 34
Hamilton, Juan, 380
Hanfstaengl, Ernst "Putzi," 89
Harding, Warren G., 150
Haring, Keith, 380
Harlem Renaissance, 95
d'Harnoncourt, René, 174, 182, 298, 306, 330, 440n
Harris, Harwell Hamilton, 220, 227
Harrison, Wallace K., 227, 259–60, 263, 270, 302, 353; Metropolitan Opera House, 259–60, 263; United Nations complex, 259
Hart, Kitty Carlisle, 380
Harvard Defense Group, 153
Harvard Graduate School of Design, 147–60, 166–71, 184, 333, 353

Harvard Society for Contemporary Art, 46–47, 92
Harvard University, 5, 11–12, 31–46, 48, 57–9, 92, 108–9, 111, 120, 143, 148, 152–3, 158–9, 165, 180, 207, 220, 233–4, 310
Haskell, Douglas, 81
Haussmann, Georges Eugene, 29, 301
Heckscher Building, 59
Heidegger, Martin, 144
Hejduk, John, 309, 332
Helmsley Palace, 380
Hemingway, Ernest, 58
Heraclitus, 140, 402, 419
Herder, Johann Gottfried von, 419
Herrick, Myron T., 15
Hester, James, 303
Hilberseimer, Ludwig, 412
Hines, Gerald, 325–7, 331, 338, 358, 360, 362, 387, 409
Hitchcock, Henry-Russell, Jr., 45, 55, 58, 60–3, 67–70, 72–4, 76–87, 90, 92–4, 100, 105, 109, 111, 118, 147, 158–9, 167, 177, 182, 200, 202, 217, 222, 224, 226, 233, 239–40, 355, 398, 401–2, 420; *The International Style: Architecture Since 1922* (with Philip Johnson), 78, 86, 111, 137, 147, 167; *Modern Architecture: Romanticism and Reintegration*, 60
Hitler, Adolf, 89–90, 106–110, 112, 115, 123, 129–30, 132–38, 141, 145, 146–47, 163, 267, 410, 412, 429n; *Mein Kampf*, 140–41
Hodgsons (family), 246
Hoffman, Burrell, 352;
Hoffmann, Josef, 181;
Hohnsbeen, John, 216–19, 264–6, 312, 314, 380, 434n
Holabird, Root and Burgee, 311
Hood, Raymond, 71, 76, 82–3; American Radiator Building, New York, 360
Houseman, John, 95
Houses of Parliament, London, 359
Howe and Lescaze, 71–2, 76, 100; Philadelphia Savings Fund Society Building, Philadelphia, 72, 100
Howe, George, 72, 81, 158, 164–5, 167, 219–21, 243, 333, 421n
Hudnut, Joseph, 147, 150, 431n

Hughes, Robert, 345
Huxtable, Ada Louise, 180, 298–9, 309, 351, 357–8, 366–7

Ictinus, 276
Ignat, Mrs. Lee, 122
Illinois Institute of Technology, 148, 166–7, 177, 179, 220, 252–3, 311
Institute for Architecture and Urban Studies, 309, 330–2, 373, 375–6; *Oppositions*, 331
International Architecture Forum, Dessau, 417–18;
International Style, 72–3, 78, 81–3, 85–6, 90, 98, 158, 166, 173, 176, 181, 200, 204, 221, 238, 251, 258, 269, 298, 307–8, 329, 347, 372, 412; definition and derivation, 78–79
Investors Diversified Services, 321
Iofan, Boris Mikhailovich, Palace of the Soviet, 418
Isherwood, Christopher, 216
Isozaki, Arata, 331

Jacobs, Jane, 274, 304
Jadwin, Edgar, 28
Jagger, Bianca, 380
Jakobson, Barbara, 316
James, Henry, 38
James, William, 38, 139, 430n
Jansen, Hendrix, 11
Jansen, William, 11
Jefferson, Thomas, 252, 378
Jencks, Charles, 349, 369–70, 377
Jenney, William LeBaron, 87
Jewell, Edwin Alden, 178
Jews, Judaism, anti-Semitism, 28, 89, 94, 108, 135–9, 141, 143–44, 163–4, 181, 238–9, 283–4, 432n
Joedicke, Jürgen, 268–69
Johanson, John M., 155–6, 227, 270, 308, 336
Johns, Jasper, 288, 314, 381
Johns Hopkins University, 58
Johnson, Alfred, 16–18
Johnson, Alfred Stutts, 9, 11
Johnson, Homer Hosea, 9–30, 32–5, 40–1, 79, 110, 115, 117–18, 121, 127–8, 272, 415, 421n, 432n
Johnson, Jeannette, *see* Dempsey, Jeannette Johnson

Johnson, Louise Pope, 11–30, 34, 38–9, 41, 45, 47–8, 51, 55, 63, 72, 76, 88, 90, 115, 127, 157, 272, 415, 421n, 424n, 431;
Johnson, Lyndon B., 163n, 300
Johnson, Melvin Blake, 12, 15
Johnson, Philip
  LIFE awards: American Institute of Architects Gold Medal, 352; Bronze Medallion of the City of New York, 352; Pritzker Prize, 352; R. S. Reynolds Memorial Award, 352; Thomas Jefferson Medal of the University of Virginia, 352; School Award, American Institute of Architects, 160; concern with urbanism, 257–60, 263, 300–7; education, early, 5–6, 22–7, 29–32, later, 33–45; formative years, 17–32; genealogy, 9–13; lovers: Ed Boysen, 156, 165; John Cage, 92, 97, 112; Jimmy Daniels, 93–5; John Hohnsbeen, 216–19, 264–6, 312, 314, 380, 434n; Cary Ross, 58–60, 62–3; Karl Schlubach, 156, 184; Jon Stroup, 184–5, 187–8, 197–8, 216–17, 434n; Peter Vranic, 265–6, 312, 380; David Whitney, 266, 287–8, 305, 311–15, 317, 374, 379–84, 386, 391, 399, 442n; John Wisner, 156, 184; period in military service (*see* Camp Devens, Fort Belvoir, Camp Ritchie, Camp Atterbury), 160–68; physical and mental condition, 3, 4–5, 24, 34–6, 39–42, 50–1, 75, 90, 115, 118, 335–6, 381–2, 386–92, 415; political career in 1930s and 1940s, 104–46, assessments thereof, 144–46; "ten greatest architectural works of all time," personal choices, 438n; tenure at The Museum of Modern Art: beginning as unsalaried department head, 71; official appointment as department head, 87; resignation, 104; unofficial resumption of duties, 171; official resumption, 181; second resignation, 225, 227
  ARCHITECTURAL WORKS AND PROJECTS AT&T Building, 344–52, 358–9, 366–7, 379, 386, 441n; Abbott House, 202; Amon Carter Museum, 275–8, 417; Asia House, 253–4; Avery Fisher Hall reconstruction, 342; Battery Park City, 302; Beck House, 296; Berlin Fantasy, 413; Boissonas House, New Canaan, Conn., 251–2, 296, 367; Boissonas House, Cap Benat, France, 296; Booth House, 186–7, 192; Boysen House, 202; Boston Public Library Addition, 320–1; Broadway Junction, 320; Burden House, 214–16, 296; Business Center, Das, 410; Celebration Town Hall, 406; Century Center, South Bend, Ind., 342; Chelsea Walk, 320; Chrysler House, 216, 296; Church intended for Greenwich, Conn., 239; contributions to Seagram Building, especially Four Seasons Restaurant, 248–9, 258, 336, 380, 394, 435–6n; Crescent, The, 56, 368; Crystal Cathedral, 337–42, 345, 352, bell tower, 341; Dade County Culture Center ("New World Center"), 352–3; Davis House, 214; 80 Field Point Road, Greenwich, Conn., 342; Ellis Island Shrine, 295–6; Farney House, 186, 211; Ford House, 202; Fort Worth Water Garden, 324–5, 335, 337, 339; Four Seasons Restaurant, *see* Johnson, Philip, architectural works and projects: contributions to Seagram Building; Geier House, 294; General American Life Insurance Company Building, 342; Hendrix College, Library, 294; Hess Gallery, 238; Hirshhorn, Joseph, town design, 258; Hodgson House, 211–12, 246; Hospital, New London, Ohio, 166; Houston, University of, Law School, 405, School of Architecture, 369–70; Hudson River Sewage Disposal Plant, 301; IBM Building, 390; IDS Center, 321–4, 329, 347, 358; International Place, 376; Johnson, Philip, houses: Cambridge, Mass., 150–1, 156–8, 166, 187, 195, 210; *see also* New Canaan, Philip Johnson home and grounds; King Faisal Foundation competition, 416; Kneses Tifereth Israel Synagogue, 238–40, 250, 284;

(*Cont.*)

Kreeger House, 296, 300, 305; *Ladies' Home Journal* House, 171–2, 432n; Leonhardt House, 214; Lewis House, 405–6, 417; Lipstick Building, 387–88, 405; de Menil House, 202–3; Mercedes-Benz headquarters, 320; Monaco, Hotel, 266–7; Munson-Williams-Proctor Institute, 252–3; Museum of Modern Art Annex ("21 Building"), 205–7, 210, 246; Museum of Modern Art East Wing, 298–9, 314; Museum of South Texas, 324; National Center for the Performing Arts, Bombay, 342; Neuburger Museum, 320; New York State Pavilion, 294–5; New York State Theater, 260–3; New York University rebuilding (galleria, Bobst Library, Tisch Hall, Kevorkian Center, Meyer Hall), 303–4, 310; Niagara Falls Convention Center, 320; Nuclear Reactor, Israel, 283–6, 294; 190 S. LaSalle Street, 368–9; 1001 Fifth Avenue, 343; Oneto House, 211; Paine House, 202; Pelican Marsh Center, 406; Pennzoil Place, 326–9, 345, 347, 358, 362, 367, 410; Peoria Civic Center, 342; Post Oak I, II and III, 326; PPG Building, 359–60, 366–7; Pre-Columbian Museum, Dumbarton Oaks, 277–81, 294, 367; RepublicBank Building, 362–4, 366–8, 410; Rockefeller Guest House, 203–5, 379; Rockefeller Sculpture Garden, Museum of Modern Art, 207–11, 258, 298, 367; Rockefeller Sculpture Pavilion, 203; Roofless Church, 281–3, 285, 294; St. Anselm's Abbedy, 277; St. Thomas, University of, campus design, 252–3, 281, chapel, 405; Sarah Lawrence College Dormitories, 277; Schlumberger Administration Building, 214; Seton Hill College Arts Center, 405; Sheldon Memorial Art Gallery, 254–7, 360; student project, Lincoln, Mass., 186; Terrace Theater, Kennedy Center, 342; Thanksgiving Square, 334–5, 417; Times Square reconstitution,

390–1, 403–4, 416; tombstones for Alfred and Margaret Barr, 386; tool storage shed, Townsend Farm, Ohio, 166; Transco Tower, 360–2, 366–7; Trump, Donald, projects for: Gulf-Western tower conversion, 417, Riverside South, 416; Two Reserve Plaza, 368; Wadsworth House, 166–8, 171; John Wiley House, 166, 171; Robert C. Wiley House, 214, 216; Wolf House, 202; Yale University: Epidemiology and Public Health Building, 277; Kline Science Center (Chemistry Building, Geology Laboratory, Kline Scinece Tower), 278–81, 294

Johnson, Philip, Ritchie and Fiore, 417
Jova, Talita, 35–6
Judd, Donald, 291
Junger, Ernst, 134
Jungian (Carl Gustav Jung) theory, 399

Kahn, Louis, 220, 243, 251, 270, 308, 336; Adler House project, Philadelphia, 251; Devore House project, Springfield Township, Penn., 251
Kahn and Jacobs, 243
Kaiser Wilhelm II, 65
Kandinsky, Wassily, 55
Karl-Marx-Allee, East Berlin, 418
Kates, George, 60
Kaufmann, Edgar, Jr., 181–2, 238
Kaufmann, Emil, 157–8, 194–6, 216; *Von Ledoux bis Le Corbusier: Ursprung und Entwicklung der Autonomen-Architektur*, 158, 194–5
Kay, Jane Holtz, 397–8
Keck, George Fred, 98; House of Tomorrow, 98
Kelly, Richard, 236
Kennedy, John F., 163n, 300
Ketcham, Diane, 377
Kiesler, Frederick, 220, 270
Kipnis, Jeffrey, 402–3, 411, 417–18; *In the Manor of Nietzsche*, 402
Kirstein, Lincoln, 46–7, 92–3, 95, 107, 164, 186–7, 198, 217, 235, 260; New York City Ballet, 260, 263, 384–6; *Films*, 92; School of the American Ballet, 92; *Hound and Horn*, 107, 129
Kirstein, Louis, 432n

Kisch, Egon Erwin, 66
Klee, Paul, 55, 412
Klein, George, 391
Kline, Franz, 236, 31
Kling, Vincent, 311
Kloman, Tony, 219
Klotz, Heinrich, 409
Kohl, Helmut, 418
Kohn, Pedersen and Fox, 404
Kollek, Teddy, 284, 286
Koolhaas, Rem, 331, 395, 417
de Kooning, Willem, 314
Kornblee Gallery, 314
Kramer, Dale, 142
Kreusel, Albert, 51
Krier, Leon, 331
Krier, Rob, 376
Kroller–Muller House, The Hague,
  435n
Ku Klux Klan, 128

Lambert, Phyllis, 240, 242–6, 418, 436n
Lanchester, Elsa, 113
Landon, Alfred, 429n
Lansky, Meyer, 266
Lauder, Ronald, 410, 413
Laughton, Charles, 113
Lassaw, Ibram, 236, 240
Le Corbusier (Charles Edouard Jean-
  neret), 4, 52, 63, 66, 71, 73, 76–7, 79,
  83, 85, 106, 158, 175, 177, 182, 194–6,
  200–1, 214, 220, 243, 266–7, 286,
  300, 305, 307, 331, 352, 408, 412;
  L'esprit nouveau, 66; *Vers une architec-
  ture*, 66, 307; Chandigarh, plan, 300;
  de Mandrot Villa, 86, 186; Pavillon
  Suisse (referred to by Johnson as
  Pavilion de la Suisse), 73; Ronchamp,
  Chapel, 240, 294; Villa Savoye, 76
Ledoux, Claude-Nicolas, 177, 191,
  193–7, 201, 214, 216, 238, 240, 369;
  House of Education, Chaux, 369
Léger, Fernand, 99
Legion for Social Justice, 124
Lemke, William, 125–6, 143
Lenin, Nikolai, 110
Le Notre, Andre, 412
Lescaze, William, 72
Levy, Julien, 73, 92
Lewis, Anthony, 377
Lewis, Peter, 406, 417

Lewis, R. W. B., 139
Libeskind, Daniel, 395
Lichtenstein, Roy, 314
Lieberman, William, 440n
Liedtke, J. Hugh, 327–8, 346
Lin, Maya, 295
Lincoln Center, 258–63, 274, 302, 384
Lindbergh, Col. Charles A., 73
Lindsay, John V., 300–02
Lipchitz, Jacques, 235–6, 283, 290; *Fig-
  ure*, 235–6, 290; *Descent of the Holy
  Spirit*, 283
Loeb, Gerald, 186
Loewy, Raymond, 182
Lonberg-Holm, Kurt, 81–2
Long, Huey, 114–25, 127, 142, 146. 164,
  180
Longman, Evelyn Beatrice, 350; *Genius
  of Electricity* ("Golden Boy") 350,
  441n
Loomis Institute, 312
Lorsch, Gatehouse, 50, 52
Louis, Morris, 314
Louis XIV, 300
Louis XVI, 73
Lowry, Bates, 440n
Luckhardt, Wassily, 66
Luckman and Pereira, 242
Luther, Martin, 430n
Lutyens, Edwin, 350
Lynes, Russell, 115, 316

Machiavelli, Niccolò, 116
MacPherson, Dr. Sandy, 35, 425n
de Maistre, Joseph, 419
Malevich, Kasimir, 197
de Man, Paul, 144, 397
Manhattan Building Department, 210
Manley, John, 392
Manny, Carter H., Jr., 149–57, 166–7,
  214, 310–11
Mantua, *see* Ducal Palace
Marden, Brice, 314
Marini, Marino, 216
Markelius, Sven, 259
Marx, Karl, 110
Massachusetts Institute of Technology,
  157, 330
Mathildenhohe, Darmstadt, 52
Matisse, Henri, 73
Matisse, Pierre, 92

May, Ernst, 66
McAndrew, John, 52–3, 55, 60, 92, 172–3, 180, 182, 207–8;
McKim, Mead and White, 299, 343, 374; Boston Public Library, 320; Century Club, 374; Judson Memorial Baptist Church, 303; Pennsylvania Station, 299
Meier, Richard, 309, 332, 375
Mendelsohn, Erich (later Eric), 66, 73, 227
de Menil, Dominique, 202–3, 281, 436
de Menils (family), 203, 303
Mephistopheles, see Goethe
Messel, Alfred, 412
Metropolitan Museum of Art, 303
Metropolitan Opera, 259–60
Meyer, Adolf, 55, 150
Micah, 282
Michelangelo, 84, 200
Middleton, Robin, 274–7, 296, 378
Mies van der Rohe, Ludwig, 4, 52, 57, 66–71, 73–4, 76, 82, 85, 100, 106–8, 129–30, 132, 148–51, 157, 166–8, 172–3, 175–80, 182, 191–4, 196–202, 207, 209, 211–12, 214, 216, 220, 223, 225, 227, 233, 235, 240, 242–54, 258, 261, 267, 269–70, 277–8, 305, 308, 311, 327, 352, 359, 367, 369, 401, 412, 418, 420, 425n, 430n, 432n, 434n, 435n, 436n; Cantor House project, Indianapolis, 193; Convention Hall project, Chicago, 216; Electricity Pavilion, Barcelona, 253; Esters House, Krefeld, 426n; Farnsworth House, Plano, Ill., 191–3; Friedrichstrasse Office Building project (referred to by Johnson as Friedrichstrasse Bahnhof project), 418; German Pavilion at Barcelona, 57, 68, 70, 86, 149, 177, 214, 253, 425n; Glass House on a Hillside project, 214; Hubbe House project, Magdeburg, 193, 211; Illinois Institute of Technology, Chicago, 167, 177, Library and Administration Building project, 167, 212, S. R. Crown Hall, 253; Kroller-Muller House project, The Hague, 192, 245; Hermann Lange House, Krefeld, 426n; Reichsbank project, Berlin, 107; Resor

House project, Jackson Hole, Wyo., 186, 202, 211; Seagram Building, New York, 221, 240–9, 258, 266, 299, 320–1, 324, 336, 345–6, 387; Tugendhat House, Brno, 68, 70, 76, 178, 426n; Wolf House, Guben, 426n
Miller, Nory, 334
Mizner, Addison, 352, 36
Mock, Elizabeth B., 173–4, 180, 226
Moderne (style), see Art Deco
Moeller van den Bruck, Arthur, 134, 140
Moholy-Nagy, László, 267–8
Moholy-Nagy, Sibyl, 267–70, 278, 315, 436n
Moral Rearmament, 422n
Mona Lisa, 395
Mondrian, Piet, 204, 255
Moore, Charles, 308, 345–6
Moore, Henry, 175
Moral Re-Armament, 422n
Morgenthau, Henry, Sr., 28
Morris, Robert, 291
Morris the Finicky Cat, 367
Moses, 344
Moses, Robert, 258
Mother Teresa, 367
Mount Holyoke College, 274–5
Mr. T., 367
Mumford, Lewis, 68–9, 76–9, 86, 104, 150, 182, 277, 309, 372
Municipal Art Society, 380
Murphy, C. F. Associates, 149, 310–11, 321; O'Hare Airport, Chicago, 311
Muschamp, Herbert, 395, 397, 399
Museum of Modern Art, The, 5, 48, 57–8, 69–71, 80, 87, 91–2, 97–101, 104, 108, 111, 114–15, 120, 126, 137, 143–4, 158–9, 164–5, 171–2, 178, 182, 191, 197, 202–11, 218, 225–27, 234, 239–40, 258, 281, 284, 298, 300, 306, 308–9, 314, 316, 330, 332, 353–7, 358, 379, 384, 386, 393–4, 398, 408, 415–16, 424n, 430n, 432n (Johnson alteration of Goodwin-Stone design), 432n (Mies van der Rohe Archive), 436n, 438n, 440n
Mussolini, Benito, 132

Nadelman, Elie, 235, 263
Nalle, Eugene, 220

National Endowment for the Arts, 393
National Fine Arts Commission, 163n
National Party, 113
National Socialism, theory and practice, 89–90, 105–10, 119, 128, 130, 133–4, 140–2, 146–7, 152, 163, 429n; Nuremberg *Parteitag*, 133–4, 239; *Sommerkurs für Ausländer*, 133
National Trust for Historic Preservation, 355, 386, 417
National Union for Social Justice (NUSJ), 124–5
Nelson, George, 182, 226
Neo-Plasticism, 77, 271
Neues Bauen, 66
Neumann, J. B., 58, 60, 71
Neutra, Richard, 75–6, 83, 113, 227, 337–8
New Canaan, Connecticut; Philip Johnson home and grounds: 187, 210, 287–93, 382–4; buildings left from previous owners, 386, 391; entry gate, 382; "Gehry Ghost House," 4, 287, 382; Glass House, 3, 56, 188–99, 201, 203–4, 212, 214, 217, 219, 223–4, 226, 235–37, 244–5, 250–1. 253–5, 261, 263, 266, 276, 283, 287–8, 292–3, 296, 305, 312, 314, 337, 339, 367, 382, 384; Guest House, 3, 194, 196, 198, 212, 235–40, 245, 254–5, 287; Library-Study, 3–4, 382–4, 392; Lincoln Kirstein Tower, 4, 287, 384; Lipchitz sculpture, 235–6, 290; Painting Gallery, 3, 287–90; Pavilion, 4, 254–5, 261; Sculpture Gallery, 3, 287–93; uncompleted buildings, 287, 384, 417
New Harmony, Christian Rappite-Owenite Settlement, 281–3
New London Power Company, 122
New York City Parks Department, 239
New York Board of Registration, 249
New York Philharmonic Orchestra, 259
New York University, 58, 302–4
New York World's Fair of 1964, 294, 303
Newman, Barnett, 314
Niemeyer, Oscar, 182
Nietzsche, Friedrich, 44, 48–9, 90. 110–11, 115–16, 134, 140, 145–6, 232, 344, 402, 419, 435n; *Also sprach*

Zarathustra, 44, 110, 145; *Umwertung aller Werte*, 110; *Der Wille zur Macht*, 110, 145;
Nixon, Richard M., 163n
Noguchi, Isamu, 350
Noland, Kenneth, 314
North, Arthur T., 82
Notre Dame, Cathedral, Paris, 345
Notre Dame, University of, 311
Nowicki, Matthew, 182, 270, 296
Noyes, Eliot F., 173, 180, 187

Oberlin College, 9, 28, 34, 40, 48
Office of Naval Intelligence, 142
Ohio Fuel & Gas Company, 122
Ohio State University, 401
Oldenburg, Claes, 291
Oldenburg, Richard, 441n
Onassis, Jacqueline, 374, 380
Ortega y Gasset, Jose, 145, *The Revolt of the Masses*, 145
Oud, J. J. P., 45, 48, 52–3, 55–6, 58, 63, 71, 73, 76, 79, 81, 105–6, 109, 137, 175–8, 191, 197, 200–1, 244; Johnson House project, Pinehurst, N.C., 76; Shell Building, The Hague, 176
Owen, Jane Blaffer, 281, 303
Owen, Robert, 281
Oxford Group, 422n
Oxford University, 41, 422n

Paley, William S., 354, 441n
Pareto, Vilfredo, 419
Parkinson, John, 316
Parthenon, The, Athens, 45, 68, 221, 233, 274
Pater, Walter, 395
Paul, Bruno, 55
Pei, Ieoh Ming, 157, 243, 270, 336, 354
Pelli, Cesar, 302; 354–5, 379; Museum of Modern Art additions, 355; Museum Tower, 379
Pennsylvania, University of, School of Architecture, 150
Pennzoil Corporation, 326
Peres, Shimon, 283, 286
Pericles, 276
Peridot Gallery, 218
Perkins, Frances, 131, 430n
Perkins, G. Holmes, 150
Perry, Ralph Barton, 152

Persius, Ludwig, 88–9, 105, 109, 168, 193
Peterson, Steven, 357
Phidias, 276
Phillips Exeter Academy, 33
Picasso, Pablo, 175, 218, 232; *Guernica*, 175
Piero della Francesca, 412
Piest, Oskar, 142
Plato, 37, 40, 44, 48, 99–100, 111, 141, 146, 231; *Philebus*, 99–100, 344; *The Republic*, 141
Plutarch's *Lives*, 116
Pollock, Jackson, 314
Pollock, Lou, 218
Pöppelmann, Matthäus Daniel, 56; Zwinger Pavilion, Dresden, 56
Pope, Alfred Atmore, 12, 38
Pope, Alton, 11–12
Pope, Edward, 12
Porter, Donald, 405
Post-Impressionism, 46
postmodernism, 332–5, 345–52, 357–70, 398, 406–7
Poussin, Nicolas, 235–6
Pratt, Henry, 374
Pratt Institute, 246
Pratt, Richard, 171
Prentice, Mrs. E. Parmelee, 208
Princeton University, 58, 330, 397
Prix, Wolfgang, 395, 417
Propylaea, Athens, 221
Prozac, 418

Radziwill, Lee, 314
Racquet Club, 399
Ranney, Omar, 121–2
Rappel a l'ordre, 66
Rauschenberg, Robert, 288, 314, 381
Rave, Paul Ortwin, 89, 105
Read, Helen Appleton, 89, 99–100
Reagan, Ronald, 351, 366–7
Reich, Lilly, 70, 129
Resor, Stanley, 186
Rhode Island School of Design, 266, 312
Richardson, Henry Hobson, 77, 87, 193; Glessner House, Chicago, 299–300
Riddle, Theodate Pope, 38; christened Effie, 422n
Riley, Robert Sanford, 31

Riley, Terence, 409
Rindge, Agnes, 92
Ritchie, Alan, 417
Riverview Park, Chicago, 126
Rizzoli Publishers, 393
Roberts, L. W., Jr., 430n
Robertson, Jaquelin, 355, 375–7
Rockefeller, Abby Aldrich (Mrs. John D., Jr.), 97, 143, 207
Rockefeller, Blanchette (Mrs. John D. III), 180, 203–4, 205, 216, 259, 315, 353–4, 379
Rockefeller Center, 259, 366
Rockefeller, David, 354, 440n, 441n
Rockefeller, John D., Jr., 208
Rockefeller, John D. III, 203–4, 259–60
Rockefeller, Nelson, 115, 172–3, 181–2, 260, 286, 300, 354, 433n
Rockefellers (family), 181, 202–3, 205, 207, 298, 303, 355, 441n
Rockwell, Norman, 346
Rodman, Selden, 223–5
Rogge, John, 162
Rohm, Ernst, 108, 113
Rohrheimer, Louis, 16
Roman Catholics and Roman Catholicism, 94, 124
Roob, Rona, 440n
Roosevelt, Franklin Delano, 117, 123–6, 138, 429n
Root, John Wellborn, 16, 87, 369; The Rookery, Chicago (with Daniel Burnham), 369
Rorschach blot, 197, 433n
Ross, Cary, 58–60, 62–3, 67
Rossi, Aldo, 331
Rothko, Mark, 314, 435–6n
Rubell, Steve, 380
Rubin, William, 355
Rudolph, Paul, 227, 243, 270, 308, 336
Ruhtenberg, Jan, 54–5, 67, 106, 425n
Ruskin, John, 434n; Ruskinian worldview, 93
Russell, Bertrand, 37, 155, 230–1, 239, 277
Russell, John, 337

S.A.S. Building, Copenhagen, 270
Saarinen, Eero, 165, 227, 243, 260, 270, 296; Repertory Theater, Lincoln Center, 260

Sachlich, Sachlichkeit, die neue Sachlichkeit, 66, 81, 107, 425n, 429n
Sachs, Paul, 92
St. Thomas, University of, 281
Salle, David, 314
Samarra, Great Mosque, 334
Scandinavian Empiricism, 86
Schacht, Hjalmar, 130
Schad, Christian, 66
Schinkel, Karl Friedrich, 88–9, 197, 201, 238, 255, 412–14; Altes Museum, Berlin, 255, 413; Bauakademie, Berlin, 413; Casino in Glienicke Park, Potsdam, 196; city planning in Berlin, 412–13; Friedrich-Werdersche Kirche, Berlin, 413, Kaufhaus project, Berlin, 413; State Library project, 413
Schlesinger, Arthur, Jr., 153, 155, 374;
Schlubach, Karl, 156, 184
Schlumbergers (family), 202
Schonberg, Harold, 260
Schrager, Ian, 380
Schuller, Robert, 337–42; "The Hour of Power," 337–42
Schweikher, Paul, 220
Scolari-Fitzmaurice, Margaret, *see* Barr, Margaret Scolari-Fitzmaurice
Scott Brown, Denise, 376, 409
Scott, Geoffrey, 234, 239; *The Architecture of Humanism,* 234
Scully, Vincent, 221, 269, 307, 351, 367–6, 372
Scutt, Der, 358
Seagram, Joseph E. and Sons Corporation, 240–9
Segal, George, 291
Serra, Richard, 291
Seton Hill College, 399
Severns, Scott, 315
Severns, Theodate Johnson, 5, 17–22, 24–7, 29, 33, 40–1, 88, 90, 95–7, 106, 112, 115, 119, 136–7, 184, 198, 216, 218–19, 272, 315, 382, 386, 421n, 424n; *Musical America,* 315, 439n
Shakespeare, William, 5, 116
Share-the-Wealth movement, 125, 128
Shirer, William L., 151–2, *Berlin Diary,* 151–2
Shrine of the Little Flower, 123
Silvertip Ranch, 316–17

Silvetti, Jorge, 357
Sinan, 278
Singh, Patwant, 300
Sixtus V, 412
Skidmore, Owings and Merrill, 182, 227, 242–3, 357, 404; Lever House, 242–3, 270
Skyscrapers: Tribune Tower, Chicago, Chrysler Building, Empire State Building, Woolworth Building, New York, 346
Smallens, Alexander, 95
Smith, Carleton Sprague, 31, 36, 422n
Smith, Gerald L. K., 125
Smith College, 92, 230, 233–4, 271
Soane, John, 237–8, 250, 379; Bank of England, London, 237; breakfast room, Soane House, London, 237
Society of Architectural Historians, *see* American Society of Architectural Historians
Socrates, 37, 61, 111, 231, 233, 306, 419
Sombart, Werner, 130; *Weltanschauung, Science and Economy,* 130, 142
Sony Corporation, 441n
Sophists, The, 146, 419
Sorkin, Michael, 143–4, 366–7, 393–5, 409
Speer, Albert, 410
Spengler, Oswald, 140
Stackpole, Theodate, 422n
Stalin, Josef, 110, 418
Stalinallee, East Berlin, 418
Statue of Liberty, 286
Stein, Gertrude, 95; *Four Saints in Three Acts,* 95
Stella, Frank, 288, 291, 413
Stephens, Suzanne, 405
Stern, Robert A. M., 220, 308–10, 333–4, 345–6, 357–8, 372, 375, 402, 417
Stettheimer, Florine, 95
Stirling, James, 308
Stone, Edward Durell, 173, 205, 207, 270, 308
Stonehenge, 174
Stout, Rex, 162–3
Stroup, Jon, 184–5, 187–8, 197–8, 216–17, 434n
Stubbins, Hugh, 270
Stuyvesant, Pieter, 11

Sullivan, Louis, 77, 87, 182, 352; Carson, Pirie, Scott Store, Chicago, 268; National Farmers' Bank, Owatonna, Minn., 268

Summers, Gene, 246, 249, 311

Suprematism, 193, 197

di Suvero, Mark, 291

Swanke, Hayden and Connell, 35

Sweeney, James Johnson, 92

Sweeney, Martin, 124

Swiczinsky, Helmut, 395

Symes, Robin, 204

Tange, Kenzo, 308

Taut, Bruno, 66; Hufeisen housing project, Berlin, 412

Tchelitchew, Pavel, 92

Tenniel, John, 210

Thomson, Virgil, 60, 90, 92–7, 218–19; *Four Saints in Three Acts*, 95; Second String Quartet, 97

Tim Costello's, 211

Toker, K. B. S., 366–7

Tomerius, Lorenz, 413

Tomkins, Calvin, 440n

Townsend Farm, 9–10, 22, 24, 32, 35, 55, 113, 120, 128. 166, 317

Townsend, Francis, 122, 124–6

Townsend, Hosea, 10

Townsend, Philothea, 9–11

Townsend Plan, 122, 124–5

Treasury of Atreus, Mycenae, 288

Trinity College, 92

Trump, Donald, 410, 416

Tschumi, Bernard, 331, 395

Tugendhat, Fritz and Grete, 68, 108

Tughlaqabad, 300

Tunnard, Christopher, 220

Twitchell, Ralph, 227

Twombly, Cy, 314

Union Party, 125–7

United Jewish Appeal, 283

U.S. Army Corps of Engineers, 226

Utley, Freda, 155

Valentin, Curt, 218

Van de Velde, Henry, 77, 435n

Vassar College, 58, 92, 172, 242

Venturi, Robert, 307–10, 332–3, 345, 379; *Complexity and Contradiction in Architecture*, 307; *Learning from Las Vegas*, 310

Versailles Treaty, 89

Vico, Giambattista, 419

Vidler, Anthony, 331

Viereck, George Sylvester, 142, 154

Virginia, University of, 252, 307, 375–6; *The Charlottesville Tapes*, 375

Vranic, Peter, 265–6, 312, 380

Vyas, Ujjval K., 419

Wadsworth Atheneum, Hartford, 92, 95; Avery Memorial Wing, 95

Wadsworth, Julius and Cleome, 167

Wagner, Martin, 147, 155

Wagner, Otto, 77, 181

Wagner, Richard, 56; *Die Götterdämmerung*, 410; *Der Ring des Nibelungen*, 133

Wagner, Robert, 258

Wagner, Siegfried, 56

Waldheim, Kurt, 143

Walker, John III, 46

Walters, Barbara, 380

Warburg, Edward M. M., 46, 92, 95, 105–6, 282–4

Warburgs (family), 91

Warhol, Andy, 288, 291, 314–15, 337, 374, 380–1; Velvet Underground, 337, 442n

Weatherill, Bernard, 264

Weber, Nicholas Fox, 284

Weese, Harry, 270

Weinstein, Richard, 355

Weiss, Heinie, 128

Weissenhofsiedlung, Stuttgart, 48, 52, 56, 67, 70

Wellesley College, 5, 11–12, 21, 29, 41, 46–7, 57, 71, 95

Wells, H. G., 145

Wesleyan University, 92, 158

Whistler, James A. McNeill, 100

Whitcomb, Janet, 13, 21

Whitehead, Alfred North, 37, 40, 43–4, 47–8, 230–1, 403;

Whiteheads (family), 39

"Whites, The," 332–4

Whitney, David, 266, 287–8, 305, 311–15, 317, 374, 379–84, 386, 391, 399, 442n

Whitney, John Hay, 181

Whitney Museum of American Art, 207–8, 375
Whitneys (family), 91, 181, 205
Wierzbowski, Stephen, 393–95
Wigley, Mark, 395–7, 402–3
Wiley, John, 165–6
Wiley, Robert C., 245, 435n
Winchester Cathedral, 39
Wisner, John, 156, 184
Wolfe, Tom, 374
Woodstock Country School, 312
Wrede, Stuart, 394, 408–9
Wren, Christopher, 386
Wright, Frank Lloyd, 4, 15–16, 71, 76–7, 80, 82–7, 100, 106, 113, 166, 168, 175–82, 200–2, 209, 220–5, 227, 243–4, 270, 305, 352, 372, 378, 420, 427n, 434n; Guggenheim Museum, New York, 221, 304, 400; "House on the Mesa" project, Denver, 76, 83; Johnson Wax Buildings, Racine, Wis., 167; Kaufmann House, "Fallingwater," Ohiopyle, Penn., 181,

427n; Taliesin East, Spring Green, Wis., 85, 179, 220, 223; Taliesin West, Scottsdale, Ariz., 223; 167
Wright, Olgivanna, 223
Wrightsman, Mr. and Mrs. Charles, 303, 315, 330
WSPD, radio station, Toledo, Ohio, 127
Wu, King-Lui, 220
Wurster, William Wilson, 270

Yale University, 58, 188, 219–21, 224–5, 251, 264, 269, 280, 296, 298, 307, 330, 333
Yale University School of Architecture, 219–20, 269; *Perspecta*, 221
Yamasaki, Minoru, 270
Yoshimura, Junzo, 227
Young Nationalists, 128, 131
Youth and the Nation, 128

Zapata Corporation, 327
Zion, Robert L., 300
Zweig, Peter, 395

PERMISSIONS ACKNOWLEDGMENTS

Grateful acknowledgment is made to the following for permission to reprint previously published and unpublished material:

Academy Group Limited: Excerpts from open letter to Philip Johnson in "Cosmorama" by Robin Middleton (*Architectural Design,* March 1967). Reprinted by permission.

ARTnews Magazine: Excerpt from "Present Trends in Architecture in Fine Exhibit" by Ralph Flint (*ARTnews,* February 13, 1932), copyright © 1932 by The ART NEWS. Reprinted by permission.

The Frank Lloyd Wright Foundation: Excerpts from letters of 1/18/32, 1/19/32, 10/3/45, 8/6/48, 9/6/48, and undated, probably 1950, from Frank Lloyd Wright to Philip Johnson. The Letters of Frank Lloyd Wright are copyright © 1984, 1994 by The Frank Lloyd Wright Foundation. All rights reserved. Reprinted by permission.

Martin Filler: Excerpts from "The Architect as Theorist" by Martin Filler (*Art in America,* December, 1979), copyright © 1979 by Martin Filler. Reprinted by permission of the author.

I.H.T. Corporation: Excerpts from "Two Quit Modern Art Museum for Sur-Realist Political Venture" (*New York Herald Tribune,* December 18, 1934), copyright © 1934 by the New York Herald Tribune Inc. All rights reserved. Reprinted by permission.

Alfred A. Knopf, Inc. and *Weidenfeld and Nicolson Ltd.:* Excerpts from *Virgil Thomson* by Virgil Thomson, copyright © 1966 by Virgil Thomson. Rights in the United Kingdom administered by Weidenfeld and Nicolson Ltd., London. Reprinted by permission.

The Museum of Modern Art: Excerpt from *Modern Architecture: International Exhibition* by Alfred Barr, copyright © 1932 by The Museum of Modern Art; excerpt from *Deconstructivist Architecture* by Philip Johnson and Mark Wigley, copyright © 1988 by The Museum of Modern Art. Reprinted by permission.

The Nation: Excerpt from "What the Man About Town Will Build" by Douglas Haskell (*The Nation,* April 13, 1932), copyright © 1932 by The Nation Company, Inc. Reprinted by permission.

The New York Times: Excerpt from "Architecture Styled International" by H. I. Brock (*The New York Times Magazine,* February 7, 1932), excerpt from an article on National Party of Blackburn and Johnson (*The New York Times,* December 18, 1934), excerpt from "He Adds Elegance to Modern Architecture" by Ada Louise Huxtable (*The New York Times,* May 24, 1964), copyright © 1932, 1934, 1964 by The New York Times Company. Reprinted by permission.

Oxford University Press: Introductory remarks by Robert Stern to "Review of Robin Boyd: *The Puzzle of Architecture*" from *Writings* by Philip Johnson (Oxford University Press, 1979). Reprinted by permission.

Michael Sorkin: Excerpt from "The Real Thing" by Michael Sorkin (*Architectural Record,* September, 1986), copyright © 1986 by McGraw-Hill, Inc. Reprinted by permission of the author.

The Village Voice: Excerpts from "Canon Fodder" by Michael Sorkin (*The Village Voice,* December 1, 1987). Reprinted by permission of the author and *The Village Voice.*

Warner Books, Inc.: Excerpts from *The Andy Warhol Diaries,* edited by Pat Hackett, copyright © 1989 by the Estate of Andy Warhol. Reprinted by permission.

PHOTOGRAPH CREDITS

(photographers' names in CAPS)

page

10 Johnson Country Home, Townsend Farm, near New London, Ohio. Courtesy Johnson family / NORTON

16 Homer and Louise Johnson residence, c. 1915. Courtesy Johnson family

17 Homer Hosea Johnson with Alfred and Jeannette, 1904. Courtesy Johnson family

17 Philip, c. 1908. Courtesy Johnson family

18 *left:* Alfred, Jeannette, and Philip, 1907; *right:* Theodate and Philip, c. 1911. Courtesy Johnson family

20 Louise Pope Johnson with Theodate, Philip, Jeannette, c. 1917. Courtesy Johnson family / NORTON

23 Philip, c. 1917. Courtesy Johnson family

25 Theodate and Philip, c. 1917. Courtesy Johnson family / NORTON

26 top Louise Johnson with Jeannette, Theodate, and Philip, Townsend Farm, c. 1918. Courtesy Johnson family / NORTON

26 bottom Johnson family, Townsend Farm, c. 1918. Courtesy Johnson family / NORTON

30 Hackley School, Tarrytown, New York, 1920. Courtesy Johnson family

42 *left:* Philip Johnson in Arab garb, Cairo, 1928; *right:* Philip and Jeannette, Nice, 1928. Courtesy Johnson family

43 Jeannette, c. 1928. Courtesy Johnson family

54 Philip, Berlin, c. 1930. HELMUT LERSKI

62 Henry-Russell Hitchcock, c. 1935. GEORGE PLATT LYNES

63 J. J. P. Oud. (n.d.) Photograph courtesy The Museum of Modern Art, New York.

76 Installation view of "Modern Architecture—International Exhibition," The Museum of Modern Art, New York. February 10 through March 23, 1932. Photograph courtesy The Museum of Modern Art, New York.

77 Lewis Mumford, c. 1938. ERIC SCHAAL

88 Theodate Johnson, Jan Ruhtenberg, and Philip Johnson; Potsdam, Germany. October, 1932. Photograph courtesy The Museum of Modern Art Archives, New York. The Margaret S. Barr Papers.

91 Alfred H. Barr, Jr.; Philip Johnson; Margaret Scolar Barr; Cortona, Italy. 1932. Photograph courtesy The Museum of Modern Art Archives, New York. The Margaret S. Barr Papers.

91   Philip, New York City, 1933. CARL VAN VECHTEN

94   Philip, 1933. CARL VAN VECHTEN

94   Jimmy Daniels, c. 1940. MORGAN AND MARVIN SMITH. Photograph and Prints Division; Schomburg Center for Research in Black Culture; The New York Public Library. Astor, Lennox and Tilden Foundations.

96   Theodate, c. 1932. Courtesy Johnson family / BACHRACH

99   Philip Johnson installing the exhibition "Machine Art," The Museum of Modern Art, New York. March 5 through April 29, 1934. Photograph by Paul Parker. Photograph courtesy The Museum of Modern Art, New York.

118   Johnson family house, c. 1935. Courtesy Philip Johnson

129   Johnson's drawing (1988) of the Flying Wedge, the symbol of the Young Nationalists.

157   Philip Johnson House, Cambridge, Massachusetts, 1942, interior looking toward court. / EZRA STOLLER © ESTO

179   Philip Johnson and Ludwig Mies van der Rohe in the galleries of the exhibition "Mies van der Rohe," The Museum of Modern Art, New York. Photograph by William Leftwich. September 16, 1947 through January 25, 1948. Photograph courtesy The Museum of Modern Art, New York.

185   Jon Stroup, c. 1949. MELTON-PIPPIN

189   Philip Johnson residence, New Canaan, Connecticut: the Glass House, 1949. ALEXANDRE GEORGES

190   Johnson residence, New Canaan: the Glass House, interior chairs, ottoman, and lounge by Mies van der Rohe with Lilly Reich; painting, *The Funeral of Phocion,* attributed to Nicolas Poussin. RICHARD PAYNE

190   Plan, the Glass House, late 1960s. Courtesy Philip Johnson

195   Johnson residence, New Canaan: the Guest House, 1949. EZRA STOLLER © ESTO

201   Left to right: Philip Johnson, Frank Lloyd Wright, Alfred Barr, c. 1950. Courtesy Philip Johnson

205   Philip Johnson. Rockefeller Guest House, 242 East 52nd Street, New York, New York. (n.d.) Patio between living room and other quarters. Photograph courtesy The Museum of Modern Art, New York.

206   The Museum of Modern Art Annex (the "21" Building), New York City, 1950. ALEXANDRE GEORGES

209   Abby Aldrich Rockefeller Sculpture Garden, The Museum of Modern Art, 1953. EZRA STOLLER © ESTO

212   Mr. and Mrs. George C. Oneto House, Irvington-on-Hudson, New York, 1951 (Landis Gores, partner). EZRA STOLLER © ESTO

213   Mr. and Mrs. Richard Hodgson House, New Canaan, Connecticut, 1951 (Landis Gores, partner). ALEXANDRE GEORGES

213   Mr. and Mrs. Robert C. Wiley House, New Canaan, Connecticut, 1953. EZRA STOLLER © ESTO

215   Mr. and Mrs. Robert C. Leonhardt House, Lloyd's Neck, Long Island, New York, 1956: view of living area. EZRA STOLLER © ESTO

215   Ludwig Mies van der Rohe. *Glass House on a Hillside,* 1934. Elevation. Ink on paper, 4¼ × 8″ (10.7 × 20.3 cm). The Mies van der Rohe Archive, The Museum of Modern Art, New York. Gift of the architect. © 1995 The Museum of Modern Art, New York.

217   Project, house for William A. M. Burden, Mt. Kisco, New York, 1956. EZRA STOLLER © ESTO

218   John Hohnsbeen, c. 1955. DONALD GAYNOR

222   Frank Lloyd Wright and Philip Johnson, c. 1953. Courtesy Philip Johnson / AUSTIN COOPER

236   Philip Johnson residence, New Canaan: the Glass House, c. 1990; interior. RICHARD PAYNE

237   Johnson residence, New Canaan: the Guest House. Remodeled in 1953. Wall sculpture by Ibram Lassaw. ALEXANDRE GEORGES

241   Kneses Tifereth Israel synagogue, Port Chester, New York, 1956. EZRA STOLLER © ESTO

241   Kneses Tifereth Israel synagogue: interior. EZRA STOLLER © ESTO

244   Philip Johnson, Ludwig Mies van der Rohe, and Phyllis B. Lambert. Mid-1950s. Photograph courtesy The Museum of Modern Art, New York.

247   Ludwig Mies van der Rohe: Seagram Building, New York City, 1954–1958 (Philip Johnson, partner). HEDRICH-BLESSING

248   Four Seasons Restaurant, Seagram Building, New York City, 1959. LOUIS REENS

251   Mr. and Mrs. Eric Boissonas House, New Canaan, Connecticut, 1956. EZRA STOLLER © ESTO

252   Classroom building, University of St. Thomas, Houston, 1957. FRANK LOTZ MILLER

254   Asia House, New York City, 1960: preliminary scheme. EZRA STOLLER © ESTO

254   Johnson residence, New Canaan: Pavilion and fountain, 1962. EZRA STOLLER © ESTO

256   Sheldon Memorial Art Gallery, University of Nebraska, Lincoln, Nebraska, 1963. EZRA STOLLER © ESTO

256   Sheldon Memorial Art Gallery: interior. EZRA STOLLER © ESTO

257   Amon Carter Museum of Western Art, Fort Worth, 1961. EZRA STOLLER © ESTO

261   Lincoln Center plaza, 1958: study for entrance arcade (rejected). Courtesy Philip Johnson

262   New York State Theater, Lincoln Center, New York City, 1964 (Richard Foster, partner). EZRA STOLLER © ESTO

262   New York State Theater, Lincoln Center: interior (Richard Foster, partner). EZRA STOLLER © ESTO

265   Philip Johnson, with photograph of the Glass House in the background, early 1950s. HOMER PAGE

279   Museum for Pre-Columbian Art, Dumbarton Oaks, Washington, D.C., 1963: plan. Courtesy Philip Johnson

279   Museum for Pre-Columbian Art, Dumbarton Oaks: interior. EZRA STOLLER © ESTO

280   Kline Science Tower, Yale University, New Haven, Connecticut, 1965 (Richard Foster, partner). RICHARD PAYNE

282   Roofless Church, New Harmony, Indiana, 1960: view toward baldachin. Courtesy Philip Johnson / GEORGE HOLTON

285   Above: Nuclear Reactor, Rehovot, Israel, 1960. Below: view of court. (Photographs © ARNOLD NEWMAN)

288   Johnson residence, New Canaan, late 1960s: swimming pool in foreground; sculpture by Jacques Lipchitz, left; Glass House in background. BILL MARIS © ESTO

289   Johnson residence, New Canaan, Painting gallery, 1965: entrance. Sculpture by Robert Bart, to the left; painting by Jasper Johns, visible through doorway. EZRA STOLLER © ESTO

289   Painting gallery: interior. Paintings, left to right, by Frank Stella, Jasper Johns, Jasper Johns, David Salle. NORMAN McGRATH

292   Johnson residence, New Canaan, Sculpture Gallery, 1970: interior. Sculptures by Claes Oldenburg, floor level; Donald Judd, on wall; Mark di Suvero, upper level. RICHARD PAYNE

295   Project, National Shrine, Ellis Island, New York, 1966. LOUIS CHECKMAN

297   Mr. and Mrs. Eric Boissonas House, Cap Benat, France, 1964. EZRA STOLLER © ESTO

297   Mr. and Mrs. David Lloyd Kreeger House, Washington, D.C., 1968 (Richard Foster, partner). EZRA STOLLER © ESTO

302   Governor Nelson Rockefeller, Mayor John V. Lindsay, and Philip Johnson, c. 1965. Courtesy Philip Johnson

313   David Whitney, c. 1975. LYNNE STERN

316   Philip Johnson and Eliza Bliss Parkinson, c. 1970. Courtesy Philip Johnson

322   IDS (Investors' Diversified Services) Center, Minneapolis, 1971 (John Burgee, partner). RICHARD PAYNE

323   IDS Center: view of Crystal Court. RICHARD PAYNE

325   Fort Worth Water Garden, Fort Worth, 1975 (John Burgee, partner). RICHARD PAYNE

326   Post Oak Central I, II, and III, Houston, 1976–1981 (John Burgee, partner). RICHARD PAYNE

328   Pennzoil Place, Houston, 1976 (John Burgee, partner). RICHARD PAYNE

334   Robert A. M. Stern and Philip Johnson, 1983. Courtesy Robert Stern

335   Thanksgiving Square, Dallas, 1977 (John Burgee, partner). RICHARD PAYNE

340 top   Crystal Cathedral, Garden Grove, California, 1980. RICHARD PAYNE

340 bottom Crystal Cathedral, Garden Grove, 1980: interior. RICHARD PAYNE

342   Facade, 1001 Fifth Avenue, New York City, 1979 (John Burgee, partner). AARON McDONALD

348   A.T. & T. (American Telephone and Telegraph) Corporate Headquarters, New York City, 1984 (John Burgee, partner). TIMOTHY HURSLEY

348   A.T. & T. Building: entry (John Burgee, partner). RICHARD PAYNE

349   Evelyn Beatrice Longman: *The Genius of Electricity*, 1916; moved to foyer of A.T. & T. Building, 1984. RICHARD PAYNE

356   The Museum of Modern Art, New York. Winter Garden, designed by Cesare Pelli, 1984, and part of the Museum Tower, seen from the Abby Aldrich Rockefeller Sculpture Garden. 1984. Photograph by Scott Frances, courtesy The Museum of Modern Art, New York.

361   PPG (Pittsburgh Plate Glass) Company Corporate Headquarters, Pittsburgh, Pennsylvania, 1984 (John Burgee, partner). RICHARD PAYNE

362   Philip Johnson and John Burgee at topping out ceremony for PPG Building, 1954. Courtesy John Burgee / BILL MITCHELL

363   Transco Tower, Houston, 1985 (John Burgee, partner). RICHARD PAYNE

364   Philip Johnson and Gerald Hines, c. 1985. Courtesy Philip Johnson

365   NCNB Center (formerly RepublicBank), Houston, Texas, 1984 (John Burgee, partner). RICHARD PAYNE

366   NCNB Center, Houston: view of foyer (John Burgee, partner). RICHARD PAYNE

368   The Crescent, Dallas, Texas, 1985 (John Burgee, partner). RICHARD PAYNE

369   College of Architecture, University of Houston, 1986 (John Burgee, partner), RICHARD PAYNE

377   Philip Johnson in his office at 885 Third Avenue, New York City, c. 1985. Courtesy Philip Johnson

381   David Whitney and Andy Warhol at opening of Art Museum of South Texas, Corpus Christi, 1972. Courtesy Philip Johnson / ROBERT SHAW

383   Johnson residence, New Canaan: Library/Study, 1980. RICHARD PAYNE

383   Johnson residence, New Canaan: Gehry Ghost House, 1985. NORMAN McGRATH

383   Johnson residence, New Canaan: Lincoln Kirstein Tower, 1985. NORMAN McGRATH

385   George Balanchine, Philip Johnson, and Lincoln Kirstein, c. 1984. Courtesy Philip Johnson

385   Philip Johnson and Edward M. M. Warburg, c. 1985. Courtesy Philip Johnson / EUGENE R. GADDIS

385   Headstones designed for Margaret Scolari Barr and Alfred H. Barr, Jr. by Philip Johnson, in Greensboro, Vermont, 1983. Photograph courtesy The Museum of Modern Art Archives, New York. The Margaret S. Barr Papers.

Photograph Credits

387   Philip Johnson in the home of Frank Lloyd Wright, Oak Park, Illinois, c. 1984. Courtesy Philip Johnson

388   Fifty-third Street and Third Avenue, New York City, 1985 (John Burgee, partner). GREGORY MURPHEY

400   Left to right: Peter Eisenman, Philip Johnson, Frank Gehry, 1991. HUGH HALESTOOKE

402   Philip Johnson and Henry-Russell Hitchcock, c. 1985. Courtesy Philip Johnson

404   Project for Times Square Center, New York City, 1989 (John Burgee, partner). Courtesy Philip Johnson /NATHANIEL LIEBERMAN

406   Project for Chapel, University of St. Thomas, Houston, 1992. Courtesy Philip Johnson

411   Das Business Center, Berlin, 1992; completion expected 1995 (drawing by Louis Blanc). Courtesy Philip Johnson

414   Project, "Berlin Fantasy," 1993. Courtesy Philip Johnson / ROBERT WALKER

416   Philip Johnson, c. 1988. Courtesy Philip Johnson

      Cover photo of Philip Johnson by LUCA VIGNELLI